MW00788315

The AEF Way of War

The American Army and Combat in World War I

MARK ETHAN GROTELUESCHEN

United States Air Force Academy

CAMBRIDGE
UNIVERSITY PRESS

CAMBRIDGE UNIVERSITY PRESS
Cambridge, New York, Melbourne, Madrid, Cape Town, Singapore, São Paulo

Cambridge University Press
32 Avenue of the Americas, New York, NY 10013-2473, USA

www.cambridge.org
Information on this title: www.cambridge.org/9780521864343

First published 2007

Printed in the United States of America

A catalog record for this publication is available from the British Library.

Library of Congress Cataloging in Publication Data

Grotelueschen, Mark E., 1969–
The AEF way of war: the American army and combat in World War I /
Mark Ethan Grotelueschen.
p.   cm.
Includes bibliographical references and index.
ISBN-13: 978-0-521-86434-3
ISBN-10: 0-521-86434-8
1. United States. Army – History – World War, 1914–1918.   2. United States. Army.
American Expeditionary Forces.   3. World War, 1939–1945 – Campaigns – Western
Front.   4. Tactics – History – 20th century.   5. Military art and science – Technological
innovations – United States – History – 20th century.   I. Title.
II. Title: American Expeditionary Forces way of war.
D570.2.G76   2007
940.4'1273 – dc22   2006009170

ISBN-13   978-0-521-86434-3 hardback
ISBN-10   0-521-86434-8 hardback

For Abigail, Grant, Caleb, and Samuel.
And in memory of the military service of their grandfathers
Paul Gerhardt Grotelueschen
U.S. Army, 1945–1948, 1951–1953
Albert Millson Gonder
USMC, 1951–1954

Contents

Acknowledgments

I am grateful for the advice and assistance of dozens of professors, historians, archivists, librarians, friends, and family members. Without their support, this book would have been impossible to complete. Professors Brian M. Linn, Joseph G. Dawson III, H. W. Brands, Arnold P. Krammer, R. J. Q. Adams, and Richard Stadelmann all read (and, in some cases, reread) the manuscript and provided helpful comments. I thank them for all their assistance and also for the encouragement they provided throughout the project.

I also thank scholars Mike Neiberg, Tim Travers, Holger H. Herwig, Dennis Showalter, and Edgar F. Raines, Jr., for advice and encouragement along the way. Professor Robert Ferrell took time away from his own research into the Meuse-Argonne campaign to discuss the AEF with me and loaned me his copy of P. L. Stackpole's diary. Major James Powell, U.S. Army, and David Campbell both provided important information.

Throughout this project, I have been blessed with the able help of a number of archivists, librarians, and research assistants. During my work at the National Archives and Records Administration, Mitchel Yockelson and Timothy Nenninger provided extraordinary research assistance, using not only their skills as archivists but also as Great War historians themselves. Also, Tim Nenninger allowed me access to important chapters of Charles P. Summerall's memoir. The staff at the U.S. Army Military History Institute, especially Dick Sommers, Richard Baker, Kathy Olson, and David Keough, helped make my visit there as productive and enjoyable as possible. Dr. Sommers' personal interest in my project ensured that I had access to important materials I did not know existed, and Ms. Olson went above and beyond the call of duty in assisting me both during and after my visit. At the Combined Arms Research Library at Fort Leavenworth, Rusty Rafferty and John Roger provided important assistance while I was on site and loaned me materials before and after my visit. Although I was unable to travel to the Donovan Research Library at Fort Benning, Ericka Loze sent me material unavailable anywhere else. Jane Yates, the director of the Citadel Archives and Museum, helped me make the most of my visit there. James W. Zobel did the same at the MacArthur Memorial and Archives, as did Andrew Woods at the McCormick Research Center of the First Division Museum. Finally, I thank the entire staff of both the Massachusetts Historical Society and the manuscripts division of the Library of Congress.

The research required for this project entailed a few lengthy trips, and a number of families graciously opened their homes to me during my travels. Thanks for all the logistical and moral support given by Corvin and Nadine Connolly, Paul and Sherri Grotelueschen, Mark and Liz Heinitz, Herb and Ruth Hohenstein, Tom and Beth Hohenstein, Jim and Tisha Powell, and John and Cindy Raquet. In some instances, their support made a trip possible; in every case, they made my travels more enjoyable.

Finally, thanks to my family for all their prayers, advice, and encouragement, and especially to Alison, my wife, whose love, support, and countless daily acts of service enabled this project to be completed. Despite all the remarkable assistance I have received throughout this undertaking, all errors of fact, faulty interpretations, and mistaken conclusions are my own.

Soli Deo Gloria

Introduction

While critiquing northern and southern generalship in the American Civil War, the distinguished historian, T. Harry Williams, claimed that the war was not just a struggle of men and material but also "a war of ideas."[1] He was referring not only to the political or social ideologies then being contested between the northern and southern states but especially to the military theories and beliefs that guided the decisions of the leading generals on each side. Williams claimed that Union generals Ulysses S. Grant and William T. Sherman adjusted their ideas of warfare to meet the strategic and operational demands of the war, while Robert E. Lee failed to adapt from his limited, Jominian, prewar conceptions. In the last few decades, historians have begun to apply Williams' assertion to other wars, which were, for the officers who directed the combat operations, just as much wars of ideas.

When such ideas are widely agreed upon in an army and codified in some way, either formally or informally, they become *military doctrine* – the officially sanctioned ideas and methods that are to govern combat operations.[2] These core beliefs should influence the army's force structure, training, armament, battle plans, and tactics. In turn, doctrine must remain in harmony with the changing conditions of the

---

[1] See T. Harry Williams, "The Military Leadership of North and South," in *Why the North Won the Civil War*, ed. David H. Donald (Baton Rouge: Louisiana State University Press, 1960; reprint, New York: Simon & Schuster, 1996), 48.

[2] The U.S. Army currently states that doctrine elucidates the "fundamental principles by which military forces guide their actions in support of national objectives." HQ Department of the Army, *FM 100-5 Operations*, Washington, D.C.: GPO, 14 June 1993, glossary-3.

battlefield – particularly, developments in weaponry, limitations in train-ing, logistical constraints, strength of the enemy force, and even terrain and climate. One need look no further than the standard interpretation of generalship in the First World War, especially during the first three years of the conflict, to see that ideas of warfare, whether or not formally codi-fied, matter a great deal and that they must develop to meet the changing conditions of the industrial battlefield.

Historians of the Great War, especially those who have studied the European and Dominion forces, have begun to examine the extent to which ideas, at various levels, influenced the way armies, corps, divisions, and other units fought. These studies have also investigated the nature and extent of doctrinal and operational adaptation and innovation. For example, historians of the British Expeditionary Force (BEF), such as Tim Travers, Robin Prior, Trevor Wilson, and Gary Sheffield, have discovered that although Field Marshal Douglas Haig, the BEF commander-in-chief, may have failed to make important adjustments to British doctrine dur-ing the war, many subordinate commanders, such as those of field armies, corps, and divisions, made significant changes to their combat style in the latter half of the war.[3] Having examined the doctrinal pronouncements, attack plans, and operations reports of various British combat organiza-tions, these historians conclude that although Haig offered few solutions to the tactical problems of the Western Front, some of the BEF's field armies managed by the end of 1917 to have developed more effective, though not bloodless, methods of attack. Some historians have claimed that even more impressive innovations occurred at the corps level of command.[4]

[3] See Tim Travers, *The Killing Ground: The British Army, the Western Front and the Emer-gence of Modern Warfare, 1900–1918* (London: Unwin Hyman, 1987), and *How the War Was Won: Command and Technology in the British Army on the Western Front, 1917–1918* (London: Routledge, 1992); Robin Prior and Trevor Wilson, *Command on the Western Front: The Military Career of Sir Henry Rawlinson, 1914–1918* (Oxford: Blackwell, 1992), and *Passchendaele: The Untold Story* (New Haven, Conn.: Yale University Press, 1996); Gary Sheffield, *Forgotten Victory* (London: Headline, 2001); and Geoffrey Powell, *Plumer: The Soldier's General* (London: Leo Cooper, 1990).

[4] For corps-level studies, see Shane Schreiber, *Shock Army of the British Empire: The Canadian Corps in the Last 100 Days of the Great War* (Westport, Conn.: Praeger, 1997); Daniel G. Dancocks, *Spearhead to Victory: Canada and the Great War* (Edmonton: Hurtig, 1987); and C. E. W. Bean, *The Official History of Australia in the War of 1914–1918* (Sydney: University of Queensland Press, 1942), vols. 5 and 6. For the accounts of two corps commanders, see Arthur W. Currie, *Canadian Corps Operations During the Year 1918* (Ottawa: Department of Militia and Defence, 1919); and John Monash, *The Australian Victories in France in 1918* (Sydney: Angus and Robertson, 1936; reprint, London: Imperial War Museum, 1993).

Taken together, these investigations have led to a more complex and more accurate understanding of what was happening in the huge combat forces along the Western Front. They have demonstrated that although some senior generals may have learned little and retained painfully anachronistic ideas of warfare, other officers adapted not only their ideas of war but also the kinds of battles they tried to fight. At times, lessons appear to have been learned and then forgotten, or misapplied, especially as the character of the fighting began to change throughout 1918. But, ultimately, this development was significant enough that certain senior generals and even entire levels of command – such as Haig and the British General Headquarters (GHQ) – may have become increasingly irrelevant at the *operational* level as the field armies, corps, and divisions waged battles according to their own ideas in the final year of the war. Such conclusions have moved the historiographical debate beyond the simple good–bad dichotomy that formerly dominated Great War histories.

These studies provide useful models for how to examine the relationship among command, doctrine, and operational adaptation in military forces, but, as of now, the American Expeditionary Forces (AEF) have not been subjected to this new, more detailed form of analysis. One reason for this is the relative lack of academic studies of any kind on the AEF, especially in comparison with the other major armies of the Great War. Although historians have examined both America's role in the war and the war's effect on America, few operational histories of the AEF's major campaigns have been written. For example, there is no scholarly study of the strategically important Aisne-Marne Offensive, although more than 300,000 Americans took part. Only one historian has written a book on the battle of St. Mihiel, the largest American battle to date when it was fought, and that work is based primarily on published sources. There are just two studies of the massive Meuse-Argonne Offensive, even though more than one million AEF soldiers participated in the forty-seven–day battle that led to 117,000 AEF casualties – certainly ranking it to this day as one of the greatest military campaigns ever fought by American forces.[5]

---

[5] The only scholarly study of the Aisne-Marne Offensive is Douglas V. Johnson and Rolfe L. Hillman's book on the fighting of the 1st and 2nd Divisions near Soissons. The actions of the other six divisions that took part in the campaign in July and August have been neglected. See Johnson and Hillman, *Soissons, 1918* (College Station: Texas A&M University Press, 1999). The sole book on the St. Mihiel Offensive is James H. Hallas, *Squandered Victory: The American Army at St. Mihiel* (Westport, Conn.: Praeger, 1995). The Meuse-Argonne Offensive is covered by Paul Braim's short but critical monograph, *The Test of Battle: The American Expeditionary Forces in the Meuse-Argonne Campaign* (Newark, Del.: University of Delaware Press, 1987); and Frederick Palmer's early work, *Our Greatest Battle* (New York: Dodd, Mead, 1919).

In lieu of sufficient campaign studies, the historiography of the AEF consists largely of the memoirs of American generals and enlisted men, some excellent biographies of a few senior officers, and general accounts of the entire American war effort. For the first fifty years after the armistice, Pershing's official version of the AEF's prowess dominated the field.[6] Then, in the late 1960s, the works of Edward M. Coffman and Harvey A. DeWeerd began to question aspects of Pershing's overly generous portrayal of American doctrine and operations.[7] Beginning in the late 1970s, a wave of revisionism began to erode what remained of the favorable interpretation begun half a century before by Pershing. A number of books, articles, and chapters by Allan R. Millett, James W. Rainey, Timothy K. Nenninger, Paul F. Braim, Donald Smythe, and David F. Trask identified what scholars more familiar with contemporary Allied impressions of the AEF already suspected – that the American army in France was not the "powerful and smooth-running machine" Pershing and others claimed it to be.[8]

The revisionists claim that the AEF was often inadequately trained, poorly supplied, and inconsistently led. Many of their assessments of AEF doctrine, training, and combat performance are particularly severe. Rainey attacks all three areas when he writes, "In having to grope its way to victory [due to poor training], the AEF succeeded not because of imaginative operations and tactics nor because of qualitative superiority in open warfare, but rather by smothering German machine guns with

---

[6] See Pershing's positive *Preliminary Report* (19 November 1918) and the more substantial *Final Report* (Paris: GHQ, September 1919), both in U.S. Department of the Army, Historical Division, *United States Army in the World War 1917–1919* (Washington, D.C.: U.S. GPO, 1948; reprint, Center for Military History, 1990), vol. 12., pp. 2–71 (hereafter *USAWW*, 12: 2–71). For other generally favorable interpretations of the AEF and its operations, see Shipley Thomas, *The History of the A.E.F.* (New York: Doran, 1920); and Arthur Page, *Our 110 Days Fighting* (Garden City, N.Y.: Doubleday, 1920). After a number of former AEF generals published memoirs, Pershing put a capstone on this favorable interpretation with his own account, *My Experiences in the World War* (New York: Frederick A. Stokes, 1931), for which he won a Pulitzer Prize. Laurence Stallings' popular account, *The Doughboys: The Story of the AEF, 1917–1918* (New York: Harper & Row, 1963), stands in this tradition. Even as late as 1977, Frank E. Vandiver included no significant criticism of AEF operational effectiveness or of Pershing's doctrinal and operational leadership in his two-volume biography of Pershing. See *Black Jack: The Life and Times of John J. Pershing* (College Station: Texas A&M University Press, 1977).

[7] See Coffman, *The War to End All Wars: The American Military Experience in World War I* (New York: Oxford University Press, 1968); and DeWeerd, *President Wilson Fights His War: World War I and the American Intervention* (New York: Macmillan, 1968).

[8] Pershing, *Final Report, USAWW*, 12: 44.

American flesh."[9] More or less, the other revisionists make similar accusations, and they provide ample evidence to support their assertions. The conclusion of the revisionists is clear: AEF combat forces were relatively ineffective, even by Great War standards.[10]

However, most of these studies, both traditional and revisionist, have been long on conclusions and short on the kind of detailed operational analysis that would move the debate away from the simple good–bad dichotomy that has come to dominate it. To be fair, the revisionist histories have typically been examinations of general officers, grand strategy, or single offensives. Many of the most important criticisms of AEF operations have been presented in short articles and chapters. Those studies generally have been done well, but none included any detailed examination of different combat organizations fighting for the duration of the war; none even attempted it. In fact, no systematic examination of AEF doctrine, training, and combat operations exists. Despite this, those who closely read the literature on the AEF will notice that each revisionist qualifies his criticism of American forces with a general statement claiming that they were improving when the war ended.[11] Although this glimmer of improvement has been mentioned repeatedly, it rarely has been demonstrated or discussed in any detail. The scholarship of the AEF as a combat force has thus remained mired in a simplistic good–bad dichotomy wrapped in a problematical discourse of "combat effectiveness."

[9] James W. Rainey, "The Questionable Training of the AEF in World War I," *Parameters: Journal of the US Army War College* 22 (Winter 1992–93): 100. Also see Rainey, "Ambivalent Warfare: The Tactical Doctrine of the AEF in World War I," *Parameters: Journal of the US Army War College* 13 (September 1983): 34–46.

[10] See David Trask, *The AEF and Coalition Warmaking, 1917–1918* (Lawrence: University Press of Kansas, 1993), 175; Donald Smythe, *Pershing: General of the Armies* (Bloomington: Indiana University Press, 1986), 217; Paul Braim, *The Test of Battle: The American Expeditionary Forces in the Meuse-Argonne Campaign* (Newark, Del.: University of Delaware Press, 1987), 143, 153; Allan R. Millett, *The General: Robert L. Bullard and Officership in the United States Army, 1881–1925* (Westport, Conn.: Greenwood Press, 1975), 411; and Timothy K. Nenninger, "Tactical Dysfunction in the AEF, 1917–1918," *Military Affairs* 51 (October 1987): 177–81, and "American Military Effectiveness in the First World War," in *Military Effectiveness*, Volume I: *The First World War*, eds. Allan R. Millett and Williamson Murray (Boston: Allen and Unwin, 1988), 116–56.

[11] See Trask, *Coalition Warmaking*, 175; Nenninger, "Tactical Dysfunction in the AEF, 1917–1918," *Military Affairs* 51 (October 1987): 181; Millett, "Over Where? The AEF and the American Strategy for Victory, 1917–1918," in *Against All Enemies: Interpretations of American Military History from Colonial Times to the Present*, eds. Kenneth J. Hagan and William R. Roberts (New York: Greenwood Press, 1986), 251; and "Cantigny, 28–31 May 1918," in *America's First Battles, 1776–1965*, eds. Charles E. Heller and William A. Stofft (Lawrence: University Press of Kansas, 1986), 181.

It is surprising that little research has been done and even less history written on how the AEF planned and conducted its battles; what it learned about modern combat in those battles; and how it adapted its doctrine, tactics, and other operational methods during the course of the war. Such a study would have to present detailed analysis of the training programs, attack plans, and operational reports that show how AEF units hoped to fight, how they actually fought, and why they fought as they did. Until this is done, our understanding of the American military experience in the Great War is incomplete.

This work attempts to accomplish this task. It examines AEF training and operations in detail, but its focus is primarily on ideas and methods and the changes in both during the war. Was the U.S. Army as doctrinally unprepared for modern industrialized combat as the revisionists have claimed? What was the link among prewar doctrine, official AEF doctrine, and the doctrine actually used within the combat divisions to attack the enemy? Did the AEF adapt its doctrine and methods during the war? If there was improvement, as even most revisionists have stated, in what ways did this manifest itself; and where did the learning and adaptation occur first: at AEF GHQ, the headquarters (HQ) of the American First Army, the various army corps, or the combat divisions? How relevant were Pershing and the AEF GHQ in 1918? What impact did they have on American combat operations? Finally, how did the U.S. Army assimilate these lessons after the war? These are the questions addressed in this study.

In short, this work exposes and examines a war of ideas waged *within* the AEF between those who adhered to the traditional, human-centered ideas of the prewar army and those who increasingly appreciated the modern, industrial ideas more prevalent in the European armies. The former set of ideas – based on infantry manpower, the rifle and bayonet, simple attack plans, the maximization of maneuver, and the hope of decisive operational and even strategic results – was summed up in the phrase "open warfare." The latter set of ideas – based on the integration of the latest weaponry, the use of meticulously prepared attack plans, the maximization of firepower, and the methodical attack of specific enemy units to achieve more modest operational results – was often called "trench warfare." With a few notable exceptions, American officers in 1917 were committed to the ideal of open warfare, but interaction with veteran Allied officers and their own experiences in the front lines in 1918 gave rise to an appreciation of the ideas and methods associated with the competing doctrine, trench warfare. Although this inquiry examines the way a number of combat organizations fought throughout the war, it is *not* intended to determine whether those units and soldiers were "good" or "bad." Rather, it discusses their strengths and weaknesses, what they learned, and, ultimately, how they used what they learned.

For a number of reasons, this investigation focuses on selected AEF combat divisions. American units engaged in offensive combat for about six months, but the various army corps exercised combat command for just about half that time, whereas the First Army did so for only about two months. Although some AEF divisions engaged in combat for only a few weeks, the most experienced division commands spent much more time directly opposing the enemy than any army corps or field army. This longer exposure, as well as the greater intensity of the experience, suggests that the division commands had the best opportunity to recognize the significant adjustments that needed to be made to AEF attack doctrine and operational methods. Also, as the largest combat organizations that retained command and control of all its subordinate units, the division commands had the necessary continuity to implement necessary modifications.[12]

Although this study confirms many of the revisionists' criticisms, it also shows that many American officers and men did a lot of learning and adapting. This was true, to various extents, of even some senior officers, a fact neglected in most histories of the AEF. Yet, learning and adaptation were even more common at lower levels. In particular, many officers in the most active American divisions learned to maneuver and communicate on the modern battlefield and, perhaps most important, to employ massive amounts of firepower in set-piece attacks to ensure successful advances at a minimal if not small cost in lives. To be sure, in certain units and in the corps, army, and GHQ staffs, some senior officers retained ideas that negatively affected combat operations. In some instances, different problems – administrative, logistical, and personal – inhibited the successful implementation of new ideas and methods that were often learned at great cost on the battlefield. But, even in those units in which the division commander remained committed to obsolete concepts, there are signs that subordinate officers – and often the men themselves – significantly adapted their methods of fighting, especially to maximize the use of

---

[12] Only minor changes were made to division organizations during the war, such as the temporary addition of a regiment for a special operation. The corps and field armies were composed of many different divisions that rotated in and out of their commands during operations.

firepower. As operational ideas changed, so did the way American units fought on the battlefield, and often with increased success. The stunning aspect of the AEF's experience is not that commanders and junior officers made strategic, operational, and tactical mistakes; that some units struggled to accomplish the missions given them; or that men got lost or straggled; but rather that so many inexperienced officers and men (at all levels) and such new units (of all sizes) managed to continue fighting, learning, and often succeeding throughout their days, weeks, and months of horrific combat in a foreign land.

In 1957, I. B. Holley first published his extraordinary study of how the U.S. Army struggled to develop the air weapon before and during the First World War, not so much due to a lack of ideas but rather to the lack of codification and acceptance of those ideas in the form of doctrine.[13] In 1917–1918, the AEF also struggled to align its ideas and its weapons, but its challenge was almost the opposite of the problem identified by Holley. If weapons-acquisition officers need to "translate ideas into weapons," combat officers immediately before and during battle are tasked with translating weapons into ideas – attack plans. During the First World War, American officers had to overcome the impediment of a somewhat unclear and in many ways impractical set of ideas, typically called *open warfare*, that threatened to force them to rely on certain traditional weapons and to employ emerging weaponry in ways that did not maximize their effectiveness. The challenge for those combat leaders was to take the instruments of war at hand and to develop pragmatic ideas to govern the use of that weaponry so as to inflict the greatest harm on the enemy at the smallest cost to one's own force. This study shows how four combat divisions met this challenge of "ideas and weapons" and, along the way, developed their own AEF way of war.

The investigation begins in Chapter 1 with a discussion of the prewar U.S. Army, its efforts to prepare itself for combat in 1917 and early 1918, and the reaction to combat of General John J. Pershing and other senior American officers at GHQ. The U.S. Army and the AEF had a number of opportunities to ensure that they were materially, organizationally, and intellectually ready for the Western Front, and although they made important strides, they did not succeed uniformly – especially in the intellectual arena – in effecting the kind of transformation required by the

---

[13] See I. B. Holley, Jr., *Ideas and Weapons* (New Haven, Conn.: Yale University Press, 1957; reprint, Washington, D.C.: GPO, 1997), 18.

modern, industrialized battlefield. It remained for the combat divisions to make up the difference.

The subsequent eight chapters describe and analyze the organization, training, and combat operations of four of the AEF's most active divisions. Two of them, the 1st and the 2nd, were labeled Regular Army divisions (formed by gathering existing Regular Army regiments); one, the 26th, was a National Guard division (formed of existing Guard regiments); and the fourth, the 77th, was a National Army division (formed of newly created regiments and filled with draftees). The actual differences between such kinds of divisions were often overstated by some senior AEF officers, but that alone warranted examining at least one of each kind. I selected these divisions not because they were considered the best of their category (at least one of them was not) but rather because they were the first of their kind to arrive in Europe and thus became, at least by some standards, the most experienced. Chapters 2 and 3 cover the 1st Division, Chapters 4 and 5 discuss the 26th Division, Chapters 6 and 7 examine the 2nd Division, and Chapters 8 and 9 analyze the 77th Division. Chapter 10 offers some concluding comments comparing the experiences of each division and the differences among the divisions and the senior commanders and staff officers at GHQ. The work closes with a short discussion of the legacy of the Great War on the U.S. Army.

AEF divisions were not simply new, larger units. They were forced to wage war with new and emerging technologies, such as machine guns, automatic rifles, grenade launchers, trench mortars, rapid-fire artillery, tanks, and aircraft. Although the AEF senior leadership often provided official guidelines for how AEF units were supposed to fight, the approved doctrine did not always provide realistic solutions to the problems and challenges of the battlefield. It was there, in the trenches, where the men in the combat divisions tested the approved doctrine. Forced with the realities of success or failure, victory or defeat, and, ultimately, life or death, divisional officers were forced to discern between good and bad doctrine, between the useful and the harmful, and sometimes between the possible and the impossible. When battlefield experience proved that aspects of doctrine were unsuitable or inadequate, they had to develop answers and make the changes. The question is, how much and in what ways did they adapt and innovate? The following chapters examine the successes and failures of those efforts.

Doctrine, Dogma, and Development in the AEF

While the major powers struggled for mastery along the Western Front during the first three years of the Great War, the United States had a unique opportunity to ready itself for possible belligerency. Yet, when Congress declared war in April 1917, the entire country, and especially the U.S. Army, was unprepared for war in Europe. For a host of reasons, the Army made few significant changes to its official combat doctrine, despite accurate reports of fighting in Europe that warned of practically revolutionary changes on the battlefield. After the American declaration of war, the Army had a second chance to prepare itself for combat on the Western Front because no American unit did any significant fighting for the next thirteen months. Although the U.S. Army and the AEF made enormous strides before the armistice in November 1918, particularly in organization and logistics, many senior leaders resisted making the intellectual adjustments necessary to effect the kind of fundamental doctrinal changes demanded by the modern battlefields in France. Senior leaders did modify official combat doctrine – but they did so belatedly, slowly, and incompletely.

The U.S. Army, 1914–1917

The extent of the U.S. Army's lack of preparedness for the First World War would come as no surprise to those familiar with the basic American attitudes toward military forces and budgets from 1800 to 1917. Furthermore, throughout its period of neutrality, 1914–1917, the U.S. Army showed little sense of urgency and made few changes that improved its ability to fight in Europe, either in its size, organization, armament and equipment, or doctrine and training.

When the Great War started in 1914, the U.S. Army was tiny by European standards, with fewer than a hundred thousand soldiers scattered from China to the Philippines to Panama and from San Francisco to Texas to Boston. About 120,000 other Americans were members of the organized militia – the National Guard. An effort to strengthen the American defense establishment with the National Defense Act of 1916, which was to have swelled the peacetime Regular Army to 165,000 and the National Guard to 450,000 men by 1921, bore little fruit before the nation declared war on the Central Powers in April 1917. By then, the Regular Army had grown to just 121,000 men and the National Guard to 181,000, of whom only about 80,000 were on active duty. There were still just 5,791 Regular officers and about 6,000 more Guard or Reserve officers.[1] The most notable sign in these "baby steps" was the proportionately heavy growth in field-artillery regiments, suggesting that some in the War Department and Congress may have been aware of the nature of the fighting in Europe. The entire U.S. Marine Corps, which was to play a small but prominent role in the AEF, had only 462 officers and 13,000 men in April 1917. The total American land force of 220,000 active-duty soldiers and Marines was still tiny by Great War standards (e.g., the British suffered 250,000 casualties in the Third Battle of Ypres in 1917). It was merely an imperial constabulary and coastal defense force and not an expeditionary army capable of battle against a major power on foreign soil.[2]

In no way were the organizational inadequacies of the defense establishment more obvious than in the structure of the Army's combat

---

[1] The figures on the prewar Army, the National Guard, and the National Defense Act of 1916 come from John Patrick Finnegan, *Against the Specter of a Dragon: The Campaign for American Military Preparedness, 1914–1917* (Westport, Conn.: Greenwood Press, 1974), 6, 13, 154–5; Allan R. Millett and Peter Maslowski, *For the Common Defense: A Military History of the United States of America*, rev. ed. (New York: Free Press, 1994), 341, 349; and Edward M. Coffman, *The War to End All Wars: The American Military Experience in World War I* (New York: Oxford University Press, 1968), 17–18.

[2] In 1915, just fifty-seven hundred officers and men were in the Field Artillery branch and nearly twenty thousand were in the Coast Artillery Corps. But, the 1916 Defense Act called for the Field Artillery to increase from six to twenty-one regiments, and by 1917, the Field Artillery had increased to about eighty-five hundred whereas the Coast Artillery experienced no increase. See Allan R. Millett, "Cantigny, 28–31 May 1918," 151. Marine Corps statistics come from Edwin N. McClellan, *The United States Marine Corps in the World War* (Washington, D.C.: GPO, 1920), 9; the number of British casualties comes from Robin Prior and Trevor Wilson, *Passchendaele: The Untold Story* (New Haven, Conn.: Yale University Press, 1996), 65, 195.

elements. The U.S. Army possessed no organized field armies, army corps, combat divisions, or brigades and very few actual regiments; those regiments that did exist were small in comparison with those then battling on the Western Front. The situation was just as unfavorable regarding the number of officers prepared for senior staff and command work because only 379 officers had completed the command and staff courses at Fort Leavenworth or the Army War College. The bulk of the Regular officer corps was also relatively young and inexperienced – only 3,885 of the 5,791 Regular officers serving in April 1917 had more than one year's service, and only Brigadier General John J. Pershing had commanded a force larger than a brigade (about 10,000 men) in action.[3]

Although the American defense establishment was scattered, small, and inexperienced by European standards, it was actually more professional and experienced than any peacetime force in the nation's history. Many of the men in both the Regular Army and the Guard were veterans of the Spanish-American and Philippine Wars, as were about one third of all officers. The 1916 Punitive Expedition against the Villistas in Mexico provided experience to many more, including a number of important AEF officers (most notably Pershing), but also to a number of future corps and division commanders as well as many senior staff officers.[4] But, those campaigns, difficult as they were, not only provided little opportunity to prepare for the kind of fighting going on along the Western Front, they also further encouraged officers to think of battle in a certain way – as a meeting engagement of small groups of infantry that relied primarily on the rifle, the bayonet, and wide, sweeping maneuvers. This prewar vision of battle, so seemingly inapplicable to the operational realities of the Western Front, was as pervasive as it was ambiguous and proved difficult to dislodge.

[3] Millett, "Cantigny," 154. Prior to Pershing's command of ten thousand men during the Punitive Expedition in Mexico, the largest American campaigns occurred during the Spanish-American and Philippine Wars. During the former effort, the U.S. Army had deployed a seventeen-thousand–man corps to Cuba under the command of Maj. Gen. William R. Shafter. The V Corps included two divisions, each of three brigades. Of those commanding officers, only Brig. Gen. Leonard Wood, who led a cavalry brigade at the battle of Santiago, was still on active duty in 1917. By then, the most senior veteran of the Philippine War was Maj. Gen. J. Franklin Bell, who commanded a brigade of about four thousand men in 1901. Both Wood and Bell had completed tours as Army chief of staff by 1917. Both commanded American divisions (i.e., Wood the 89th, Bell the 77th) during their months of training in the United States, but neither saw any action in France. See Millett and Maslowski, *For the Common Defense*, 289, 312, 337.

[4] Other senior AEF officers who served with Pershing along the Mexican border were Robert L. Bullard, Omar Bundy, John L. Hines, Robert Alexander, Hugh A. Drum, and Harold B. Fiske.

The available armament of the prewar Army was consistent with the lessons of its last three major campaigns. The standard service rifle was the key weapon, and the Army had a good one, although not nearly enough of them. The Springfield Model 1903 was a superb piece for long-range marksmanship – quite possibly the best in the world. But only six hundred thousand guns were on hand. Although the supply could equip a force of about one million men, it was inadequate for the Army that reached four million by the end of the war. Despite this lack of preparedness, the Springfield was the prized weapon of the U.S. Army, and its relative importance in the prevailing vision of battle can be judged by the lack of supporting weaponry for the infantry.[5]

Despite reports from Europe between August 1914 and April 1917, the U.S. Army had made only halting and inadequate steps to integrate emerging technologies, such as the machine gun, into its combat organizations or its vision of battle. The 1912 tables of organization, in effect until the wartime reorganization in 1917, called for just four machine guns per infantry regiment. In comparison, the German Army had by 1917 placed at least thirty-six machine guns in each infantry *battalion* and was, as historian Allan R. Millett writes, making the machine gun its "national weapon."[6] Furthermore, the Army did not possess a single automatic rifle, light trench mortar, or light infantry cannon such as the 37mm gun. Few soldiers had ever seen much less held a grenade, and none had ever fired a rifle grenade.[7] In the prewar army, the infantryman was a rifleman, nothing more and nothing less.

The U.S. Army was similarly lacking the other weapons then dominating the battlefields of the Western Front, such as artillery, tanks, and aircraft. Although it had a decent light field piece in its 3-inch gun, it had few of these and no other heavier field artillery to complement it. In 1917, the French alone had seventeen hundred aircraft at the front, but

---

[5] Leonard P. Ayres, *The War with Germany* (Washington, D.C.: GPO, 1919), 63; Millett, "Cantigny," 153.

[6] Millett, "Cantigny," 155.

[7] In 1917, American machine-gun units were equipped with the 1909 model Benét-Mercié gun, which had been recognized by officers as unsatisfactory as early as 1913. Machine-gun companies were still organized as they had been in 1908. David Armstrong insists that "American interest in machine-gun tactics" actually "declined after 1910." Even after the Great War started, Army officers were convinced that the extraordinary reports of massive machine-gun use in France were the result of the "special conditions" at play on the Western Front, and potential lessons were dismissed by officers who rarely considered having to join the fighting there. See David A. Armstrong, *Bullets and Bureaucrats: The Machine Gun and the United States Army, 1861–1916* (Westport, Conn.: Greenwood Press, 1982), 189, 195, 204.

the entire aerial complement of the U.S. Army consisted of fifty-five obsolete aircraft and just fifty-six flying officers. The Army did not possess a
single tank.[8]

For all its organizational and material weaknesses, the Army's prewar
combat doctrine may have been its greatest handicap. The prewar doctrine, as set forth in the *Field Service Regulations* and expressed in the
corporate knowledge of the officer corps, indicated the Army's vision
of combat in the next war. Both the official regulations and the equally
important beliefs expressed in the Army's professional journals present a
picture of an army more focused on fighting human-centered battles with
small, mobile units in the American Southwest or the Philippines rather
than giant offensives with the huge masses of men and longer-range automatic weapons of the Western Front. Firepower, in the limited way it was
defined prior to 1917, was important but not decisive.

The 1914 *Field Service Regulations* (FSR), revised slightly in 1917 and
again in 1918, formed the basis of official American combat doctrine
throughout the entire world war era.[9] The regulations explained the roles
and duties of each of the combat branches (i.e., infantry, artillery, and cavalry) and described how those forces were to fight on the battlefield. They
were not obviously anachronistic when first issued, especially considering
they were written before the shocking developments in the fall and winter of 1914, when the operational stalemate developed on the Western
Front. However, U.S. Army doctrine was based more on traditional views
of warfare than on existing or emerging technologies. In fact, American

---

[8] Ayres, *The War with Germany*, 80, 85; James J. Cooke, *The U.S. Air Service in the
Great War* (Westport, Conn.: Praeger, 1996), 11; and Coffman, *War to End All Wars*,
188.

[9] The *Field Service Regulations*, printed initially in 1905, were completely revised and
updated at odd intervals, such as 1910, 1913, and 1914. Occasionally, instead of printing a
completely revised edition, the U.S. Army made minor corrections to the existing editions
and simply printed them with titles like *Field Service Regulations, 1914 (with changes
Nos. 1 to 7)*, which was done in 1917 and then again in 1918. Neither minor revision
impacted the roles of the combat arms or use of firepower in battle. In essence, the 1914
edition, with the few changes made by 1918, remained the official Army doctrine until the
next complete revision was published in 1923. Similarly, the 1911 version of the *Infantry
Drill Regulations* underwent only minor changes in 1917 and was deemed authoritative
throughout the war. See William O. Odom, *After the Trenches: The Transformation of
U.S. Army Doctrine, 1918–1939* (College Station: Texas A&M University Press, 1999),
6; War Department, Document No. 394, *Infantry Drill Regulations, United States Army,
1911* (Washington, D.C.: GPO, 1911); and U.S. Infantry Association, *Infantry Drill Regulations, United States Army 1911, with Changes 1–18* (Philadelphia: J. B. Lippincott,
1917).

doctrine in 1914 mirrored operational thinking in most European armies before the fighting in Europe began.[10]

The U.S. Army's leaders, like most European officers before the war, believed that speed and mobility were the keys to warfare. Although the 1914 *FSR* made it clear that "fire superiority" was a crucial element of combat success, a closer reading of the text reveals that the American doctrine possessed great continuity with the Army's history and tradition of fighting in large open places with highly maneuverable units of riflemen.[11] The regulations demonstrated this in three substantial ways. First, American doctrine was explicitly based on the use of lightly armed infantry formations, called "the principal and most important arm." These units were "charged with the main work on the field of battle," and they ultimately decided "the final issue of combat."[12] The other arms, especially the artillery, existed solely to assist the infantry in accomplishing its crucial role of closing with the enemy ranks and defeating them in man-to-man combat.

Second, while some parts of the 1914 *FSR* seem to emphasize the importance of "fire superiority," other sections, including some that would be crucial to waging modern war, exposed just what officers meant by the term. In 1914, American forces were to achieve "fire superiority" by massing infantry rifles at least as much as by using rapid-fire artillery and other modern weapons. The 1903 Springfield was a fine rifle, but the Army placed much greater emphasis on its long-range accuracy than its rate of fire. At its best, it was still a far cry from the faster-firing automatic rifles and light machine guns that became so prevalent in the European war. Making the rifleman the decisive element of battle put the focus squarely on manpower and single-shot accuracy, not on overwhelming firepower. The regulations implied that the artillery would merely assist

---

[10] Both the French and the British placed more emphasis on maneuver than firepower and sought to fight a war of movement. Although somewhat more prepared to employ increasing numbers of howitzers and machine guns on the battlefield, the Germans too planned to fight a war of movement based on traditional rifle companies. For comparisons of prewar doctrine in the French and German armies, see Bruce I. Gudmundsson, *On Artillery* (Westport, Conn.: Praeger, 1993), Chapters 2–4; for a detailed examination of British prewar doctrine, see Bidwell and Graham, *Fire-Power*, Chapters 1–3. As Dennis Showalter asserts, the war plans of all the great powers "were predicated on manœuvre: constant offensives at strategic, operational, and tactical levels." Showalter, "Manœuvre Warfare: The Eastern and Western Fronts, 1914–1915," in *The Oxford Illustrated History of the First World War*, ed. Hew Strachan (New York: Oxford University Press, 1998), 39.

[11] U.S. War Department, Office of the Chief of Staff, *Field Service Regulations: United States Army, 1914, Corrected to July 1, 1914* (Washington, D.C.: GPO, 1914), 67.

[12] Ibid., 68.

the infantry in gaining and maintaining fire superiority. In light of the reality of the Western Front, this relationship seems altogether backwards if not ridiculous. Furthermore, both machine guns and heavy artillery, two key weapons that came to the fore in the first year of the Great War, were minimized. Machine guns were described as "emergency weapons" whose "effective use will be for short periods of time – at most but a few minutes – until silenced by the enemy."[13] Similarly, "heavy field artillery" was viewed as almost useless in field battles. Due to its "limited mobility," it was to be kept "well to the rear of all combatant units" until the appearance of the special conditions that warranted its occasional employment.[14]

The third way in which the 1914 *FSR* demonstrates the Army's traditional approach to combat rests simply in the type of battle that it described in its section on "offensive combat." The regulations presented a battle script more akin to a Civil War meeting engagement than to the massive battles of attrition on the Western Front. The regulations envisioned battles starting with a meeting of the opposing forces, after which the American commander would select whether to turn the enemy's flank or envelop him completely. Either plan required a "holding attack" and at least one "turning movement." Then, after weakening the enemy with fire from a distance – delivered as much by long-range rifles as by artillery – the infantry made the main assault, culminating in a bayonet charge. Successful attacks ideally were followed by a "pursuit" phase, leading not just to the enemy's defeat but also to its "destruction."[15] In this way, as well as in the emphasis on infantry predominance and the limited definition of fire support, the *FSR* of 1914 clearly put a premium on the traditional human-centered element of maneuver in combat and minimized the increasingly important role of using technology to dominate the modern battlefield with firepower.

One method of determining how officers interpreted and understood the official regulations is to examine the views presented in the articles and editorials of the professional military journals, such as the *Infantry Journal*, the *Field Artillery Journal*, the *Cavalry Journal*, and the *Journal of United States Artillery*.[16] In their understanding of the roles of the different

---

[13] Ibid., 72.

[14] Ibid., 70.

[15] Ibid., 82–8.

[16] The *Infantry Journal*, *Field Artillery Journal*, and *Cavalry Journal* had the most articles dealing specifically with combat doctrine. The *Journal of United States Artillery*, written by and for officers in the Coast Artillery, printed many articles on firing techniques and procedures but understandably few on Army combat doctrine.

branches, their beliefs in which weapons were most valuable, and their expectations of the type of battle they would fight, Army officers overwhelmingly confirmed the doctrine presented in the *FSR*. These articles give an even clearer picture of the very traditional, human-centered view of combat that dominated the U.S. Army until it joined the fight in Europe and, in many cases, continued through 1918.

Although the different journals tended to focus on issues relating most specifically to their own branch, each usually agreed with – or at least refrained from directly disputing – the Army's prevailing doctrine. It is not surprising that the infantry and cavalry journals printed one article after another that defended the *FSR* dogma regarding the primacy of human or animal forces on the battlefield. A lengthy editorial published just after the start of the world war gave a clear description of the type of battle American soldiers expected to fight, as well as of the continued dominance of infantry on the field. It argued that in modern combat, the infantry would advance, crawling and bounding forward with nothing but rifles and bayonets, which it would hardly use until almost face to face with the enemy. Only when "fractions of the first line" of infantrymen were "unable to advance further without the support and aid of their weapons" would they

leap up, come together and form a long line which is lit up [with fire] from end to end. A last volley from the troops, a last rush pellmell of the men in a crowd, a rapid making ready of the bayonet for its thrusts, a simultaneous roar from the artillery...a dash of the cavalry from cover emitting the wild yell of victory – and the assault is delivered. The brave men spared by the shot and shell will plant their tattered flag on the ground covered with the corpses of the defeated enemy. Such is the part played by infantry on the field of battle today [1914].

In case there was any doubt in the reader's mind, the writer made it plain: "in real war infantry is supreme...it is the infantry which conquers the field, which conducts the battle and in the end decides its destinies."[17] The other arms mattered, but the infantry remained the key to victory.

A more common method of demonstrating the traditional perspective in the *Infantry Journal* between 1914 and 1917 was to place great emphasis on the infantry's most basic weapons, the rifle and bayonet. While in Europe hundreds of thousands of infantrymen were massacred by artillery and machine guns every few months, American officers continued to focus on the weapons they knew and loved best. Editorials regularly stressed the

---

[17] "Effect of the New Tactics on the Operations of Infantry," *Infantry Journal* 11 (September–October 1914): 242–6.

importance of the individual marksman and the power of the well-trained rifle.[18] Possibly more telling is that issue after issue contained articles on bayonet exercise, bayonet training, and bayonet combat. Of course, one would expect to see a few articles on this still-important aspect of combat, but the sheer number of articles on the topic, probably the single most written about aspect of warfare between 1914 and 1917, reveals much about how U.S. Army officers viewed combat and the role of firepower in achieving success.[19]

As information from the war in Europe began in pour in, the various branches were forced to address the shocking roles of firepower on the Western Front. While the *Field Artillery Journal*, not surprisingly, did not hesitate to print reports from Europe that clearly detailed the unprecedented use of and greater reliance on field guns and howitzers of all sizes, the editorials tended to focus their warnings more on dangerously outdated American techniques and procedures than on an apparently antiquated U.S. combat doctrine.[20] An analysis of *Infantry Journal* articles indicates that the accounts from Europe tended, ironically, only to reinforce existing beliefs in the importance of discipline, mobility, and maneuver. American officers were unwilling to admit that either firepower had overcome maneuver or artillery had superseded infantry. As they understood the relationship of those elements in the delicate balance of combat, if firepower ruled combat, then artillery truly was the "king of battle"; for infantry to remain the "queen of battle," maneuver had to be emphasized more than ever.

---

[18] See Editorial Department, "Rifle and Bayonet," *Infantry Journal* 12 (February 1916): 734–6; General Cherfils, French Army, "Infantry Fire in the Present War," *Infantry Journal* 12 (November 1915): 347–9. In this translated article, which stressed the importance of infantry on the Great War battlefield, the author insisted, "the complete weapon of the infantry is the rifle with a bayonet," p. 349.

[19] For example, see 2nd Lt. L. H. Drennan, "The Psychology of the Bayonet," *Infantry Journal* 11 (September–October 1914): 169–71; Lt. Roger H. Williams, "Bayonet Combat Instruction," *Infantry Journal* 11 (November–December 1914): 390–1; 2nd Lt. C. N. Sawyer, "The Stiff Bayonet," *Infantry Journal* 12 (November 1915): 396–405; 2nd Lt. J. M. Moore, "Bayonet and Bayonet Combat," *Infantry Journal* 12 (March 1916): 908–19; Maj. L. S. Upton, "Bayonet Melee," *Infantry Journal* 13 (July–August 1916): 32–5; "Bayonet Training," *Infantry Journal* 13 (May 1917): 733–50; Maj. Percy Hobbs, "Bayonet Fighting and Physical Training," *Infantry Journal* 14 (August 1917): 79–85; Capt. Allan L. Briggs, "Bayonet Training," *Infantry Journal* 14 (October 1917): 336–40; and Capt. William H. Wilbur, "Bayonet Instruction," *Infantry Journal* 14 (December 1917): 414–21.

[20] "New Field Artillery Classification," *Field Artillery Journal* 7 (January–March 1917): 29; Col. Henry J. Reilly, "Fontainebleau in War Time," *Field Artillery Journal* 7 (April–June 1917): 109–13.

For most American officers, the dominance of highly mobile and lightly armed infantry was simply a principle of warfare, as unchanging as the importance of fighting on the offensive and maintaining unity of command. Writers insisted that "Fire[power] is ... an aid, but only an aid ... Mobility, i.e., the ability to 'git thar fustest with the mostest men,' is the predominant factor."[21] To the extent that the conditions on the modern battlefield had changed, the infantry would simply have to deal with reality and get on with carrying out its traditional role. As one editorial put it, "If the intensity and range of modern fire have increased, if the difficulty of driving home an attack has become greater, so much the greater will be the demand made on the infantry for its utmost effort, for the supreme sacrifice without which victory ... cannot be won."[22] According to American dogma, no matter how hard the infantrymen's task became, the decision in combat always rested with them. To the growing European realization that the infantry was becoming increasingly marginalized on the modern battlefield, due to both the greater range and lethality of artillery as well as the relative impotence of traditional infantry weapons, American officers asked rhetorically, "What shall we think of the school that denies both the possibility of aimed [rifle] fire and the efficacy of the bayonet? If the correctness of such a view is admitted, what is the function of the man in battle? There is only one answer: cannon fodder."[23] That may have been exactly what was happening in Europe, but most American officers were unwilling to admit it. They agreed with the *FSR* that asserted that the only proper way to fight was to attack aggressively with lightly armed infantry, assist the attack with whatever fire support was available, drive the enemy back in disorder, and pursue the enemy with infantry and cavalry until it was destroyed.

Some of these articles suggest that the "cult of the offensive," so prevalent in the European armies before the war, had its adherents in the U.S. Army as well.[24] During the decade before the war, no American military theorists rivaled the fame of such Frenchmen as Ferdinand Foch and Louis

---

[21] Editorial Department, "The Function of Fire," *Infantry Journal* 12 (November 1915): 487–91.

[22] Editorial Department, "Some General Deductions," *Infantry Journal* 11 (November–December 1914): 433–6.

[23] Ibid.

[24] For a discussion of the role of the offensive in the European armies before the war and the psychological and moral aspects of the offensive, see Michael Howard, "Men against Fire: The Doctrine of the Offensive in 1914," in *Makers of Modern Strategy from Machiavelli to the Nuclear Age*, ed. Peter Paret (Princeton: Princeton University Press, 1986), 510–26.

de Grandmaison (who argued that it was "more important to develop a conquering state of mind than to cavil about tactics"), but some Americans agreed that the moral element was supreme in war.[25] The American focus on the offensive, and more specifically on the infantry attack that culminated in a bayonet charge, rested on the psychological and moral component almost as firmly, or as precariously, as did the European.

Both through its service branch journals and in the Fort Leavenworth schools, Army officers were taught to value the moral factor, sometimes above all else. Even in 1915, the editorial department of the *Infantry Journal* approvingly quoted a French colonel who confirmed, "it is the infantry which we have to proclaim today. It is vain to speak of ballistics and pyrotechnics. The soul stands very much above them. And in battle, it is the most resisting soul that triumphs."[26] Some American officers openly concurred with this assessment, writing of "the all importance of man himself" and claiming that the key to successful training was the proper disciplining of the soldier's moral element, not making him a master of tactics, technique, or technology.[27] Other writers took direct issue with reports that the fighting in Europe had become an "artillery war" in which the "human element" played a diminished role.[28]

At the Fort Leavenworth schools, where many influential AEF officers learned what graduate Major General Robert Alexander called "true tactical doctrine," the psychological component was also emphasized, but less directly.[29] Perhaps the most significant of the American tacticians in the prewar years was Major John F. Morrison, who distinguished himself during a six-year teaching tour at Fort Leavenworth. Like his European counterparts, Morrison did not so much deny the reality of defensive

[25] Ibid., 520.

[26] Editorial Department, *Infantry Journal* 12 (December, 1915): 513.

[27] See 1st Lt. James L. Frink, "Method of Training Troops," *Infantry Journal* 12 (September–October, 1916): 139–55.

[28] Editorial Department, "The Character of the Present War," *Infantry Journal* 12 (November–December, 1916): 352–7; Editorial Department, "The Battle of the Future," *Infantry Journal* 12 (November–December, 1916): 357–61.

[29] Robert Alexander, *Memories of the World War, 1917–1918* (New York: Macmillan, 1931), 2–3. Alexander wrote, "If there is one tactical principle which all wars, including the last, have demonstrated to be unshakably correct it is that no operations can be decisive save those carried on in the open." He harshly criticized senior officials in the War Department in 1917 for yielding to the defensive-minded "heresy of the trench warfare cult." He claimed that the Leavenworth schools had "thoroughly imbued" enough Regular officers with "true tactical doctrine" that such a mistake should have been avoidable, and he blamed the error on the lack of Leavenworth training among officers then in the War Department.

firepower as discount it by overcompensating with other factors – such as training, leadership, and a superior psychological attitude. As an observer of the Russo-Japanese fighting in Manchuria in 1904–5, Morrison learned what so many European attachés also seemed to discover: that even in the face of trenches, barbed wire, and the firepower of machine guns and modern artillery, "the right kind of infantry can carry anything if you have enough of it. It is cheaper to do it some other way than by frontal attack if possible but frontal attacks can win." As Timothy K. Nenninger notes, "Morrison was very much attuned to the vagaries of the human element in warfare and the psychological impact of fire superiority."[30] He therefore taught that good leaders had to possess the courage to continue an attack once begun and be able to maintain the morale of the men ordered forward. Perhaps the clearest proof, as well as the most damaging effect, of the human-centered view of battle that dominated the Fort Leavenworth courses was the curriculum's blatant neglect of recent technological developments – including those in such crucial areas as artillery, machine guns, aircraft, and automobiles.[31] If the prewar Army's appreciation of the moral element of war was not as pronounced as in some European circles, it remained sufficiently potent to lead many future American combat commanders, including the AEF commander-in-chief, to eventually stress the importance of individual discipline and aggressiveness to an extent consistent with the greatest European proponents.[32]

[30] Quoted in Timothy K. Nenninger, *The Leavenworth Schools and the Old Army: Education, Professionalism, and the Officer Corps of the United States Army, 1881–1918* (Westport, Conn.: Greenwood Press, 1978), 88. Morrison commanded various training units in United States during the war but never led a division in France. Alexander claimed that he was "removed from his divisional command, ostensibly on account of failing health" but "actually because he dared protest against the erroneous system of [trench warfare] training embarked upon by the Allied officers attached to his division." In all likelihood, if Morrison was eliminated from service in France due to ill health, it was probably at the urging of General Pershing, who demanded the War Department remove from command any officer not meeting his standards of youth, vigor, and health. See Alexander, *Memories*, 3.

[31] Nenninger, *Leavenworth Schools*, 103.

[32] For references to the importance of aggressiveness and other psychological characteristics in the AEF, see Pershing to Henri Pétain, in "Report of G-5," Appendix 31, Divisional Training, pp. 7–8, Folder 246, Commander-in-Chief Reports, Entry 22, RG 120, NA; "General Principles Governing the Training of Units of the American Expeditionary Forces," *USAWW*, 14: 305. "Final Report of Assistant Chief of Staff, G-5," 30 June 1919, *USAWW*, 14: 306–7; HQ First Army, "Combat Instructions," 12 October 1918, Folder 50.9, Box 12, 77th Division Historical File, RG 120, NA; Pershing to Robert Alexander, 24 October 1918, Robert Alexander File, Box 9, JJP Papers, LOC; Pershing, *My Experiences*, 1: 152, 2: 237; Alexander, *Memories*, 16–17, 37, 44–5.

Although the human-centered view of battle may have been stated most clearly by infantry and cavalry officers, few artillerymen were willing to challenge the dominant doctrine prior to arriving in France. No articles written by artillery officers stationed in the United States openly suggested that American doctrine should treat the artillery as an equal of the infantry or that modern firepower was fundamentally changing the battlefield. However, in a few instances, the *Field Artillery Journal* offered hints that some artillerymen were becoming convinced that modern weaponry was upsetting the balance on the battlefield between man and machine, between infantry and artillery, and between firepower and maneuver. For whatever reasons, whether the fear of professional ostracism or simple institutional inertia, most of the direct challenges to the status quo came from American artillery officers assigned as observers in Europe. Although most officers back in the States were not willing to present their views in a public and official forum like the journal, some apparently did discuss them privately. One such glimpse into this muted debate appears in a footnote of an article written by Captain Oliver L. Spaulding that explained the most promising infantry formations that could help units advance with a minimum of casualties from artillery. Spaulding, a prominent artillery officer recognized as an expert in gunnery tactics and procedures, felt compelled to announce that while he sometimes may have appeared "to claim exaggerated effect for artillery fire," he had "never belonged to the school known as the 'destroyers,' who believe that they can annihilate anything within range." He further insisted that he never claimed artillery fire to be "all-powerful."[33] Such a school of officers, apparently composed exclusively of artillerymen, must have existed, but they were unwilling to publicly challenge the Army's traditional views on doctrine. Eventually, some lost their inhibitions.

Between 1914 and 1917, what little training the Army accomplished was based strictly on such traditional doctrine. Infantry training consisted

---

[33] Capt. O. L. Spaulding, "Infantry under Artillery Fire," *Infantry Journal* 11 (March–April 1915): 641. A rare exception to this public silence was in 1915 when the ordnance chief of the General Staff wrote, "It appears that although the field artillery has played an important role in all modern wars, its use has now been extended to the point where it becomes a question as to whether it does not actually make the main attack, which is rendered permanently effective by the infantry advance, instead of, as formerly considered, being used to prepare the way for the main attack to be made by the infantry." Millett notes that this was viewed as "heresy" by cavalry and infantry officers. See Millett, "Cantigny," 151.

mainly of close-order and extended-order drill on open grounds and rifle marksmanship practice. The field artillery did less firing and none of it under conditions similar to those prevalent on the Western Front, where massed barrages, based primarily on map coordinates, were the rule even at night and in bad weather. American officials considered such firing a waste of ammunition and prohibited it. Most important, combined training between infantry and artillery forces almost never occurred. The lack of artillery fire was not merely a result of budget restrictions. Colonel Conrad H. Lanza, a career artillery officer who later served in the AEF's First Army during its two great battles at St. Mihiel and the Meuse-Argonne, caustically noted that in the official prewar doctrine, "the artillery was considered an auxiliary, sometimes useful, never necessary, and sometimes a nuisance."[34]

Although the U.S. Army was authorized by Congress to improve its size between 1914 and 1917, it made practically no change in its doctrine. The official regulations, such as the *FSR* and the *Infantry Drill* (i.e., tactical) *Regulations*, showed no significant development, even regarding infantry tactics and the employment of machine guns and artillery. This doctrine continued to be preached with particular fervor at the Army's staff and command courses at Fort Leavenworth, where the most promising young officers were treated to descriptions of battle that bore no semblance to the fighting then raging in Europe. Fewer than three months before America declared war, Harold B. Fiske, then a major and leading instructor at Fort Leavenworth, gave insight into the infantry tactics deemed so powerful by existing doctrine: "The object was to maneuver infantry forces so as best to bring infantry fire upon the opposing infantry. As rapidly as possible, the firing line was to be built up so that 'fire superiority' could be gained. Once gained, the stage was set for the ultimate act, the bayonet charge."[35] The joining of such ideas about infantry tactics with the beliefs that the infantry was the key to victory, the rifle and bayonet the most important weapon, and the artillery an occasionally necessary auxiliary bore bitter

---

[34] Col. Conrad H. Lanza, "The Artillery Support of the Infantry in the A.E.F.," *Field Artillery Journal* 26 (January–March 1936): 62.

[35] Johnson and Hillman, *Soissons*, 153. Fiske was not alone. As Millett notes, other officers such as John F. Morrison and Oliver L. Spaulding, who were recognized as two of the Army's most important tacticians, described battles in which the main role of the artillery was simply to weaken enemy resistance enough that the infantry could get within rifle range and work its way forward under the power of its own weaponry and spirit. See Millett, "Cantigny," 152–3.

fruit on the battlefields near Belleau Wood, Soissons, the Vesle, and the Meuse-Argonne, where American units slowly learned the obsolescence of such ideas.

Several factors contributed to the stagnation of American doctrine during a three-year period when the U.S. Army might have made significant adjustments to prepare itself to fight in the war it ultimately joined. A lack of raw information about the conditions on the Western Front was *not* a handicap because numerous American observers sent back reports and descriptions of modern combat.[36] Essentially, the doctrinal stasis resulted from an unwillingness to believe the Army would soon have to fight on such a scale or in such an environment and an inability to devote the resources to preparing for possible operations in Europe while meeting other existing demands. Most American military officers, like the vast majority of their fellow citizens, suffered from an utter disbelief that Americans would ever have to fight on the Western Front. President Woodrow Wilson's chastisement of General Staff officers who were reported to be developing contingency war plans for a possible war with Germany made it clear to others that the U.S. Army was not to prepare itself to join the conflict.[37]

The Army's preoccupation with its more immediate concerns, particularly the Punitive Expedition in Mexico that completely taxed not only the Regular Army but also drew tens of thousands of National Guardsmen into federal service, also inhibited preparation for the world war. The Army had to close its primary field-artillery training and experimentation center, the School for Fire at Fort Sill, Oklahoma, just to field the forces necessary to meet the border emergency. More important, the Army also dissolved the Field Artillery Board – the group of senior officers charged with analyzing all reports from Europe regarding artillery issues and ensuring that the branch's *Drill and Service Regulations* were updated and properly interpreted. Such organizational disruptions, along with the need to meet all the other urgent requirements of missions along the Mexican border, ensured that senior American officers in charge of military organization, armament, and doctrine continued to focus primarily

---

[36] Even a casual reading of the Army service journals cited previously shows the number of reports from France.

[37] David R. Woodward cites the example of Wilson accusing the Chief of the U.S. Army's War College Division (i.e., the General Staff division responsible for war planning) of possessing plans for an offensive war with Germany (the division chief later insisted there was no offensive plan). See Woodward, *Trial by Friendship: Anglo-American Relations, 1917–1918* (Lexington: University Press of Kentucky, 1993), 18–19.

on continental defense, a responsibility they expected to be an ongoing concern long after the Punitive Expedition and even the Great War were over. In that light, James L. Abrahamson is correct in asserting that, "contrary to the old cliché suggesting that in peacetime generals invariably spend their energies in vain preparation to refight the last war, during the three-year period before America's intervention in the world conflict, its military leaders prepared neither for the last war, nor indeed for the present war, but instead for the next war."[38] However, those officials expected such future campaigns to be waged most likely in a limited war and in accordance with the traditional infantry-based doctrine that favored maneuver over firepower and manpower over machines. Whether such a doctrine might have been useful in future operations in northern Mexico, the Philippines, or along the eastern seaboard will never be known. As of April 1917, the doctrine was destined to be applied on the Western Front in Europe.

Pershing and the Creation of the AEF, 1917–1918

In June 1917, the first convoy of American soldiers under the command of General Pershing sailed to Europe. As general-in-chief of the new AEF, Pershing was charged with creating a large American field army and conducting a decisive offensive on the Western Front to win the war and ensure American dominance of the postwar peace talks.[39] Considering the organizational and material condition of the forces at his disposal – and the doctrinal stagnation of the previous three years – Pershing had much work to do to get the fledgling AEF ready to carry out such a mission. In fact, most senior military officers did not expect the AEF to conduct a major offensive until 1919.[40]

---

[38] James L. Abrahamson, *America Arms for a New Century: The Making of a Great Military Power* (New York: Free Press, 1981), 162. For more information on the negative effects of the Punitive Expedition on the field artillery branch, see Mark E. Grotelueschen, *Doctrine Under Trial: American Artillery Employment in World War I* (Westport, Conn.: Greenwood Press, 2001), 4.

[39] For a discussion of Wilson's goals for the AEF, see Trask, *The AEF and Coalition Warmaking*, 6, 12–13, and "The Entry of the USA into the War," in *The Oxford Illustrated History of the First World War*, 242–6.

[40] For discussion of the initial plan developed by Pershing and GHQ for the 1919 offensive, see Millett, "Over Where? The AEF and the American Strategy for Victory, 1917–1918," in *Against All Enemies: Interpretations of American Military History from Colonial Times to the Present*, eds. Kenneth J. Hagen and William R. Roberts (Westport, Conn.: Greenwood Press, 1986), 238–9. See also Daniel R. Beaver, *Newton D. Baker and the American War Effort 1917–1919* (Lincoln: University of Nebraska Press, 1966), 111, 120.

John J. Pershing, Commander-in-Chief of the AEF.

Although the AEF, like the U.S. Army as a whole, started with a small core, it rapidly grew to an historically unprecedented size. By May 1918, when the AEF began its first offensive engagements, 667,000 men had arrived in France. By August, when Pershing formed the American First Army, the number was 1,473,000. When the war ended in November, the total surpassed two million. Thanks to a smoothly run draft back in the United States and a relatively trouble-free Allied convoy system, raw numbers of men were not a major problem for Pershing or his GHQ.[41]

More troubling was the small core of experienced officers and men available to assume leadership positions in the growing AEF. The tiny

---

[41] A full accounting of the size of the AEF during each month of the war is in American Battle Monuments Commission (ABMC), *American Armies and Battlefields in Europe: A History, Guide, and Reference Book*, Washington, D.C.: GPO, 1938; reprint, Center for Military History, 1995, 502. The AEF did ultimately suffer manpower shortages, and Pershing even reduced the authorized strength on infantry companies to about 174 men in October 1918. But, in comparison with the British, French, and Germans, the AEF's manpower troubles were minor.

cadre of professional officers and noncommissioned officers (NCOs) was quickly supplemented by an equally small number of less professional officers and NCOs from the National Guard. However, Pershing and many other senior AEF officers viewed Guardsmen with dislike, distrust, and sometimes both. Considering the low level of training and experience in the National Guard and the prevalence of political and social factors that sometimes compromised the professionalism of Guard units, such Regular bias was not always without warrant. Yet, such beliefs caused serious problems because the War Department and the AEF gave each combat division one of three essentially permanent designations: divisions were either Regular, National Guard, or National Army (i.e., those supposedly formed from draftees). During the course of the war, these distinctions became increasingly irrelevant; as Regular officers took command of battalions, regiments, and brigades in Guard and National Army divisions, and as draftees and inexperienced volunteers joined all three kinds of divisions as replacements in large numbers, the important distinctions receded. But, in many cases, Regular officers retained prejudicial opinions and made biased decisions regarding Guard divisions and, to a lesser extent, National Army divisions. In fact, concerning the experience level of the junior officers and troops at the start of AEF operations, nearly all divisions were the same – they were all green.

One major organizational decision the AEF GHQ had to make immediately concerned the sizes of the various combat units, from infantry company to division. The GHQ invariably settled on the largest potential figure for each unit. Infantry companies were to be 250 men (i.e., five times the peacetime strength), in battalions of more than 1,000. Regiments had 3,800 officers and men (i.e., triple the size of the standard peacetime regiment) and infantry brigades nearly 8,500. With two giant infantry brigades, a five-thousand–man artillery brigade, as well as a host of other support troops, each AEF division numbered more than twenty-eight thousand officers and men, well over twice the size of most Allied or German divisions.[42]

Historians have offered various explanations for the reasons behind the giant AEF division, including GHQ's awareness of the dearth of officers

[42] During 1918, typical British divisions averaged 11,800 men, French divisions just 11,400, and German divisions about 12,300. For each nation, the official authorized strength of the division was about fifteen thousand men. Certain British divisions, such as the Canadian and Australian, were larger – with a total strength of about twenty-one thousand men; some French divisions, such as the 1st Moroccan, were close to that size. See ABMC, *American Armies*, 501; Schreiber, *Shock Army*, 20–21.

qualified for division command and a desire to put Regular officers in command of all divisions, especially those from the Guard. Although those factors likely played a part in the decision, one influential GHQ officer stressed another concern – one that touched on AEF doctrine. James G. Harbord, who served as Pershing's first chief of staff in France, claimed that the primary consideration was "tactical." Harbord insisted that the large division was essential to wage the kind of offensive American doctrine demanded – a crushing blow using infantry to crack the enemy lines, race through the breach, and destroy the enemy remnants out in the open. Aware that it was "quite a problem" to replace one division in line with another during an offensive, and apparently equally mindful of the casualties likely to be suffered while battering forward for several days in the early stages of the attack, GHQ created divisions it considered large enough – especially in infantry strength – to make a "decisive stroke" and continue attacking "until a decision was reached."[43] Thus, the huge AEF division can be taken to demonstrate the early understanding by Pershing and GHQ that casualties would be heavy, as well as their expectation that AEF units were to continue attacking until they broke into the open.

In accordance with American prewar doctrine, Pershing and the GHQ believed the key component of the AEF division was its large complement of twelve thousand riflemen. But GHQ's apparent awareness of the hard fighting in the first stages of any major attack forced them to add a number of other weapons to the integral strength of the division. Each had an artillery brigade with two twenty-four–gun regiments of light guns, a third regiment of twenty-four large howitzers, and a twelve-gun battery of 6-inch trench mortars. Each infantry regiment was supported by 192 automatic rifles, sixteen heavy machine guns, six 3-inch Stokes mortars, and three 37mm guns. Each infantry brigade also had its own sixty-four–gun machine-gun battalion, and a third similar battalion reported directly to the division staff.[44]

For the basic weapon of the rifleman, the War Department supplemented existing Springfield rifles with a modified version of the British Enfield, then in mass production in many American plants. The U.S. Enfield Model 1917 rifle, rechambered to take Springfield 0.30-caliber

---

[43] James G. Harbord, *The American Army in France, 1917–1919* (Boston: Little, Brown, 1936), 103. Strangely, Pershing never offered his reasons for the giant division in either his *Preliminary Report*, his *Final Report*, or his memoirs. See James W. Rainey, *Ambivalent Warfare: The Tactical Doctrine of the AEF in World War I*, 13 (September 1983): 40.

[44] Each division could also equip thousands of machine-gun troops and the regiment of combat engineers with rifles, and this was done on more than one occasion. See the tables of organization, *USAWW*, 1: 339–88.

ammunition, was of comparable quality to the 1903 Springfield, but all other divisional armament was completely new to American soldiers. Due to the material unpreparedness of the peacetime U.S. Army, the sluggish pace of development in the ordnance section of the War Department, and a slow transition to wartime production in some sectors of American industry, the AEF relied heavily on Allied weaponry. In some cases, this proved adequate: the French Hotchkiss heavy machine gun, 37mm gun, 75mm light artillery piece, and 155mm Schneider howitzer were all fine weapons, though not without weaknesses. The famous "French 75," with its light shell and rapid rate of fire, was a good fit for a war of movement, but it did limited damage to troops protected by deep trenches or dense woods. The Hotchkiss was a reliable weapon, but it was the heaviest machine gun then in use and was therefore impracticable except under the most stabilized conditions. Similarly, the Schneider howitzer was a powerful weapon, with a 130-pound shell capable of great destruction. But, it required at least one eight-horse team just to move the weapon over good ground, and it needed many more to keep it supplied with ammunition. For its automatic rifle – an increasingly important infantry weapon on the Western Front – the AEF accepted the French Chauchat, a poor weapon with serious jamming and accuracy problems that made it especially inadequate for continuous or long-range fire. One divisional machine-gun officer claimed it was good, like the Hotchkiss and the Schneider howitzer, only for "trench to trench warfare."[45] Only at the very end of the war did some lucky units get a small number of the new

---

[45] Division Machine Gun Officer to Chief of Staff, 1st Division, 3 August 1918, Folder "First Division-Memoranda and Instructions," Box 14, Charles P. Summerall Papers, LOC. The AEF used about thirty-four thousand Chauchats during the war. The much-superior BAR, which was used throughout the Second World War and the Korean War, was being produced in large numbers by March 1918, but they were only slowly given to American divisions. Nearly seventy thousand were produced during 1918 and twenty-nine thousand made it to France before 1 November, but only about forty-six hundred were used in combat. Coffman suggested that a breakdown in transportation prevented more BARs from getting to the divisions during the war. Ayers claims that the delay in employing the new weapon was the result of "a deliberate and most significant judgment" by Pershing, who thought the BAR "so greatly superior" to any automatic rifle then in use that they needed to be held back until they could be issued en masse throughout the AEF. He feared that if the guns were used piecemeal, the Germans would capture one, mass produce them, and reissue them in time to negate any American advantage on the battlefield. As in other matters, the officers and men in the divisions saw things differently. Division commanders such as Summerall and Edwards tried to replace their Chauchats with BARs as soon as possible, and many automatic riflemen simply appropriated them whenever they could get their hands on them. See Ayers, *The War with Germany*, 66–9; Coffman, *The War to End All Wars*, 39; and William G. Dooley, Jr., *Great Weapons of World War I* (New York: Walker and Co. Publishing, 1969), 91–2.

Browning Automatic Rifle (BAR), which was the best automatic rifle used in the war. Some American divisions received old-model trench mortars that were impossible to move with any speed. Furthermore, the AEF was dependent on the Allies for tanks, aircraft, gas shells, and telephone wire, and American units rarely secured the numbers of these weapons that they requested. In sum, the AEF was adequately armed, especially for combat in the trenches, but it was not particularly well equipped to carry out any rapid campaign of maneuver.[46]

Although Pershing made great strides in overcoming the organizational and material inadequacies of the prewar American Army, little development occurred in the intellectual arena. Whereas U.S. Army doctrine may have mirrored European thinking before the war, by 1917 a wide gulf had developed between the two.[47] Most combat officers in both the French and British armies, though perhaps not all staff officers, had realized that the only way to achieve any measure of success on the battlefield was to rely heavily on firepower and to have the infantrymen do whatever maneuvering they could to get to and into the enemy trenches. But, when Pershing observed Allied attacks in 1917 based on "the doctrine of destruction" or, as French General Henri Pétain tritely proclaimed, the idea that "artillery conquers, infantry occupies," he was not impressed.[48]

Pershing was a devout believer in the prewar doctrine as elucidated in the 1914 *FSR*. A 1914 *Infantry Journal* editorial quoted then–Brigadier

---

[46] For additional information on the AEF's reliance on the French Army, see Robert Bruce, *A Fraternity of Arms: America and France in the Great War* (Lawrence: University Press of Kansas, 2003).

[47] According to Lieutenant Colonel C. N. F. Broad, a British officer, "Tactics before the war usually meant fire and movement of infantry supported by such artillery as was available; one of the main essentials being a large infantry reserve." This closely mirrored American doctrine in 1914. C. N. F. Broad, "The Development of Artillery Tactics – 1914–1918, Part I," *Field Artillery Journal* 12 (September–October 1922): 375–96.

[48] An excellent description of the European "doctrine of destruction" was given in a 1917 *Field Artillery Journal* article: "No attack is possible until after an intense and effective artillery preparation, which has for its objects: (a) To destroy the enemy's barbed wire; (b) To disintegrate and destroy enemy's trenches and dugouts, and to destroy or annihilate their defenders; (c) To prevent, or at least interfere with, hostile artillery action; (d) To prevent the passage of the enemy's reserves by curtain (barrage) fire; and (e) To destroy the machine guns wherever they can be located." "Notes on Artillery," *Field Artillery Journal* 7 (April–June 1917): 179–81. For further discussions of the developments in European doctrines during the war, see Shelford Bidwell and Dominick Graham, *Fire-Power: British Army Weapons and Theories of War, 1914–1945* (London: Allen and Unwin, 1982); J. B. A. Bailey, *Field Artillery and Firepower* (Oxford: The Military Press, 1989); and David T. Zabecki, *Steel Wind: Colonel Georg Bruchmüller and the Birth of Modern Artillery* (Westport, Conn.: Praeger, 1994).

General Pershing's statement that "the importance of well-trained infantry as the prime essential to military success can hardly be overestimated."[49] Such a statement was entirely justified, if delivered within a context that recognized that the infantry's reliance on firepower was equally difficult to overestimate. But, Pershing's statement should be understood in light of an official doctrine that neglected this latter point. His attitude apparently underwent little change in the following three years. Shortly after arriving in Europe, Pershing recognized that Allied combat methods not only differed from American doctrine, they often directly contradicted it. In no way was their deviance more egregious to Pershing than in their reliance on firepower and their diminished emphasis on the rifle-and-bayonet armed infantryman. Significantly, he despised those Allied attacks that he said were "based upon the cautious advance of infantry with prescribed objectives, where obstacles had been destroyed and resistance largely broken by artillery." Although this brief description may sound like an effective system of fighting on the modern conventional battlefield, Pershing meant it as a harsh criticism. He also denounced the French infantryman in particular for not relying enough on "his rifle" and for not making use of "its great power."[50]

To ensure that the American forces sent to Europe would not be easily converted to any heretical ideas, Pershing sent a flurry of messages back to Washington directing that all military training stress the crucial role of infantry in battle, the preeminent value of the rifle and bayonet, and the American version of mobile fighting. He insisted that all soldiers be taught that "the rifle and the bayonet remain the supreme weapons of the Infantry soldier" and that "the ultimate success of the army depends upon their proper use in *open warfare*."[51] As late as October 1917, then, he either downplayed or failed to appreciate automatic rifles, machine guns, grenades, mortars, and infantry cannon.

Those last two words, *open warfare*, became Pershing's slogan for employing the U.S. Army's prewar doctrine on Europe's modern battlefields. The AEF commander believed that "to bring about a decision the [enemy] army must be driven from the trenches and the fighting carried

[49] "General Pershing's Opinion of Infantry," *Infantry Journal* 11 (July–August 1914): 83.

[50] John J. Pershing, *My Experiences in the World War.* 2 vols. (New York: Frederick A. Stokes, 1931), 2: 237.

[51] Cablegram No. 228-S, 19 October 1917, Report of Chief of Artillery, AEF, Inclosures-Part II, "Field Artillery Training," p. 15, Folder 382, Commander-in-Chief Reports, Entry 22, RG 120, NA (italics added).

out into the open."[52] Once this was accomplished, the traditional American vision of battle, as described in the *FSR*, was to be carried out to its natural conclusion with an envelopment, an assault, and a vigorous and final pursuit that destroyed the enemy army. To Pershing and most other senior American officers, victory in "open warfare" would come when the AEF waged an "aggressive offensive based on *self-reliant infantry*" [emphasis added].[53] This extraordinary terminology was not accidental; Pershing truly wanted and expected his infantry to be capable of fighting without any significant use of heavy firepower. The expression also was consistent with other phrases he and other senior officers at GHQ used that always accentuated – or rather exaggerated – the physical and moral capabilities of the human element and minimized the role of modern machines and weapons technology. Pershing wanted the infantry trained to the point that each soldier felt he was "as a bayonet fighter, invincible in battle."[54] The statements of many other senior commanders and staff officers confirm that these views were widely shared throughout the AEF, at least until midway through 1918.

As far as the AEF high command was concerned, the Army's human-centered prewar doctrine was to govern American operations in Europe, at least during offensive operations. Strangely, many American officers showed a surprising appreciation for the latest tactical ideas for defensive operations, including a heavy reliance on firepower and the finer points of what became known as the *defense-in-depth*, or the *elastic defense*. Many times during the fighting in the spring and summer of 1918, American division commanders demonstrated a superior understanding of these defensive methods than the French corps and army commanders under whom they had to serve. When on the offensive, however, most American officers, including influential GHQ officers and many division commanders, seemed to agree that the Army's infantry-based prewar doctrine – what they all referred to as "open warfare" – was still applicable.[55]

---

[52] Pershing, *My Experiences*, 2: 12.

[53] Pershing, *My Experiences*, 2: 237. Pershing and other officers at GHQ used this term regularly.

[54] Report of G-5, Appendix 31, "Divisional Training," pp. 7–8, Folder 246, Commander-in-Chief Reports, Entry 22, RG 120, NA.

[55] These defensive adjustments appear to have been the result of rapidly appreciated new ideas, not accidentally applicable remnants of the prewar doctrine. One AEF officer understood the 1914 *FSR* description of defensive preparations as "strong front line, weak supports, strong reserves, weak outposts, little depth, and incomplete organization of the ground." This bore little resemblance to the elastic defense of 1918. See Edward S. Johnston, "A Study of the Nature of the United States Infantry Tactics for Open Warfare

The term "open warfare" and other similar terms such as "war of movement" and "maneuver warfare" were also regularly used by many senior Allied and German officers throughout 1918. In some cases, British, French, and German officers even agreed with Pershing that their own troops reacted poorly when forced to fight on ground devoid of deep trenches and barbed wire, as happened on a number of occasions between the battle of Cambrai in November 1917 and the end of the war. In December 1917 and again in April 1918, General Henri Pétain, the head of the French Army, issued memoranda directing that units prepare for a phase of fighting in which "elaborately and developed positions on and under the ground have disappeared." Such training was to stress the following:

> ... rapidity of offensive movement; brief orders instead of elaborate plans; flexible formations; out-flanking in place of frontal attacks; assignment of general directions to larger units, specific objectives to small ones; adaptation of artillery fire to the ground and the conditions, rather than rigid barrage; direct fire of machine guns to support and accompany the attack; use of the rifle as the all-important arm of the infantryman; close tactical connection of all arms, including air forces and tanks; broader fronts for units in attack. To sum up: rapidity and violence in preparation, flexibility in execution by both infantry and artillery. The artillery hammers the strong parts of the enemy's armor; the infantry seeks the weak spots, slips through, and takes him in reverse.[56]

Similarly, one British division commander reported that the main lesson of his division's operations in the summer of 1918 was "the necessity for adapting ourselves at once to the requirements of more open warfare," and many British memoranda discussed the methods necessary to fight under such conditions.[57] The German Army's emphasis on elite

on July 18, 1918, and of Their Points of Difference as Contrasted with the United States Army Tactics as Taught in 1914," Student Monograph IR-124-1931, Command and General Staff School, Combined Arms Research Library (CARL), Fort Leavenworth, Kans.

[56] See Memorandum, *Armees du Nord et du Nord-Est; Etat Major*, 3 Bureau, No. 8810, 9 April 1918, which references a previous memorandum of 30 December 1918, cited in Oliver J. Spaulding and John W. Wright, *The Second Division, American Expeditionary Force in France, 1917–1919* (New York: Hillman Press, 1937), 9–10.

[57] At the same time, Canadian officers were noticing the same problem. The commander of the 1st Canadian Brigade criticized his division because "trench warfare ideas still apparently prevail.... The training of officers in open warfare still leaves much to be desired." The problems existed despite the special period of training in open-warfare methods that the Canadian Corps underwent in May and June of 1918, during which the troops learned a new "diamond formation," a "battalion 'scatter' maneuver, and infantry envelopment methods." Travers notes that even two successful Canadian brigades reported

stormtroop units and infiltration tactics is well known, and they represent the German method of waging "open warfare." In this light, the main issue was not that AEF leaders talked about open warfare but rather what they meant when they used the term.

Most senior American officers approached the idea of open warfare very differently from their counterparts in the Allied and German armies. The latter generally treated open warfare as a certain phase of combat that needed to be dealt with or an opportunity to be exploited, but American officers considered it a necessity and a superior form of war. AEF leaders viewed trench warfare as a horrific aberration and insisted that open warfare was the natural state of affairs, even though the war, from beginning to end, showed just the opposite: stabilized conditions in the trenches proved the more typical situation, and most open conditions were merely transitory events between periods of trench stabilization.[58]

An unfortunate result of this difference was that whereas European forces chose only specific times, places, and situations for employing open-warfare methods, American officers were encouraged to initiate open warfare and to employ open-warfare methods anywhere and everywhere. American doctrine and official AEF pronouncements insisted not only that it was possible to do so, but also that it was the only proper way to fight. Officers committed to AEF doctrine failed to apprehend that tactics and techniques used successfully by the Germans in the open terrain and against the poor defensive arrangements of the British Fifth Army near St. Quentin in March 1918, and by the British on similar open ground and against the even weaker defensive positions (and more demoralized troops) of the German Second Army at Amiens five months later, did not guarantee equally impressive results when attempted by American troops against the Hindenburg Line positions in the wooded, broken terrain between the Meuse River and the Argonne Forest.

"the failure to coordinate arms and weapons systems after the support of the artillery and tanks had been outrun, despite earlier training," and he concludes that "if the innovative Canadian Corps was experiencing the pains of organizing the cooperation of all arms in the new warfare, so must the rest of the BEF have been experiencing similar or worse difficulties." See Travers, *How the War Was Won: Command and Technology in the British Army on the Western Front, 1917–1918* (London: Routledge, 1992), 149–52. For a discussion of open-warfare methods in British and Germany forces, see HQ I Army Corps, "Notes on Recent Fighting: Extracts from an Order Issued by the 6th Bavarian Division for the Attack on Merckam Front (Belgian), 4 April 1918," 6 June 1918, Folder 50.1, Box 32, I Army Corps Historical File, RG 120, NA.

[58] This was the case during the British attack at Cambrai in 1917, during the German Spring offensives in 1918, and the Allied counteroffensives from July 1918 to the end of the war.

Perhaps the most important difference between the American and European understanding of open warfare lay in the relative emphasis of the role of firepower in such fighting. Both perspectives admitted the importance of infantrymen making a maximum use of the service rifle – a reasonable admonition for the hundreds of thousands of soldiers for whom the rifle and bayonet were the *only* weapons under their control. But, European officers on both sides of the trenches had learned that rifle proficiency was no longer the *sine qua non* of victory, and they placed much more emphasis on artillery, machine guns, automatic rifles, mortars, grenades, flamethrowers, poison gas, tanks, and aircraft. German stormtroopers were not so much expert riflemen as coordinators of the most devastating firepower-producing weapons available and whose reliance on Colonel Georg Bruchmüller's massive artillery fire plans could not be overstated. For the Allies, the reliance on the "auxiliaries" was equally dramatic – even on open terrain, tanks, artillery, automatic weapons, and grenades were deemed more crucial to success than the British Enfield or French Lebel service rifles. Most Allied officers also had concluded that often the only reasonable course of action was to make limited, meticulously planned, set-piece attacks based on crushing artillery barrages. Many AEF officers recognized this tendency but, instead of emulating it, they criticized it.[59]

American officers including Pershing, high-ranking officers at GHQ, and many other senior commanders remained committed to prewar doctrine. Official documents insisted that "the essential principles of war have not changed," that "the fundamental principles governing the conduct of fire for field artillery remain essentially unchanged," and that "the ultimate object" of all operations was "warfare in the open conducted in all essential elements according to the principles found in our standard manuals" – the latter a clear reference to the *FSR* and *Infantry Drill Regulations*.[60] This established the rifleman as the crucial element of all AEF attacks, minimized the importance of auxiliary weapons, treated such essential techniques as the rolling barrage as a crutch not fit for open warfare, and made attacks with unlimited objectives preferable to set-piece assaults.

---

[59] For descriptions of the German stormtroopers and their methods, see Holger H. Herwig, *The First World War: Germany and Austria-Hungary 1914–1918* (London: Arnold, 1997), 189, 253, 413–14; and Bruce I. Gudmundsson, *Stormtroop Tactics: Innovation in the German Army, 1914–1918* (Westport, Conn.: Praeger, 1989).

[60] See *USAWW*, 3: 316–17, 326.

These views hindered the full utilization of both existing weaponry such as artillery, mortars, and automatic rifles and emerging technologies such as tanks, chemical weapons, and aircraft. None of those weapons could be fully utilized in a doctrine that dogmatically sought to preserve the traditional role and methods of the rifleman as described in prewar regulations. In the words of Brigadier General Samuel D. Rockenbach, the head of the AEF tank corps: "Tanks were to conform to the tactics of Infantry. They were an auxiliary arm and must conform."[61]

Although most senior AEF officers – and, no doubt, many junior ones as well – may have been convinced that American doctrine was reasonably settled, at least one officer was willing to voice a dissenting opinion almost immediately after seeing the Western Front with his own eyes. The only recorded debate among senior American officers regarding combat doctrine occurred in July 1917, when a group of officers from the War Department met with Pershing's staff. The War Department had ordered a special fact-finding team called the Baker Mission, composed of officers from all combat branches, to visit various French and British commands, learn all it could about fighting successfully on the Western Front, discuss its findings with Pershing's staff, and then report back to Washington. Colonel Charles P. Summerall, a hard-charging artillery officer with a sterling record both in combat and in peacetime service, was the senior artilleryman on the mission, and during the meeting with GHQ, he forcefully argued that the amount of firepower GHQ planned to use to support American attacks was "inadequate."[62] Summerall insisted that GHQ needed to more than double the number of guns that it planned to allocate to attacking combat divisions. Furthermore, he contended that attacking divisions had to be provided more of the light- and medium-sized field guns and howitzers "without which," according to Summerall, "the experience of the present war shows positively that *it is impossible for infantry to advance*" [emphasis added].[63]

---

[61] S. D. Rockenbach, "Lecture on Tanks and their Operations with the First American Army at St. Mihiel and in the Argonne, Sept. 11th to Nov. 11th," Box 30, Clarence R. Edwards Papers, Massachusetts Historical Society, Boston, Mass.

[62] One report of the meeting between the Baker Mission and the AEF staff is in *USAWW*, 1: 109–14.

[63] Although some historians fixate on the discussion over types of artillery (e.g., Summerall advocated 105 mm howitzers whereas GHQ wanted 155mm pieces) and suggest that the meeting showed that GHQ wanted more firepower to fight a war of attrition, this is a misreading of the debate. Summerall understood that the 75mm gun fired too small a shell for many missions and that the 155mm piece was too heavy for practically any movement in the field, nor could it fire the kind of rapid-fire rolling barrage he thought necessary.

GHQ did not agree with Summerall's admonitions. Harbord, Pershing's chief of staff at the time, criticized Summerall for wanting "a disproportionately large amount of artillery."[64] Others accused him of "arrogance" and of misrepresenting the amount of artillery used by the British in some of their more successful attacks. But, the key issue was that they simply were unwilling to admit that American infantrymen – trained to maneuver properly, shoot accurately, and fight skillfully with the bayonet – would require that much fire support throughout a battle.[65]

Summerall insisted that the nature of combat on the Western Front demanded a reliance on firepower that was indeed out of all proportion with previous American experience or current American doctrine. In the mission's final report to the War Department, he wrote:

> It may fairly be stated that losses in war today are inversely proportional to the volume and efficiency of friendly artillery fire. If we are to produce a decided effect upon the issue of the war, we must strive to develop some form of a rolling offensive over a very considerable area and for this purpose, artillery must be furnished in quantities not hitherto contemplated.[66]

Summerall failed to convert the AEF staff to his position, but he did not give up the fight. In subsequent correspondence to the War Department, the contentious artilleryman made it perfectly clear that he believed the

He believed the 105 mm howitzer, with twice the explosive power of the 75 mm gun but the same tactical mobility, to be the best all-round field piece, a belief validated by the Army some years after the war. More important, Summerall wanted each attacking AEF division to be supported by 259 dedicated guns from the division, corps, and army artillery groups, whereas the AEF staff planned to use just 122 guns for the same scenario. Despite a curious line in one report of the meeting that the 155 mm piece would be acceptable because of the "belief that the present war would not assume the form of a war of any considerable movement" (a phrase anathema to Pershing, who was at the meeting and tried to get Summerall to agree to the GHQ proposal), reports from both sides in the debate agree that Summerall was advocating more firepower for the division than GHQ. See *USAWW*, 1: 109–14. For Summerall's report, see Artillery Section of Military Mission to England and France, to Adjutant General of the Army, Subject: Organization of Field Artillery, 21 July 1917, Folder 1, Box 11, CP 10, Charles P. Summerall Papers, Citadel Archives and Museum, Charleston, S.C.; and James W. Rainey, "Ambivalent Warfare: The Tactical Doctrine of the AEF in World War I," *Parameters: Journal of the US Army War College* 13 (September 1983): 38.

[64] Harbord, *American Army in France*, 101.

[65] Summerall claimed that after making his proposal, he was "viciously attacked personally and officially by officers of the staff whom I hardly knew for trying to promote a lot of artillery generals, for advocating the light howitzer and for such a quantity of artillery." Charles P. Summerall, "The Way of Duty, Honor, Country," p. 86, unpublished memoir, First Division Foundation, Cantigny, Ill. See also DeWeerd, *President Wilson Fights His War*, 205; and Smythe, *Pershing*, 36.

[66] *USAWW*, 1: 68.

course settled on by GHQ was not just a minor organizational error but rather a blunder that would lead to disastrous consequences in combat:

The artillery proposed by the [GHQ] Operations Section is inadequate in both types and quantity. It is further believed that our infantry will suffer great and unnecessary losses if it attempts to advance over any reasonable front under any artillery fire that can be established by the plans of the Operations Section.... The lives of many thousands of our infantry depend upon a decision with reference to this all-important subject.[67]

He not only attacked the amount of firepower that Pershing's staff expected to employ, he also directly challenged the very foundation of American combat doctrine. In Summerall's vision of battle, the infantry never was expected to be "self-reliant," and riflemen did not have to fight their way forward with whatever fire support was available. Instead, he insisted, "with proper employment of artillery ... the task of the infantry is to follow the barrage, mop up the trenches as taken, and consolidate the final objective."[68] Obviously, this form of attack placed greater emphasis on firepower than on maneuver, or on the rifle and bayonet, or on the infantry as a whole. This was the first serious challenge to the American prewar doctrine, but it would not be the last.

Just a month later, Lieutenant Colonel John H. Parker, a controversial officer considered to be the prewar Army's machine-gun expert, conducted a tour of a French training center for automatic weapons with another American officer. Apparently, the experience was enlightening. In the report he submitted after his visit, Parker heretically announced: "We are both convinced ... the day of the rifleman is done. He was a good horse while he lasted, but his day is over.... The rifleman is passing out and the bayonet is fast becoming as obsolete as the crossbow." As expected, the report was not received warmly at GHQ; Lieutenant Colonel Paul B. Malone, then heading the GHQ training section, scribbled on his copy of the note, "speak for yourself, John."[69] Neither Summerall nor Parker convinced Pershing or GHQ to modify official AEF doctrine – only struggles on the battlefield would do that. In the meantime, GHQ shifted its attention from the formulation of doctrine to its transmission to the troops.

---

[67] Memorandum, Artillery Section of Military Mission to England and France to Adjutant General of the Army, Subject: Organization of Field Artillery, 21 July 1917, Folder 1, Box 11, CP 10, Charles P. Summerall Papers, Citadel Archives and Museum.

[68] Ibid.

[69] Quoted in Rainey, "Ambivalent Warfare," 38, 45, note 21.

By Pershing's own admission, intensive training was a crucial factor in preparing to wage war and especially to successfully wage open warfare on the Western Front. He later wrote that, considering the AEF's reliance on an inexperienced "citizen soldiery," training was "the most important question" to be solved before engaging in combat.[70] He also made it clear that such training was to focus on open warfare. This was especially necessary because Pershing and many other American officers were convinced that trench warfare was much simpler than open warfare and that "any officer who had mastered open warfare...could get in a hole in the ground and take care of the situation at hand" should he be forced to fight in the trenches.[71] These officers believed that troops needed only to master a few special techniques to fight in the trenches but, as Pershing stated, fighting in the open required "individual and group initiative, resourcefulness, and tactical judgment," as well as aggressiveness and superb marksmanship. According to Pershing and GHQ, for AEF units to have any chance of waging open warfare on the Western Front, they would have to dedicate themselves wholeheartedly to the effort. Yet, despite GHQ's efforts to ensure that troops both in Europe and in the United States received sufficient training in open warfare, all AEF divisions ultimately received much more training in trench-warfare techniques than in the skills supposedly so necessary for open warfare.

For those units that began their training in the United States, most of the instruction focused on fighting in and around the trenches. Some of this was the result of an early decision by officers in the War Department to begin training troops for the kind of combat they were most likely to see in Europe. As late as December 1917, Pershing was still receiving War Department pamphlets that he claimed were "not in harmony" with his recommendations for training and doctrine. One such pamphlet openly stated in the first paragraph that "in all the military training of a division, under existing conditions, training for trench warfare is of paramount importance," and it subordinated "all instruction to training for trench warfare."[72] Only early in 1918 did Pershing successfully get the War Department to agree with his training priorities.

Training in Europe was equally problematic. The first American divisions to arrive in France, the 1st and 26th, had conducted no significant

---

[70] Pershing, *My Experiences*, 1: 150.

[71] Department of Gunnery, School of Fire for Field Artillery, "American Drill Regulation and 'Artillery Firing,'" *Field Artillery Journal* 8 (July–September 1918): 364.

[72] Pershing to War Department, Cable No. 348-S, 7 December 1917, *USAWW*, 3: 318.

training in the United States. Nevertheless, even under the watchful eye
of Pershing and GHQ, both divisions received much more preparation to
fight in the trenches than in the open, although arguably not enough to
be considered experts even in the former. The same was true with divisions that arrived later, such as the 2nd and 77th. The standard AEF
training plan in Europe for all but the first divisions to arrive (i.e., for
those expected to have conducted a number of months of initial training
in the States) included one month for small-unit training in and around
the practice trenches behind the lines, a second month of training under
the tutelage and command of an experienced Allied division in a quiet
sector of the front-line trenches, and a third month of training devoted
to open-warfare methods and large-unit maneuvers.[73] Yet, for a host of
reasons, including the crisis of the German Spring offensives in 1918, no
American division completed this schedule and, in every case, the final
phase of open-warfare training was either greatly abbreviated or eliminated altogether.

One reason so much of the training focused on trench fighting was
that the AEF had to rely on experienced Allied officers to serve as instructors. French and British units designed and performed demonstrations
and maneuvers in front of AEF units. Allied officers served as instructors
and advisers to American commanders at all levels, ran all of the special
courses to train troops in the auxiliary weapons (i.e., artillery, machine
guns, automatic rifles, and grenades), and taught courses in the AEF's new
staff school at Langres. Not only did AEF units learn to use the weapons
and methods of trench warfare but, in countless ways, they also were
exposed to the dominant operational doctrine in the French and British
armies, one largely based on firepower and often completely at odds with
AEF dogma.[74]

At the AEF staff school, Allied instructors taught that infantry was far
from "self-reliant" and could not successfully attack unless the artillery
kept under heavy fire "all during the attack . . . the immediate objectives
of the attack, the flanking defenses which could paralyze the attack, and

---

[73] James B. Bowen, "Commander-in-Chief Report," *USAWW*, 3: 313.
[74] Many AEF officers were trained exclusively in Allied schools. Most of the six thousand
replacement officers sent to Europe by the War Department after completing their initial
officer training in the United States did their advanced training in British schools or in
one of the two special schools set up early on by the GHQ and manned by French instructors. See "Final Report of Assistant Chief of Staff, G-5," 30 June 1919, *USAWW*, 14:
297–8.

the rear lines from which the enemy could fire on the attacking forces."[75] The French and British had concluded that the artillery even had to provide protective fire for the infantry after the attack had succeeded. They preached that artillery support was so essential and infantry capabilities so limited that divisions could "progress only step by step, towards limited objectives" – a direct challenge to the AEF beliefs that unlimited objectives were superior and that extensive results were possible and expected.[76] Although the 1917 American *FSR* claimed that "preconcerted plans" were "objectionable" for attacks because they limited initiative and flexibility, Allied instructors insisted that because of the strength of enemy defensive positions, "preconcerted plans covering all phases of the attack, far from being objectionable, now prove to be the only ones likely to meet with any success."[77] These Allied officers even claimed that during the pursuit stage of an attack – supposedly the most open phase of open warfare – infantry still needed to be "constantly supported by artillery."[78] One lecturer cautioned American officers to "never venture Infantry in an attack against organized positions without having carefully prepared this attack." He then explained that the term "organized positions" meant not only "trenches and wire entanglements" but also "strong points, hastily organized as they may be; every possible strong point which has to be attacked or outflanked must be taken under strong artillery fire." He insisted such firepower-based tactics were "the only way for preventing tremendous and useless losses."[79] These comments exposed the significant differences between American and Allied combat doctrine and the difficulty for AEF officers who sought to find a place for "self-reliant infantry" on the modern battlefield as described by veteran Allied officers.

Neither Pershing nor many other officers in GHQ appreciated such heretical teaching. As late as August 1918, Pershing commented in his

---

[75] "Artillery III: The Use of Artillery in the Offensive" (Lecture 28 at the 1st Course, AEF General Staff College, Langres, 24 December 1917), G-5 Schools File, Entry 362, RG 120, NA.

[76] "Division in the Offensive (I)" (Lecture 20 at the 1st Course, AEF General Staff College, Langres, 19 December 1917), G-5 Schools File, Entry 362, RG 120, NA.

[77] Ibid.; War Department, *Field Service Regulations: United States Army, 1914, Corrected to July 31, 1918* (Washington, D.C.: GPO, 1918), 91.

[78] "Exploitation of Success" (lecture for Conference 107 at the 2nd Course, AEF General Staff College, Langres, 29 April 1918), G-5 Schools File, Entry 362, RG 120, NA.

[79] Col. Hoechlin-Schwartz (French Army), "Artillery in War of Movement" (lecture given to the 2nd Course, AEF General Staff College, Langres, 2 May 1918), G-5 Schools File, Entry 362, RG 120, NA.

diary, "I consider some of the instruction which we have received from the British to be a positive detriment."[80] He felt much the same about the training and doctrine offered by the French. Earlier that summer, Harold Fiske, then a colonel and the chief of training at GHQ, wrote that the French were purposefully trying to "impregnate the American units with French methods and doctrine.... the tactics and techniques of our Allies are not suited to American characteristics or the American mission in this war.... their infantry is consequently entirely too dependent upon a powerful artillery support.... what we build up, they to a certain extent pull down.... the assistance of our Allies has become not an asset but a serious handicap in the training of our troops."[81]

Aside from strictly doctrinal disagreements, two factors must also be considered when seeking to understand the unwillingness of Pershing and other senior AEF officers to accept the advice of the Allies. First, although American officers may not have been rigorously examining the Great War between 1914 and 1917, they were well aware that neither the Allies nor the Germans had demonstrated any extraordinary offensive abilities on the Western Front. The initial AEF contingent to reach France arrived just in time to witness the disastrous results of French General Robert Nivelle's misbegotten offensive that led to perhaps 200,000 casualties, as well as mutinies (in one form or another) in most French divisions. Then, during the autumn months, American officers either saw or read about the British offensive near Passchendaele, which seemed to offer little worth emulating and much to avoid. In the spring of 1918, American officers finally were treated to a series of tactically successful campaigns – but they were carried out *against* the Allies, not by them. Americans, especially Pershing, sought to emulate the German tactics (though most did not fully understand them or the elaborate preparations and training that preceded them), but their confidence in the Allies diminished further.

Second, Pershing and other senior American officers may have sought to mark out their own "American doctrine and methods" to add more weight to their arguments against repeated Allied efforts to amalgamate American troops directly into French and British units.[82] From the beginning of U.S. belligerency, French and British officers lobbied to secure American manpower to bolster their weakened armies. Some proposals included placing hundreds of thousands of individual American soldiers

---

[80] Entry for 25 August 1918, Pershing Diary, JJP Papers, LOC.
[81] Fiske Memorandum to Chief of Staff, Subject: Training, 4 July 1918, *USAWW*, 14: 304.
[82] "Final Report of Assistant Chief of Staff, G-5," 30 June 1919, *USAWW*, 14: 304.

directly into Allied infantry battalions, whereas others asked for entire American units of various sizes – from platoons to regiments. To the great displeasure of the Allies, Pershing emphatically resisted all these efforts and, in doing so, he stood on solid legal ground. The Secretary of War, Newton D. Baker, had charged him with creating and employing a "separate and distinct" American force, "the identity of which must be preserved."[83]

Although it is impossible to say for sure, Pershing and other senior AEF officers may have magnified the importance of their doctrinal differences for political reasons. At times fighting for the very existence of his army and his own chance to command it, Pershing may have seized on the doctrinal and tactical differences as an additional reason why AEF men and units needed to fight under American command. Pershing argued that Americans differed from their European associates, with special inherent characteristics and capabilities, as well as distinct traditions, and he claimed that they needed to fight with a doctrine that matched their national character. This is not to say that Pershing did not honestly believe this or that he contrived the argument merely to support his position on amalgamation, but it might help explain the emphasis he placed on the uniqueness of AEF doctrine and its particular American-ness.

Pershing later explained that he also feared too much training for trench warfare would create forces that "lacked the aggressiveness to break through the enemy's lines and the knowledge of how to carry on thereafter."[84] But, regarding training, the AEF had little choice. GHQ simply did not have enough experienced American officers to do all the teaching and training required, especially early on. Beyond that, the German offensives in 1918 threw off all training schedules. Pershing intended to train his divisions for a war-winning offensive in 1919, but the events of

---

[83] Baker's instructions are quoted in Smythe, *Pershing: General of the Armies*, 11. However, due to the crisis of the German Spring offensives in 1918, Pershing ultimately allowed temporary amalgamation of American units (but never individual soldiers) into Allied armies, corps, and even divisions. Ironically, after all the effort made by Wilson, Baker, and Pershing to keep America and the AEF distinct from the Allies so that it could wage a decisive, independent campaign to win the war, events beyond their control would force amalgamation to occur, leading to the very effect they fought so hard to avoid. In the end, for most Allied soldiers, amalgamated American units were all they knew of the American military effort. In fact, until the last two months of the war, the only American units to see combat anywhere in Europe did so as parts of Allied armies, corps, and divisions. See Trask, *The AEF and Coalition Warmaking, 1917–1918* (Lawrence: University Press of Kansas, 1993), 168.

[84] Pershing, *My Experiences*, 1: 152; C.G. III Army Corps to chief of staff, AEF, 22 July 1918, Folder 56.0, Box 29, III Army Corps Historical File, RG 120, NA.

1918 forced him to accelerate the training program of nearly all divisions. Ironically, the heavy interaction between the Allies and AEF combat officers and units exposed the Americans to doctrine and methods that were more appropriate than the official AEF dogma.

By any standard, though, many American soldiers and units were not well trained for combat and certainly not sufficiently trained for the kind of fighting called for by official AEF doctrine – and much documentary evidence suggests that Pershing and other members of GHQ knew that to be the case. After the war, Pershing admitted both the inexperience and "lack of technical skill" of American troops, and even Harold Fiske, then a brigadier general in charge of all AEF training, wrote that "to the end most of our divisions were lacking in skill."[85] George C. Marshall, one of the few senior staff officers to have spent considerable time in a combat division, also acknowledged "the limited amount of training and complete lack of experience on the part of the men and young officers."[86] In this light, the senior AEF leadership's relentless insistence that AEF units should wage open warfare (supposedly the most difficult kind of fighting), and their development of extremely aggressive attack plans that were based on such fighting capability become all the more surprising.

In the end, historian Douglas Johnson's description of combat training in the United States was sadly appropriate for much of the limited training throughout the AEF as a whole: "It produced infantry that attacked in linear formations of the decades gone by. It produced infantry that only knew how to attack straight ahead. It produced infantry unfamiliar with its normal supporting arms. It produced infantry willing to be killed in straight-ahead attacks because it knew no better."[87] Many units rose above this, but generally they did so more despite official AEF doctrine than because of it.

Doctrinal Development in the AEF, 1918

Despite the inability or unwillingness of U.S. Army and AEF leaders to make appropriate doctrinal adjustments during the years of neutrality and the first year of belligerency, senior officers did make certain

---

[85] For Pershing's words, see *My Experiences*, 2: 293; for Fiske's comments, see "Final Report of Assistant Chief of Staff, G-5," 30 June 1919, *USAWW*, 14: 309.

[86] George C. Marshall, *Memoirs of My Services in the World War, 1917–1918* (Boston: Houghton Mifflin, 1976), 122.

[87] Douglas V. Johnson II, "A Few 'Squads Left' and Off to France: Training the American Army in the United States for World War I" (Ph.D. diss., Temple University, 1992), 247.

changes after American forces began fighting. The horrific casualties suffered by American divisions between the end of May and August 1918 (i.e., more than sixty thousand), especially during the Aisne-Marne Offensive, prompted Pershing to demand a reexamination of American combat methods on 7 August 1918. He admitted to his chief of staff, Major General James McAndrew, "perhaps we are losing too many men," and he even recognized that the answer might be found in "tanks or possibly by artillery."[88]

The resulting investigations by officers in the operations sections at GHQ and the new American First Army led to the first significant adjustment of American tactical doctrine and methods since 1914. Within a month, AEF staff officers prepared two important documents that distinguished between various battlefield environments and elucidated the different methods to be employed. The first, entitled "Combat Instructions for Troops of First Army," was completed on 29 August 1918 and immediately issued to the combat divisions.[89] The document's main purpose was to help officers identify "the tactical problems or difficulties which they may be called to solve and to lay down certain principles to be followed."[90] Specifically, it described "the differences in the tactical methods to be employed and preparation required for the assault of a highly organized position as compared to a hastily or partially organized position." As George Marshall explained, the document was still to be used for operations involving "a break through carefully fortified positions, followed by fighting in the open" – very aggressive goals in line with existing American doctrine.[91] But, at least the tactics and procedures described admitted that in certain phases of major offensives, many of the most important elements of AEF doctrine – such as its reliance on infantry, maneuver, and the rifle, as well as its lack of emphasis on comprehensive attack plans and employment of heavy firepower – were disregarded.

[88] Quoted in Rainey, "Ambivalent Warfare," 41.

[89] Most likely, this document was prepared by George C. Marshall, who had just left the 1st Division and become the assistant chief of staff for operations (G-3) for the First Army. Marshall later wrote that shortly after joining the staff in August, Hugh Drum, the First Army chief of staff, ordered him to "draw up a set of combat instructions" for all units in the army. Marshall admitted that he drew on his experiences with the 1st Division, as well as "copies of Ludendorff's most recent tactical instructions for the German Army." See Marshall, *Memoirs*, 126.

[90] HQ First Army, "Combat Instructions for Troops of First Army," 29 August 1918, issued as HQ 1st Division Memorandum, 1 September 1918, *WWRFD*, vol. 2.

[91] Marshall, *Memoirs*, 126.

The instructions divided major attacks into three phases and explained that different tactics and procedures were required in each. The most innovative section was the first, entitled "Preparation of Forward Zone (trench warfare)," because it validated the doctrine and tactics that had been developed and used by the Allied armies. It announced that attacks against the first 3 to 4 kilometers of a prepared enemy position required "trench warfare methods.... the operation must be planned in great detail and carried out according to a fixed schedule ... the advance of the troops should be covered by a dense artillery barrage and facilitated where possible by tanks and heavy neutralization fire on suspected enemy strong points. All must move according to schedule and along carefully defined or determined lines." After a heavy preliminary artillery bombardment, tanks with teams of engineers and infantry were to open gaps in the wire. The "front line teams" were to "follow the barrage closely" and be covered by automatic-rifle teams and lots of smoke. Furthermore, throughout the entire area covered by trenches and wire,

...the rate of progression of the [rolling] barrage must be slow and should include long pauses on strong positions.... the infantry must hug the barrage closely in order to reach the enemy's successive trenches before he has time to man them after the barrage has cleared. This is a matter of seconds.... The leading infantry waves must progress steadily towards their objective. Following elements must methodically clean up the partially conquered ground, according to the detailed program worked out in advance.

In this phase, the best infantry formations for such attacks were not linear waves or even the old prewar skirmish lines but rather "small squad or platoon columns preceded by a leader and followed by a driver."[92] Such tactics were entirely consistent with recent doctrine in the European armies (sometimes called "worms" in the BEF), but they had no precedent whatsoever in the official doctrine of either the prewar Army or the AEF. Yet, as AEF divisions became more experienced, they increasingly carried out these kinds of attacks and then stopped to regroup.

However, the "Combat Instructions" continued on with discussions of the tactics to be used in subsequent attacks in the "Advance Across the Intermediate Zone" and finally during the period of "Exploitation." Only in these sections did any semblance of the existing AEF doctrine appear. In the intermediate zone, supposedly the 5 to 10 kilometers behind the enemy's main line of resistance and divisional artillery line, "the

---

[92] HQ First Army, "Combat Instructions for Troops of First Army," 29 August 1918, issued as HQ 1st Division, Memorandum, 1 September 1918, *WWRFD*, vol. 2.

entire character of the conduct of the operation" was to be "completely changed." There were to be no more "barrage and infantry time tables, minutely regulated movements, close lateral contact, etc." Infantrymen were to be given only an "axis of advance" and told to push forward "as rapidly as possible." Enemy strong points were to be "instantly taken under fire, first by rifle and then successively by machine guns, Stokes mortars and 75s [French 75mm artillery pieces accompanying the infantry] as rapidly as the infantry battalion commander can bring these to bear." Meanwhile, other infantry were to work around the enemy flank to take the enemy position "from the flank or rear or both." Battalion commanders were again reminded to use "every possibly means to secure fire superiority and then drive forward by the flanks of the smother strong point under the cover of this fire superiority." Reinforcements were only to be "thrown in where 'the going is good' and not piled up against strong resistance."[93]

In many ways, this section demonstrates the American fascination with and emulation of the German tactics used in the 1918 Spring offensives, and such improvements represented the AEF's most realistic description of at least some form of open warfare. Even so, serious problems remained. The importance of communication and liaison, both between front and rear and from side to side, was neglected. The logistical challenges of keeping the machine guns, mortars, and accompanying artillery in close support of the infantry were ignored. And, for all its apparent emphasis on firepower, the burden of continued progress was still placed squarely on the infantry battalion, whose resources were still rather limited in that regard. In general, the document offered no appreciation for the extraordinary difficulties of actually carrying out such tactics against a skilled and determined defender in partially fortified positions on difficult ground.

The "Combat Instructions" asserted that "the foregoing phase of operations, which depends upon individual initiative, rapidity of decision, resolute daring and driving power, should afford the American officer and soldier the opportunity to display his best known national characteristics to their greatest advantage." Such appeals to national pride and character were a dubious basis upon which to expect success in so challenging an endeavor. As the German Army discovered in its Spring attacks, superbly trained units could achieve remarkable tactical results against a surprised enemy in an imperfect and untested defensive system. But, even then, the losses in killed and wounded among the attackers were very high. When

[93] Ibid.

less well-trained German units were thrown in to continue the attacks, the casualty rates rose even higher. Success had to be based on training, experience, equipment, and an accurate understanding of the enemy, not on supposed "national characteristics."[94] Most AEF units simply did not have the training, experience, or weaponry required to carry out the tactics in "Combat Instructions." Furthermore, the failure of the German stormtroop units against the French Fourth Army along the Marne on 15 July 1918 should have shown that even the best trained and equipped forces could be stopped by experienced troops using an elastic defense when the element of surprise had been lost. In the end, it was left to the American combat divisions themselves to more accurately match the doctrine and tactics to the capability of the troops.

The other major statement of doctrinal adjustment was dated 5 September 1918, issued under Pershing's authorship, and entitled simply, *Combat Instructions*. Many of the August document's strengths and weaknesses reappeared. Even more clearly than the First Army instructions, this document was GHQ's answer to Pershing's concern that AEF units suffered excessive losses in the open or semi-open warfare of the Aisne-Marne Offensive. As such, it dealt almost exclusively with that form of warfare and went into greater detail in defining it and explaining the organizational and tactical changes required to wage it. Pershing apparently agreed so strongly with the document that he issued it directly under his own name.

Combat Instructions began with a reproof of the methods used in many Aisne-Marne attacks: Formations were "everywhere too dense.... Waves are too close together.... Lines are frequently seen with the men almost elbow to elbow.... All formations are habitually lacking in elasticity; there is almost never any attempt to maneuver."[95] As subsequent chapters show, these were valid criticisms. But, the frequent insistence from the highest offices in the AEF that the prewar doctrine and methods of the old regulations were still appropriate probably contributed to those very mistakes.

---

[94] As Travers shows, the "innovative German stormtroop tactics were not sufficiently maintained ... and the German casualties mounted when traditional mass tactics were used." Such tactics led to nearly one million casualties from 21 March to mid-July 1918, even against a British defensive system that "was not understood, did not work and did not properly exist at all." He concludes that even the German tactics "however ingenious, never really solved the problem in 1918 of continuously attacking defences that fought back with large amounts of firepower, whether artillery, machine guns, or Lewis guns." Travers, *How the War Was Won*, 50, 65, 108.

[95] John J. Pershing, *Combat Instructions* (AEF GHQ, 5 September 1918), 3.

Pershing went on to claim that "the essential difference between open and trench warfare . . . is characterized by the presence or absence of the rolling barrage ahead of the infantry." Considering Pershing's well-known dislike for trench warfare, such a statement could be interpreted as a lack of appreciation for the importance of the rolling barrage, an essential element of nearly all successful attacks throughout 1918. But, the commander-in-chief's main point was that "the method of combat in trench warfare presents a marked contrast to that employed in open warfare." For example:

Trench warfare is marked by uniform formations, the regulation of space and time by higher command down to the smallest details, absence of scouts preceding the first wave, fixed distances and intervals between units and individuals, voluminous orders, careful rehearsal, little initiative upon the part of the individual soldier. Open warfare is marked by scouts who precede the first wave, irregularity of formations, comparatively little regulation of space and time by the higher command, the greatest possible use of the infantry's own fire power to enable it to get forward, variable distances and intervals between units and individuals, use of every form of cover and accident of the ground during the advance, brief orders, and the greatest possible use of individual initiative by all troops engaged in the action.[96]

Pershing insisted that "the attempt by assaulting infantry to use trench warfare methods in an open warfare combat will be successful only at great cost." In fact, the exact opposite was at least as true and probably more applicable to the kinds of problems AEF units experienced during the war; attempts to fight according to official AEF open-warfare methods when in trench-warfare situations, or even most semi-open-warfare situations, resulted in disaster. Few senior AEF commanders or staff officers, and certainly not Pershing, seemed to appreciate the amount of firepower required to successfully attack even hastily organized enemy positions. Against a skilled enemy using an elastic defense, the old infantry-based tactics were never enough to carry assaults on their own. The "firing line" of riflemen, occasionally supported by whatever auxiliaries could be brought to bear, was almost never sufficient to successfully attack even a greatly outnumbered enemy that made a maximum use of automatic rifles, machine guns, and artillery. The Allied and German armies had learned this in the first couple of years of the war and had made changes to their doctrine and tactics. Many senior American officers simply did not appreciate the enormity of this problem.

[96] Ibid.

Despite these problems of prewar dogma and limited training, AEF doctrine and methods improved during the last four months of the war in a number of ways. First, an increased appreciation of the demands of fighting against the enemy in prepared positions led AEF planners to create attack plans for both the St. Mihiel and Meuse-Argonne Offensives that were impressive in many respects. The initial assault for each major offensive was supported by a brief but massive saturation bombardment, a dense rolling barrage, and detailed infantry plans with numerous intermediate objectives. At St. Mihiel, most AEF divisions advanced about 8 kilometers on the first day. By the end of the third day of the Meuse-Argonne Offensive, nearly all AEF divisions had driven the German lines back more than 9 kilometers. Both offensives were generally successful in the initial stages, and in neither case did American units suffer heavy casualties. Perhaps more important, commanders of the most experienced American divisions had by then learned to maximize the use of all kinds of firepower and to prepare and execute set-piece attacks. Increasingly, division commanders eschewed the supposedly more decisive infantry-based attacks of open warfare in favor of the firepower-based tactics of trench warfare.

Second, as shown in the two combat-instruction documents issued in the late summer of 1918 by GHQ and HQ First Army, even many senior staff officers increasingly understood that the infantry needed to use more than the rifle and bayonet to have any chance of success. Both documents, as well as others, stressed that all weapons, especially automatic rifles, machine guns, mortars, 37mm guns, tanks, and even 75mm guns, had to be used. Even so, these changes were slow to be accepted by some senior officers. After the war, Major General Robert Alexander, who commanded the 41st Depot Division (i.e., a replacement training unit) for many months in 1918 before assuming command of the 77th Division, proudly claimed,

in all instruction one dominating principle was insisted upon – that training for the open was of primary value and of that training the utilization of the rifle as a firearm was indispensable to success.... Instruction was of course also given in the use of the bayonet, hand and rifle grenades, the automatic rifle (Chauchat) and the other auxiliaries, *but that they were merely auxiliaries and could never replace the ability to maneuver,* which in turn must be accompanied by the ability to use *the fire-power of the rifle,* was always insisted upon [emphasis added].[97]

[97] Robert Alexander to Adjutant General, U.S. Army, Subject: Operations of 41st (1st Depot) Division, 13 December 1919, General Robert Alexander File, Box 9, JJP Papers, LOC.

Furthermore, even the increasing emphasis on the auxiliary infantry weapons appears to have also been an attempt by GHQ to make a more heavily armed infantry more "self-reliant," according to the original AEF doctrine, rather than to admit that infantry required heavy artillery support in almost all situations.[98]

However, despite its developing appreciation of the role of artillery and other infantry-support weapons, the AEF displayed a lack of vision respecting the use of aircraft in a ground-attack role. American combat divisions knew the importance of aircraft, and unit commanders regularly reported the loss of morale, the disruption of command, and the casualties suffered from enemy airpower. Yet, nearly all divisional officers limited their concerns about Allied aircraft to observation and reconnaissance missions, as well as to requests to clear out enemy aircraft. In no case did a division commander order aircraft to attack enemy troops or positions in support of an assault. Even at the corps and army level, attempts to use aircraft for ground attack and close interdiction were extraordinarily rare, despite the fact that the Allies and Germans had from late 1917 on shown the value of such missions during major offensives.[99]

Regarding other new technologies, the record was similarly mixed. GHQ tried to secure more than five hundred tanks for the St. Mihiel attack and did not receive either the number or types requested. Although sources vary widely as to how many actually took part in the forty-seven-day Meuse-Argonne Offensive, historian Timothy Nenninger claims the First Army received fewer than a quarter of the tanks it originally hoped to employ there.[100] Although generally complimentary of the logistical

---

[98] Pershing showed this to be the case throughout his *Combat Instructions*.

[99] Throughout my investigation, I did not find a single case in which a division commander attempted to employ firepower from aircraft during an attack. I discovered only three instances of corps and army commanders using aircraft for ground attack and close interdiction during a major offensive: the bombing of the town of Vigneulles on 13 September in St. Mihiel – which Maj. Gen. George H. Cameron, the V Corps commander, claimed to have hit American troops already in the town; the bombing of the German positions in and around the village of La Bézace in the 77th Division sector on 3 November by 182 planes, which Robert Alexander, then the 77th Division commander, personally witnessed but admitted to having had no advanced warning of; and Major General John L. Hines' order, as the III Corps commander in October, for a bombardment of a certain strong point then holding up one of his divisions.

[100] See Nenninger, "American Military Effectiveness in the First World War," *Military Effectiveness*: Volume I: *The First World War*, eds. Allan R. Millett and Williamson Murray (Boston: Unwin Hyman, 1988), 136. Dale Wilson writes that the initial plans for the assault on the St. Mihiel salient called for 369 light tanks and 150 heavy British tanks, but the First Army received only 409 light Renault tanks instead. Other sources list only 267

support he received from his Allies, Pershing admitted that the AEF was
"less fortunate" in receiving tanks than other weapons because the "Allies
barely had sufficient tanks to meet their own requirements."[101] In any
event, the rough, broken, and forested ground there did not lend itself
to large-scale tank employment. Nor did the AEF consistently make adequate use of chemical weapons in the war. As with tanks, the main problem may have been logistical because GHQ's initial plans for the start
of both the St. Mihiel and Meuse-Argonne Offensives included massive
gas bombardments. Due to a shortage of gas shells, poor leadership at
GHQ, a hesitancy on the part of certain corps and division commanders
to employ gas ahead of attacking infantrymen, or a combination of all
three, gas missions were often not executed. However, by late October, no
such factors apparently stood in the way, and an official historian for the
Army's chemical-warfare service later claimed the gas bombardment for
the 1 November attack "was the best that could have been devised, and
it succeeded exactly as planned."[102] In sum, although GHQ's inclusion
of tanks and gas was not all it could have been, the AEF did attempt to
integrate those important weapons into its major offensives.

AEF doctrine did increasingly stress the need for infantry units to
use open, flexible formations in the attack and to rely on flanking and

tanks at the battle. During the forty-seven days of the Meuse-Argonne, Ayres claims 324
tanks were employed, and other sources cite a figure as low as 189, including Pershing in
his *Final Report*. Wilson again claims 419 were used. Only fifteen were available for the
last major attack on 1 November. See Pershing, *Final Report*, in *USAWW*, 12: 42; Dale
E. Wilson, *Treat 'em Rough! The Birth of American Armor, 1917–20* (Novato, Calif.:
Presidio Press, 1989), 98, 100, 136, and 160, note 31; Ayres, *The War with Germany*,
113; and Braim, *Test of Battle*, 96.
[101] Pershing, *Final Report*, *USAWW*, 12: 60.
[102] Rexmond Cochrane, *The Use of Gas in the Meuse-Argonne Campaign, September–
November 1918*, Study #10, U.S. Army Chemical Corps Historical Studies: Gas Warfare in World War I (Washington, D.C.: GPO, 1958), 91. Cochrane blamed corps and
division commanders for not carrying out the gas bombardment at the start of the
Meuse-Argonne campaign and insisted there was no shortage of gas shell. Col. John W.
Schulz, the chief gas officer of First Army, never identified a lack of shell as a problem,
but he claimed Pershing's unwillingness to announce the length of the preliminary bombardment at both St. Mihiel and in the Meuse-Argonne limited the use of gas. However,
two senior AEF artillerymen, Col. Conrad H. Lanza of the First Army Artillery and
Maj. Gen. Charles P. Summerall, both claimed that gas employment was only limited by
"the supply that could be obtained." See John W. Schulz, "Explanation and Execution
of Gas Plans for St. Mihiel and Argonne-Meuse Operations," 13 January 1919, Box 30,
Edwards Papers, MHS; and Charles P. Summerall, "Comments by the Corps Commander upon the Operations of the Fifth Army Corps," p. 4, Folder 11.2, Box 2, V Army
Corps Historical File, RG 120, NA; Lanza, *The Army Artillery, First Army* (n.d., n.p.,
USAMHI), 11.

infiltration tactics rather than rigid lateral lines (e.g., "building up the firing line") and frontal assaults. Yet, most AEF attacks continued to have too many infantrymen packed into the attack sector, making maneuver more difficult and almost always leading to higher casualties due to, if nothing else, the increased number of targets. Often, this excessive troop density was a direct result of the huge AEF division attacking in an excessively narrow sector. Under such conditions, even when junior infantry commanders diligently resisted ordering too many men into the assault line – as happened so often in early attacks – American divisions tended to suffer heavier casualties because so many troops were present in the support and reserve units that followed up the advance throughout the attack sector.

Some AEF veterans suggested that open-warfare ideas, and especially the doctrinal adjustments between September and November 1918, constituted an American version of either German stormtroop tactics or the maneuver-warfare practices of the Allied armies.[103] Although certain elements of the latest infantry tactics were incorporated into AEF doctrine, the remaining differences were substantial. The Germans and the Allied armies were all striving to improve their ability to fight in the open; however, despite Pershing's insistence that such activity validated his emphasis on infantry, the rifle, and open warfare in general, the continued criticism of AEF doctrine and tactics in the French and British armies as well as GHQ's continued faultfinding with French and British doctrine and tactics demonstrated the enduring differences between the Americans and the Europeans.[104]

The more important question is how, in light of those doctrinal improvements made, the official AEF doctrine so loudly proclaimed by Pershing and GHQ influenced the combat operations of the AEF. First, GHQ's consistent accentuation of the rifleman and its unwavering stress

---

[103] Spaulding and Wright, *Second Division*, 9–10; Robert Alexander, *Memories*, 32–3.

[104] On more than one occasion, Pershing and GHQ insisted that the Allies came to agree with the AEF's official ideas on open warfare. Pershing wrote, "the soundness of our methods is now accepted by the French, who themselves have published similar orders on instruction of troops," and GHQ claimed that "the time came when ... the correctness of American doctrine and methods received somewhat general recognition." Yet, even well into 1918, Pétain criticized AEF training for spending too much time on "small operations, having but little relation to actual warfare. ... Americans dream of operating in open country, after having broken through the front. This results in too much attention being devoted to this form of operations, which the Americans consider as superior." For the comments of Pershing and GHQ, see *USAWW*, 12: 324, 304. For Pétain's comments, see "Training of American Units with French," *USAWW*, 3: 292–5.

on the continued applicability of *all* prewar doctrine called for American officers to continue relying on anachronistic and obsolete ideas. Infantry needed to use new formations and tactics on the Western Front, not mimic the old prewar guidance. The AEF needed to employ the latest communications technologies, not rely on runners. At first, GHQ minimized the importance of all firepower beyond the rifle, and although it made some improvement in this regard, it continued to minimize the necessity of heavy artillery. And, even then, some open-warfare purists such as Pershing, Fiske, and Alexander never really understood the limitations on the old rifleman on the modern battlefield. They remained dissatisfied with Allied training because it focused too much on the use of auxiliary weapons, and they seemed to never fully understand the amount of firepower required to successfully attack even in situations that might be termed open warfare.

Second, the official admonition that commanders get their troops to fight out in the open exaggerated the capabilities of the typically inexperienced and unsupported AEF infantry on the modern battlefield, under both trench- and more open-warfare conditions. It also underestimated the importance of control, communication, and coordination, especially regarding infantry–artillery cooperation, a factor essential under nearly all battlefield conditions. AEF soldiers and units were simply not prepared to fight in the open; many were not even ready to fight under the more controlled conditions of trench warfare. Only under the most rare conditions could the AEF open-warfare doctrine have been applicable; however, even then, it must be admitted that a doctrine that might have been acceptable for highly trained and adequately equipped German stormtroop battalions was not satisfactory for poorly trained and inadequately armed Americans – regardless of their supposed "natural characteristics."

Third, GHQ never sufficiently corrected the prewar underestimation of the importance of heavy firepower. Its doctrinal leanings, along with its misinterpretation of such atypical battles as those at Cambrai and Soissons, encouraged it to mistakenly order general attacks without either sufficient tanks or enough preliminary artillery bombardment to take strong defensive positions held by defenders fully expecting an attack, as was done in the Meuse-Argonne on 4 October 1918. Some early attacks by American divisions even lacked a rolling barrage and the full use of machine guns, 37mm guns, and mortars in direct support of the infantry assault. Early attacks by all the American divisions evaluated in this study suffered from one or more of these problems.

Fourth, the open-warfare doctrine encouraged the creation of extraordinarily aggressive and optimistic attack plans for both the St. Mihiel and the Meuse-Argonne Offensives. These plans, especially for the attack of 26 September, established such ambitious – indeed, essentially unlimited – objectives that they were completely unattainable by the forces employed. The weak resistance and ultimate German withdrawal at St. Mihiel obscured this problem in that attack, but in the Meuse-Argonne, the distant objectives caused heavy losses and severe disorganization in the American infantry units that tried to make continued advances after their initial successes. Some units needed days to sort themselves out, and others, such as those in the 35th Division, became so utterly confused that they were mauled by German counterattacks and had to be hurriedly replaced earlier than GHQ expected.[105]

All four of these problems could have been minimized by the use of more tightly controlled, set-piece attacks in which meticulous planning, limited objectives, and overwhelming firepower made the greatest use of the aggressiveness of the American soldier and compensated for his lack of experience and inadequate training. Instead, after each offensive began, senior commanders continuously ordered the men and units forward. This was especially true in the Meuse-Argonne, despite supposed pauses between different phases of the campaign. Regarding the absence of comprehensive fire plans and set-piece attacks after the initial attack, Major General W. S. McNair, the chief of artillery for the First Army, admitted, "Between September 26th and October 31st, there were no general offensives involving the whole of the Army Artillery, although various attacks incident to a continuing operation were conducted under First Army Field Orders."[106] Individual divisions simply tried to grind their way forward – a sign of an absence of substantive leadership at the top.

Pershing's own diary entries demonstrate the nature and extent of his influence on the battle. On the third day of the offensive, when advances slowed to a halt and casualties rose sharply, Pershing recorded that he visited his subordinate commanders and "gave orders for the advance to be resumed," confident he had "done all in my power to instill an aggressive spirit in the different Corps headquarters." On 4 October, he wrote, "Our men have had to fight for every 100 yards they have gained, and it looks as though we will have a slow, hard advance. . . . There is no course except

[105] For a succinct account of the 35th Division's troubles in the Meuse-Argonne, see Coffman, *The War to End All Wars*, 311–12. For a more thorough treatment, see Robert H. Ferrell, *Collapse at Meuse-Argonne: The Failure of the Kansas-Missouri Division* (Columbia: University of Missouri Press, 2004).

[106] W. S. McNair, "Explanation and Execution of Plans for Artillery for St. Mihiel Operations and Argonne-Meuse Operations to November 11, 1918," 23 December 1918, Box 30, Edwards Papers, MHS.

Hunter Liggett, commander of the I Corps in the Aisne-Marne, St. Mihiel, and Meuse-Argonne Offensives, before succeeding General Pershing as commander of the American First Army in the Meuse-Argonne.

to fight it out." Again on the 5th he confided, "there is only one course left and that is to keep on driving. This is what we will do." Finally, on the 14th, he bluntly commented, "Hope for better results tomorrow. There is no particular reason for this hope except that if we keep on pounding, the Germans will be obliged to give way..."[107] Although Pershing seems to have thought there was no other way to proceed, he was wrong. For more than two years, some Allied generals had achieved a moderate level of success by methodically using limited, firepower-based, "bite-and-hold" attacks. Ironically, only after Pershing yielded the First Army to Major General Hunter Liggett in mid-October – who finally ceased all attacks and set about preparing a comprehensive firepower-based plan for what became the AEF's final 1 November attack – did the AEF achieve anything even approaching the kind of breakthrough for which Pershing and GHQ had been dreaming about for a year and a half.

[107] Entries for 28 September and 4, 5, and 14 October, Pershing Diary, JJP Papers, LOC.

In sum, it took much more firepower and better coordinated fire-power, as well as smaller, more flexible infantry formations to take smaller objectives than AEF leaders generally thought. The very best infantry could take enemy positions with lower casualties than a less well-trained and less experienced infantry, but even the best infantry divisions – such as the elite German stormtroop units, the Canadians, the Australians, and other British and French divisions – all earned their successes in large part by learning how to coordinate massive amounts of firepower, not by rely-ing on the rifle and the bayonet or even solely on infantry auxiliaries.[108] Furthermore, for his part, Pershing should not have had illusions about the technical abilities of his infantry regiments, which were typically run through abbreviated training programs and then, after suffering heavy losses in their first engagements, were filled up with even less well-trained replacements. Pershing and others at GHQ allowed prewar dogma and national chauvinism to mask a reality that they did not want to face: American units were not adequately trained, especially to carry out the kind of deep, decisive attacks his doctrine required, and the battlefield did not recognize any "inherent" superiority of the American character to fight in any certain way. Instead, they needed a doctrine that matched their limitations in skills, abilities, training, and weaponry.

The equation in the minds of many senior AEF leaders between open warfare and American warfare probably inhibited open discussions about doctrine because doctrinal heresy (bad enough at the time) could have been seen as a form of almost traitorous sentiment. A free discussion of doctrine and methods might have helped the AEF more properly align its doctrine with its capabilities. Despite Napoleon's old maxim that "with a new army it is possible to carry a formidable position, but not to carry out a plan or design," many AEF divisions proved they could successfully carry out the kind of limited set-piece assaults – or bite-and-hold attacks – used by some of the best British and French generals.[109] The follow-ing division studies show, among other things, how the combat divisions learned, more or less, to turn their attacks into these kind of set-piece battles.

---

[108] As Travers writes, "In summary, the Canadian Corps seems to have been more successful when engaged in set-piece attacks, such as 27 September, or earlier on 8 August at Amiens . . . rather than in continuous attempts to follow up such set-piece victories"; see Travers, *How the War Was Won*, 166.

[109] B. H. Liddell Hart, *The Real War 1914–1918* (Boston: Little, Brown, 1930), 460. Among senior British generals, Henry Rawlinson and Herbert Plumer were noted for "bite-and-hold" attacks.

How did the AEF learn to fight? Chiefly by fighting and, often, from the bottom up. As one junior infantry officer claimed: "It was the grim common sense of the 'doughboy' and not our obsolete and impossible tactics that won us ground. Oh! The precious time wasted in our elaborate, useless, murderous 'science' called 'musketry.' It is as much out of style as the musket from which it takes its name. Teaching it should be made a court-martial offense. It is murder in print. Battles were not fought in lines."[110]

In many ways, learning in the AEF flowed up from the divisions, to the corps, to the army, and finally to the GHQ. Some division commanders, like Robert Alexander, confused doctrine with dogma and showed little willingness or ability to adapt. But, others such as Robert L. Bullard, Charles P. Summerall, John A. Lejeune, and even the much maligned Clarence R. Edwards learned a great deal. The most applicable elements from the doctrinal adjustments issued by Pershing in early September 1918 had already been learned by the best division commanders in June, July, and August. The bulk of the development at the corps and army levels occurred when the best division commanders, such as Summerall and John L. Hines, were promoted to corps command. The same process occurred at the head of the First Army, where Liggett seemed to have a much better appreciation of the battlefield than Pershing. In his study of the BEF in 1918, historian Tim Travers notes that often "the further the commander was from the battlefield the less grasp he had of reality."[111] In many ways, the criticism applies to the AEF as well.

The most important learning, adjustment, and adaptation occurred within the AEF divisions, and that is where this investigation now moves.

---

[110] Hervey Allen, *Toward the Flame: A War Diary* (Pittsburgh: University of Pittsburgh Press, 1968), 139.

[111] Travers, *How the War Was Won*, 130–1. The differing viewpoints of divisional combat officers and the senior commanders and staff officers at GHQ often led to hostility between the two groups. Many officers admitted it, but none so brashly as Summerall, who wrote, "all during the war, there was an impassable gulf between G.H.Q. and the troops. G.H.Q. knew little of the real conditions or difficulties and was always ready to sacrifice anyone who might be blamed." Summerall, "Duty, Honor, Country," p. 94.

2

The 1st Division

Training for and Waging Trench Warfare

The 1st Division was the showcase unit of the AEF. It was the first to arrive, the first to enter and complete training, the first to enter the line, and the first to attack the enemy. As such, Pershing took an extraordinary interest in the division's training and operations. It received the most extensive training of all the AEF divisions. It fought in all three major offensives in which the AEF was a significant or dominant factor: the Aisne-Marne Offensive in July, the St. Mihiel Offensive in September, and the Meuse-Argonne Offensive of September through November. By all accounts, the 1st Division became one of the most successful AEF divisions.[1]

Many senior officers in the 1st Division were handpicked by Pershing and the AEF General Staff. Nevertheless, the division increasingly fought in a style that maximized firepower to secure limited objectives at a minimum cost in human life. Although the unit received more open-warfare training than any other in the AEF, its methods ultimately betrayed a commitment to a style of fighting at odds with the official AEF doctrine that stressed self-reliant infantry, the rifle and bayonet, unlimited objectives, and aggressiveness at all costs. Although the division's relatively lengthy training period allowed it to train for open warfare more than other American units, the unit also spent significant time training under French tutelage and encountering the challenges of living and fighting in the trenches. These experiences may have encouraged many officers

---

[1] The main units in the 1st Division were the 1st Infantry Brigade, composed of the 16th and 18th Infantry Regiments; the 2nd Infantry Brigade, composed of the 26th and 28th Infantry Regiments; and the 1st Field Artillery Brigade, with the 5th, 6th, and 7th Field Artillery Regiments.

in the division to gain a greater appreciation of the importance of fire-power, combined arms, and limited objectives early on in their time in France.[2]

Training in France, June 1917–May 1918

Although the AEF referred to the 1st Division as a "regular" division, it was so only in organizational nomenclature because its infantry regiments existed in the prewar U.S. Army. In reality, the division that arrived in France in June, July, and August 1917 was almost as much a new creation of inexperienced officers and soldiers as the other divisions that followed. Shortly after the units began to arrive in France, they were put under the tutelage of the crack French 47th Division, whose senior officers expected to quickly teach the essential details of fighting on the Western Front to the pick of the American Army and then send them into the line. When confronted with the overly aggressive and advanced French training schedule, the 1st Division's first commander, Major General William S. Sibert, wrote a letter to the 47th Division's commander in an attempt to disabuse him of his faulty notions regarding the first contingent of American "regulars." He announced that well over half the division's soldiers were fresh recruits "entirely without training," that "few of the present noncommissioned officers have had longer service than two years" (in fact, most of these were privates only weeks before, all the best NCOs having been immediately commissioned as lieutenants), and that "practically all of the officers

---

[2] After arriving in France, the 1st Division trained in and around the trenches of Europe for ten months, including time holding quiet sectors of the front. In comparison, other Regular divisions such as the 2nd, 3rd, and 4th trained for about seven, four, and six months, respectively, though some units in the 2nd Division exceeded this figure, and I have subtracted about two months to account for the time spent by the latter two divisions in getting organized, traveling to Europe, and restarting training there. Of the National Guard divisions, the 26th and 42nd Divisions each had about eight months of training time, each with about a month in the United States and the rest in France; whereas the 32nd trained in the United States for about four months and in Europe for about five more. Of the National Army divisions, the 77th Division trained for about six months in the United States and another three in Europe, and the 89th trained for about nine months in the United States and another two in France. However, most of the Guard and National Army divisions organized between August and October 1917, such as the 32nd and 89th Divisions, spent considerably longer than two months getting organized and traveling to Europe because they had to wait on later drafts of troops. Furthermore, most divisions had to yield thousands of partially trained replacements to fill up units embarking for Europe and then received completely untrained drafts to fill up their own vacancies. See Ayres, *The War with Germany*, 33–4.

below the grade of captain have been appointed less than six months." Organizationally, he noted that members of the division, brigade, and regimental staffs "were assembled for the first time" after landing in France.[3] So, neither the division nor its elements nor its officers and men could in any meaningful respect be described as experienced. With the possible exception of its few senior officers, the division needed the most basic remedial training.

Sibert secured permission to carry out a basic-training regimen for his infantry in late July and August that stressed physical conditioning, close-order drill, and marches with full packs. Although the troops began some basic familiarization with French trench-warfare weapons, such as hand and rifle grenades, automatic rifles, 37mm guns, and machine guns, all under the close guidance of the attached French units, the basic combat skills to be learned at this time were, in keeping with American doctrine, bayonet training and rifle target practice up to ranges of 300 yards.[4] Only in September did the division begin to actually practice small-unit maneuvers when, in addition to continued small-arms practice, its units began to solve "problems in minor tactics, offensive and defensive."[5] From August into late October, the artillery regiments trained separately at the artillery camp at Valdahon, where French instructors taught them the latest methods and techniques, including rolling barrages. The impact of the French trainers was so pervasive during these months that Sibert felt compelled to issue a memorandum exclaiming "the time has come for the 1st Division to stand alone. Its officers must be required to solve for

[3] George C. Marshall, an early member of the division staff, explained what happened to each of the supposedly "regular" infantry regiments after the war declaration. From an initial size of about seven hundred men in May 1917, half this number of "trained personnel" was stripped to provide cadre for other units, and then the unit was filled up to about two thousand men with raw recruits. See Marshall, *Memoir of My Services in the World War 1917–1918* (Boston: Houghton Mifflin, 1976), 19. Letter from Commanding General (C.G.), 1st Division, to C.G., 47th Division, French Army, 18 July 1917, *USAWW*, 3: 426.

[4] Marshall also mentions the need to train "raw recruits" in "the elementary duties of a soldier." These men, who generally were "not impressive," "undersized," and often could hardly speak English, were issued their first rifles when en route for the transport ships at Hoboken. The only positive element of the new division was that it did receive the best fifteen to twenty newly commissioned officers from each of the new training camps around the nation. Unfortunately for the division, many of these were stripped for other duties before May 1918. See Marshall, *Memoir*, 8, 19; and HQ 1st Division, Memorandum for Brigade and Regimental Commanders, 2 August 1917, *USAWW*, 3: 432.

[5] Society of the First Division, *History of the First Division in the World War, 1917–1919* (Philadelphia: John C. Winston, 1931), 25, hereafter *History of the First Division*.

themselves problems in trench warfare, giving the necessary orders and executing the problems without the help of French officers."[6]

At this very time, Pershing and his GHQ began to have serious reservations about the kind of training the Allied instructors were giving the Americans, particularly regarding the emphasis on methods of trench fighting (so clearly mentioned in Sibert's memorandum) and on the weapons that dominated that kind of warfare. The divisional officers clearly perceived the high command's attitude, but they also noted GHQ's somewhat confused and ineffective response. George Marshall wrote that GHQ "did not approve of the French methods of instruction, but did not order us to discontinue them. At the same time, however, they did give us very drastic orders to conduct certain training along American lines."[7] Certainly, the training "along American lines" was a reference to the open-warfare ideas; however, although it was easy for GHQ to vent its doctrinal convictions, having those ideas dominate the 1st Division's training while it was so heavily under the control of the French instructors was a more difficult task.

In early October, the division carried out a special training exercise, and it was thoroughly trench-warfare–oriented, involving a battalion occupation of a "center of resistance . . . in the face of the enemy and under intermittent artillery bombardment," under "hostile aerial reconnaissance," and with "the probability of gas attack."[8] Later in the month, although the division continued to use such traditional methods as close-order drill and target practice, it also increased its training of the machine-gun companies, the Stokes mortar teams, and the 37mm-gun crews. The division even laid out "an extensive set of practice trenches, about which the initial training centered."[9] The division history states plainly, "as was to be expected . . . almost all instruction was in trench warfare."[10]

The next phase of training, the four-week period from late October to late November in the front-line trenches near Sommerville under the instruction of the French 18th Infantry, could not in any way have made

[6] HQ 1st Division, Memorandum for Brigade Commanders, 21 September 1917, *USAWW*, 3: 43. See also HQ 1st Division, Memorandum for Brigade Commanders, 10 September 1917, *USAWW*, 3: 439.

[7] See Marshall, *Memoir*, 20; and Millett, *The General*, 322.

[8] HQ 1st Division, Memorandum for Brigade Commanders, 5 October 1917, *USAWW*, 3: 440.

[9] HQ 1st Division, Memorandum for Brigade Commanders, 12 October 1917, *USAWW*, 3: 446.

[10] *History of the First Division*, 20.

the division more proficient in waging open warfare. This training, however, did improve the division's ability to stay alive and fight in the
trenches, employ and rely on the weapons that dominated the trench
environment, and further appreciate the ideas and methods of warfare
that reigned in the French combat divisions. The division history claimed
that the training in the trenches "was of the greatest value."[11]

In late November, the division left the trenches to return to its training
area near Gondrecourt for what one regimental history called the "final
stage of training" and what should have been the unit's immersion into
those skills needed to carry out GHQ's plans for a war of movement
based on open-warfare methods.[12] The division did begin training for
open warfare, but it continued to train for trench warfare as well – spending nearly half of its training hours over the next three weeks practicing
trench-warfare methods and carrying out trench-warfare maneuvers. The
scenario for one brigade-level maneuver carried out during this period,
entitled "Trench Warfare – Attack of 3 Successive Objectives," envisioned
a preliminary artillery preparation of four days. The actual assault, including both infantry regiments, received the cover of both creeping artillery
and machine-gun barrages and had three clearly limited objectives. The
artillery barrage advanced at 50 yards a minute (intentionally very fast to
decrease the danger to the troops in this live-fire exercise) with a pause
at each objective. As the combat experience of the 1st Division demonstrated, if senior AEF officers considered this to be the definition of trench
warfare, then the AEF hardly engaged in anything but trench warfare during the entire war.[13]

Whatever the nature and extent of the division's open-warfare training
during the period, transfers of officers and men in and out of the division negatively disrupted its proficiency as a combat unit. The division's
War Diary noted that during just one November week, nine of the twelve
infantry battalion commanders left for training in the AEF's growing system of staff schools. The diary included the commentary that these kinds
of changes, bringing a wave of "very young and inexperienced" officers,

---

[11] Ibid., 30.
[12] "Historical Sketch of the 7th Field Artillery Regiment," p. 2, Folder 11.4, Box 102,
 1st Division Historical File, Record Group 120, National Archives (hereafter RG 120,
 NA).
[13] Records of the 2nd Brigade show that this third period of training, from 25 November
 to 15 December, included 46 hours of training in trench warfare and just 54 hours in
 open-warfare maneuvers and exercises. See 2nd Brigade, Memorandum, 20 November
 1917, Folder 50.4, Box 68, 1st Division Historical File, RG 120, NA.

"seriously handicapped" the regimental commanders – many of whom were new themselves – just as they began the period of regimental- and brigade-level training. Despite the supposed emphasis on open-warfare training in the upcoming weeks, the diary stressed that the new officers were "not prepared to give any instruction or to carry out regimental orders in the tactics of trench warfare," a sign that the divisional leadership continued to be concerned about that kind of fighting.[14]

Few junior officers understood their duties during open warfare either. Brigadier General Beaumont B. Buck, the commander of the 2nd Infantry Brigade, noted after certain open-warfare exercises in early December that his command was filled with young officers unable to perform such basics of open warfare as "Advance and Rear Guard" and "Patrolling and Scouting." He claimed that, regarding the skills required for open warfare, the brigade had "over the past six months . . . lost a great deal of our former efficiency in these duties and these defects should be remedied at once."[15] The weather also conspired to further inhibit this period of open-warfare training, as many maneuvers had to be conducted in ice and snow during one of the worst winters in French history. A history of the 7th Field Artillery Regiment claimed that "rain and mud and later snow and ice made maneuvering and drilling almost impossible." The same source also recorded that the unit had few horses, certainly an important element for any artillery training in open warfare. In this case, the men "courageously pulled guns and caissons by hand over the ice covered roads."[16] One wonders just how much maneuvering could have characterized such training.

Further examination of the actual open-warfare training conducted shows that the emphasis was on control of troops during marches "in the presence of the enemy" and then in "the occupation of a defensive position."[17] There is no record of any training that might have enabled the regiments, brigades, or the division as a whole to learn how to combine fire and maneuver in some form of mobile attack in an environment devoid of trenches and overwhelming defensive firepower. However, even though senior commanders were not comfortable with the capabilities of

---

[14] 1st Division War Diary entry for 26 November 1917, *USAWW*, 3: 456. See also Marshall, *Memoir*, 15.

[15] 2nd Brigade Headquarters, Memorandum, 10 December 1917, Folder 50.4, Box 68, 1st Division Historical File, RG 120, NA.

[16] This unit history makes no mention, explicitly or implicitly, of *any* open-warfare training. In fact, it never uses those words at all. "Historical Sketch of the 7th Field Artillery Regiment," p. 3, Folder 11.4, Box 102, 1st Division Historical File, RG 120, NA.

[17] 1st Division War Diary entry for 18 December 1917, *USAWW*, 3: 459.

Robert L. Bullard, commander of the 1st Division at Cantigny as well as the III Corps in the Aisne-Marne and Meuse-Argonne. In October 1918, he took command of the new American Second Army.

their small-unit commanders, especially regarding their abilities on the open field, by late December the division was again preparing for trench warfare. Marshall claimed that in late December and early January, the unit "carried through a series of divisional maneuvers in trench warfare tactics," and this training culminated with both infantry brigades accomplishing a "Problem in Trench Warfare" on 6 January, closing with a movement into real front-line trenches near the town of Seicheprey along the St. Mihiel salient.[18]

Three other important changes occurred in the division at this time. First, in December, General Robert Lee Bullard gave up command of the

[18] Marshall, *Memoir*, 53. The details of this trench-warfare training are unknown, but most references to such training entailed practicing trench-to-trench attacks and resisting such attacks. Another example of the continuing problem of personnel turbulence in the division occurred on 1 January 1918, when the 7th Field Artillery Regiment received

Charles P. Summerall, commander of the 1st Division in the Aisne-Marne, St. Mihiel, and the Meuse-Argonne Offensives. He was given command of the V Corps for the last month of the Meuse-Argonne campaign.

1st Brigade and replaced Sibert as division commander. During his subsequent six months of command, Bullard showed an increasing willingness to absorb the lessons and methods of French advisors and senior commanders. Second, Bullard arranged to have Charles Summerall assigned as the commander of the 1st Field Artillery Brigade, and the artilleryman brought with him his emphasis on firepower maximization. Third, Summerall immediately instituted an increasingly effective system of liaison and communication between the infantry and artillery units of the division. He "permanently" detailed artillery liaison teams, with officers, enlisted men, and their own horses, to each of the infantry brigades and regiments and charged them with consulting with the infantry commanders, understanding all infantry movements, and coordinating all artillery support with their own artillery unit. Summerall stressed the crucial nature

thirty new officers, equal to nearly half of the regiment's authorized officer strength, whose "total military experience consisted of but one training camp and three months training in France." See "Historical Sketch of the 7th Field Artillery Regiment," p. 7, Folder 11.4, Box 102, 1st Division Historical File, RG 120, NA; *USAWW*, 3: 460.

of artillery liaison teams during combat, asserting that "the success or failure of a considered movement would depend upon their skill, understanding and thoroughness."[19] Summerall had laid the groundwork for what would soon become an effective relationship between the infantry and artillery units of the 1st Division.

When the division arrived at Seicheprey in mid-January, the 1st Brigade held the trenches while the 2nd Brigade began another round of training just behind the lines. On 7 March, they changed places. By late March, both brigades were holding sectors at the front because the French had to withdraw veteran divisions to respond to the huge German offensive of 21 March.[20] Uncertain of the division's capabilities in open warfare and apparently suspicious of the extent to which the division's officers had accepted French doctrine, AEF GHQ ordered the individual infantry brigades to accomplish more open-warfare training during this period. It sent each brigade a detailed four-week training program. The programs included a total of 140 hours of training; the largest amount, some 66 hours, was in "small unit" tactics for sections, platoons, and companies.[21] Because GHQ never identified small-unit training as having either trench- or open-warfare specialization, this may mean that the AEF leadership recognized that, at this level of minor tactics, the distinctions between the two kinds of warfare were unimportant and the skills required were essentially the same. However, for training at the battalion, regiment, or brigade level, GHQ ordered 38 hours for open warfare and, strange as it may seem, 36 more hours in trench warfare.

Although the nearly equal training time for open and trench warfare may betray an awareness in GHQ that AEF units really did have to be proficient in trench warfare (including executing trench-to-trench attacks, resisting enemy attacks, and carrying out counterattacks) and that perhaps the skills inherent in that effort were not so easily obtained, the accompanying language of the GHQ program was filled with doctrinal traditionalism. It demanded that every soldier "fire the full [rifle]

[19] See HQ 1st F. A. Brigade, "Instructions for Artillery Liaison Officers with Brigades and Regiments of Infantry," 30 December 1917, Folder 32.11, Box 93, 1st Division Historical File, RG 120, NA; and Millett, "Cantigny, 28–31 May 1918," 161.

[20] During this period, the 1st Division became the first American unit to take full command of a sector of the front lines. Until 5 February, the command of the division sector was held by the neighboring French division, though the 1st Division held a front of 7.5 kilometers. On 5 February, Bullard took tactical command of the sector. *USAWW*, 3: 460.

[21] GHQ AEF to C.G., 1st Division, 27 January, 1918, Subject: Training Program, 2nd Brigade, Folder 50.4, Box 68, 1st Division Historical File, RG 120, NA.

qualification course at 600 yards" and emphasized that "the final measure of efficiency of any command is its action in open warfare. Only
by the solution of problems of manoeuvre, can sureness of decision be
cultivated in all commanders and smoothly working teams be produced.
Tactical schemes and problems of open warfare must therefore not be
slighted."[22]

The 2nd Brigade began the new GHQ program on 4 February and carried out three brigade-level exercises – two in open warfare and a third in
trench warfare. The first open-warfare maneuver called for the brigade to
"seize and hold a defensive position in the path of a superior force, pending
the arrival of reinforcements," and the second simulated that the brigade
"while marching will be attacked by a represented enemy, the point and
direction of the attack being unknown previous to the attack."[23] So, both
open-warfare exercises were defensive in nature, a fact that flies in the face
of Pershing's demands for a war-winning campaign based on an aggressive war of movement. Possibly this was a natural reaction to the common expectation that a major German offensive was imminent in early
1918. Again, they stressed unit-maneuvering more than unit-assault tactics. Further examination of the brigade's open-warfare maneuvers shows
the unit employing many trench-warfare methods. In the first exercise,
one of the brigade commander's first orders after directing his regiments
into position was for "the Pioneers [engineers] of each regiment" to be
"utilized under sector commanders in construction of defensive works,
clearing fields of fire, and improving roads leading to their positions."
And, under special instructions, "where the orders require that troops
will entrench, clear fields of fire, improve roads, etc., the actions will be
simulated. Trenches will be outlined with stone." Other orders show that
machine guns were used extensively in the maneuver.[24] Except for the lack
of discussion in the brigade plans regarding artillery (which may not have
been available for the exercise and were not brigade assets anyway), the
maneuver seemed to settle into a typical trench-warfare situation rather
than an aggressive attack or counterattack that could lead to the dramatic
destruction of the enemy force.

[22] Ibid.
[23] HQ 2nd Brigade, Memorandum, "Training Program," 3 February 1918, Folder 50.4,
Box 68, 1st Division Historical File, RG 120, NA.
[24] "Field Orders No. 19, Sixth Period of Training of 2nd Brigade," 11 February 1918, Folder
50.4, Box 68, 1st Division Historical File, RG 120, NA.

Although no records reveal how well the brigade did in the open-warfare maneuvers, General Buck lauded the brigade for its performance of the one trench-warfare exercise. He noted that "the specially difficult feature was the successful passage through the narrow streets of the village just before reaching the initial points for the regiments.... The occupation of the trenches, both those which were actually dug and those which were simulated, was very satisfactory.... The firing by the Stokes Mortars and 37mm guns was specially good, and showed excellent gun crews...The resistance of the enemy's attack, the counter attack and the raid were all satisfactory." Buck's comments offer two important details regarding the brigade's trench-warfare training. First, the training included some clearly offensive aspects; and second, at least the brigade commander, who only recently was highly critical of his brigade's performance in the December open-warfare maneuvers, was fully satisfied that his unit could perform well in a limited, highly organized, trench-to-trench battle.[25]

While one infantry brigade was training behind the lines, the other was manning the trenches and learning more about defensive trench warfare. Although the division had its difficulties and suffered casualties, by all accounts it became proficient in holding the sector. In fact, the division leadership appeared to be ahead of many French corps and army commanders regarding the need to fully implement a system of defense-in-depth, or elastic defense. After receiving full reports of the German attack methods used at Caporetto in Italy and then later against the British, officers in the division pressed the French corps commander to allow the division to place "only a screen of men" in the most forward line of trenches; create a "strong support line, well back" as "the main line of resistance"; and have ready behind that line designated groups of reserves "held for reinforcement or counterattack." The supporting artillery was to be withdrawn out of enemy-gun range and sited-in on No Man's Land and the front German trenches.[26]

The division had also demonstrated satisfactory infantry–artillery coordination in the stable trench-warfare environment, even during some minor offensive operations. Bullard showed a willingness to use an inordinate amount of artillery support on the smallest operations, demanding that all infantry incursions into No Man's Land be supported by

---

[25] HQ 2nd Brigade, Memorandum No. 17, 18 February 1918, Folder 50.4, Box 68, 1st Division Historical File, RG 120, NA.

[26] Charles P. Summerall, "The Way of Duty, Honor, Country," p. 95.

prearranged artillery fire-support plans.[27] Front-line company commanders applauded the speed and accuracy with which the artillery responded
to infantry calls for fire support. One company commander recorded
that "in this company we all feel the utmost confidence and friendship
for the artillery."[28] Although the division's first trench raids failed to
secure German prisoners due to poor operational security, the fire support for them was considered excellent, and the raiding parties suffered no
losses.

On 3 April, the American 26th Division replaced the 1st Division in
the trenches near Seicheprey. GHQ arranged for the 1st Division to begin
a final brief period in division-level open-warfare training prior to being
released for full service anywhere on the front. Although the division executed some form of an open-warfare demonstration for observers from
GHQ (including Pershing), as well as a French Army delegation, this training never occurred in the manner intended. By 24 April, the 1st Division
was back in the front trenches, this time near the little village of Cantigny,
where it remained until early July honing its skills in trench warfare and
doing little to improve its abilities to fight in the open field.[29] During this
period, the division carried out the first of its four significant attacks. Even
though it had not had its last day of training, the division was henceforth
considered a trained division ready for combat operations. Just what kind
of battle it was capable of waging would soon be apparent.

The 1st Division completed a number of training hours in open warfare, but it practiced much more for trench warfare, including three different lengthy tours in the front-line trenches. Nearly all of this training
was under the guidance of French instructors, most of whom dismissed
Pershing's ideas of open warfare. Furthermore, its exercises in trench

---

[27] Bullard also noted the need for more air support, expressing frustration at the way the
French allowed the enemy unchallenged opportunities to reconnoiter, strafe, and bomb
his positions. Millett, *The General*, 343.

[28] Field Message from C.O., Company L, 18th Infantry to C.O., 2nd Battalion, 6th Field
Artillery, 1 March 1918, Subject: Cooperation of Artillery and Infantry, Folder 33.6,
Box 76, 1st Division Historical File, RG 120, NA.

[29] Although some historians have claimed that the division accomplished full-division
maneuvers in open warfare in April, the weight of evidence indicates that although such
maneuvers were scheduled and detailed plans and orders were drawn up for a large-
scale maneuver against the 42nd Division, the exercise was canceled without having
taken place. Instead, the division was ordered to the front near Cantigny. Marshall wrote
that after arriving in the sector, the division was able to spend a couple of days accomplishing some hastily organized exercises in "mobile warfare," emphasizing "the lessons
which had just been learned by the French in opposing the enemy's great offensive." See
Marshall, *Memoir*, 77. Also see Millett, "Cantigny," 164, and *The General*, 356.

warfare appear to have included realistic combat missions, especially the delivering and resisting of attacks. But, the open-warfare training seems to have been less well defined and less relevant to combat on the Western Front. To the extent that it dealt directly with battle, it was often defensive in nature, heavily based on infantry marches with the need to quickly respond to a surprise enemy attack on an advancing column, rather unlike any combat missions the division was subsequently ordered to perform. Sometimes the open-warfare training was even trench-like in form. The division leadership understood it was capable of performing adequately in the trench environment. Other observers, especially French officers, also complimented the division's efficiency in typical trench operations, including living in, maintaining, defending, and attacking the extensive trench networks that dominated the Western Front.

Far from fearing that the Allied instructors and liaison officers attached to the division were polluting the unit with heretical European doctrines, senior officers in the 1st Division credited the division's development as a combat unit to their French trainers and advisors.[30] Although officially on record as a supporter of "American methods" of warfare, Bullard increasingly considered heretical tactical notions. He wanted more artillery, machine guns, and even tanks added to the integral strength of the division, and he noted in his diary that the new firepower weapons were dominating the battlefield; they were doing all the killing, while the infantry did little but walk and die. He showed signs of accepting many French ideas, such as restructuring the rifle companies to increase the number of men dedicated to using rifle grenades, hand grenades, and carrying ammunition.[31] At one point, he relieved one of his infantry regimental commanders, Colonel Ulysses Grant McAlexander, who apparently agreed so strongly with Pershing's warnings against French training and methods that he openly resisted Bullard's direction to visit an experienced French unit to learn and appreciate some of the new special trench-warfare techniques. At times, Bullard's praise of French generalship was so generous that GHQ worried about his commitment to the AEF, its goals, and its methods. Bullard even suggested to some AEF leaders that they consider using experienced Allied officers as small-unit commanders in American

[30] "Historical Sketch of the First Division, AEF," pp. 1–2, Folder 11.4, Box 11, 1st Division Historical File, RG 120, NA.

[31] HQ 1st Division, Instructions No. 29, Subject: Provisional Tactical Organization of Infantry Rifle Companies, 13 May 1918, *World War Records, First Division, A.E.F., Regular,* vol. 12 (Washington, Society of the First Division, 1928–30), hereafter cited as *WWRFD.* This collection of records is unpaginated. See also Millett, *The General,* 347.

divisions.[32] On the other hand, although Pershing told Marshal Ferdinand Foch in mid-April that the division was "ready for active service" because it had "received thorough training," an inspection by the division leadership concluded that the infantry battalions did not have enough trained marksmen and were not fully qualified for open warfare.[33] As the division's combat operations proved, it was not ready for open warfare but was both willing and able to execute highly organized, firepower-based, trench-warfare attacks.

Cantigny, 28 May 1918

Whatever else the 1st Division needed to learn about trench warfare after the completion of its training period, it learned during its long, arduous tour in the front lines near Cantigny. The sector was exceptionally active from the time the division took command on 24 April. At the tip of the new salient created by the initial German Spring offensive, no proper trenches existed, and American platoon commanders noted the front line was marked by "nothing but foxholes."[34] Twice in recent weeks the French had recaptured the village of Cantigny, only to lose it again to German counterattacks. Veteran French officers in the sector compared the incessant shelling to the artillery fire at the battle of Verdun. The troops found it practically impossible to dig trenches or lay wire. A newly formed American Flash and Sound Ranging Section served in the French corps that commanded the sector, and it identified more than ninety German batteries that fired into the American lines. During one 3-hour period in early May, the Germans fired more than fifteen thousand high explosive and mustard gas shells into a village behind the front lines,

[32] Lt. Gen. Hunter Liggett, the commander of the fledgling U.S. I Corps that possessed nominal administrative control over the 1st Division in the spring of 1918, told Bullard that if he suggested to AEF GHQ that they put Americans under Allied officers, he would be immediately relieved of command. It is interesting that Col. Alexander was quickly given command of a regiment in the 3rd Division, commanded by Maj. Gen. Joseph P. Dickman, an old cavalry officer who also strictly adhered to the prewar doctrine of the U.S. Army. Hunter Liggett, *A.E.F.: Ten Years Ago in France* (New York: Dodd, Mead, 1928), 52; see also Millett, *The General*, 335, 341.

[33] *USAWW*, 3: 489–90. See also Millett, "Cantigny," 165.

[34] Welcome P. Waltz, "Personal Experience of a Machine-gun Officer at Cantigny, 28th–30th May 1918," p. 2, U.S. Army Command and General Staff School (CGSS) Monograph, IR-6-1933, Fort Leavenworth, Kans. Waltz was a platoon leader and company commander in Company C, 3rd Machine Gun Battalion, 1st Division.

causing heavy casualties to an infantry regiment resting there. German air-craft constantly strafed and bombed the American positions. With the full approval of the French corps and army commanders, Generals Charles A. Vandenberg and Marie E. Debeney, respectively, Bullard ordered so much return artillery fire – averaging more than ten thousand rounds per day – that Summerall's gunners ruined about one 75mm gun a day due to overuse.[35]

This level of activity continued well into May. As casualties mounted, Bullard increasingly stressed to his men the importance of minimizing all unnecessary exposure to the enemy. Although the French corps and army commanders were increasingly impressed by the division's performance, some members of GHQ were suspicious that Bullard was becoming too comfortable in waging trench warfare. They may have been correct, but it should not have troubled them at all. In the division's subsequent attack and seizure of Cantigny, the 1st Division demonstrated that when given a limited objective, sufficient time to plan, and ample resources, it was surprisingly capable of delivering a highly organized and well-executed blow to the enemy, and of holding on to its gains. Although some AEF staff officers, and even a number of civilian historians, have claimed that this successful attack justified Pershing's insistence on open-warfare methods, the attack actually showed nothing about the AEF's ability to wage war in the open.[36] Instead, it was proof that at least some AEF units, even early in their combat experience, possessed the ability to carry out the limited, firepower-centered attacks that were the apex of trench-warfare methods. The attack also showed that for all GHQ's bluster of the need for and superiority of open warfare, the importance of unlimited objectives, the preeminent role of infantry, and the supposed power of the rifle and bayonet, when it came to the first test in actual offensive combat – not

---

[35] Between 25 April and 8 July, the 1st F.A. Brigade fired 566,536 75mm rounds and 91,647 155mm rounds, including 31,475 rounds of gas. HQ 1st F.A. Brigade, "Ammunition Expenditure by the 1st F.A. Brigade, A.E.F.," 27 February 1919, Folder 33.6, Box 97, 1st Division Historical File, RG 120, NA; *History of the First Division*, 69–77; Marshall, *Memoir*, 85; and Millett, "Cantigny," 165.

[36] Forrest Pogue called the Cantigny assault "the first American success in the open warfare for which they were being especially prepared." Pogue, *George C. Marshall: Education of a General, 1880–1939* (New York: Viking Press, 1963), 166. Although Millett admitted that the attack did not offer "a full test" of Pershing's open-warfare doctrine, he might have written that it provided no test at all. Rather it was, as he says later, an attack of "limited objectives, deliberate planning, and set-piece design." Millett, "Cantigny," 179–80.

just for the 1st Division but also for American forces as a whole – an American division could plan and execute, with GHQ's full approval, a limited, set-piece, firepower-based attack.

In early May, Generals Debeney and Vandenberg decided that it was time for the Allied forces to try and push the Germans back a little, and they developed a plan for an ambitious corps-sized attack in which the 1st Division played the central role. But, shortly after the French XX Corps and the three designated divisions prepared orders for this attack, Debeney canceled it after becoming suspicious that the Germans were planning a larger attack of their own to the immediate north. Anxious to do something other than continue to absorb heavy casualties while sitting on the defensive, Vandenberg and Bullard convinced Debeney and Pershing to let the 1st Division carry out a much smaller attack that would take and hold Cantigny. Although some tactical and operational justification existed for the attack because it could deprive the enemy of some high ground in the sector and eliminate a small German salient, the primary motive for the attack appears to have been moral. The Americans were eager to prove themselves as soldiers, to the French and Germans alike, and French commanders were eager to show their tired troops that, finally, after a year of belligerency, American forces were ready to pick up a share of the burden of combat.[37]

Although the French provided impressive support for the 1st Division assault, the attack plan itself was an American creation. Bullard assigned Summerall and Marshall, his G-3 (i.e., assistant chief of staff for operations) to develop the plan. Casting aside any notions of a traditional American style of fighting, they designed an attack that relied on the latest methods of trench warfare. Strictly limited in objective, meticulous in every detail, and based on overwhelming fire support, the plan left nothing to chance. Intelligence gathered on the German positions identified the enemy units to be attacked, the machine guns to be silenced, the trench mortars to be knocked out, and the strong points to be reduced.

The plan called for the three infantry battalions of Colonel Hanson E. Ely's 28th Infantry Regiment to assault, surround, and hold the village "after a short but very violent artillery preparation" of 1 hour

---

[37] Another possible motive might have been to overwhelm the negative publicity flowing from a recent beating absorbed by the 26th Division during a strong German raid in the trenches near Seicheprey. HQ 1st Division, Field Orders No. 15, 10 May 1918, *WWRFD*, vol. 1; Millett, "Cantigny," 168; and Millett, *The General*, 360–1.

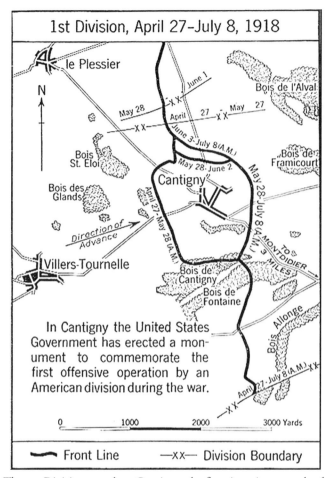

MAP 1: The 1st Division attack at Cantigny, the first American attack of the war.

(see Map 1).[38] Each attacking battalion advanced with a machine-gun company, Stokes mortars, and 37mm guns so that "each company will be provided with the necessary means to overcome machine guns." Two battalions had French flamethrower teams attached, and the center battalion also had the dedicated support of twelve tanks manned by Frenchmen. After seizing the village and its outskirts, the infantry and attached engineers were to immediately organize the positions in depth for defense

---

[38] An "Advanced Copy" of the attack order specified only 30 minutes of preparatory artillery fire, but it was doubled in length in the final draft. HQ 1st Division, Field Orders No. 18, Operation Against Cantigny, 20 May 1918, *WWRFD*, vol. 1.

against enemy counterattacks. The division was given control of a couple of "infantry planes" and a balloon to monitor the attack's progress, while other aircraft assisted the artillery and fought off enemy aircraft.[39]

To ensure success and minimize casualties, all attacking units were removed to a specially prepared, full-sized training ground with a mockup of the village, where they rehearsed the attack a number of times over two days. For almost all the attacking troops, this was the first demonstration of flamethrowers, and some noted that the weapons were "quite impressive."[40] The regiment also practiced fighting and communicating with the tankers, ensuring that the special French-speaking American liaison teams understood their tasks. Colonel Ely concluded the practice sessions with detailed critiques, and the full dress rehearsal on the second day demonstrated to all observers that the unit was ready for the attack.

However, the most striking feature of the attack plan was not the tanks or flamethrowers, or even the rehearsals behind the lines, but rather the amount of firepower dedicated to the attack. Summerall's brigade of seventy-two guns and twelve old trench mortars was augmented with eighty-four additional 75mm guns, twelve more 155mm howitzers, twenty heavy 220mm and 280mm howitzers, and twenty-eight more trench mortars ranging in size from 58mm to 240mm, giving this regimental size attack with a frontage of about 2,200 meters and a maximum depth of 1,600 meters the dedicated support of 234 pieces. In addition, the supporting corps artillery gave counterbattery support by dedicating two guns to every known enemy battery. Summerall calculated that he possessed one 75mm gun for every 15 meters of front and one 155mm, 220mm, or 280mm piece for every 38 meters, even exclusive of the trench mortars.[41] This was to be no attack of "self-reliant infantry."

Beyond the sheer number of tubes supporting the attack, Summerall's fire-support plan demonstrated an impressive ability to coordinate the weaponry to provide the infantry maximum support. The artillery fire plan consisted of three distinct phases. During the last few days before

---

[39] Marshall was so concerned that the envelopment of the town would lead to friendly fire on the far side that one early draft of the attack plan included the decidedly un-American instruction that the fighting on the far side of the village would have to be fought primarily with grenades.

[40] Waltz, "Personal Experience," 4–6; and Millett, "Cantigny," 170.

[41] HQ 1st F.A. Brigade, "Report on Operation Against Cantigny, May 28, 1918," File 33.6, Box 96, 1st Division Historical File, RG 120, NA; Maj. Gen. C. P. Summerall to Deputy Chief of Staff, AEF, Subject: Artillery, HQ V Army Corps, 4 January 1919, Folder 31.23, Box 13, V Army Corps Historical File, RG 120, NA; and HQ 1st Division, Field Orders No. 18, Operation Against Cantigny, 20 May 1918, *WWRFD*, vol. 1.

the attack, "the slow and methodical fire of destruction already begun on Cantigny" was to be "completed by the long heavy artillery (220s and 280s) placed at the disposal of the division." To disguise its intentions, the brigade was to carry out similar fire missions on other distinctive targets on the front, and registration fire was minimized. One hour before the attack, all the divisional artillery was to begin a "violent" bombardment of the "zone of attack and points selected for diversions." Fifteen minutes before the attack, some guns were to shift to smoke shell to obscure enemy observation. For the attack itself, a rolling barrage would advance ahead of the infantry, first jumping 100 meters every 2 minutes; then, after a brief halt, slowing to 100 meters every 4 minutes all the way to the final objective. Guns not firing in the barrage would execute "neutralization fire on ground commanding the zone of attack" and interdiction fire on probable counterattack routes. Three groups of machine guns, between six and twenty-four guns apiece, would fire barrages during the assault. After the attack (a crucial phase of the operation because the Germans were sure to counterattack, and the American advance was not to be deep enough to seize the enemy artillery positions), the brigade was to maintain a box barrage and interdiction fire for some time after taking the final objectives and was to be prepared to destroy counterattacks. The corps artillery was to begin its important counterbattery firing 2 minutes before H hour (i.e., when the infantry jumped-off) and was to continue its support until "the end of the operation." Also, "throughout the whole of J day [i.e., the attack day] and the following days," the corps guns were to "be ready to intervene in case of violent enemy artillery reaction on the conquered position."[42] By 26 May, the gunners had stacked six days' worth of ammunition in the battery positions, and all was ready.

Despite the comprehensive plans and preparations, two events during the last days prior to the attack threatened the operation. The first, the discovery of a missing soldier who might have compromised the attack, ultimately caused no trouble. The second event, the start of the third German Spring offensive on 27 May, had much more significant consequences. To stop the huge German breakthrough in the French lines along the Chemin des Dames area south of Cantigny, the French high command began withdrawing units and guns from along the entire front and sending them to the area in crisis. Some of the French corps guns were ordered

---

[42] HQ 1st Division, Field Orders No. 18, Operation Against Cantigny, 20 May 1918, *WWRFD*, vol. 1.

to leave the Cantigny front as soon as the American assault concluded, thus weakening the important postattack counterbattery effort.

Despite these concerns, the attack began on time on the morning of 28 May. All the troops were in position well before the jump-off time. Promptly at H-1 hour, the artillery opened up on the German lines and made a remarkable impression on the waiting assault troops. Lieutenant Welcome P. Waltz, a young machine-gun officer, claimed his troops stood in awe of the bombardment, which was "very impressive... all of us, at once, sensed the power of our own artillery and felt that with that kind of protection the enemy would be helpless... the results were inspiring... words could not describe this magnificent picture."[43] Captain S. D. Campbell, an infantry company commander, reported that the bombardment was "a sight never to be forgotten.... I have previously seen heavy preparation fire while on the British front but in this case it did not seem possible that the air could contain so many shells going and coming."[44] Colonel Ely called it "tremendous and most effective."[45] In about an hour, the village was nearly obliterated. Just before the jump-off time, some guns fired smoke shells to conceal the tanks that rolled into No Man's Land to lead the infantry forward. On schedule, at 0645 hours, the 75mm guns shifted into a thick rolling barrage that led the tanks and the infantry to and through the town in about 35 minutes. Although the flanks of the attack experienced more than a little trouble and suffered some casualties in the initial advance, within an hour and a half the regiment had established a new defensive position beyond the town, complete with wire, shallow trenches, a line of resistance, and three strong points, all supported by automatic rifles and well-sited machine guns. After mopping up the village, the attackers counted 255 prisoners and about 300 dead Germans. A French liaison officer concluded that the two German battalions holding the front lines at Cantigny were "practically annihilated," while Ely estimated his attacking troops suffered just sixty to eighty casualties during the assault.[46] Despite the minor difficulties on

[43] Waltz, "Personal Experience," 10.
[44] Memorandum from C.O., Company "E," 18th Infantry to C.O., 2nd Battalion, 18th Infantry, 5 July 1918, Subject: "Positions Occupied, Situation and Events that Took Place Before, During and After the Battle of Cantigny by "E" Co., 2nd Bn., 18th Infty.," Folder 33.6, Box 76, 1st Division Historical File, RG 120, NA.
[45] HQ 28th Infantry, "Report of capture of Cantigny and consolidation of position," 2 June 1918, Folder 33.6, Box 87, 1st Division Historical File, RG 120, NA.
[46] Captain Crochet, "Attack of the 1st DIUS on Cantigny," 29 May 1918, *WWRFD*, vol. 12. Ibid.; Marshall estimated just thirty-five to seventy-five casualties. Marshall, *Memoir*, 95.

the flanks, the seizure of the town had to be considered a resounding success, especially for a division carrying out its first attack of the war.

Although the regiment had successfully taken the town, the battle was only beginning. Starting the first afternoon and continuing over the next two days, the Germans made as many as six counterattacks to throw the Americans out of the town. Even though all of these were repulsed, a testimony to the fortitude and skill of the troops while on the defensive and to the effectiveness of Summerall's artillery fire, the casualties suffered in the following days were severe. Most resulted not from counterattacking enemy infantry but from the terrible pounding of the German artillery. Throughout 28 May, the supporting French artillery, so crucial to the counterbattery effort, was continuously withdrawn. By midnight of the first day, it was all gone. According to Summerall, from that point on, the artillery support was "altogether inadequate and our infantry suffered heavily in consequences."[47] When Ely's regiment was replaced in the front lines on the night of 30–31 May, it had lost 45 officers and 822 men, about a quarter of the unit's authorized strength.[48]

[47] Summerall to Deputy Chief of Staff, AEF, Subject: Artillery, HQ V Army Corps, 4 January 1919, Folder 31.23, Box 13, V Army Corps Historical File, RG 120, NA. The casualty figure comes from Ely's official report after the battle, HQ 28th Infantry, "Report of capture of Cantigny and consolidation of position," 2 June 1918, Folder 33.6, Box 87, 1st Division Historical File, RG 120, NA. Other sources give a figure as high as 1,067 American casualties. Millett estimates the total casualties for the three German regiments engaged in the Cantigny fight at 1,750 men. See Millett, "Cantigny," 179; Marshall, *Memoir*, 95–6; "Historical Sketch of the First Division, AEF," Folder 11.4, Box 11, 1st Division Historical File, RG 120, NA.

[48] The 867 casualties represented 22.6 percent of the 3,832 officers and men authorized in an AEF infantry regiment. Whether or not the regiment was at full strength at the start of the battle is unknown. All told, the division suffered about 942 total casualties during the battle, about 3 percent of the division's authorized strength. To provide some historical comparison, it was not uncommon for units in the Great War, even entire divisions, to lose more than a quarter of their strength in a day of hard fighting. In fact, even during the famous "hundred days" campaign of the expert Canadian Corps from August to November 1918, the Canadians suffered 45,830 casualties out of a total of about 105,000 men engaged – an overall casualty rate of 43.6 percent during the campaign. The Canadian Corps achieved great rewards in captured enemy troops, guns, and ground, but the casualty rate should not go unnoticed. Current U.S. Army standards state that a unit is considered fully "combat capable" as long as it retains 85 percent of its strength. Units with losses from 16 to 30 percent are considered "combat capable with minor deficiencies"; those with losses between 31 and 50 percent are considered "combat ineffective." Units with less than 50 percent of their strength require "reconstitution before next mission." See Department of the Army, *FM 101-5-1, Operational Terms and Graphics* (Washington, D.C.: GPO, 1997), p. C-1. The statistics on the Canadian Corps come from Schreiber, *Shock Army*, 133. The 28th Infantry Regiment statistics come from HQ 28th Infantry, "Report of capture of Cantigny and consolidation of position,"

Although military officers and historians have placed much emphasis on the heavy casualties suffered by the 1st Division at Cantigny – the division suffered more than five thousand casualties during its seventy-three-day assignment in the sector – only the preparations and execution of the 28 May attack offer significant details regarding the doctrinal development and offensive capabilities within the unit.[49] The 28 May assault proved the division's ability to plan and carry out a certain kind of attack. As Summerall wrote in his report of the battle, "The most notable features of the operation were firstly, the enormous power the Artillery was capable of displaying, and secondly, the enormous amounts of ammunition which were expended."[50] Regarding both points, some might respond that this attack merely confirmed the adage that quantity has a quality all its own, and that the division's success resulted simply from the overwhelming number of guns supporting the attack. Such claims minimize the division's demonstrated ability to coordinate and execute the complex battle plan that converted the superiority of weapons into a successful attack. In contrast, the First World War offers numerous examples when attacking divisions, corps, and armies failed to do this.[51]

By all accounts, the superb fire support for the attack was not simply a matter of quantity but also a result of the quality of the plan and the technical ability of the troops. The infantry was as impressed with other aspects of the artillery work as they were with the preliminary bombardment. Ely reported that the rolling barrage was "extremely accurate, enabling the infantry to follow at less than fifty yards in general and keeping practically all elements of the defense under cover and depriving them of all aggressive action."[52] Other infantry officers confirmed that they could follow the barrage safely even at a distance of 30 to 50 yards. Captain Campbell

2 June 1918, Folder 33.6, Box 87, 1st Division Historical File, RG 120, NA. Millett offers the full division casualty figure in "Cantigny," 179.

[49] The division's 5,163 casualties during these weeks near Cantigny represented 18 percent of its authorized strength. See ABMC, *American Armies*, 417.

[50] Each of the 75mm regiments fired more than sixteen thousand rounds on 28 May, and the 155s fired more than four thousand rounds. HQ 1st F. A. Brigade, "Report on Operation Against Cantigny, May 28, 1918," Folder 33.6, Box 96, 1st Division Historical File, RG 120, NA; Memorandum from C.G., 1st Field Artillery Brigade to Chief of Staff, III Army Corps, 6 May 1919, Folder 11.4, Box 91, 1st Division Historical File, RG 120, NA.

[51] The battles fought at Neuve-Chappelle, Loos, and the Artois in 1915; at Verdun and the Somme in 1916; and especially Robert Nivelle's attack along the Chemin des Dames and Douglas Haig's Passchendaele offensive in 1917 all proved that a superiority of artillery did not guarantee success.

[52] HQ 28th Infantry, "Report of capture of Cantigny and consolidation of position," 2 June 1918, Folder 33.6, Box 87, 1st Division Historical File, RG 120, NA.

described the barrage as "splendid." The box barrage fired in front of the new line of resistance after the attack was thick and accurate, enabling the troops to prepare the new defensive line without suffering from enemy attacks. Finally, although the divisional artillery was unable to silence the enemy artillery – a mission no divisional artillery could do well during the war – Summerall's gunners proved superb at helping stop the enemy counterattacks. It responded so rapidly that it destroyed more than one of them before the defending American infantry even had to open fire.[53]

The success of the attack also resulted from the generally well-executed assault by the infantry, machine-gunners, and tanks. As with any attack, a few enemy machine guns survived the bombardment, and some infantry reports note that those machine guns in and around the town that survived the artillery fire were handled by the tanks or taken by "flank attack."[54] The commander of the French tank detachment praised the American troops highly, rating the tank–artillery coordination as excellent and stating that "the cooperation of the Tanks and the Infantry was accomplished in a manner beyond expectations.... The American Infantry showed a remarkable knowledge of how to use tank assistance, following them closely without allowing themselves to be held up by them." He summarized the attack by reporting that "this operation was well planned and was executed with perfect cooperation between a spirited and intelligent infantry and a Tank Battalion which was anxious to do its part."[55] General Vandenberg, the corps commander, reported that "the spirit of the American troops was magnificent. The success obtained will have a great moral effect on them." He also noted that "the artillery, *using our methods*, fired very well" and closed by writing that, in summary, it was an "excellent operation from every point of view" [emphasis added].[56]

---

53 Memorandum from C.O.,Company "E," 18th Infantry to C.O. 2nd Battalion, 18th Infantry, 5 July 1918, Subject: "Positions Occupied, Situation and Events that Took Place Before, During and After the Battle of Cantigny by "E" Co., 2nd Bn., 18th Infty.," Folder 33.6, Box 76, 1st Division Historical File, RG 120, NA. See also Edward S. Johnston, "A Study of the Nature of the United States Infantry Tactics for Open Warfare on July 18, 1918, and of Their Points of Difference as Contrasted with the United States Army Tactics as Taught in 1914," Student Monograph IR-124–1931, CGSS. Johnston served as a junior officer in the 28th Infantry.

54 Memorandum from C.O., Company "E," 18th Infantry to C.O. 2nd Battalion, 18th Infantry, 5 July 1918, Subject: "Positions Occupied, Situation and Events that Took Place Before, During and After the Battle of Cantigny by "E" Co., 2nd Bn., 18th Infty.," Folder 33.6, Box 76, 1st Division Historical File, RG 120, NA.

55 "Report: On the Participation of the 5th Tank Battalion in the Operation of the 1st US I.D. on Cantigny," 28 May 1918, WWRFD, vol. 12.

56 "Report of Commander of the 10 Army Corps," 29 May 1918, WWRFD, vol. 12.

Despite these accomplishments, the attack also exposed some problems, which – although minor in such a small, set-piece attack – could be much more serious in the kinds of large-scale attacks the AEF General Staff had in mind for American divisions. First, the infantry, due to either inexperience, poor training, overconfidence in the artillery support, or a combination of all three, attacked in formations that would not work well under different circumstances. Marshall wrote that "the long waves of infantry moved out in perfect alignment."[57] One company commander reported that "their line was perfect and they looked as if they were taking part in a drill movement."[58] Edward Johnston, an infantry lieutenant in the attack, claimed that only a few company-level officers had trained their men, as he had, "to advance by rushes from cover to cover, while still following the barrage," something he learned only from the more experienced French trainers.[59] Some of the troops made a similar mistake after the assault was over by making conspicuous targets of themselves while walking around the ruins of the village. Equally serious was the problem of bunching forward; lines of troops in the support and rear waves moved forward so fast they nearly ran into the assault waves. This made maneuvering difficult and increased the potential for casualties from enemy machine guns and artillery. Others identified the tendency of commanders at and above the battalion level to excessively reinforce the front lines after the attack, leading to increased casualties. Although German prisoners confirmed the incapacitating nature of the artillery support, some reported that at least one strong point that got its machine guns going was taken not by American fire and flanking maneuvers but by "a brilliant bayonet charge" and "hand to hand fighting."[60] The brigade commander, Beaumont Buck, admitted that communications with the very front line were poor just a few hours after the initial assault. Finally, Summerall, Ely, and no doubt others noted the inadequate support of the infantry by the division's own artillery brigade, unavoidable in this

---

[57] Marshall, *Memoir*, 95.
[58] Memorandum from C.O., Company "E," 18th Infantry to C.O., 2nd Battalion, 18th Infantry, 5 July 1918, Subject: "Positions Occupied, Situation and Events that Took Place Before, During and After the Battle of Cantigny by "E" Co., 2nd Bn., 18th Infty.," Folder 33.6, Box 76, 1st Division Historical File, RG 120, NA.
[59] Johnston, "A Study of the Nature of the United States Infantry Tactics for Open Warfare," Appendix 4, p. 2.
[60] "Notes on Recent Fighting: Attack of May 28 According to Prisoners' Statements," from 1st French Army Bulletin, 30 May 1918, Folder 50.1, Box 32, I Army Corps Historical File, RG 120, NA.

case, after the first phase of the attack was accomplished.[61] None of these problems, except the dearth of artillery, was severe enough to cause major trouble in such a set-piece, limited-objective, firepower-based attack. They would cause more harm in larger operations in the future.

Despite those difficulties, the ultimate conclusions of the officers of the 1st Division and the French Army must be granted. After the attack, Pershing cabled the War Department to announce the victory, claiming the attack "was well planned and splendidly executed."[62] He too was correct. The division proved it was capable of carrying out limited trench-warfare attacks. But, it had shown nothing of its ability to wage open warfare. That would come in the division's next great battle, at Soissons.

The Aisne-Marne Offensive, 18–22 July 1918

Between the battle of Cantigny and 8 July, the 1st Division remained in the front lines of the sector, resisting enemy raids and attacks and carrying out a number of successful raids itself.[63] When the French command finally pulled it out of the line, members of the division hoped they were going to a training area in the rear to assimilate the nearly five thousand replacements that had joined the division since it entered the sector in mid-April. Some commanders, perhaps still uncertain as to the division's ability to fight in a more traditionally American fashion, hoped the unit would get the chance to accomplish more open-warfare training. However, after being sent to a training area, it quickly received orders to move to another front-line position, where it was to play a prominent part in a battle considered by many to have marked a turning point in the war. At the battle of Soissons, part of the giant Franco-American offensive to eliminate the huge salient created by the third German Spring offensive, the division displayed great aggressiveness, perhaps to the point of recklessness. Although the 1st Division made an impressively deep advance, proved it had the stamina

[61] HQ 2nd Brigade, Memorandum, "Report of Incidents Immediately Prior to and During the Operation Against Cantigny Carried Out on 28 May, 1918," 29 May 1918, Folder 33.6, Box 67, 1st Division Historical File, RG 120, NA.
[62] *USAWW*, 2: 434.
[63] During the fourth German Spring offensive of 9–13 June, called the Noyon Defensive by the AEF, the 1st Division successfully resisted all German attacks and, at a cost of 567 casualties, held secure a 5-kilometer sector on the elbow of the new salient. The French division to its immediate right quickly withdrew more than 2 kilometers in the face of attacks. The French army and corps commanders noted that the 1st Division was the only division to carry out its orders to resist the attacks without withdrawing. *History of the First Division*, 88–90; Millett, *The General*, 369.

to fight hard over many days, and ultimately succeeded in reaching its objective, it also showed an inability to coordinate sufficient firepower and to control its infantry attacks in conditions approaching open warfare.[64]

Much more than at Cantigny, the French Army dominated the Soissons attack. French commanders determined the strategy behind the offensive, the French Army took complete responsibility for transporting and supplying the attack divisions, French army and corps commanders determined the amount of artillery support and directed the operations of the divisions during the battle, and French units attacked on both of the division's flanks. Yet, the battle reveals much about the 1st Division's combat abilities and inabilities and about the way the unit attempted to adapt its methods. Summerall, who replaced Bullard as the division commander on the eve of the battle, showed in this first experience with open warfare the determination – if not always the capability – to mass firepower as much as possible during subsequent days of the offensive and to advance his units by small, limited steps instead of by great breakthrough-inspired bounds.[65]

Just one day after arriving at the Dammartine training area on 14 July, the division received orders to proceed immediately to the zone of the French XX Corps of the French Tenth Army, just west of the major transportation center of Soissons. While en route, the division staff learned that they were to take part in a major offensive, and provisional field orders were prepared. By 17 July, the division had arrived "in the rear" of the corps sector and on that day finally received confirmation from the corps commander that it was scheduled to attack at 0435 hours on the following day.[66] On 18 July, all four French field armies surrounding the German salient from Reims to Compiègne were to attack, but the main blow was to be delivered by the three divisions of General Pierre E. Berdoulat's XX Corps as part of General Charles Mangin's Tenth Army. The 1st Division was to attack as the XX Corps' left flank division, with

---

[64] Summerall, "Duty, Honor, Country," p. 100; and "Historical Sketch of the First Division, AEF," Folder 11.4, Box 11, 1st Division Historical File, RG 120, NA.

[65] Summerall officially assumed command of the division on 15 July. Bullard took command of the newly formed U.S. III Corps. Although Bullard's III Corps held official administrative control over the U.S. 1st and 2nd Divisions in the Soissons attack, it retained no operational command of them. Col. L. R. Holbrooke, one of the artillery regiment commanders, assumed command of the artillery brigade. Col. John L. Hines moved from his regimental command to take over the 1st Infantry Brigade. Col. Ely left his regiment to command a brigade in the 2nd Division.

[66] HQ 1st Division, Memorandum, Subject: "Report on Operations of First Division South of Soissons, July 18–24, Inclusive," 27 July 1918, *WWRFD*, vol. 12.

the famous 1st Moroccan Division to its immediate right in the center of the corps and the American 2nd Division to the right of the Moroccans. The three divisions were to spearhead the drive to cut the road and rail lines that ran south from Soissons (approximately 9 kilometers beyond the jump-off) and then, if possible, to press another 6 kilometers beyond to the plateau northeast of Hartennes. If successful, the attack would force nearly forty German divisions in the salient to withdraw behind the Aisne and Vesle Rivers, for some of them a retreat of about 40 kilometers.[67] Also, with the German defenses in the area considered weak, this attack offered the opportunity for the attacking division to break through and fight out in the open. Mangin even had a cavalry corps ready to exploit any such success (see Map 2).

To ensure surprise for the attack, the French high command took some extraordinary risks in this offensive. Mangin prohibited any increase in artillery fire before the attack by his army, meaning there would be no artillery registration or preliminary bombardment. To compensate for this, he secured the greatest concentration of tanks by the French Army in the war, 343 in his army alone. Of even greater significance for the attacking divisions was the decision to wait until the last moment to bring the attacking troops into the sector and divulge the plans to them.

Although this effort succeeded in maintaining security for the operation, it caused great hardship for the 1st Division and possibly even more for the 2nd Division. After arriving a number of kilometers behind the lines on 17 July and holding a conference with the unit commanders, Summerall had to develop his attack orders, find his units somewhere in the French transportation system, move them all the way to the jump-off trenches after dark that night, and still get them into attack position on time to follow the rolling barrage at H hour.[68] Yet, the last-minute nature of the attack preparations caused such terrible traffic jams and logistical chaos all along and behind the front that the division was unlikely to get all of its units, with all of their weapons, in position on time. Finally, the drawing up of orders and the movement into attack positions were complicated by the fact that, due to some recent local fighting, the XX Corps could not tell the 1st Division exactly where the current front lines

---

[67] In all, thirty-five Allied divisions attacked on 18 July. See *USAWW*, 5: 231; HQ 1st Division, Memorandum, Subject: "Report on Operations of First Division South of Soissons, July 18–24, Inclusive," 27 July 1918, *WWRFD*, vol. 12.

[68] George A. Davis, "A Critical Analysis of the Aisne-Marne Offensive," p. 7, Student Monograph IR-99–1933, CGSS.

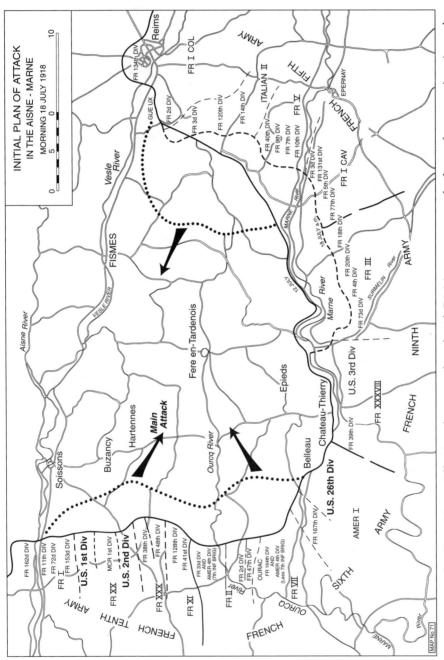

MAP 2: During the Aisne-Marne Offensive, the 1st, 2nd, and 26th Divisions were part of a force of 300,000 Americans that helped the French Army eliminate the huge salient created by the third German Spring Offensive of 1918.

86

were. Few officers had the opportunity to see the battlefield before they attacked.

The division attack plan specified the northern and southern boundaries for the generally eastward attack. It also identified the three successive intermediary objectives laid out by the French senior commanders. The first was a line about 2 kilometers ahead, the second about 2.5 kilometers farther, and the third another 1.5 kilometers beyond that. At each objective, some attackers were to organize the line for defense while others pushed on. Even after the third objective, commanders were to push out patrols and, "if possible," continue the advance. Apparently, if all went well, the infantry would outrun its artillery support and have to continue attacking under its own power. This, finally, held the prospect for testing Pershing's open-warfare ideas and the capabilities of "self-reliant infantry."

The two infantry brigades were to form abreast, each putting both of its regiments in line so that, from left to right, the division had the 28th, 26th, 16th, and 18th regiments attacking. Each regiment had its three battalions "echeloned in depth" or stacked in assault, support, and reserve positions. Brigade orders specified that the leading platoons would form in "2 waves" with men about 7 to 8 meters apart, while all other platoons followed in "small columns." The 2nd Brigade was supposed to have eighteen tanks to support the attack; the remainder, as many as forty-eight tanks, would aid the 1st Brigade, which was expected to make the deepest advance.[69]

For artillery support, the 75s would put down a barrage just beyond the official "jump-off line" and have it remain there for 5 minutes while the infantry worked its way up to it. The guns then were to advance the barrage to the first objective at a rate of 100 meters in 2 minutes, halting for 20 minutes on that line. Then, "all the available artillery" was to cover the advance to the second objective, moving 100 meters every 3 minutes, where the barrage would rest for 40 minutes. Any 75mm guns unable to cover the advance to the second line were to begin advancing to more forward positions. The guns that could still fire would continue the barrage through the third objective, at the same rate, and then cease firing. Each of the four 75mm battalions in the artillery brigade was assigned to cover the advance of one infantry regiment. The artillery brigade was augmented by one French thirty-six–gun regiment of 75s, ordered to superimpose its fire over the barrage fire of the 6th and 7th Artillery Regiments. Twelve guns

---

[69] HQ 1st Division, Field Orders No. 27, 16 July 1918, *WWRFD*, vol. 2; HQ 2nd Brigade, Field Orders No. 34, Folder 32.1, Box 64, 1st Division Historical File, RG 120, NA.

were to fire in the sector of the 2nd Brigade and the remaining twenty-four were to support the advance of the 1st Brigade. In fact, after the first 2 hours of the attack, nearly all the light guns would be moving to more forward positions, meaning that only the twenty-four 155s would still be in position and have the range to support the infantry in the latter stages of the attack. The 155mm howitzers were directed to focus some of their fire on the deep Missy Ravine, which ran north to south through the 2nd Brigade sector about 4 kilometers into the advance. Otherwise, the big howitzers were ordered "especially to protect the advance of the 1st Brigade which has the most important mission." Yet, all told, the division had a total of just 108 guns to cover an attack frontage of more than 3 kilometers. Additional corps guns were to provide counterbattery support, but they were not under Summerall's control. Later, Summerall computed that he had one 75mm gun for every 35 meters of front and just one 155mm piece for every 125 meters. The order closed by reminding the division that "surprise is the essential factor in this operation."[70] Judging by the lack of firepower available and the absence of detail in the fire plan, the attack would need all the surprise it could get.

The attack orders included a strange mix of instructions betraying an ambivalence to the operation's supposed goal of a breakthrough and reliance on open-warfare methods. Despite giving such aggressive injunctions as "contact with the enemy must not be lost. Holding troops will be reduced to a minimum," the orders also stressed that "liaison between infantry and accompanying artillery must be very close throughout." The orders from the acting artillery brigade commander, Colonel L. R. Holbrooke, confirmed a common AEF perception that the end of a rolling barrage meant the beginning of open warfare. He directed that after the guns had reached maximum range and had to advance, they would "resume firing only at request of the infantry." He added the ideal concept that after the rolling barrage, artillery commanders "will be in close liaison with the infantry for the opening of fire on first request, considering that conditions become from this time on those of open warfare."[71] This makes

---

[70] HQ 1st Division, Field Orders No. 27, 16 July 1918, WWRFD, vol. 2; HQ 1st Division, Memorandum, "Changes and additions to F.O. #27, 17 July 1918"; HQ 1st Division, Memorandum for Infantry Brigade Commanders, "Change in time of departure of barrage and Infantry from second objective," 17 July 1918, WWRFD, vol. 2; Maj. Gen. C. P. Summerall to Deputy Chief of Staff, AEF, Subject: Artillery, HQ V Army Corps, 4 January 1919, Folder 31.23, Box 13, V Army Corps Historical File, RG 120, NA.
[71] The artillery brigade field order for 18 July is included in "Notes on the First Division in the Battle of Soissons, with Special Reference to the Employment of Artillery," n.d., Folder 4, Box 11, Summerall Papers, Citadel Archives and Museum.

it all the more interesting that the division orders stressed the absolute importance of the rolling barrage by stating, "the assaulting troops must follow the rolling barrage" and by announcing that "the Commanding Officers of first line battalions can demand the rest of the rolling barrage before their lines if they encounter prolonged resistance." They could also "demand the resumption of the rolling barrage" by using so-called "conventional signals" such as shooting certain colored flares.[72] This reliance on the rolling barrage hints that certain officers entered the battle with some tactical concepts more closely related to trench than open warfare.

In nearly every respect, this attack was dramatically different than the Cantigny assault. At Soissons, all four infantry regiments had to advance 6 kilometers over varying terrain. If they reached that objective – and no Allied attack in 1918 had as of yet penetrated so deeply in a single stroke – they would be ordered to attack again immediately. The officers had not even seen the initial ground to be attacked, they knew little of the enemy, and there certainly was no rehearsal behind the lines. The attack orders gave few details, it promised to be a race with the clock to get all units into attack positions on time, and most important, there was less than half the artillery support for an attack on a larger front by four times the amount of infantry. In fact, the artillery support was certain to *decrease* as the attack moved forward. Soissons promised to be a very different kind of battle.

In soldiers' memoirs and unit histories, the night of 17–18 July was universally regarded by members of the 1st Division as one of the most trying of the war. Small-unit commanders had to find their way forward along jam-packed roads and through dark woods while a terrific thunderstorm turned the ground into a quagmire. One participant claimed that "the congestion and confusion was beyond all description."[73] The most significant aspects of the approach to the battle are that not all the units were in position to attack at H hour and that some of the units that did attack on time had to do so without important weaponry and other supplies. Some of the infantry regiments had to leave their 37mm guns in the rear areas due to the road congestion, and none of them could get enough hand or rifle grenades from the chaotic French supply system. Only four of the twenty-four divisional howitzers were ready to fire at H hour. No officers below the battalion commander received maps, a fact that complicated

[72] HQ 1st Division, Memorandum for Commanding Generals Brigades, "H hour, J day and other information," 17 July 1918, *WWRFD*, vol. 2.

[73] HQ 6th Field Artillery, "Report on Operations South of Soissons," 1 August 1918, Folder 33.6, Box 101, 1st Division Historical File, RG 120, NA. For other descriptions of the arduous movement into the attack positions, see the operations reports listed in footnote 75.

the march to the front and was to cause more trouble in this deep advance across unknown terrain. One infantry battalion commander reported that "we were short most everything but rifle ammunition."[74] Few of the tanks made it into the assault position on time, and most of them ended up following the infantry, sometimes hundreds of meters to the rear of the assault troops, instead of being out front clearing a path for them.[75]

Despite these significant difficulties, most leading waves of the exhausted infantry made it to the jump-off line on time and attacked at 0435 hours on 18 July behind a rolling barrage from the 75mm guns, which also barely reached their firing positions in time (see Map 3).[76] Within the hour, all the 155s finally reached their positions and began

---

[74] "Report, 1st Bn. 16th Inf. Aiane [*sic*] Marne July 18,18" Folder 33.6, Box 73, 1st Division Historical File, RG 120, NA.

[75] The 16th and 28th Infantry Regiments both claimed they were unable to get any 37mm guns or Stokes mortars to the attack position due to road congestion. Both regiments of the 2nd Brigade claimed their companies were short of grenades. In some cases, the French guides, responsible for getting the companies correctly into the front lines, took the troops to the wrong places. Even those units that were in position at H hour claimed to have arrived there only a few moments before the attack began. By all accounts, the traffic jams, congestion, and confusion behind the lines of the French Tenth Army must have equaled if not surpassed the more famous troubles behind the lines of the American First Army in the Meuse-Argonne. For information on the approach to battle and the fighting itself, see HQ 16th Infantry, "Report on Operations South of Soissons, July 1918," 9 August 1918, Folder 33.6, Box 73, 1st Division Historical File, RG 120, NA; HQ 1st Infantry Brigade, "Report on Operations South of Soissons July 16–23, 1918," 4 August 1918, Folder 33.6, Box 61, 1st Division Historical File, RG 120, NA; Lt. Col. C. R. Huebner, "The Twenty-Eighth Infantry in the Aisne-Marne Offensive, July 18–21, 1918," Folder 33.6, Box 87, 1st Division Historical File, RG 120, NA; HQ 28th Infantry, "Messages," Folder 21.16, Box 85, 1st Division Historical File, RG 120, NA; HQ 28th Infantry, "Report of Offensive July 18–22, 1918," 26 July 1918, and "Report on Operations South of Soissons, July 1918," 4 August 1918, Folder 33.6, Box 87, 1st Division Historical File, RG 120, NA; HQ 2nd Brigade, "Report on Action South of Soissons, July 1918," 5 August 1918, Folder 33.6, Box 67, 1st Division Historical File, RG 120, NA; HQ 5th Field Artillery, "Operations South of Soissons during July, 1918," 1 August 1918, Folder 33.6, Box 100, 1st Division Historical File, RG 120, NA; HQ 7th Field Artillery, "Report on Action of the 7th Field Artillery in the Soissons Area," 2 August 1918, Folder 33.6, Box 104, 1st Division Historical File, RG 120, NA; HQ 1st F. A. Brigade, C.O., 1st F.A. Brigade to C.G., 1st Division, Subject "Report of Operations South of Soissons, July 18–24 (inclusive)," 4 August 1918, and "Operations North [*sic*] of Soissons, July 18–24 (inclusive)," n.d., *WWRFD*, vol. 12.; HQ 1st Division, Memorandum, Subject: "Report on Operations of First Division South of Soissons, July 18–24, inclusive," 27 July 1918, *WWRFD*, vol. 12; "Notes on the First Division in the Battle of Soissons, with Special Reference to the Employment of Artillery," n.d., Folder 4, Box 11, Summerall Papers, Citadel Archives and Museum.

[76] For more detailed discussions of the fighting near Soissons, see Douglas V. Johnson II and Rolfe L. Hillman, Jr., *Soissons, 1918* (College Station: Texas A&M University Press, 1999); and *History of the First Division*, Chapter 5.

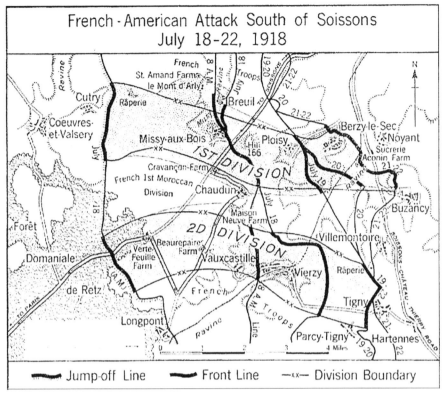

MAP 3: The attack of the 1st and 2nd Divisions near Soissons at the start of the Aisne-Marne Offensive.

firing their missions, and the infantry progressed on schedule through the first objective. On the right, the 1st-Brigade attack continued successfully all the way to the third objective, suffering moderate casualties through the second objective and heavier losses in the final advance. But, on the left, the 2nd Brigade finished the day just east of the second objective. The infantry of the 28th Regiment suffered heavy casualties during brutal fighting in the Missy Ravine. All efforts to advance to the third objective met severe enemy fire, not only from the front but especially from its left, where the adjacent French 153rd Division lagged behind.[77] Division

---

[77] One officer in the 26th Infantry claimed that the progress in his regiment was so good that only the slow American barrage initially kept it from going farther. See R. K. Whitson, "Study of the Operation of the First Division in the Soissons Offensive, 16–25 July 1918," Student Monograph IR-98–1931, CGSS. Whitson was a captain in the 26th Infantry.

headquarters received confused reports regarding its own progress, as well as that of its neighboring divisions. Total casualties on the first day were later estimated at about fifteen hundred.[78]

Despite the casualties and the confusion, the attack was a striking success. The division advanced between 4 and 6 kilometers along its entire front, keeping pace with the celebrated Moroccan Division on the right and outdistancing the French 153rd Division (also filled predominantly with North African troops) on the left. The 1st Division captured between fifteen hundred and two thousand German troops on the first day, took thirty enemy artillery pieces in and around the Missy Ravine alone, and grabbed more along the rest of the line. The 1st Division had helped crack the German line.

Yet, that afternoon, Summerall issued some surprisingly conservative orders. He claimed that "the most vital necessity is the maintenance of our advanced positions against counter attack," and he directed his units to "organize your positions in depth . . . and with the freshest battalion held in reserve in the regimental zone." He closed by demanding that "the exact position of the front lines in each regimental zone must be gotten to the supporting artillery and to these headquarters as soon as possible."[79] Although Summerall was rightly considered to be a "driver" by his wartime contemporaries, and he certainly possessed an aggressive personality, his orders at the end of the first day are those of a commander thinking in terms of successive steps, not decisive breakthroughs.[80]

Other commanders had different ideas. Early in the day, the senior French commanders were so overly optimistic about the progress that they issued special instructions to certain French divisions regarding objectives that ultimately were not taken until four days later. As late as midnight the first night, French army and corps staffs claimed that the Moroccans and the 153rd Division were both 2 kilometers ahead of where their front

---

[78] The fifteen hundred casualties were about 5 percent of the division's total authorized strength; losses in infantry and machine-gun units probably reached 10 percent. HQ 1st Division, Memorandum, Subject: "Report on Operations of First Division South of Soissons, July 18–24, Inclusive," 27 July 1918, *WWRFD*, vol. 12.

[79] HQ 1st Division, Memorandum for Commanding Generals Infantry Brigades, "Organization of Defensive Positions for the Night," 18 July, *WWRFD*, vol. 2.

[80] Although Summerall never explicitly mentioned the reasons behind his conservative handling of the battle, his actions were consistent with his appreciation of defensive firepower and an awareness of the tired and ill-equipped condition of his division when the battle began.

lines really were. This caused substantial confusion in the 1st Division.[81] General Mangin was so excited by the results of the attack that he ordered the French II Cavalry Corps to advance to the front during that night to exploit the supposed "breakthrough."[82] By midday, the German GHQ understood the Allied attack was remarkably successful, and it sent orders to the Crown Prince's army group directing it to "make preparations to withdraw the fighting troops in line south of the Marne."[83]

Late that night, Summerall received the corps order directing the division to continue the attack at 0400 hours on 19 July, reach the line of Berzy-le-Sec southeast to Buzancy, and then, optimistically, "push out offensive reconnaissance parties until contact with the enemy was gained."[84] The division attack order for the second day, issued at 0135 hours in the morning, directed the 2nd Brigade to advance to the line of the 1st Brigade and then both to continue to the final objective. As with the first attack, in compliance with higher directives, the orders specified "no artillery preparation" prior to the infantry advance, which would be covered by a rolling barrage from only the light guns. However, serious doubt over the exact location of the front lines forced the division to arbitrarily determine that the barrage would start "at a safe distance before yesterday's third objective." The barrage was to "stand for 45 minutes and then advance at the rate of 100 meters every 3 minutes," and it was to cover the entire advance all the way to the final objective. Possibly, the order to have the barrage stand for 45 minutes was more than an effort to allow the infantry enough time to close up on it. It might have been a way of ensuring some kind of preliminary fire despite the wishes of French senior commanders. Any tanks that survived intact the first day were to

[81] HQ 1st Division, Memorandum for Commanding Generals Brigades, "Organization of Defensive Positions," 18 July 1918, 1050 hours, *WWRFD*, vol. 2; HQ 1st Division, Field Orders No. 28, 19 July 1918, 0135 hours, *WWRFD*, vol. 2.

[82] Much regarding the use of cavalry at Soissons is unclear. Some studies claim that Mangin ordered the cavalry to attack and that it was "cut to pieces by machine gun fire." Davis, "A Critical Analysis of the Aisne-Marne Offensive," 9. Other reports also claim that the horses were shot up by enemy aircraft and machine guns, while the most favorable assessments of the cavalry assert that it never actually attacked but rather merely clogged the roads as it moved forward in the sector, and then again as it left the sector. Johnson and Hillman, *Soissons*, 88–91.

[83] Ludendorff had approved the Crown Prince's hastily prepared plan of withdrawal by 2030 hours that night. Davis, "A Critical Analysis of the Aisne-Marne Offensive," 9.

[84] French XX Corps, Orders No. 1,262/3, 18 July 1918, *USAWW*, 5: 299.

assist the advance, but the infantry was to fight its way forward to take
and hold the final objective even if the tanks were held up.[85]

At 0400 hours on 19 July, the 1st Brigade advanced well on the right,
hugging its barrage and gaining another 2 kilometers while maintaining
liaison with the Moroccans. But, on the left, the 2nd Brigade struggled
to advance at all. Troops from the 26th and 28th Infantry received the
attack order very late (e.g., just 5 minutes before H hour in the 28th
Infantry) and met severe German fire from the northeast, as they ran into
the forward positions of a stout defensive line called the Vauxbuin Position
that began just beyond the Paris-Soissons road. After advancing only
about 1 kilometer, the attack stalled and casualties were severe. The 153rd
Division on the left made no advance that morning, thus subjecting the
2nd Brigade to heavy fire from the north and northeast. The 1st Brigade,
2 to 3 kilometers ahead of the 2nd Brigade, suffered similarly. Although
the attack was unsuccessful from the American perspective, it nevertheless
brought more trouble to the Germans because it proved that the French
Tenth Army was intent on cutting the essential transportation routes south
of Soissons. The Crown Prince ordered three German divisions and a
number of individual infantry and artillery regiments to the front of the
Tenth Army and ordered the Vauxbuin Position to be held "at all costs"[86]
(see Map 4).

To get his division into more proper alignment, Summerall ordered the
2nd Brigade to make a second attack in the late afternoon. The attack
order specified the jump-off time as 1730 hours, coinciding with the time
the 153rd Division was to make another effort to advance. The 28th
Infantry, on the left flank, was to make the main effort, and the 26th
Infantry was to push forward as well. The 16th Infantry was merely to
adjust its line to maintain contact with the 26th. Summerall released a

---

[85] The attack order seems to be unclear as to whether both brigades were to jump-off at
0400 hours or if only the 2nd Brigade was to do so in order to push up to the line of the
1st Brigade. Although the order seems to indicate that both brigades attack at 0400, it
also directs that the "2d Brigade will move forward along its axis of yesterday until it
attains the line of the 1st Brigade. Both Brigades will then move forward on line to the
final objective and consolidate." This could be the first indication of an attempt to use
the kind of massed artillery and echeloned infantry attacks that Summerall ordered with
such good effect in the Meuse-Argonne. If this was his intent, he was misunderstood,
because both brigades attacked at the same time. HQ 1st Division, Field Orders No. 28,
19 July (1:35am), *WWRFD*, vol. 2.

[86] Whitson, "Study of the Operation of the First Division in the Soissons Offensive, 16–25
July 1918," 8.

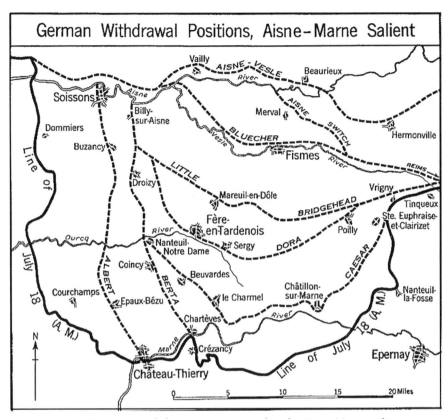

MAP 4: The German defensive positions within the Aisne-Marne salient.

fresh reserve infantry battalion to join the operation. Although the attack order did not specify any artillery fire plan, the artillery brigade did support the assault. Infantry reports and messages confirm that some amount of artillery preparation occurred before the advance and that a rolling barrage came down as well. The division history claimed that "all the 75's were employed to fire a rolling barrage in front of the 2nd Brigade to assist it forward, while the 155's were to fire concentrations on the known enemy organizations on the left flank and in the Ploisy ravine."[87] After the brief artillery bombardment to the north, northeast, and east of the 2nd Brigade, the rolling barrage began. Aided also by machine-gun fire from the 16th Infantry into the enemy flank and rear, the infantry surged

---

[87] *History of the First Division*, 124.

forward up to 3 kilometers – placing it practically on a line with the 1st Brigade.[88]

The casualties for the day's two attacks were severe, estimated at about three thousand. Total losses since 18 July were at least forty-five hundred.[89] But, the division had driven in nearly 8 kilometers and had taken approximately two thousand German prisoners. The German high command was by this time throwing all available reserves against it and its flanking divisions to prevent it from cutting the vital transportation lines out of Soissons, which lay about 2 kilometers beyond the American front lines. Despite all this, the battle was just getting started.

During the night of 19–20 July, Summerall received orders from the corps headquarters to attack again on the 20th. Due to the slow progress and heavy casualties of the 153rd Division on the left, the corps reassigned the taking of Berzy-le-Sec to the 1st Division. Summerall called for an attack at 1400 hours, with the 2nd Brigade taking Berzy-le-Sec on the left and the 1st Brigade advancing to the town of Buzancy on the right. This time, the divisional artillery was to "deliver a strong and powerful preparation for 2 hours before the assault."[90] A barrage was to stand from 1315 to 1400 hours on a line west of Berzy, then roll forward at H hour at the rate of 100 meters in 4 minutes to a line east of Berzy, where it would stand for 1 hour. Each brigade was to stop, dig in, and

---

[88] It is unclear whether the division actually massed all of its artillery on the front of the 2nd Brigade on the afternoon of 19 July. The division history insists that this happened, and a detailed manuscript on the use of artillery at Soissons found in Summerall's papers also claims that "The entire artillery was used to cover the advancing echelons and a part of the heavy howitzers were assigned." See "Notes on the First Division in the Battle of Soissons, with Special Reference to the Employment of Artillery," pp. 35–7, n.d., Folder 4, Box 11, Summerall Papers, Citadel Archives and Museum. The report of operations from the 6th F.A. Regiment, which was generally assigned to support the 1st Brigade at Soissons, mentions assisting the infantry of the 26th Regiment on the 19th; the 7th F.A. appears to have fired in front of the 2nd Brigade, as expected, on that day as well. However, the after-action reports of other units involved do not specifically confirm this innovative fire plan. Although the operations report of the 28th Regiment admits that the artillery fired before the attack and gave a rolling barrage and some artillery reports mention firing that afternoon, none of the reports from the artillery brigade or the artillery regiments describes the massing of all artillery on a narrow front, which one might have expected them to mention because the tactic was a novel one at the time. Also, the infantry reports that do mention artillery do not claim it was as powerful as one might expect if the tactics had been used. HQ 1st Division, Memorandum, Subject: "Attack at 5:30 P.M. July 19th, 1918," 19 July 1918, *WWRFD*, vol. 2.

[89] The forty-five hundred casualties were more than 16 percent of the division's authorized strength. Losses in many infantry and machine-gun units surpassed 30 percent.

[90] HQ 1st Division, Memorandum for Commanding Generals, Infantry Brigades, Subject: "Attack on Berzy-le-Sec and straightening out of line," 20 July 1918, *WWRFD*, vol. 2.

reorganize to hold the new line. This attack, although larger, deeper, less organized, and supported by much less firepower and weaponry, was yet more like the Cantigny attack than the first attack at Soissons on 18 July. It was a limited, set-piece assault, seeking to maximize firepower support for the infantry. Unfortunately, the division, especially the 2nd Brigade, was simply not capable of sufficiently organizing itself and carrying out such an attack on the third day of a brutal battle in which it had already lost nearly five thousand men.[91]

As with the other attacks, the 1st Brigade made decent progress, advancing another 2 kilometers. The 2nd Brigade had more trouble. The commander of the 28th Infantry reorganized his horribly depleted units into groups of about sixteen men and used the protection of the rolling barrage and the surrounding terrain to try and "filter" his way into Berzy-le-Sec from the north. After some of his men made it to the outskirts of the town, the lieutenant leading the attack determined the enemy machine-gun fire was too strong to continue the attack in the daylight. Although the regimental commander had decided to take the town with a night-infiltration attack, he called it off when informed that the division was already planning an attack for early the next morning, complete with an extensive artillery bombardment of the town.[92]

While Summerall developed what was to be his final attack of the battle, the other Allied divisions around him were being relieved or augmented. The American 2nd Division had been relieved on the evening of the second day, after making the deepest two-day advance of the entire offensive. The Moroccans, who only advanced slightly on the afternoon of the 20th, were relieved that night, and the troubled 153rd Division was strengthened by the addition of a fresh infantry regiment from a reserve division to help it continue its attacks. All had suffered heavy casualties, but only the 1st Division remained from the initial lineup of 18 July.

Late on 20 July, Summerall ordered that the division attack again with the rest of the Tenth Army at 0445 hours the next morning, in an effort to take and hold the objectives of the previous day's attack. Actually, Summerall ordered his two brigades to attack separately, with the 1st Brigade jumping-off at 0445 and the 2nd Brigade at 0830. Three factors

[91] HQ 1st Division, Memorandum, Subject: "Report on Operations of First Division South of Soissons, July 18–24, Inclusive," 27 July 1918, *WWRFD*, vol. 12.

[92] HQ 28th Infantry, "Report of Offensive July 18–22, 1918," 26 July 1918; and "Report on Operations South of Soissons, July 1918," 4 August 1918 both in Folder 33.6, Box 87, 1st Division Historical File, RG 120, NA.

led Summerall to attack "by echelon," as he called it.[93] First, he learned
that the French 87th Division on his right, having replaced the Moroccans, would attack at 0445, but the reinforced 153rd Division would
attack at 0800. Summerall thus adjusted his brigade attacks to those of the
flanking divisions to ensure flank support. Second, the early attack of the
1st Brigade, along with the advance of the 153rd Division, might force the
Germans to evacuate Berzy before the exhausted 2nd Brigade assaulted
it. But, the third reason for the change in time and the reason Summerall
stressed after the battle was to allow his artillery to concentrate all its
power on two separate attacks.

To ensure that no German machine-gunners would appear in the immediate front of the infantry, the close line for the supporting artillery fire
was set so near the American lines that the order had to warn subordinate commanders to withdraw any elements that might have been forward
of the line. At 0445 hours, the artillery was to fire a massed rolling barrage at the rate of 100 meters in 3 minutes to lead the 1st Brigade to its
objective, then maintain a protective box barrage beyond that line for a
full hour to help with the consolidation. Other guns were to fire a protective barrage all along the exposed left flank of the brigade. After the
1st Brigade attack, all the division guns were to make "a powerful artillery
fire for destruction" on Berzy until 0830 hours, when the 2nd Brigade
was to assault the town.[94] Whereas the division attack order strangely
directed, for some unknown reason, that there would not be a rolling
barrage for the 2nd Brigade attack, General Buck's attack order to his regiments clearly stated that his attack "will be covered by a rolling barrage
commencing at 8:30 A.M. and advancing 100 yards every 3 minutes."[95]

On 21 July, both brigades attacked as ordered, and for the first time in
the battle, both gained their objectives. Elements of the 1st Brigade drove
well beyond the Soissons-Château Thierry road, and the 2nd Brigade took
Berzy, establishing a new line east of the town. Each brigade advanced
between 1 and 2 kilometers. The two French divisions in the XX Corps
also advanced across the road, but both were thrown back with heavy

[93] HQ 1st Division, Field Orders No. 29, 20 July 1918, *WWRFD*, vol. 2.
[94] Ibid.
[95] HQ 2nd Brigade, Field Orders 36, 21 July 1918, Folder 32.1, Box 64, 1st Division
Historical File, RG 120, NA. There is no adequate explanation about why the division
staff, which used rolling barrages in all previous attacks and would use them in every
future attack, ordered that no rolling barrage would be used in the attack of the 2nd
Brigade. Equally odd is the fact that the 2nd Brigade order announced that one would be
fired. The division operations report confirms that the brigade advanced under a barrage.

casualties by German counterattacks. The reinforced 153rd Division never crossed the road at all. The 1st Division held its new line for the remainder of the 21st and throughout the 22nd, and was finally relieved that night by the Scottish 15th Division.[96]

The 1st Division had fought for five days, advanced 11 kilometers, taken thirty-five hundred German prisoners, and captured ninety-six enemy artillery pieces. No other Allied division had accomplished so much thus far in 1918. Senior officers, from Mangin to Pershing, lauded the division's feat of arms. By the evening of 21 July, German divisions were actively withdrawing from the salient. Yet, the cost of the 1st Division's success was astounding – approximately seven thousand casualties between 18 and 23 July.[97] Summerall estimated that the division lost 60 percent of its officers and 75 percent of field-grade infantry officers. It was his responsibility to ensure that the division learned from the experience, and he claimed to have held a conference and conducted "a critique of the battle" with his remaining officers shortly after the unit left the front lines.[98] Somehow, they had to account for the terrific casualties and make improvements to keep losses down in the future.

The severe casualties resulted from a number of causes, some beyond the division's control, some well within it. Four external challenges caused particular trouble for the 1st Division. First, the chaos and confusion behind the French lines before the battle ensured that the attacking units knew little of the terrain, did not have enough maps, began the attack nearly exhausted, and, in some cases, lacked important weapons and ammunition. Second, the amount of artillery support given to the division by the French high command proved wholly inadequate for the strength of the German defenses from the latter half of the first day until the end of

---

[96] The only adjustment to the division's line on 22 July was a small attack on a sugar factory to eliminate German sniper fire. *History of the First Division*, 133–6; Johnson and Hillman, *Soissons*, 136.

[97] The ABMC, *1st Division Summary of Operations in the World War*, claims a total of 7,041 casualties; the ABMC, *American Armies and Battlefields in Europe*, accounts for just 6,870. Such losses reduced the division by one quarter of its authorized strength but, as always, the casualties were not evenly distributed throughout the division. Infantry and machine-gun battalions suffered much higher casualties than other combat units and most support units suffered hardly any losses at all. When all the stragglers were rounded up, many infantry and machine-gun units had lost half their strength. Ayres claims that, overall, about a sixth of all U.S. casualties in the war were men killed in action. Of the wounded admitted to hospitals, about 80 percent were returned to duty, although often not to their original unit. About 6 percent later died of wounds. Ayres, *The War with Germany*, 122, 130.

[98] Summerall, "Duty, Honor, Country," p. 105.

the battle. The large ravines, such as the Missy Ravine, were known to be enemy strong points; however, instead of ensuring that they were drenched with firepower, Mangin advised attacking divisions to simply avoid them – an impossibility considering the ravines' size and strength. Third, the slow progress of the French 153rd Division, which had even more trouble with the Missy Ravine than the Americans, left the 1st Division's left flank open to severe enemy fire on every day of the battle. Finally, beyond the brittle front-line positions, the German defenses deeper in the sector were stronger than expected. The Vauxbuin Position, although initially weakly held in numbers, bristled with machine guns. After the German high command sent in all available reinforcements and ordered the line to be held at all costs, the task of the attackers became that much more difficult. The defenses became more substantial as the attacks progressed.

No detailed casualty figures for the French divisions in the attack are available, but French losses also were severe. In fact, a French corps report on 19 July noted that casualties "seem to have been more marked in the Moroccan Div. than in the two Allied [i.e., American] Divisions" and later stressed that "the infantry of the Moroccan division fought bravely and suffered rather heavy losses."[99] All the French divisions were either removed from the battle or given significant reinforcements by the end of the battle's third day. Even the replacement divisions suffered heavy casualties and hardly advanced the line at all.[100]

However, the 1st Division also suffered heavily from its own mistakes and inadequacies. Some of the problems experienced at Cantigny reappeared in a less benign form at Soissons, especially regarding the tactics and techniques of the infantry. One infantry officer reported that during the initial advance, "the men were not allowed to advance by rushes and take advantage of the shell holes made by our barrage but were required to follow the barrage, walking slowly at the rate of one hundred

---

[99] French XX Army Corps, Operation Report, 19 July 1918, *USAWW*, 5: 297–8.

[100] During the 21 July attack, the French 87th Division, which replaced the Moroccans, suffered more than one thousand casualties while advancing the line about 1 kilometer. The French 58th Division, which replaced the U.S. 2nd Division and was supported by the guns of the 2nd Division, two additional French artillery regiments, and as many as ninety tanks, suffered nineteen hundred casualties and finished the day where it started. When the 15th Scottish Division took over the 1st Division sector and attacked on 23 July, the unit suffered heavy casualties and did not advance the line at all. Simply put, there were no large, low-cost advances after 18 July, whether by French units, Scottish units, old units, or fresh units.

yards in three minutes, the losses were very heavy."[101] As at Cantigny, the men of the different attack waves tended to bunch forward, and at Soissons, this gave German machine-gunners and artillerymen excellent targets. One observer admitted witnessing "old conventional attack formations...with no apparent attempt to utilize cover." During the latter phases, when no barrage existed, "the officers and men were too reckless," often charging enemy machine guns instead of outflanking them.[102] Even the division commander remarked that generally "there was no time wasted in flanking these obstacles; the men...took them all by frontal attack and at the point of the bayonet."[103]

Buck reported that his "leading waves" were "not thin enough," and he wanted at least eight to ten paces between riflemen when advancing under fire. "Better still," he suggested,

would be an irregular line of small columns at wide intervals, each small column being an independent unit whose mission is to gain the flank or rear of machine gun nests, with the permission to advance rapidly or slowly according to conditions of the resistance met, always picking its way through barrages or areas swept by machine gun fire. These small columns (4, 6, or 8 men each) should have Chauchat rifles, or V-Bs [rifle grenades], or hand grenades, but the absence of any or all of these should not alter the action or purpose of the group.[104]

In many respects, Buck described the kind of tactics and techniques used with such success by German stormtrooper units in their 1918 Spring offensives and by the best BEF units in their 1918 attacks.

In fact, the reports of some junior officers show that the men were learning those lessons during the fight. One infantry officer, Edward S. Johnston, claimed:

It was by observation of the Moroccans in this action that the regiment learned the method of advance ordinarily utilized by European veterans, whereby the assault line, having lost the barrage, progressed steadily forward, individuals, under the eye of their squad leaders, moving at a run from shell-hole to shell-hole. When stopped by resistance, – usually a machine gun, – the squad, section, or platoon

[101] "Report, 1st Bn. 16th Inf. Aiane [*sic*] Marne July 18, 18," Folder 33.6, Box 73, 1st Division Historical File, RG 120, NA. See also HQ 1st Battalion, 26th Infantry, Memorandum, 3 August, Folder 33.6, Box 81, 1st Division Historical File, RG 120, NA.

[102] Johnston, "A Study of the Nature of the United States Infantry Tactics for Open Warfare," Appendix 4, p. 2.

[103] "Notes on the First Division in the Battle of Soissons, with Special Reference to the Employment of Artillery," pp. 31–2, n.d., Folder 4, Box 11, Summerall Papers, Citadel Archives and Museum.

[104] HQ 2nd Brigade, "Report on Action South of Soissons, July 1918," 5 August 1918, Folder 33.6, Box 67, 1st Division Historical File, RG 120, NA.

engaged it by fire from the front, while flankers immediately worked around with rifles and grenades to take it from the flank. It was a common saying in the 1st Division that the Moroccans taught them how to fight.

This officer believed that although such tactics were "standard practice" in the veteran European armies, they were "nowhere adequately treated in our training manuals." He insisted that "the 1914 conception of 'building up the firing line' had become passé" and claimed that in future attacks, "small columns at wide intervals were recommended as more suitable."[105]

Beyond infantry formations and tactics, the division also struggled to adequately employ its available firepower. Quite possibly due to an honest attempt to maximize the firepower for the attacking infantry, the machine-gun companies were typically attached to the leading assault waves, but this led to three significant problems. First, the machine-gun crews, and even the automatic-rifle teams (whose guns and ammunition supplies were much heavier than that of the standard rifleman), struggled to keep up with the rapid initial advance. More serious, neither those machine-gunners or automatic riflemen that kept up nor those that fell behind were given fire missions to support the infantry advance. But, worst of all, the men struggling to keep up with the leading waves suffered tremendous casualties the first two days. Most of the crews were effectively destroyed, and those that continued forward lost so many of their ammunition carriers that their automatic weapons lacked enough ammunition to be of any use.[106] These troubles, when added to the unavailability of the 37mm guns and Stokes mortars and the high attrition rate among the tanks, meant that once the infantry advanced beyond the range of the thin artillery barrage they had little more than the rifle and the bayonet to press the attack.

The division's officers took a number of actions to solve these problems. Junior officers who reported that "Infantry is handicapped against organized machine gun nests without the mortars or one pounders [37mm]" made certain they always went forward with those pieces in the future, and they learned to make good use of them.[107] Summerall ordered an

---

[105] Johnston, "A Study of the Nature of the United States Infantry Tactics for Open Warfare," Appendix 4, p. 2.

[106] HQ 1st Infantry Brigade, "Report on Operations South of Soissons July 16–23, 1918," 4 August 1918, Folder 33.6, Box 61, 1st Division Historical File, RG 120, NA; HQ 1st Division, Memorandum, "Notes on use of machine guns in the operations of the 1st Division south of Soissons and recommendations based thereupon," 5 August 1918, *WWRFD*, vol. 2.

[107] "Report, 1st Bn. 16th Inf. Aiane [*sic*] Marne July 18,18," Folder 33.6, Box 73, 1st Division Historical File, RG 120, NA.

investigation into the use of machine guns and automatic rifles, directed changes to the way the guns were to be advanced during battle (i.e., always "from cover to cover" behind the leading waves, with a forward observer looking for prospective fire missions), made improvements in their method of ammunition supply (i.e., *every* rifleman would carry a clip for the Chauchat), and stressed the importance of their fire during the attack (i.e., he claimed that one of the primary "lessons" of Soissons "was the great advantage of employing all of the machine guns in the most powerful manner to support the infantry").[108] Summerall even announced the heresy that "the service rifle" was "greatly inferior in value" to the automatic rifle, and he directed that every rifleman be trained to shoot the automatic.[109]

The division made only slightly better use of its artillery. Although Summerall appears to have tried to maximize the effect of his guns, the artillery support was ultimately insufficient. Infantry reports described the artillery barrages as "ineffective," "very light," and "inappreciable."[110] Summerall went even further, calling the artillery support "hopelessly inadequate" due to the lack of reinforcing guns for his division. He claimed "it was necessary to combine all the artillery to fire in front of one regiment or of one brigade for successive advances" and bitterly reported that "as usual, the losses of the infantry paid for the deficiency in artillery."[111]

As in other areas, the division also had its own internal problems in employing its artillery. First, as occurred in many of the Allied divisions in the rapid advance near Soissons – even the elite 1st Moroccan Division – communication within the infantry units and between the infantry and

[108] "Notes on the First Division in the Battle of Soissons, with Special Reference to the Employment of Artillery," n.d., Folder 4, Box 11, Summerall Papers, Citadel Archives and Museum.

[109] HQ 1st Division, Memorandum, 25 August 1918, *WWRFD*, vol. 2. See also HQ 1st Division, "Notes on use of machine guns in the operations of the 1st Division south of Soissons and recommendations based thereupon," 5 August 1918, *WWRFD*, vol. 2. Summerall apparently also tried to replace as many Chauchats as possible with BARs but was generally unsuccessful in this effort before the war ended. Some division automatic riflemen apparently acquired BARs on their own.

[110] See HQ 16th Infantry, "Report on Operations South of Soissons, July 1918," 9 August 1918, Folder 33.6, Box 73, 1st Division Historical File, RG 120, NA; HQ 26th Infantry "Report on the Operations South of Soissons," 3 August 1918, Folder 33.6, Box 81, 1st Division Historical File, RG 120, NA; Lt. Col. C. R. Huebner, "The Operations of the 28th Infantry in the Aisne-Marne Offensive, July 18–21, 1918," Folder 33.6 Box 87, 1st Division Historical File, RG 120, NA; and HQ 2nd Brigade, "Report on Action South of Soissons, July 1918," 5 August 1918, Folder 33.6, Box 67, 1st Division Historical File, RG 120, NA.

[111] C. P. Summerall to Deputy Chief of Staff, AEF, Subject: Artillery, HQ V Army Corps, 4 January 1919, Folder 31.23, Box 13, V Army Corps Historical File, RG 120, NA.

artillery units broke down.[112] Infantry regimental and brigade commanders struggled to identify the front lines of their most advanced units,
which was crucial to determine the starting point for any artillery support in subsequent attacks. For nearly every attack, if not all, the division
used rolling barrages to simplify infantry–artillery coordination during the
attack; however, because the barrages were so thin and the German resistance so tough, the infantry often needed to contact the artillery for additional special fire support during the attacks. The division rarely accomplished this difficult task, and infantry battalion commanders reported
that "the infantry and the artillery were unable to cooperate due to lack
of liaison."[113] The number of shells fired by the artillery regiments – on
average, they shot just a quarter of the shells per day that they fired
at Cantigny – suggests that the guns were not fully utilized.[114] Reasons
for this communications breakdown ran from a lack of wire to poorly
designed communications networks to a tendency by commanders to rely
solely on slow, casualty-prone runners. Even the division and brigade
attack orders often took hours to work their way forward, giving the
assaulting infantry little time to prepare the attack and the artillery little
time to compute the supporting firing data.[115]

---

[112] The commander of the Moroccan Division reported that although his division advanced
about 11 kilometers and took fifteen hundred prisoners, "it is nonetheless true however,
that in this entirely new form of fighting, which tends to develop open warfare, the
various echelons of the Command reported certain difficulties which they encountered
during their advance." During the attacks from 18–20 July, "information often reached
the Colonels and Brigadiers very late. The front could not always be exactly known
and this made it difficult for the Command to cause artillery to take a useful part in
the operations." Colonels' command posts were "often too far from the first line ... the
transmission of orders was often very slow.... Commanders must be sure that there is
enough time to write and transmit attack orders when choosing attack times." HQ 1st
Moroccan Division, "Remarks on Attacks of July 18th to 20th, 1918," 6 August 1918,
Folder 11.4, Box 4, III Army Corps Historical File, RG 120, NA.
[113] "Report, 1st Bn. 16th Inf. Aiane [*sic*] Marne July 18,18," Folder 33.6, Box 73,
1st Division Historical File, RG 120, NA. See also HQ 1st Battalion, 26th Infantry,
Memorandum, 3 August, File 33.6, Box 81, 1st Division Historical File, RG 120, NA.
[114] From 18–24 July, the two 75mm regiments fired about twenty-five thousand rounds, an
average of about 3,572 a day, and the 155mm regiment fired ten thousand rounds, an
average of about 1,429 a day. On 28 May, the 6th and 7th F.A. Regiments each fired
sixteen thousand rounds, and the 5th Regiment shot more than four thousand shells.
Memorandum from C.G., 1st FA Brigade to Chief of Staff, III Army Corps, 6 May 1919,
Folder 11.4, Box 91, 1st Division Historical File, RG 120, NA.
[115] "Report on Operations South of Soissons July 16–23, 1918," HQ 1st Infantry Brigade,
4 August 1918, Folder 33.6, Box 61, 1st Division Files, RG 120, NA; Memorandum,
HQ 1st Battalion, 26th Infantry, 3 August 1918, Folder 33.6, Box 81, 1st Division Files,
RG 120, NA; "Report on Action of the 7th Field Artillery in the Soissons Area," HQ
7th Field Artillery, 2 August 1918, Folder 33.6, Box 104, 1st Division Historical File,
RG 120, NA.

The communications problems in the 1st Division at Soissons demonstrated how much more difficult it was to coordinate firepower for attacks during a continuous, deep, and occasionally rapid advance than for a typical limited, set-piece assault. Nevertheless, Summerall issued orders to correct the communications problems exposed during the battle. By mid-August, the division had "completely reorganized" its signal communications, implemented a new system of "automatic liaison in semi-open warfare," and successfully convinced all subordinate commanders to create and rely on a redundant system of the latest scientific communications methods.[116] As future attacks would show, these changes improved the division's ability to improve the quality and the quantity of firepower support in future battles.

That Summerall was intent on maximizing his use of firepower was demonstrated in his use of preliminary bombardments, his reliance on the rolling barrage, and his practice of having the barrage stand for a number of minutes to give the infantry more time to close on it. His attempts to mass artillery on narrow fronts and his use of echeloned infantry attacks to achieve limited objectives on the latter days of the battle, however imperfectly executed at Soissons, strengthen the case. Even one infantry battalion commander noted in his operations report that "during the last two days of the action, trench warfare tactics were used instead of open warfare tactics."[117] The learning process continued well after the battle ended. In the weeks that followed, hardly any element of the division escaped significant changes. Summerall took steps to alleviate the causes of the internal supply problems that had plagued some units (though he could do little to guard against the more serious Allied logistical failures at the start of the battle except to ensure that the American and French high commands knew what had happened), and he corrected the serious communications problems that occurred during the battle. But, the greatest changes appear to have been mental – or doctrinal – as the division leadership became more committed to making highly controlled, firepower-based advances instead of unlimited-objective, rifle-based attacks.

[116] For an analysis of the changes made to signal communications procedures after Soissons, see Henry L. P. King, "A Critical Analysis of the Employment of Signal Communications by the 1st American Division at Soissons," Student Monograph IR-61-1933, CGSS.

[117] HQ 1st Battalion, 26th Infantry, Memorandum, 3 August 1918, Folder 33.6, Box 81, 1st Division Historical File, RG 120, NA.

3

The 1st Division

The Search for a "Sufficiently Powerful Fire"

After a couple of days behind the lines near Soissons, the 1st Division moved into the quiet Saizerais sector at the end of July. For the next month, the division not only commanded the new sector and absorbed seven thousand replacement troops but each of its infantry battalions, when rotated out of the front lines, also underwent a new period of training that was, according to the division history, "especially valuable in applying the experience gained at Soissons in reducing machine gun nests; in the disposition and employment of machine guns, automatic rifles, 37mm guns and Stokes mortars; in liaison to preserve cohesion and formations; and in marking the line so that it could be located by friendly aviators."[1]

These ten-day training events were described as "exercises for open warfare," but they were conducted primarily by "small groups" and never entailed units larger than a battalion.[2] More important, they focused on the kinds of outflanking maneuvers that were equally valuable for assaults on enemy trench positions as on the enemy on the open field. Although Summerall directed that much of the training be spent on target ranges, he specified that all shooting would be done on "short range target ranges" and ordered that firing be done not just with the Springfield rifle but also with the automatic rifle, machine gun, Stokes mortar, and 37mm gun.[3] Each day, the infantry battalion commanders in training were to

---

[1] *History of the First Division*, 145–6.
[2] Ibid.
[3] HQ 1st Division, "Preliminary instruction as to program of work and training in Saizerais Sector," 9 August 1918, WWRFD, vol. 2; HQ 1st Division, "Instructions on automatic weapons in front line battalions, inspection, drill and target practice in third line battalions, gas drill," 12 August 1918, WWRFD, vol. 2.

hold a conference with their officers "for the purpose of discussing tactical questions regarding the employment of the battalion, the use of the auxiliary weapons, [and] the reduction of strong points."[4] Yet, the regimental, brigade, and division commanders probably gained little in these supposed "open-warfare" exercises, and none of the training appears to have involved artillery, which was all in firing positions at the front.

During this period, Summerall also issued a directive specifying how he wanted his infantry to fight, and it shows that he expected it to make maximum use of its available firepower:

> Hostile strongpoints and machine guns must not impede the advance of any part of the line not obstructed by them. They will be vigorously reduced by the intense fire of machine guns, automatic rifles, Stokes mortars and 37mm guns, and the accompanying artillery. Under cover of this fire the infantry must advance by rushes around the flanks, in small groups or individually, accompanied by automatic rifles.[5]

The standard service rifle was conspicuously absent from the list of crucial infantry weapons. Also, in keeping with the directives of Pershing's newly issued *Combat Instructions*, Summerall intended to employ a few light guns as accompanying artillery pieces to give the infantry more power. He likewise directed that all twelve machine guns of each machine-gun company would be used to advance the infantry in all attacks, and that each gun was to follow all infantry advances with a minimum of twenty-five hundred rounds. Furthermore, Summerall established the rule that during any attack, each infantry brigade commander could, under his own authority, halt or recall that portion of the rolling barrage covering his advance. The division commander did warn that this should not be done simply because one part of the line was checked by the enemy – under such conditions, the infantry should exploit the other areas of success – but rather the barrage could be halted when the whole brigade was stopped.[6]

[4] HQ 1st Division, "Battalion Conferences," 16 August 1918, *WWRFD*, vol. 2.

[5] HQ 1st Division, "Offensive Exercises and Operations," 29 August 1918, *WWRFD*, vol. 2.

[6] The closer one looks at this training, the more one appreciates the increasing amount of firepower that was expected to be used even in simple infantry attacks. Before one battalion-level exercise on the attack of a strong point, Buck warned his troops that Summerall was going to inspect the maneuver and, therefore, "the maneuver ground must be selected with a view to actually using 37mm guns, stokes mortars, V-Bs, hand grenades and rifle and machine gun fire in the assault." The role of the rifle was again downplayed. Memorandum from C.G., 2nd Brigade to C.O., 26th Infantry, "Battalion Maneuvers," 22 August 1918, Folder 50.4, Box 68, 1st Division Historical File, RG 120, NA.

The St. Mihiel Attack, 12–14 September 1918

Finally, in late August, the division left the quiet sector to begin more detailed training for its role in what would be the first truly American offensive of the war and, in fact, the largest battle in American history to that time – the reduction of the St. Mihiel salient. Pershing and the AEF GHQ had initially planned for the attack on the giant salient to be immediately continued through the German support lines and straight towards Metz, nearly 20 kilometers behind. The St. Mihiel attack was to be the start of the decisive American offensive that would win the war. However, in early September, Marshal Ferdinand Foch, the Allied generalissimo, convinced Pershing to limit the attack to the reduction of the salient so that the American First Army could attack in the Meuse-Argonne sector no later than 26 September. For this reason, Pershing's first offensive as commander of the First American Army became a giant but limited set-piece operation.

As with other set-piece attacks, the plans for the St. Mihiel offensive were highly organized and very detailed. In this respect, it more resembled the Cantigny assault than Mangin's attack near Soissons. As at Cantigny, the attacking troops were forced to run through a series of maneuvers, practically rehearsals, to ensure that they were ready for the attack. The 1st Division did just that during a ten-day period of "intensive training" in the Vaucouleurs training area. The exercises began at the squad level and progressed through the larger units, until finally culminating in a division maneuver that included an advance of several kilometers through a dense forest.[7] Whether this rehearsal for a deep but limited-objective set-piece attack would have helped the division fight battles against weak enemy forces in wide-open terrain is impossible to determine, but it was a training improvement over continued assignments in quiet front-line sectors. Information on the rehearsals of other divisions that were training for the St. Mihiel Offensive shows that the maneuvers included some aspects typically (and mistakenly) associated with open warfare, such as a prohibition on telephone communications, but also other features akin to trench warfare, such as highly regulated advances of 100 meters in 3 or 4 minutes.[8] Regardless of whether the training was technically considered primarily for trench or open warfare, the maneuvers seem to have helped the division prepare to carry out its detailed orders for the upcoming attack on the St. Mihiel salient.

---

[7] *History of the First Division*, 150.
[8] See the information on the pre–St. Mihiel maneuvers of the 2nd Division in Grotelueschen, *Doctrine Under Trial*, 77.

The attack orders for the elimination of the St. Mihiel salient were developed in large part by George C. Marshall, who had left the 1st Division following the Cantigny battle to serve as a staff officer for the First Army and GHQ. After going through several drafts, changing the number of divisions in the attack from six to ten to fourteen and, ultimately, to sixteen American and six French divisions, the final attack plans were essentially completed by early September. In the initial assault, units from nine American divisions and one French division, spread out in three corps, were to attack the salient from both sides (see Map 5). Three additional French divisions, holding the tip of the salient, were to follow up the assault to ensure that the defending Germans in front of them would have to make a slow, fighting withdrawal and could therefore be cut off by the Allied troops driving in from the two sides. Other divisions remained in reserve behind those making the assault.

All told, as many as 550,000 American and 110,000 French soldiers were to participate in the attack in some form, whether in the attacking and reserve divisions, in the supporting corps organizations, as part of the air or tank forces, or providing immediate logistical and staff support.[9] For all the talk of self-reliant infantry and the power of the rifle, Pershing's staff gathered a tremendous amount of supporting weaponry for the offensive, including some fourteen hundred aircraft under the command of Colonel William "Billy" Mitchell, more than four hundred French tanks (although the British backed out of an agreement to provide 150 heavy tanks, each with two 6-inch guns and four machine guns), and more than three thousand pieces of artillery.[10] Anyone unfamiliar with the official AEF doctrine that glorified the infantryman, his rifle and bayonet, and the primacy of maneuver might be forgiven for concluding the attack was based rather on overwhelming numbers and massive firepower.

The huge salient, some 30 kilometers deep and 40 kilometers wide, had remained continuously in German hands since its creation in September 1914. Repeated French attacks throughout 1915 all failed to retake the 600-square-kilometer protrusion that jutted to the southwest just

[9] Marshall wrote that the initial plan for reduction of the salient in late July and early August had just six divisions. When much of this plan was about done, Brig. Gen. Fox Conner told him to plan for ten divisions. As Marshall completed that plan, fourteen divisions became available. Finally, sixteen American and six French divisions were made available – allowing heavy attacks on both sides of salient and reserve divisions in each of the attacking corps. Marshall, *Memoirs*, 124.

[10] Although most general sources claim that only 267 tanks took part in the attack, the most detailed study of tanks in the battle claims a total of 419. Dale E. Wilson, *Treat 'em Rough! The Birth of American Armor, 1917–1920* (Novato, Calif.: Presidio Press, 1989), 100.

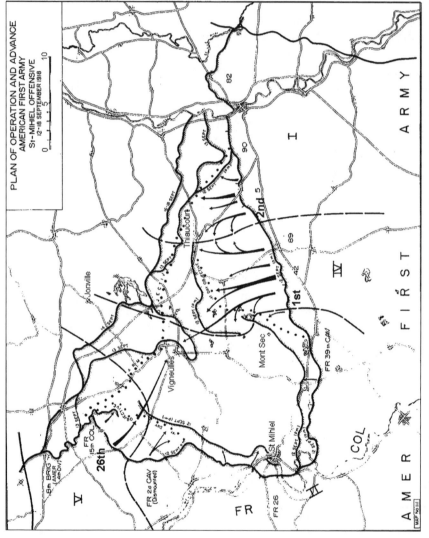

MAP 5: The American First Army's attack at St. Mihiel, where the 1st, 26th, and 2nd Divisions played major roles eliminating the German salient.

20 kilometers south of Verdun. After the Germans used the salient as a staging area for its attacks on Verdun in 1916, the entire area settled down into a tacitly agreed upon "rest sector," one that was so stable most AEF divisions accomplished their initial front-line training in its quiet trenches. The German Army defended the salient with just eight front-line divisions and one special brigade. Only one division was rated as first class, and all were tired and under-strength. Two additional divisions were held in reserve in the immediate area. However, the Germans had significantly strengthened their defensive positions over the years by adding concrete pillboxes, massive beds of wire, huge dugouts, preregistered artillery pieces, and interlocking machine-gun nests. It was a formidable defensive position (see Map 6).[11]

The American First Army planned to seize the salient by converging attacks from both sides. The main attack would be delivered by the two American corps on the south face, with Hunter Liggett's I Corps (i.e., 2nd, 5th, 90th, and 82nd Divisions) on the right and Joseph Dickman's IV Corps (i.e., 1st, 42nd, and 89th Divisions) in the center. To complete the envelopment, George Cameron's V Corps (i.e., 26th, French 15th Colonial, and 4th Divisions) would drive in from the western face. The 1st Division, on the extreme left of the IV Corps, had the difficult mission of attacking while the French divisions in the French II Colonial Corps to its left made only token attacks and follow-up advances. The 1st Division would have to protect its own left flank throughout the attack.

As the attack day of 12 September approached and the forces gathered in the area, Douglas Haig, the commander of the BEF, told Pershing

---

[11] Exactly how many German soldiers were defending the salient is unclear. Although Trask writes that only twenty-three thousand German troops held the salient, or what he calls "the effective strength of seven divisions usually on line," this seems much too low. German divisions were under-strength, but they typically numbered more than three thousand men. If the eight divisions holding the front trenches had only five thousand troops each, that would put about forty thousand in the front lines alone. Including the two reserve divisions near the base of the salient gives a total figure of near fifty thousand for the divisional troops. Because the American First Army captured some sixteen thousand Germans during the battle, must have killed and wounded about as many, and both the German and American army commanders noted that a significant number of German troops successfully evacuated the salient, the figure of at least fifty thousand seems much more accurate than Trask's lower number. Hunter Liggett, the I Corps commander in the battle, later estimated German troop strength as high as eighty thousand to one hundred thousand. Compare Trask, *The AEF and Coalition Warmaking*, 106; James H. Hallas, *Squandered Victory: The American First Army at St. Mihiel* (Westport, Conn.: Praeger, 1995), 46; and Hunter Liggett, *A.E.F.: Ten Years Ago in France* (New York: Dodd, Mead, 1928), 149.

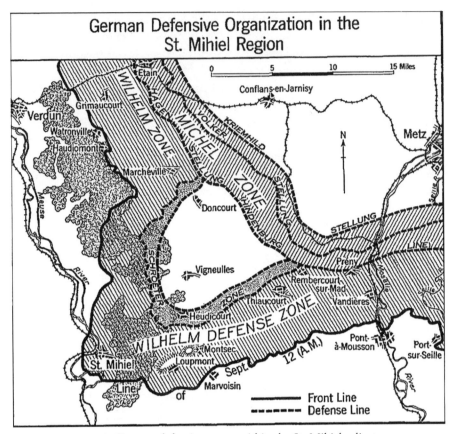

German Defensive Organization in the St. Mihiel Region

MAP 6: German defensive zones within the St. Mihiel salient.

he could not afford to loan him the 150 heavy tanks the Americans were counting on to cut the massive beds of German wire in the salient. Marshall claimed that this suddenly made the length of the preliminary artillery preparation "the critical question" of the attack. Many attacks over the previous three years of war had failed because the infantry was shot down while struggling to work its way through the enemy wire. After considering preliminary bombardments as long as 22 hours, Pershing decided to attack without any preliminary fire at all. When Marshall, whose experience with the 1st Division had given him an appreciation of the difficulties of offensive operations, suspected this to be the case, he took the extraordinary step of writing a special unsolicited letter to the army commander "appealing to him not to undertake the attack without artillery preparation," which would be little more than a "gambler's chance."[12] He recommended an 18-hour preparation, but Pershing settled on 4 hours of intense fire.

With the final issues settled by the high command, the 1st Division concluded the training and planning for its part in the attack. The army and corps orders directed that the division make an aggressive advance of about 13 kilometers over a two-day period. To do this, the division plan placed the 2nd Brigade on the right, in liaison with the adjacent 42nd Division, and the 1st Brigade on the left. On the first day, both brigades were to drive forward about 7 kilometers on a 3-kilometer front, seizing the Quart de Reserve woods and the town of Nonsard. On the far left, the 18th Infantry had the difficult mission of guarding the division's flank, which was certain to be exposed throughout the attack because the adjacent French division attacked an hour after the 1st Division. The advance was divided into four clear phases, each with its own objective, and covered entirely by a thick rolling barrage moving forward 100 meters every 3 or 4 minutes, depending on the terrain. At the first objective, the front enemy trench-line within the first kilometer, the barrage halted 20 minutes to pound the defensive position and allow the bridging of a small river called the Rupt de Mad. Also at this time, a box barrage was fired to protect troops and tanks maneuvering on the north bank of the river. At each of the following objectives, the barrage would halt for a period to allow for reorganization of the attacking units. The order specifically warned that each objective "will be the limit of the infantry advance. In front of these limits the artillery barrage will fall."[13] After reaching the fourth objective, the leading battalions were to consolidate it during the night and wait for orders to begin the second day's advance to the final objective of the battle. This was to be a tightly controlled advance, not a wild rush forward as Mangin had ordered at Soissons.[14]

---

[12] Marshall claimed that it took five hundred rounds of 75mm shells to blast open a gap in the enemy wire just 5-by-10 meters wide. See Pershing's diary entries for 10 and 11 September, in "Diary, September 1918–Jan 27 1919," Box 5, JJP Papers, LOC; Col. Conrad H. Lanza, *The Army Artillery, First Army*, p. 65, n.d., typescript unit history commissioned by the U.S. War Department, USAMHI; Marshall, *Memoir*, 136; and Pershing, *My Experiences*, 2: 265.

[13] HQ 1st Division, Field Orders No. 36, 9 September 1918, *WWRFD*, vol. 2.

[14] As late as 9 September, when the division attack order was written, the division staff still did not know the exact date and time of the attack, nor did it know whether any preliminary artillery fire would be allowed. The artillery brigade was therefore ordered to "prepare a plan for destructive fire of 14 hours prior to H hour, to be used if necessary." HQ 1st Division, Field Orders No. 36, 9 September 1918, *WWRFD*, vol. 2.

The brigade orders also show the extent to which the division viewed the battle as a giant, set-piece, trench-like attack. Although Frank Bamford, the new commander of the 2nd Brigade, directed his platoon leaders to "push" their men forward, being sure to outflank all machine-gun nests, his orders gave the most elaborate instructions for the mopping-up phases of the operation.[15] He ordered that "mopping up of captured ground will be executed according to detailed plans worked out by Regimental and Assault Battalion commanders in conference." After taking each enemy trench system, three prearranged groups, each under the command of an officer, were to carry out their distinct missions: one group, from the assault companies, was to take care of the front and support trenches; a second group, from the support companies, was to clean out the enemy dugouts; and the third group, from the follow-on battalions, was to "thoroughly mop up" trenches, dugouts, machine-gun emplacements, and battery positions, "covering all of the captured terrain and ensuring liaison."[16] These kinds of arrangements were standard operating procedure for detailed trench attacks but certainly were not a typical part of open warfare. No such details were included in the initial plans for fighting at Soissons.

Summerall also had a good deal more firepower to support this attack than he had at Soissons. The division received all but one battalion from the 58th Field Artillery Brigade, formally of the 33rd Division, a regiment of 75mm guns from the 3rd Field Artillery Brigade of the 3rd Division, and two batteries of 8-inch howitzers. Summerall concluded that his division had the dedicated support of 120 75mm guns and 48 155mm or 8-inch howitzers, giving him one light gun for every 24 meters of front and a heavy howitzer for every 60 meters.[17] The artillery was divided into five groupings – two groups of light guns dedicated to "direct infantry support," two groups of howitzers given special targets, and

---

[15] HQ 2nd Brigade, Field Orders No. 47, 10 September 1918, in Folder 32.1, Box 64, 1st Division Historical File, RG 120, NA. Bamford, former commander of the 16th Infantry, replaced John Hines after the latter took command of the 4th Division. Also in August, Frank Parker gave up command of the 18th Infantry to replace Buck in the 1st Brigade. Buck took command of the 5th Division. Holbrooke left the 1st F.A. Brigade to take command of the 152nd F.A. Brigade, 77th Division, and was replaced by Brig. Gen. H. W. Butner. "Historical Sketch of the First Division, AEF," pp. 5–6, Folder 11.4, Box 11, 1st Division Historical File, RG 120, NA.

[16] HQ 2nd Brigade, Field Orders No. 47, 10 September 1918, Folder 32.1, Box 64, 1st Division Historical File, RG 120, NA.

[17] HQ 1st Division, Field Orders No. 36, 9 September 1918, WWRFD, vol. 2; Maj. Gen. C. P. Summerall to Deputy Chief of Staff, AEF, Subject: Artillery, HQ V Army Corps, 4 January 1919, Folder 31.23, Box 13, V Army Corps Historical File, RG 120, NA.

one combined group of 75s and 155s that fired special barrages and gas-saturation missions to protect the left flank. From H hour to H plus 10 minutes, a number of light guns fired gas concentrations, while the remainder began a standing barrage on the first enemy lines and rolled the fire forward only when the infantry had advanced up behind it. The division's trench mortar battery blasted the front trenches as the infantry advanced to the barrage.[18] To put "depth in the barrage," one battery in each of the direct support groups fired 200 meters in advance of the others. Smoke shells were to be intermixed liberally with the standard high-explosive rounds. One of the light-gun battalions superimposed its fire all along the barrage line and was made available to fire on any anti-tank guns located by a special forward observer, while one battalion of howitzers was kept available to execute emergency counterbattery missions identified by a designated aircraft. The rates of fire were high enough that the artillery order directed all batteries to keep water nearby to cool down the guns.[19]

The deep advance specified by the army and corps orders meant that some divisional batteries would not be able to fire the full rolling barrage from their initial positions, but Summerall ensured that the barrage would be maintained for the entire advance. If the presence of the rolling barrage was the difference between open and trench warfare, Summerall seemed intent on guaranteeing that his troops avoided open warfare and fought an artillery-centered battle. Four battalions of light guns advanced 216 minutes after H hour and picked up the barrage from new positions, two more moved forward only after the first four were firing again, and two more – those with the most forward initial positions – advanced 6 hours after the attack's start. The artillery plan included a detailed schedule of forward displacement showing which guns moved at what time, to which forward positions, and by what routes. Also assisting the infantry were four accompanying artillery pieces, placed "at the complete disposal of the Infantry Regiment supported"; eight additional mortar teams from the attached 1st Gas Regiment, dedicated to covering the infantry with smoke and knocking out enemy machine guns; as well as the dedicated support of forty-nine light tanks, all with American crews.[20] Teams of

---

[18] The crews for the division's old, immobile 58mm trench mortars fired only in the initial assault, then left their pieces and marched forward to fire captured German pieces during the battle. HQ 1st Division, Addendum to Field Orders No. 36, 10 September 1918, *WWRFD*, vol. 2.

[19] HQ Divisional Artillery, 1st Division, "Artillery Plan," 11 September 1918, *WWRFD*, vol. 2.

[20] Ibid.

engineers with bangalore torpedoes, wire cutters, and axes accompanied the leading waves. Finally, General Dickman, an old cavalry officer, gave Summerall a detachment of cavalry to exploit any dramatic success. Summerall gave them no specific orders in his attack order. All considered, the division plan was an impressive display of the unit's willingness and ability to creatively employ all the firepower at its disposal.

Unlike at Soissons, the entire division was in place hours before the attack started.[21] Promptly at 0100 hours on 12 September, the guns of the division joined with those throughout the First Army in initiating what was at the time the largest battle in American history. The divisional artillery fired gas concentrations, cut enemy wire (the 6th Field Artillery alone had to cut nine breaches in the wire), and blasted apart enemy defenses. At 0500 hours, the light guns began the rolling barrage, and the big howitzers shifted to their special targets in advance of the barrage. The leading infantry battalions followed the barrage through the enemy positions, advancing with a thin line of skirmishers to the front, followed closely by "special automatic rifle teams" and wire cutting crews, and with other troops in "small columns" behind them.[22] The machine guns, Stokes mortars, and 37mm guns all advanced with the leading battalions. All along the line the troops found weak resistance, took each of their four objectives on time, and reported that all enemy troops encountered were "killed, captured or driven back."[23] By 1230 hours, the infantry was consolidating its fourth and final first-day objective, and casualties were light. Brigadier General Frank Parker, the new commander of the 1st Brigade, correctly reported that regarding the initial attack, "the operation was carried out exactly as planned."[24]

---

[21] Although the American First Army has been pilloried for its supposed logistical chaos and transportation congestion, all 1st Division accounts show that the American effort at St. Mihiel was much better organized than Mangin's arrangements at Soissons. Although both entailed a movement into the attack positions after dark on the day before the jump-off and the weather turned foul in both instances, the American commanders noted that everything went more smoothly at St. Mihiel. All units were in position on time and went into battle better rested, better supplied, and with all their weaponry.

[22] HQ 1st Infantry Brigade, "Report on Operations of Sept. 12th–13th, 1918," 19 September 1918, Folder 33.6, Box 62, 1st Division Historical File, RG 120, NA; HQ 6th Field Artillery, "Report on Recent Operations," 18 September 1918, Folder 33.6, Box 101, 1st Division Historical File, RG 120, NA.

[23] HQ 1st Division, "Report on Operations of 1st Division against St. Mihiel Salient September 12–13, inclusive," 21 September 1918, *WWRFD*, vol. 13.

[24] HQ 1st Infantry Brigade, "Report on Operations of Sept. 12th–13th, 1918," 19 September 1918, Folder 33.6, Box 62, 1st Division Historical File, RG 120, NA.

In fact, the American advance throughout the IV Corps seemed so smooth that just as the division took its third objective, around 1000 hours, Dickman directed the 1st Division to eliminate any further planned pauses and "to push on to the first day's objective as soon as the division was ready for the new phase of the operation."[25] Apparently taking Dickman's instruction more as a suggestion than an order, Summerall demurred. He later reported that:

under the circumstances and in view of the fact that it was necessary to bring up artillery to support the further infantry advance it was decided not to unduly hurry this advance but to resume the advance as per schedule at H plus 6 hours. In accordance with this decision the infantry went forward at 11:00 hrs., covered by a rolling barrage, and took the first day's objective at about 12:30 hrs.[26]

Summerall's decision was a decidedly conservative response to an aggressive corps instruction and only makes sense in light of both his appreciation of the need to provide adequate fire support to his troops and his desire to maintain the limited, set-piece nature of the battle.

As the front-line troops prepared their new positions for an expected enemy counterattack from the west and the attached cavalry worked its way forward, fires in the distance showed that the Germans were destroying their stores and beginning a formal withdrawal from the salient. Shortly after this, Dickman began to make arrangements to order his corps forward and begin taking the second-day's objectives. At 1345 hours, after requesting permission from the First Army HQ to accelerate the advance (but apparently before receiving that permission), Dickman directed Summerall to let the cavalry attack. Summerall ordered it to advance past Nonsard and "reconnoiter" along the division's eventual axis toward Vigneulles, disrupting enemy communications as much as possible.[27] Shortly after 1600 hours, the cavalry passed through the leading infantry lines, but they accomplished little. Although the German defenses were collapsing and a full evacuation of the salient had been ordered, the horses made much too large targets and carried far too little firepower to advance even under such conditions. The horsemen managed to capture a few stray German stragglers, but they could not overcome

---

[25] HQ 1st Division, "Report on Operations of 1st Division against St. Mihiel Salient September 12–13, Inclusive," 21 September 1918, *WWRFD*, vol. 13.

[26] Ibid.

[27] Ibid.

even the slight resistance encountered. After quickly suffering a number of casualties, they fell back in disarray.[28]

By 1500, Dickman had received permission to order his entire corps forward immediately. However, mindful of the troubles met by the cavalry, at 1610 hours, Summerall ordered infantry from the 2nd Brigade to advance, not in a rash pursuit to crush a beaten enemy but rather in standard formation to take and hold a position on the Vigneulles to St. Benoit road, about 5 kilometers ahead of the current line. In his report, Summerall explained his retention of standard formations. After admitting that the enemy's last organized position was "on the Lamarche-Nonsard line" of the division's final first-day objective, he reported that:

thereafter the division pushed forward principally in the hours of darkness to exploit its success. Every effort was made, however, to maintain the formation of the division as a unit...it is believed that this policy permitted a more complete exploitation than if small organizations had been shot out independently. The provisional squadron of cavalry, for instance, was not able to continue to advance against the opposition it encountered on the advance of September 12th. The infantry, however, was able to advance as soon as ordered, and to wipe out all opposition.[29]

And that is generally what happened, although the infantry advance started later and took longer than it should have. Bamford passed the order forward at about 1700 hours, and after extricating themselves from their newly created defensive positions, troops from the 28th and 26th Regiments began the advance around 1800 hours. As they worked their way forward, eventually moving through thick woods in the dead of night, the most advanced troops eventually reached the distant road sometime after 2200 hours. They were almost immediately ordered forward again, with the 26th Infantry to take Hattonville and the 28th Infantry to seize Vigneulles. By 0800 the next morning, they had reached those villages, linked up with the 26th Division, and closed the salient. Within hours,

---

[28] Years after the war, Summerall gave the following description of the use of cavalry in the battle: "The day of cavalry on the field of battle had ended.... Dickman tried to discredit me for not having it charge. He knew nothing of conditions and he was totally ignorant of battle." Summerall, "Duty, Honor, Country," 108; See also Col. Hugh A. Drum, C. of S., First Army to Col. Stuart Heintzelman, C. of S., IV Corps, 12 September 1918, 1500 hours, *USAWW*, 8: 256; HQ 1st Division, "Report on Operations of 1st Division against St. Mihiel Salient September 12–13, inclusive," 21 September 1918, *WWRFD*, vol. 13; and Hallas, *Squandered Victory*, 157–8.

[29] HQ 1st Division, "Report on Operations of 1st Division against St. Mihiel Salient September 12–13, inclusive," 21 September 1918, *WWRFD*, vol. 13.

the last skirmishing died out, and the 1st Division's part in the battle was over.

By the end of 13 September, the fighting was practically over throughout the First Army. The AEF had obliterated the four-year-old German salient, captured nearly 16,000 German prisoners, killed and wounded many more, and taken 450 artillery pieces. Although some AEF staff officers had suspected that as many as fifty thousand casualties would have been a normal number of losses for such an operation, the First Army suffered fewer than seven thousand casualties during its two-day advance. Congratulations poured in to Pershing and his new army.[30]

The performance of the 1st Division was at least as impressive as that of any other division in the battle. It advanced 14 kilometers in about 19 hours, and some of its units covered 19 kilometers in 34 hours, much of that through woods in the dark. It captured 1,195 Germans and 31 guns, suffered fewer than 600 total casualties, and accomplished all this while fighting the entire battle with an exposed left flank. When Summerall submitted his report of the battle a week after it ended, he could accurately report, "The division has never been in better shape."[31]

However, after the pounding endured in the trenches near Cantigny and the severe losses at Soissons, most veterans in the division could not help but focus on the weakness of the German resistance at St. Mihiel. The reports of all commanders, whether from battalions, regiments, or brigades, commented on the enemy disorganization and lack of morale. Immediately after the battle, rumors began to circulate that the Germans were already evacuating the salient before the Americans attacked. One unit history, notably from an artillery regiment, claimed that "what we had expected to be a battle proved to be little more than a foot race to Nonsard."[32] Even Summerall thought that the enemy must have begun its withdrawal before the assault. However, although the German command had expected an attack on the salient, ordered a rearward shift of its main

[30] HQ 2nd Infantry Brigade, "Report on Operation against St. Mihiel Salient," 19 September 1918, and HQ 28th Infantry, "Report of Operations against the St. Mihiel Salient," 18 September 1918, both in Folder 33.6, Box 87, 1st Division Historical File, RG 120, NA; HQ 26th Infantry, "Report on Operations against St. Mihiel Salient," 17 September 1918, Folder 33.6, Box 81, 1st Division Historical File, RG 120, NA; Pershing, *My Experiences*, 2: 270; and Marshall, *Memoir*, 146.

[31] HQ 1st Division, "Report on Operations of 1st Division against St. Mihiel Salient September 12–13, inclusive," 21 September 1918, WWRFD, vol. 13; *History of the First Division*, 169–70.

[32] "Historical Sketch of the 7th Field Artillery Regiment," p. 10, Folder 11.4, Box 102, 1st Division Historical File, RG 120, NA.

line of resistance, moved out some heavy equipment, and had *planned* to eventually order a full withdrawal, the order to evacuate the salient was not given until after the attack was well underway. The German garrison was in a confused, unsteady, and demoralized state, and it proved unable to put up a properly organized defense, but it was not carrying out a full evacuation of the salient before the attack started. In fact, senior German generals were outraged at the poor defensive reaction of their forces in the salient.[33]

[33] Many historians have minimized the American effort at St. Mihiel by misunderstanding the timing and extent of the German withdrawal from the salient. Donald Smythe claims that German orders to evacuate the salient were issued on 10 September. Trask concludes that the German army, planning to withdraw anyway, simply did so "when it recognized the extent of the American attack," thus giving credence to the allegation that "in effect the Americans simply relieved the Germans in their trenches, hardly an imposing feat of arms." See Trask, *Coalition Warmaking*, 113. However, the German records give a very different picture. First, the German GHQ viewed the St. Mihiel battle as a humiliating disaster, not some kind of unforeseen acceleration of their prearranged withdrawal plan. As early as 13 September, Hindenburg was investigating what went wrong, asking why the two main reserve divisions "were not kept closer to the front." He had already concluded that "only in this neglect can I see the reason for the deep penetration in the direction of Thiaucourt" on the morning of 12 September. Even more inexplicable, if the withdrawal had already begun before the battle, was his question of "why the center of Composite Army C was immediately withdrawn" into the reserve "Michel Position" at the base of the salient so early on the 12th. On 17 September, clearly still not satisfied, Hindenburg wrote Gallwitz again, exclaiming that "the severe defeat of Composite Army C on September 12 has rendered the situation of the Group of Armies critical...caused for the most part by faulty leadership.... There is now nothing left for us to do but offer stubborn defense...the Group of Armies will bear the responsibility for this." Gallwitz replied that although he knew before battle that the salient would have to be evacuated eventually, he concluded that "the actual withdrawal of the troops from the positions, and hence the abandonment of these positions, should be delayed as long as the tactical situation would at all permit." Although the divisions had been ordered to shift their main line of resistance back a few kilometers (hardly equal to an evacuation of the salient), Gallwitz reported that some divisions, far from withdrawing too fast, actually made the defensive changes too slowly, and at least one continued to pack too many men in their original forward trenches. He confirmed that before any full evacuation was ordered, the reserve divisions in the salient were directed to *counterattack*, not withdraw. In fact, on 11 September, the commander of Army Composite C announced to his troops, "The attack preparations of the enemy on the south front continue. On the west front also an enemy attack against the left wing of the Fifth Army and the right of the Composite Army seems to be in the preparatory stages. *Composite Army C will prepare to repulse these attacks.*" He further directed that "the modern heavy artillery assigned to the Mihiel and Gorz Groups *will be put in position so that they can be used from the forenoon of September 12 on to harass the enemy's attack preparations*" [emphasis added]. These orders suggest that the Germans were not evacuating the salient when the First Army attacked but rather preparing to resist it, and that the German command's first reaction to the attack was not a full withdrawal but rather a counterattack. Only when the American attack threatened to cut off all the German

Although the success of the attack can, in large part, be attributed to the weak resistance of the German defenders, the 1st Division's achievements also resulted from its excellent attack plan and impressive combat execution. Especially during the initial 7-kilometer advance to Nonsard – the set-piece portion of the attack – the division performed well. Most of the errors identified in the first battles at Cantigny and Soissons seem to have been corrected. The attacking infantry no longer strolled forward in neat linear waves. Liaison, from side to side and from front to rear, was much improved. Completely absent are the reports of troops charging enemy machine-gun nests from the front. On the contrary, all the infantry reports stress that when infantrymen met enemy strong points, they "were in every case taken by flanking movement" aided by a "concentration of fire" from all the infantry weapons, including automatic rifles, rifle grenades, 37mm guns, Stokes mortars, and machine guns.[34] One battalion commander concluded that his unit's use of firepower proved that, in many cases, "the ordinary strong point can be taken with fire alone, if the proper use of all arms are utilized [*sic*]."[35] Many infantry units proudly described the specific enemy strong points taken in this manner, such as the large position in the Quart de Reserve woods, and rattled off the profuse amount of ammunition used by the automatic weapons. Instead of unsuccessfully trying to march forward with the leading waves of infantry and suffering heavy casualties while firing little, the machine-gun crews stayed close behind the infantry, advanced by bounds, and regularly gave fire support.[36]

Commanders also commented favorably on the artillery support. The troops had "no difficulty in following the barrage," described as "excellent" and "deep and effective."[37] The movement of the light guns forward

troops at the tip of the salient did the German commander order the evacuation. Many of the pertinent German records are included in *USAWW*, vol. 8. See especially Operations Section Memorandum No. 2784, Composite Army C, 11 September 1918, pp. 300–301; Von Hindenburg to Group of Armies von Gallwitz, 1143 hours, 13 September 1918, p. 304; Von Hindenburg to Group of Armies von Gallwitz, 17 September 1918, p. 312; Group of Armies von Gallwitz to Supreme Headquarters, 21 September, p. 323. See also Smythe, *Pershing*, 185.

[34] HQ 28th Infantry, "Report of Operations against the St. Mihiel Salient," 18 September 1918, Folder 33.6, Box 87, 1st Division Historical File, RG 120, NA.

[35] C.O., 2nd Battalion, 28th Infantry to C.O., 1st Division, "Tactical Lessons Learned," 18 September 1918, Folder 33.6, Box 87, 1st Division Historical File, RG 120, NA.

[36] HQ 1st Infantry Brigade, "Report on Operations of Sept. 12th–13th, 1918," 19 September 1918, Folder 33.6, Box 62, 1st Division Historical File, RG 120, NA.

[37] See HQ 26th Infantry, "Report on Operations against St. Mihiel Salient," 17 September 1918, Folder 33.6, Box 81, 1st Division Historical File, RG 120, NA; Memorandum

to extend the rolling barrage was carried out well, even though the roads were so crowded that the gunners had to take their pieces across country. General H. W. Butner, the commander of the artillery brigade, reported that this movement ensured that the division's "advance in the intermediate zone was covered by Artillery barrage," despite the fact that the latest explanation of AEF doctrine minimized artillery support in the "intermediate zone."[38] However, the road congestion did prevent any of the big howitzers – too heavy to be pulled over the wet, broken terrain – from getting into advanced positions until late on the 12th, and the entire regiment was not set up in forward firing locations until the night of the 13th, long after the division's fighting was over. The lack of these guns certainly would have weakened any effort of the division to overcome an enemy line of resistance of any appreciable strength and depth beyond the initial day's attack. Yet, the divisional artillery certainly did a good deal more firing on the two days of combat than it did at Soissons, and that fire contributed to further weaken enemy resistance. From the preliminary preparation to the end of the fighting on the morning of 13 September, each of the division's light-gun regiments fired about 14,200 rounds and the 5th Field Artillery Regiment shot 7,100 of their 155mm shells, almost all on the first day. These rates of fire dramatically exceeded the average rates of fire during the fighting near Soissons. The gunners supporting the 1st Division attack fired 9,692 rounds of gas and 9,124 of smoke shell alone. The only pieces that seem to have done no good, anywhere, were the accompanying 75mm guns.[39]

Finally, the success of the 1st Division on 12 September can be compared to the poor showing of the French divisions that attempted to carry out much less difficult missions on that day. The trouble experienced by a number of the French divisions, as reported by the French II Colonial Army Corps, also showed that the German defenders were capable of putting up a not-so-insignificant level of resistance. The French 39th Division, to the immediate left of the 1st Division, attacked an hour after

from C.G., 1st F.A. Brigade to Chief of Staff, III Army Corps, 6 May 1919, Folder 11.4, Box 91, 1st Division Historical File, RG 120, NA; HQ 1st F.A. Brigade, "Ammunition Expenditure by 1st F.A. Brigade, A.E.F.," 27 February 1919, Folder 33.6, Box 97, 1st Division Historical File, RG 120, NA.

[38] HQ 1st F.A. Brigade, "Report on Operation against St. Mihiel Salient," 19 September 1918, Folder 33.6, Box 96, 1st Division Historical File, RG 120, NA.

[39] As previously noted, from 18 to 24 July, the two 75mm regiments fired an average of about 3,572 a day, and the 155mm regiment fired an average of about 1,429 a day. Memorandum from C.G., 1st F.A. Brigade to Chief of Staff, III Army Corps, 6 May 1919, Folder 11.4, Box 91, 1st Division Historical File, RG 120, NA.

the Americans. It advanced no more than a couple of kilometers, except on its right flank, which was dragged forward by the 1st Division for another kilometer, before being stopped cold by machine-gun fire from the Bois Bruly. According to the operations report of the French II Corps, the French 2nd Cavalry Division (dismounted), attacking next to the U.S. 26th Division, launched an attack at 1130 hours that "met with strong resistance" and "required a new artillery preparation."[40] The same report stated that the attacks of the French 26th Division against the long stretch of front around the tip of the salient near the town of St. Mihiel "made slow progress" initially and then were discontinued entirely when the division "found the enemy's lines still occupied." It did not enter St. Mihiel itself, just 2 kilometers behind German lines, until the morning of 13 September. Even giving full consideration to the fact that the offensive was to be an American show and that the French attacks were to be of a supporting nature, the failure of the French units to more earnestly press the withdrawing Germans illuminates both the extent of the French effort and the level of German resistance.[41]

The First Army's striking success on 12 and 13 September led a number of officers to conclude that the American divisions should continue the offensive toward Metz and take the city. Douglas MacArthur, a brigade commander in the 42nd Division, claimed to have slipped through the enemy lines on the night of 13 September and found Metz "practically defenseless for the moment."[42] That night, GHQ asked the First Army staff whether it favored continuing the general advance. Marshall later wrote that, had the original attacks of 12 and 13 September not been of a strictly limited nature, there was "no doubt in my mind but that we could have reached the outskirts of Metz by the late afternoon of the 13th, and quite possibly could have captured the city on the 14th, as the enemy was incapable of bring up reserves in sufficient number and formation to offer an adequate resistance."[43] Despite the problems faced by the cavalry he sent into the battle on the first day of the attack, Dickman claimed that "we could doubtless have made a further deep advance in the direction of Briey, with immediate menace to the enemy's line of communication."[44] It is not surprising that Pershing agreed and later wrote that "without a

---

[40] French II Colonial Corps, Operations Report, 12 September 1918, *USAWW*, 8: 275.
[41] Ibid.
[42] Douglas MacArthur, *Reminiscences* (New York: McGraw-Hill, 1964), 63.
[43] Marshall, *Memoir*, 146.
[44] Joseph T. Dickman, *The Great Crusade* (New York: D. Appleton, 1927), 159.

doubt, an immediate continuation of the advance would have carried us well beyond the Hindenburg Line and possibly into Metz."[45]

However, other officers disagreed. Marshall admitted that when asked about continuing the attack on the night of the 13th, he "vigorously" opposed the proposal because he was convinced that, by then, "the attack had lost its momentum."[46] Also, any continuation was sure to cripple the effort, already underway, to move the First Army to the Meuse-Argonne sector for the upcoming attack there. Liggett, the I Corps commander, acknowledged that "the possibility of taking Metz and the rest of it, had the battle been fought on the original plan, existed, in my opinion, only on the supposition that our army was a well-oiled, fully coordinated machine, which it was not as yet."[47] Finally, immediately after the war, Summerall offered his own estimation of the situation:

> On the third day, the resistance stiffened and it was unmistakable that the enemy had occupied a new line in considerable strength. . . . Even if the [American First] Army had not devoted the troops to other missions [i.e., the upcoming Meuse-Argonne Offensive], there would soon have come a period of temporary stabilization during which the enemy would have constantly strengthened his lines and we should have made preparations for an attack on his organizations in much the same manner as at the beginning.[48]

In other words, the original attack had spent itself in the first two days. To break through the new German defensive line at the Michel Position, part of the Hindenburg Line, the American army and the individual divisions that comprised it needed to gather themselves for another highly organized, firepower-based, set-piece attack. Summerall and Liggett knew, if others did not, that ordering the divisions to press forward in their increasingly disorganized condition and to attack with hurriedly prepared plans (or no plans at all) was a prescription for massive casualties and little movement. The First Army would prove this in its next great battle, in the Meuse-Argonne.

In sum, the handling of the St. Mihiel offensive by the newly created American First Army highlights some significant developments in AEF doctrinal development. The AEF General Staff certainly proved its willingness and a reasonable amount of ability to employ massive firepower

---

[45] Pershing, *My Experiences*, vol. 2, p. 270.

[46] Marshall, *Memoir*, 146.

[47] Liggett, *A.E.F.*, 159.

[48] Maj. Gen. Charles P. Summerall, "Comments by the Corps Commander upon the Operations of the Fifth Army Corps," Folder 11.4, Box 2, V Army Corps Historical File, RG 120, NA.

at the start of an operation. However, its optimistic estimates for deep advances in a highly developed sector, the eagerness of senior commanders to employ obsolete horse cavalry in an exploitation role, and its conclusions regarding the chances for additional success had the attacks continued toward Metz betrayed the doctrinal biases and unrealistic expectations that still remained in some circles. However, the way the 1st Division fought the battle demonstrated how much it valued the maximization of firepower in controlled, set-piece attacks and proved its ability to fight in such a manner.

The Meuse-Argonne Offensive, 1–12 October 1918

After departing the St. Mihiel battlefield, Summerall held another conference "to discuss the battle and profit by our experience."[49] He knew, if some of his newer officers did not, that the attack had not been an accurate reflection of the strength of the German Army. Summerall also initiated a new training program to continue the division's progress in small-unit tactics. The division was in the middle of carrying out this training "in battalion assault problems, in marching through woods and at night by compass bearings, and in gun squad drills" when the American First Army began its largest offensive of the war on 26 September in the Meuse-Argonne.[50]

Unlike the St. Mihiel battle, the Meuse-Argonne Offensive was not the result of months of planning. The AEF had fewer than three weeks to coordinate all preparations for the massive campaign and had to do so while completing the arrangements for and actually fighting the battle at St. Mihiel.[51] By all estimations, AEF staff officers, and particularly George Marshall, accomplished a seemingly impossible task by successfully withdrawing the First Army from the St. Mihiel front and getting it – along with the necessary army corps, combat divisions, and special support units – into the new sector before the jump-off time. But, one of the costs of this success was that the First Army had to make its initial attack not with its best and most experienced divisions as it had at St. Mihiel but rather with whatever divisions were available. Of the nine front-line divisions that attacked on 26 September, five had not completed the AEF's most

[49] Summerall, "Duty, Honor, Country," p. 108.
[50] *History of the First Division*, 174.
[51] Marshall was ordered to begin planning the Meuse-Argonne concentration on 8 September. Marshall, *Memoir*, 137.

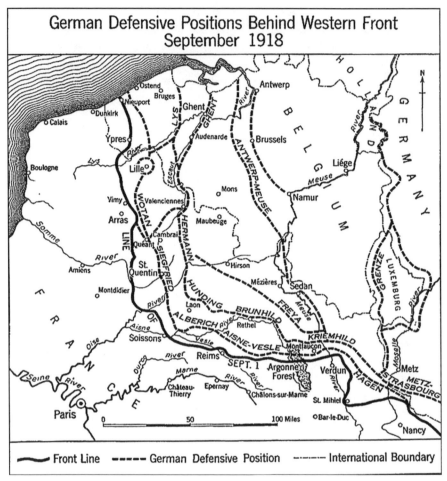

MAP 7: Major German defensive positions along the Western Front.

abbreviated training program and had no significant combat experience, three had never faced the enemy before under any conditions, and three would not be supported in the attack by their own divisional artillery brigades, which were scattered elsewhere in the rear areas.[52]

The German positions to be attacked were undoubtedly some of the most challenging anywhere on the Western Front (see Map 7). On the western edge of the First Army sector was the massive Argonne Forest,

---

[52] Only the 77th, 33rd, 28th, and 4th Divisions had done any significant fighting before 26 September, and some of them received thousands of replacements just days before the attack. Marshall, *Memoir*, 160; and Coffman, *War to End All Wars*, 305.

filled with steep hills and deep ravines and so densely overgrown that the
soldiers thought it resembled "a tropical jungle."[53] Some 30 kilometers to
the east lay the unfordable Meuse River, guarded on its northeastern bank
by high bluffs and serving as the attack's eastern limit. In the center rose
the dominating height of Montfaucon, used by the Germans to survey and
control the entire sector. The ground between these obstacles restrained
any rapid advance. Too rough and broken for much farming or livestock,
most of area was covered by "wild vegetation."[54] Furthermore, as the
army moved north, it would encounter a series of wooded ridges and
brush-filled valleys, making the terrain difficult to simply walk through
much less fight over. General Hugh A. Drum, the First Army chief of staff,
claimed it was "the most ideal defensive terrain I have ever seen or read
about."[55]

Senior French generals took note of the ground between the Meuse
River and the Argonne Forest and, after failed attempts to seize Montfaucon in 1914 and 1915, never attempted another offensive in the sector. Nevertheless, German forces did not fail to improve on the terrain's natural strength. The series of fortified defensive positions that
the Germans had built all along the Western Front extended through the
Meuse-Argonne sector (see Map 8). Unfortunately for the AEF, these three
or four successive defensive positions all converged as they approached
the Meuse, so that whereas the distance between the initial No Man's
Land and the third defensive line was 30 kilometers near Cambrai, about
40 kilometers in the sector northeast of Arras, and up to 60 kilometers
near Laon, it was compressed to just 18 kilometers in front of the First
Army. This convergence of lines resulted in part from the German Army's
need to protect its main supply and transportation artery running through
Sedan, just 55 kilometers from the American lines. Therefore, American
divisions would have to move through nearly 20 kilometers of almost
continuous fortified enemy positions constructed in terrain of remarkable
natural strength. Marshall admitted that the AEF staffs knew "a desperate
defense . . . could be counted upon."[56]

---

[53] *History of the First Division*, 173.

[54] Ibid.

[55] Drum is quoted in B. F. Caffey, Jr., "A Division G-3 in the World War: The 1st Division,
AEF, in the Meuse-Argonne, 26 September–11 October, 1918," p. 5. Student Monograph
IR-15-1932, CGSS. Caffey was in the operations section of the 1st Division staff during
the Meuse-Argonne. He is described in glowing terms by Marshall, who supervised him.
Marshall, *Memoir*, 181–2.

[56] Marshall, *Memoir*, 159. See also Pershing, "Final Report," *USAWW*, 12: 40–41; Braim,
Test of Battle, 89.

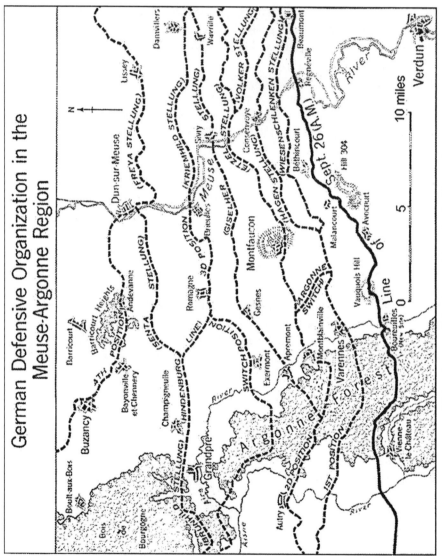

MAP 8: Major German defensive positions in the Meuse-Argonne.

Despite these factors, the AEF planners at GHQ and HQ First Army developed an extraordinarily aggressive attack plan. The nine initial divisions, supported by some 2,700 guns, 189 tanks, and 821 aircraft, were to surge forward 16 kilometers and *then* break through the German third line of resistance, the *Kriemhilde Stellung* of the Hindenburg Line, within the first two days (see Map 9).[57] Surely aware that an attack as rapid and deep as the army plans directed would outrun its initial artillery support, Pershing and his planners apparently counted on the infantrymen to use their own skills and weaponry to fight through the enemy main line of resistance without much if any artillery fire. If the infantry could do this, Pershing no doubt hoped they and other supporting troops would break into the open and carry out a decisive war-winning campaign using open-warfare techniques. Staff officers later explained that this optimistic plan was in part driven by the desire to crack the German lines before enemy reinforcements could be sent in, which might have doomed the attack to a slow, ponderous advance. However, this does not explain why they thought that the AEF divisions, especially inexperienced ones, could accomplish such a tremendously difficult mission in the first place. The only answer comes from Pershing's memoir: He admitted "it was thought reasonable to count on the vigor and the aggressive spirit of our troops to make up in a measure for their inexperience."[58] As four years of war had already shown the Allies, and as the Meuse-Argonne campaign would further prove, this assumption was entirely unreasonable.

Nevertheless, by the end of the first day of the offensive on 26 September, the AEF divisions had, by Great War standards, done a remarkable job. Many had advanced more than 5 kilometers, some more than 7. Only in the Argonne and in front of Montfaucon did divisions move as little as 2 or 3 kilometers. By the end of the third day, all the divisions except the 77th, which had slugged forward 5 kilometers in the Argonne, had advanced nearly 10 kilometers. Only when compared to the extraordinary demands of the First Army attack plan were these advances a failure.

During these days, Pershing visited his corps and division command posts and incessantly prodded them forward. When on 28 September, the new commander of the 35th Division, Major General Peter E. Traub, reported to Liggett, the I Corps commander, that his rookie division had entered the town of Exermont, more than 10 kilometers past the

[57] The numbers of guns, tanks, and aircraft available for the initial assault come from Pershing, "Final Report," *USAWW*, 12: 42.

[58] Pershing, *My Experiences*, 2: 293.

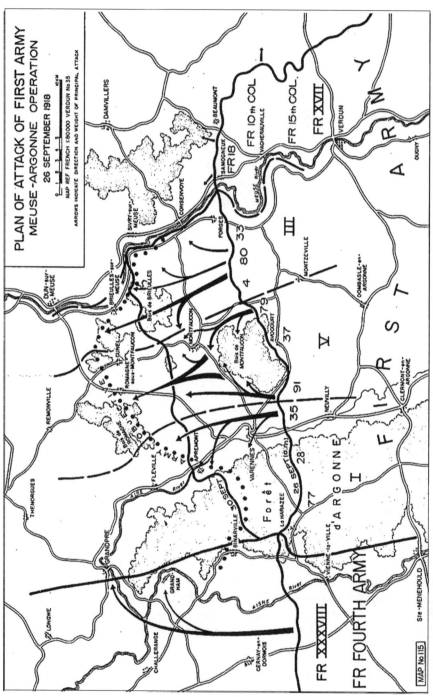

MAP 9: The American First Army's plan for the initial attack in the Meuse-Argonne Offensive required that a number of inexperienced divisions make deep advances through rugged terrain and strong German defenses.

jump-off, and needed to dig in on that line to reorganize, all Liggett could do was remind him that Pershing's order "was to keep on pushing."[59] Other divisions throughout the First Army received the same advice. That day, Pershing visited the various corps headquarters and directed Liggett's chief of staff, Malin Craig, to "call each Division Commander and in his name tell him that he must push on regardless of men or guns, night and day."[60] That evening, Liggett met Pershing, and after the latter again stressed the need to "drive and push" the men forward, the corps commander tried to give him "some notion of the terrain, the insidious character of the opposition, and the handicap all the divisions suffered from by reason of inexperience, lack of training, new officers, losses of officers, and poor ones."[61] Only the next day, after a couple of tired, disorganized American divisions not only proved they were completely incapable of continuing the advance but were also sent reeling by German counterattacks did Pershing allow an official pause in the offensive. He also ordered that three veteran divisions, including the 1st, be sent into the battle.[62]

The 1st Division immediately began a long march forward to replace the worn-out and disorganized 35th Division. On the 30th, the troops took up forward positions and early the next morning, the division took command of the sector. The division was ordered to attack early on 2 October, but after the staff produced a hurried attack order, the advance was postponed. While the staff prepared more detailed attack orders for its role in the First Army's next big push on 4 October, the troops spent the following two days familiarizing themselves with the terrain and, in many instances, trying to determine the exact enemy front line. They found the sector to be as active as any they had ever seen, and the division suffered as many as five hundred casualties on each day even though no attacks were made. The terrain to the front – a succession of hills and ridges with "densely wooded tops" and "bare glacis-like slopes" – promised to be a nightmare for any attacking troops.[63]

---

[59] P. L. Stackpole Diary, p. 236, George C. Marshall Research Library, Lexington, Virginia. Professor Robert Ferrell graciously loaned me his typescript copy of this diary, written by Liggett's aide.

[60] Ibid., 237.

[61] Ibid., 238.

[62] Cyril Falls notes that the Anglo-Belgian forces operating in Flanders had to halt their offensive at this same time and for the same reasons. Pershing Diary, entry for 29 September 1918, JJP papers, LOC. Cyril Falls, *The Great War, 1914–1918* (New York: Capricorn Books, 1961), 357.

[63] *History of the First Division*, 181–5.

After calling a halt to the general offensive at the end of September, Pershing decided to change one important element in his handling of the battle. He noted in his diary that he had finally "decided that for the next advance I will assign successive objectives ... in order to allow the green troops to reform now and then before continuing the advance."[64] Of course, division commanders like Summerall had learned this lesson months before and had been fighting their battles accordingly. It is interesting that Pershing cited only the need of "green" infantrymen to reorganize, and he made no mention of the need to ensure that adequate fire support was maintained throughout the attack, which was the other main benefit of successive objectives. However, despite Pershing's personal epiphany on this issue, the change had little apparent effect on the next phase of the battle, beginning on 4 October.[65]

As the 1st Division staff prepared its attack plan, its members may have been disturbed by three decisions made by the corps and army staffs. First, shortly after the worn-out infantrymen of the 35th Division withdrew from the sector, they were followed by all their divisional artillery, which were also relieved from the battle. The seventy-two additional guns would have dramatically increased the 1st Division's firepower. Second, no preliminary artillery fire was to precede the upcoming attack. Although such a tactic might have made sense for surprise assaults, with heavy tank support against an enemy in weak defensive positions (e.g., in the British attack at Cambrai and Mangin's at Soissons), it made little sense on 4 October, when an enemy in strong defensive positions fully expected a new American attack, and Pershing had few tanks to give his divisions. Third, although the corps orders did set definite limits for the attack, they were rather deep – at least 4 to 5 kilometers from the jump-off – and the orders warned the divisions they should "be prepared to advance from the Corps objective at H plus 5 hours, this advance to be covered by later orders."[66] If that was what Pershing meant by "successive objectives," the new idea was not going to bear much fruit.

For the 4 October attack, the 1st Division put the 1st Brigade on the left and the 2nd on the right (see Map 10). Each brigade put each of its regiments in line to cover the 4-kilometer front so that the 16th, 18th,

---

[64] Pershing Diary, entry for 30 September 1918, JJP papers, LOC.

[65] On 3 October, just days after Pershing supposedly settled on step-by-step attacks, Stackpole noted that Pershing visited I Corps HQ and gave Liggett personal instructions "to keep the Corps going tomorrow without stopping at any objective, and until stopped by the enemy." Stackpole Diary, p. 245.

[66] HQ 1st Division, Field Orders No. 47, 2 October 1918, WWRFD, vol. 3.

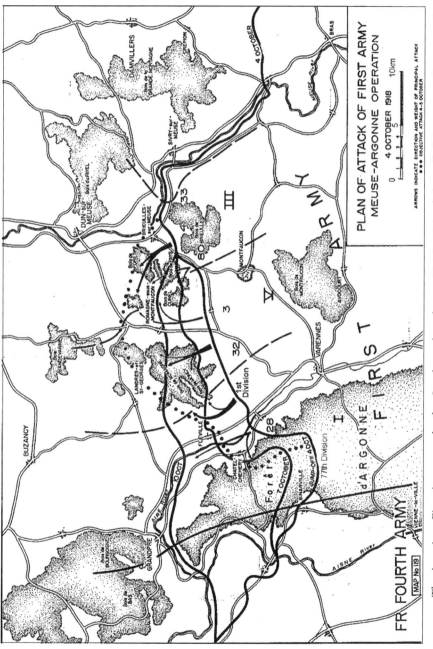

MAP 10: The American First Army attack of 4 October, when the 1st Division joined the stalled American offensive in the Meuse-Argonne.

28th, and 26th Regiments, from left to right, all took part in the initial advance. Small patrols on the days before the attack suggested that both the German defenses and the terrain were stronger on the left; therefore, Summerall directed the 2nd Brigade to make the main effort and specifically instructed the 16th Infantry, on the far left, to keep "wide intervals and distance" between its elements to reduce casualties from the enemy guns on the high ground to the north and northwest. Summerall repeatedly stressed the importance of keeping the assault waves thin and of using firepower and flanking maneuvers to overcome all opposition. His subordinate commanders apparently understood, for they included phrases like "great use will be made of the Stokes and 37mm guns during the advance" in their accompanying orders.[67] Thirty light tanks joined the advance, some with the leading waves to "attack strong points and machine gun nests" and others following to help in the "mopping up." Each infantry battalion received two light guns as accompanying artillery, doubling the number used at St. Mihiel. The machine-gun battalion fired a number of barrages during the assault, while other machine-gun companies were to follow the advance "by bounds" and be constantly ready to fire support missions.[68]

The 1st Field Artillery Brigade was augmented by a number of French 75mm and 155mm batteries. Summerall noted that he had eighty-four light guns and thirty-six howitzers under his command, giving him one light gun for each 47 meters of front and a howitzer for each 111 meters. Although the corps artillery was to fire the counterbattery missions, Summerall claimed that "it did not protect the infantry." He angrily described the number of guns as "pitifully inadequate."[69] At H hour, the light guns were to fire a rolling barrage that advanced 100 meters every 4 minutes and the heavy howitzers fired on targets directly in advance of it. The barrage was to halt for 30 minutes at both the first and second intermediary objectives, stand for 20 minutes beyond the corps objective, and then cease. Summerall ordered lethal gas "to be used freely on favorable targets and under favorable weather conditions" and directed a smoke screen to be fired on the woods to the front for the first 45 minutes of

[67] HQ 28th Infantry, Field Orders No. 16, 3 October 1918, Folder 32,1 Box 84, 1st Division Historical File, RG 120, NA.

[68] HQ 1st Division, Field Orders No. 47, 2 October 1918, *WWRFD*, vol. 3; HQ 1st Division, Memorandum, Subject: H Hour, D Day & Supplementary Instructions, 3 October 1918, *WWRFD*, vol. 3.

[69] Maj. Gen. C. P. Summerall to Deputy Chief of Staff, AEF, Subject: Artillery, HQ V Army Corps, 4 January 1919, Folder 31.23, Box 13, V Corps Historical File, RG 120, NA.

the attack.[70] As at St. Mihiel, a preprogrammed schedule regulated the staggered forward displacement of the guns.

At 0525 hours on 4 October, the division began its last great battle of the war. The rolling barrage came down, but as the troops advanced, they met strong enemy fire. Although Summerall had suspected his left regiment would have the most trouble, it was the only unit in the entire First Army to achieve its objective that day, advancing a good 4 kilometers that morning after difficult fighting. The other three regiments fought their way forward 2 kilometers and had to stop. When it became clear that the infantry was unable to keep pace with the barrage, Summerall gave each brigade commander direct control of a light-gun regiment to fire on the targets they deemed most appropriate for the remainder of the day. The German resistance was so severe during the day's attacks that only three of the original thirty tanks survived intact.[71]

During the night of 4 October, despite the troubles all along the First Army front, the division received word that the advance was to continue at 0630 hours the next morning. Instead of ordering all his lines forward at H hour, Summerall divided the next attack into three distinct parts, each with its own limited objective. Whether authorized or not, he ordered a 15-minute preliminary bombardment that fired only on targets threatening the advance to the first objective. At 0630, the three infantry regiments on the right were to follow a massed rolling barrage that led them forward 1 kilometer, where they should stop for 60 minutes while protected by a standing barrage. During the halt, other guns and howitzers were to pound the enemy zone up to the second objective. The barrage was then to roll forward again another kilometer, up to the line gained by the 16th Infantry the prior day, and stop again for another hour. Only then would all four regiments advance together, following a third rolling barrage to seize the corps objective. Summerall also directed "all available tanks" to assist the initial advance.[72]

Although the advance started well and the first objectives were taken easily all along the line, the next advance met heavy resistance and separated the infantry from the barrage. When the leading battalion commanders reported this to their regimental commanders, they were told *not* to press on under their own power but rather to dig in and wait for a new rolling barrage. Colonel Hjalmer Erickson, the commander of the 26th

[70] HQ 1st Division, Field Orders No. 47, 2 October 1918, *WWRFD*, vol. 3
[71] *History of the First Division*, 193–4.
[72] HQ 1st Division, Field Orders No. 48, 5 October 1918, *WWRFD*, vol. 3.

Infantry, repeatedly told his assault units: "Do not advance until you get orders from me . . . dig in. . . . Do not advance until your protective barrage begins."[73] A new rolling barrage was arranged to start from the stalled line at 1400 hours that afternoon, and only then was the advance continued. The ability to recall a rolling barrage was a rare and impressive achievement during the war, and it demonstrates the level of communication and coordination present in the division, as well as the commitment to maximize fire support even if it meant holding up the attack. That afternoon, the three lagging regiments successfully continued their advance to bring them abreast of the 16th Infantry. By controlling its rolling barrage, the 26th Infantry fought its way forward more than 2 kilometers at a cost of just three hundred casualties. After receiving reports of the Germans' strength on and around Hill 272, positions "literally studded with machine gun nests and *minnenwerfer* emplacements," Summerall concluded that another "especially prepared assault" would be necessary to seize the next objective.[74]

By this time, the 1st Division was well ahead of those on its flanks, and it received permission from the corps to hold its current line for three days while it prepared for its next assault. That attack became the crowning achievement of Summerall's set-piece, firepower maximization attacks as a division commander. As the infantry carried out small patrols to gather information on enemy positions, seized weakly held enemy outposts, and fought off strong enemy counterattacks, Summerall prepared his most elaborate attack plan to date.

On 9 October, the division was to make three small but distinct set-piece attacks, two of which were even broken down into multiple phases. First, the division's remaining fresh battalion, the 1st Battalion of the 16th Infantry, would assault Hill 272 at H hour, following a dense barrage by all the divisional artillery. Twenty-two minutes later, all the guns were to shift to fire a dense rolling barrage in front of the 2nd Brigade, which was to advance up to the new line, then halt for 2 hours while the guns pounded the next objective. At H plus 3 hours, a new rolling barrage would begin and lead only the 2nd Brigade forward again to the second objective. In the second attack, preceded by a 30-minute artillery

[73] See "Field Messages," Folder 32.16, Box 79, 1st Division Historical File, RG 120, NA.
[74] George R. F. Cornish, "The Twenty-Sixth Infantry (U.S.) in the Meuse-Argonne Offensive." Student Monograph IR-104–1931, CGSS. Cornish commanded the HQ Company during the operations and was with the regimental commander throughout the offensive. *History of the First Division*, 200.

preparation by all the divisional guns, another massed rolling barrage would lead the 1st Battalion, 16th Infantry, forward at H plus 290 minutes to its second objective. For the third attack, preceded by another 30-minute massed artillery preparation and dense rolling barrage, the remainder of the 1st Brigade, on the far left, would drive forward to the second objective. All rolling barrages, except the first 15 minutes of the initial assault, were to move very slowly – just 100 meters every 6 minutes. All the available machine guns were to fire coordinated rolling and standing barrages as well and were required to keep twenty thousand rounds at each gun emplacement. Crews from the American 1st Gas Regiment fired smoke and thermite into selected enemy positions. And, because this attack could not count on any amount of surprise, Summerall ordered all his guns to begin blasting the enemy lines a full day before the attack, drenching them with gas and high-explosive rounds. Although Summerall may have thought the amount of firepower given his division "pitifully inadequate," he developed a plan to get the maximum benefit from the weapons he had.[75]

At 0830 on 9 October, the attack began and by the early afternoon, the division had – for the first time in the Meuse-Argonne – taken all its objectives (see Map 11). Some company commanders even reported that they met "little resistance" before digging in on the new line, and another reported the advance was accomplished "without great difficulty."[76] The division captured more than six hundred prisoners in the set-piece attack, advanced the line about 2 more kilometers, and shattered the enemy resistance in the area. Although Summerall sought to maximize the use of his artillery, the infantry did much more than just walk behind the rolling barrages in neat rows. Descriptions of the infantry tactics often assert that the "fighting was by individual groups," using the same combination of firepower and flanking maneuvers that they showed at St. Mihiel.[77]

Late that night, the I Corps ordered the division to continue the advance early on 10 October. Either because he was aware of the broken nature of the enemy resistance to his front or because he did not think his tired

[75] HQ 1st Division, Field Orders No. 49, 8 October 1918, *WWRFD*, vol. 3.
[76] "Field Messages," Folder 32.16, Box 79, 1st Division Historical File, RG 120, NA.
[77] HQ 28th Infantry, "Report of the Operations East of the Argonne Forest from October 1 to October 11," 18 October 1918, Folder 33.6, Box 87, 1st Division Historical File, RG 120, NA. See also Cornish, "The Twenty-Sixth Infantry (U.S.) in the Meuse-Argonne Offensive."

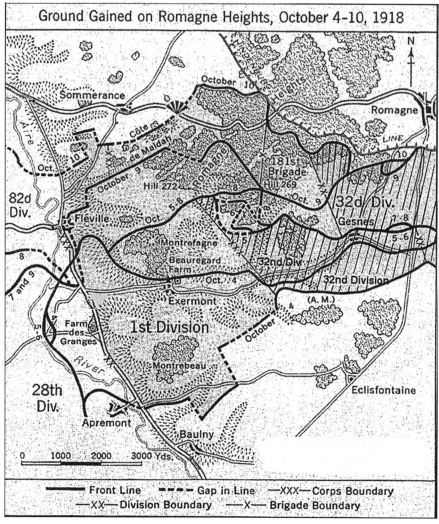

MAP II: 1st Division advances in the Meuse-Argonne from 4 to 10 October.

division could mount another full attack, Summerall ordered his troops to merely "exploit its successes" by carefully advancing through a series of "exploitation lines." At 0700 on the 10th, each regiment was to push out small patrols. If no resistance was encountered, the patrols were to "immediately advance and occupy the best possible defensive position." However, he ordered that "if resistance is encountered, artillery assistance will be demanded and after artillery preparation patrols will again go forward to keep contact with the enemy."[78] Each brigade could call directly on its dedicated artillery regiment for immediate support as needed. That day, the lines were advanced between 1 and 2 kilometers, at light cost. When the I Corps ordered the division to attack again on 11 October, Summerall gave essentially the same orders but with more strict admonitions to rely solely on artillery fire to smash enemy resistance. When his patrols ran into the enemy's main defensive line, the *Kriemhilde Stellung*, he determined the position was too strong for his division and made no attack at all.[79] The First Army finally relieved the division on the night of 11 October, and Pershing promoted Summerall to command the V Corps the next day.

The division's fighting during the First Army's darkest days in the Meuse-Argonne Offensive marked in some ways both the high and low points of its entire wartime experience. Regarding the latter, the division suffered approximately eight thousand casualties during its longest and most brutal period of combat.[80] Unlike at Soissons, the division never made a surprisingly deep and rapid advance, never forced a huge enemy withdrawal, and could not claim it took part in a "turning point" of the war. Yet, the division also achieved some impressive results – driving forward more than 7 kilometers in about as many days of actual attacks, battering to pieces parts of eight German divisions, taking more than fourteen hundred prisoners, and capturing thirteen guns.

Even more impressive than the raw statistics was the manner in which the division fought the battle. The infantry continued to show dramatic improvement from its attacks in early July, even on much more challenging terrain. All accounts stress the ability of the infantry battalions to combine the massed fire of their 37mm guns, mortars, rifle grenades, and automatic weapons with flanking and infiltration maneuvers to overcome enemy resistance. The junior officers kept their men well organized without bunching them together, and senior commanders had no trouble determining the actual front lines. The artillery continued to demonstrate its ability to provide accurate barrages and special fire. Equally important was the level of coordination between the two arms, as numerous infantry officers reported the successful recalling of barrages that were running away from slow-moving infantry. Many infantry commanders

---

[78] HQ 1st Division, Field Orders No. 50, 2330 hours, 9 October 1918, *WWRFD*, vol. 3.

[79] HQ 1st Division, Field Orders No. 52, 2230 hours, 10 October 1918, *WWRFD*, vol. 3.

[80] The ABMC lists 7,772 casualties for the period, as well as an additional 459 for losses in the attached 181st Infantry Brigade. *American Armies and Battlefields*, 327.

agreed with a division staff officer who identified the "excellent cooperation with the artillery" as one of the salient features of the campaign.[81]

Each of these achievements was in large part the result of the decisions
made by the division commander, who did everything he could to turn the
division's participation in a huge general offensive into a series of smaller,
firepower-based, set-piece battles. This conceptual shift enabled the division to mass its limited artillery support in an unprecedented fashion. It
allowed the infantry to maximize its own firepower during short, controlled advances that seized one or more limited objectives.[82] It helped
the smaller infantry and artillery units maintain almost constant communications with their own higher commanders and with each other.
Perhaps most important, it encouraged throughout the division a different view of combat, one that appreciated the realities of the modern
battlefield and demanded not just more men, effort, and suffering but
also better ideas – and ideas that accurately accounted for the current
abilities and limitations of the unit itself. This development enabled the
division to turn what could have been a futile bloodbath into a slow but
steady advance against a desperate enemy, waging a tenacious defense,
on a battlefield that favored the defender as much as any during the
entire war.

Conclusions

When the 1st Division left the Meuse-Argonne in October, its activity
in the war was not over, but it had fought its last significant battle.
Despite the confusion and controversy surrounding the Sedan incident
in early November (i.e., when the division crossed paths with two other
divisions in a race to take Sedan), the division finished the war with a

---

[81] See Caffey, "A Division G-3 in the World War," p. 24; HQ 26th Infantry, "Report on
Operations of the 26th Infantry Northeast of Verdun, Sept. 30, 1918 to Oct. 11, 1918,"
18 October 1918, Folder 33.6, Box 81, 1st Division Historical File, RG 120, NA; HQ 2nd
Infantry Brigade, "Report of Operations of the Second Infantry Brigade, in the Sector
North-East of Verdun, September 29–October 12, 1918," 20 October 1918, Folder 33.6,
Box 67, 1st Division Historical File, RG 120, NA; also see Cornish, "The Twenty-Sixth
Infantry (U.S.) in the Meuse-Argonne Offensive."

[82] On many days during the Meuse-Argonne fighting, the light-gun regiments fired fourteen
thousand or more rounds, and the howitzers shot off more than four thousand rounds,
totals that approach or equal the high rates achieved in the ultrastabilized, set-piece environment at Cantigny on 28 May 1918. HQ 1st F.A. Brigade, "Ammunition Expenditure
by 1st F.A. Brigade, A.E.F.," 27 February 1919 in Folder 33.6, Box 97, 1st Division
Historical File, RG 120, NA.

reputation as one of the finest units in the AEF and, ironically, as Pershing's favorite.[83] The irony rests in the fact that throughout its training and combat experience, the 1st Division seemed to become more and more capable of fighting in the style that Pershing supposedly most despised. As early as the Cantigny attack, the division demonstrated its ability to plan and execute limited, firepower-intensive, set-piece attacks.

Although it succeeded strategically in the Aisne-Marne Offensive, with its deep penetration near Soissons, it also failed tactically there, as it tried to fight in a manner more consistent with the AEF's approved open-warfare doctrine than with its own abilities. Already, by the end of that grim battle, the division was increasingly trying to execute the kind of limited, set-piece attacks that most officers recognized as essentially related to trench warfare. At St. Mihiel, the division showed that it had learned a great deal about fighting on the modern battlefield and, although some of its techniques such as its infantry infiltration tactics had been accepted by AEF GHQ, its efforts to adhere to highly regulated infantry advances covered entirely by rolling barrages never became official doctrine. Finally, in the Meuse-Argonne, the division showed both its willingness and ability to plan and execute limited, set-piece attacks, supported to the greatest extent by infantry and artillery firepower. All divisions in the Great War, in every army, had to make their attacks with the limited resources given them. During those trying days of October, the 1st Division proved it had come a long way toward matching its plans with its abilities and maximizing the results from its limited means. Far from suffering interminably from a flawed open-warfare doctrine imposed from on high by Pershing and GHQ, the 1st Division developed a remarkable appreciation and an impressive ability for making limited, firepower-based attacks.

---

[83] After a brief period of rest, the addition of some replacement troops, and a little more training, the division reentered the offensive in early November. But, after the First Army smashed through the German Army's last established line of defense on 1 November, the division's final three days of operations from 6 to 8 November were filled with much more marching than fighting. Neither its essentially unopposed 6-kilometer drive to the Meuse River nor its subsequent misbegotten advance on Sedan (when the division marched through the sectors of 77th and 42nd Divisions without their knowledge) offered the division any opportunity to further demonstrate its offensive prowess. Although the "race to Sedan" operation was fascinating and controversial, it showed little about doctrinal development in the division or the AEF. The division suffered just a few hundred casualties during its final days of marching through scattered German resistance.

4

The 26th "Yankee" Division

Doctrine, Discipline, and Discrimination

No AEF division was as controversial as the 26th Division. Composed of National Guard units from throughout New England, it was the first National Guard division and the second American division overall to get to France and begin training.[1] Only the 1st Division preceded it. Many observers noted early on the division's high morale and unique esprit de corps. One of the first divisions to enter the front lines, it fought the first major engagement against the enemy, then participated in the AEF's three major campaigns in the Aisne-Marne, St. Mihiel, and the Meuse-Argonne Offensives. When the war ended, only the 1st Division had spent more time opposing the enemy. However, the 1st Division became Pershing's favorite and was widely regarded as among the AEF's best units, but many senior American officers considered the Yankee Division a troubled unit and a major disappointment.[2]

Although much of this notoriety was due to the reputation and behavior of the Yankee Division's controversial commander, Major General Clarence R. Edwards, some of it was the result of the division's performance.[3] Despite receiving more training than most AEF divisions

---

[1] The 26th Division was composed of the 51st Infantry Brigade, with the 101st and 102nd Infantry Regiments; the 52nd Infantry Brigade, with the 103rd and 104th Infantry Regiments; and the 51st Field Artillery Brigade, with the 101st and 102nd F.A. Regiments of 75mm guns and the 103rd F.A. Regiment of 155mm howitzers.

[2] Ayres, *War with Germany*, 114.

[3] Edwards graduated last of fifty-two in the West Point class of 1883. In 1899, after a number of tours in the American West and service as a general's adjutant in the Philippine War, Edwards joined the War Department as Chief of the Customs and Insular Affairs Division (later called the Bureau of Insular Affairs). During his twelve years in that powerful post, Edwards was promoted to colonel and then brigadier general. He made numerous political

Clarence R. Edwards (center), commander of the 26th Division from its inception until his relief in October 1918. Here, he reviews troops from the 101st Infantry Regiment.

and spending many months in the front trenches supposedly honing its skills and strengthening its organization, the division became known as a group of confused, undisciplined complainers that could not – or would not – perform well on the battlefield. To Pershing and many staff officers, the division did not train well, it showed many weaknesses even while holding "quiet" front-line sectors, it struggled in its first efforts to push the enemy back during the Aisne-Marne Offensive in July, and it made slow progress against weak resistance during the early part of the St. Mihiel attack. They noticed that the 26th Division failed to make significant advances during the Meuse-Argonne Offensive in late October and became embroiled in an embarrassing fraternization incident during that engagement. To many senior AEF officers, the Yankee Division gave

connections, especially to the various secretaries of war including William Howard Taft, with whom he became particularly close, as well as Jacob McGovock Dickenson and Henry L. Stimson. In 1912, Edwards left the War Department to command the 6th Brigade in Wyoming, then other commands in Hawaii and Panama. After the declaration of war, Edwards took command of the Northeast Department, where he became popular with many of the governors, legislators, and other prominent civilians. See the brief biography of him in the "Guide to the Clarence R. Edwards Papers, 1879–1937," Massachusetts Historical Society (MHS), Boston.

lackluster performance for a unit with so much time in France, and they blamed the division's senior officers – particularly Edwards – for ruining an otherwise fine group of soldiers.

The 26th Division had many weaknesses and it struggled at times on the battlefield, but Regular officers often exaggerated its operational problems. In many ways, the biases and poor decisions of senior AEF officials actually contributed to the division's troubles. Many staff officers and senior commanders at corps, army, and GHQ levels were harshly critical of the AEF's first National Guard division from the start; they did not ensure that it had sufficient training opportunities; they gave the division onerous and inglorious missions; they failed to send it sufficient replacements; and they left it under a commander who they agreed was undisciplined and unreliable, then replaced him in the middle of the division's most difficult and costly battle. Whatever the failures of the 26th Division were, senior AEF officers were partially to blame.

Despite its spotty operational record, even the 26th Division made important tactical and doctrinal changes during the war. For all his other problems, Edwards quickly developed an impressive understanding of the importance of maximizing firepower; opening up infantry formations; relying on infiltration and flanking maneuvers instead of frontal assaults; and applying other emerging technologies such as the tank, the airplane, the telephone, and the wireless radio during attack. Indeed, the division had more successes than some AEF leaders admitted, but other problems, both internal and external, prevented the unit from reaping the full benefits of its doctrinal and tactical developments.

Organization in the United States, August–September 1917

In August 1917, the War Department created the 26th Division from a number of small National Guard units throughout New England, such as the 2nd Connecticut Infantry and the 1st Massachusetts Field Artillery. Some of these units had distinguished service records dating back to the War of Independence. More important, many of the men in these units had recently returned from service on the Mexican border during 1916 and others had been on active duty training and guarding installations since the declaration of war in April. By all accounts, these were some of the most experienced Guardsman in the nation.[4]

---

[4] One unit history even claimed that "a large majority of the troops" had been on active service for many months by the time the division was created. "Summary History of the Twenty-Sixth Division," p. 3, n.d., Folder 11.4, Box 6, 26th Division Historical File, RG 120, NA.

The existing organizational structure and committed personnel of the New England National Guard units proved to be both a blessing and a curse for the 26th Division. The Guard organization enabled the 26th Division to be the first division fully formed in the United States and shipped overseas. Whereas the War Department was still gathering troops for most other divisions in the late fall, all it had to do for the 26th Division was assign it a number of experienced officers for the staff and command positions, fill the vacancies in the ranks, and get it on the transport ships. By early November, the Yankee Division was in France training for war while most other divisions were just getting organized and assembled in the United States.

Although the War Department assigned the division a contingent of Regular officers – naming Edwards, the former head of the Northeastern Department, as division commander; Brigadier Generals Peter E. Traub and William L. Lassiter as brigade commanders; and Lieutenant Colonel George H. Shelton as the chief of staff – nearly all the other officers, including many of higher rank, were Guardsman.[5] Many Regular officers considered this a liability, and the combination of their dislike of Edwards as a commander and distrust of the part-time militia officers as small-unit leaders led to a strained relationship between many AEF leaders and the division.[6]

---

[5] The commander of the 52nd Infantry Brigade, Peter Traub, was a classmate of Pershing in the West Point class of 1886. A cavalry officer, he served in the Philippine War with distinction, taught languages at West Point, and served at the Army Signal School. William Lassiter was also a West Point graduate and a close-enough friend of Pershing to have attended his wedding. He was regarded as an excellent artillery officer and a superb staff officer. In the spring of 1917, he was serving as a military attaché to Great Britain. His reputation was such that in late 1917, when Robert Bullard took command of the 1st Division and was told by Pershing that he could draw on the best of the AEF to fill important positions, Bullard asked for either Lassiter or Charles Summerall to take over the artillery brigade. Bullard got Summerall in that instance, but when Bullard took command of the American Second Army in October 1918, he made Lassiter his chief of artillery. Shelton was a West Pointer and an infantryman with twenty years of service. He served on the Army's General Staff for two years, and his credentials were sufficiently impressive to enable him to serve as the editor of the *Infantry Journal*. See Emerson Gifford Taylor, *New England in France: 1917–1919: A History of the Twenty-Sixth Division U.S.A.* (Boston: Houghton Mifflin, 1920), 20–22. Taylor was a major in the 26th and served on the division staff, eventually as acting assistant chief of staff. Millett, *The General*, 334; and Vandiver, *Black Jack*, 2: 703.

[6] The commander of the 51st Infantry Brigade, Charles H. Cole, had been the Adjutant General of Massachusetts before retiring in 1916. After the U.S. declaration of war, he immediately enlisted as a private; however, when the 26th Division was created, he was given command of the brigade and promoted to brigadier general. Albert Greenlaw, the former Adjutant General of Maine, did the same thing but only secured a position as a captain in an infantry regiment in the new division. Coffman, *War to End All Wars*, 147; and Taylor, *New England in France*, 21.

However, the Guardsman may have had one advantage over their Regular counterparts – they were less likely to be dogmatically committed to the anachronistic elements of prewar U.S. Army doctrine. These officers, though less experienced in command and supposedly less committed to the importance of obedience and discipline, gave the division the opportunity to develop its own combat doctrine or at least to examine the official AEF doctrine with an open mind.

Whatever the tactical and doctrinal leanings of the Yankee Division's officers, they had practically no time to develop them or train according to them in the United States before shipping to Europe. Most of the units remained at their state training camps in August and early September gathering supplies, equipping the men, and accomplishing the parade-ground drill and rifle-target practice that were the basis of all military training during the era. By 7 September, just three weeks after the division was formed, the first units shipped out, and by late October, the entire division was in France and ready to begin the training regimen prescribed by GHQ.[7]

Within weeks of its arrival, the division began drawing negative attention from Pershing and the GHQ staff. This was partly because of Edwards' reputation as an ambitious and unreliable commander but also because of the long-standing dislike and distrust of the part-time militia Guardsman by professional officers of the Regular Army. Regular officers were suspicious of the political, personal, and social factors that seemed to determine the rank and position of Guard officers and NCOs.[8] The

---

[7] While one history of the 51st Infantry Brigade notes that there was little time for any drill or training before going to France, Lawrence Stallings claims that the men of the 26th Division had completed plenty of rifle practice. "History of the 51st Infantry Brigade," n.d., 26th Division Boxes, World War I Survey Collection, USAMHI; and Lawrence Stallings, *The Doughboys: The Story of the AEF, 1917–1918* (New York: Harper & Row, 1963), 48.

[8] Although this sentiment seems to have been held somewhat by Pershing and perhaps even more so by many of the staff officers of the "Leavenworth clique," other Regular officers showed no sign of it. Many of the Regular officers who commanded Guard divisions insisted that their officers and men were every bit as intelligent and devoted as any they had ever served with. Furthermore, Pershing seemed to show no similar hostility to other Guard units, such as the 42nd, 28th, or 32nd Divisions. Hervey Allen, a young officer in the 28th Division formed from Pennsylvania Guard units, admitted that the personal and political element of the old militia system came to France with the new Guard divisions. He wrote, "It seems impossible that Pennsylvania politics could reach to France, even in a guard regiment, but they did. In the old days, a lot of the men had been appointed non-commissioned officers to salve up the folks at home in the fourth ward, or for some such reason, and it was necessary to change this now. I tried to get the right man in the right place." Allen, *Toward the Flame: A War Diary* (Pittsburgh: University of Pittsburgh Press, 1968), 12.

division also may have gotten off on the wrong foot when Edwards supposedly appropriated the shipping designated for the 42nd "Rainbow" Division, though this would seem to have been a source of concern more for those in the War Department and the 42nd than for anyone in the AEF. More troublesome was the interaction between Pershing and the division after it arrived. Although Pershing's memoir account of his first inspection of the 26th Division is favorable, other sources claim he was "cruelly critical" of the un-martinet-like, former part-time soldiers, referring to them as "Boy Scouts."[9] Within a few weeks, Pershing heard rumors that Edwards had openly criticized senior American officers and the AEF's chances for success in front of both distinguished civilian visitors and junior officers. Pershing, who viewed loyalty with the utmost seriousness, sent him a stern personal note warning that in the future such behavior would be grounds for dismissal.[10] Throughout the 26th Division's period of training and operations in France, more reports of poor performance and bad leadership continued to surface, while important tactical and doctrinal improvements went unappreciated.

Training in France, November 1917–March 1918

Despite the doctrinal desires of Pershing and GHQ, the 26th Division was immersed in the trench-warfare environment of the Allies throughout its training period. In fact, the division probably received less open-warfare training than any of the other three "pioneer divisions" (i.e., 1st, 2nd, and 42nd Divisions) and received no such training until late August 1918 – a month *after* its first major offensive. The evidence shows that the 26th Division, possibly due to the doctrinal openness of its Guardsmen officers but also to the awareness of some of its senior Regular leaders, rapidly gained an appreciation of the value of firepower on the Great War battlefield. Some of these ideas were included even in early division attacks, and any trouble in applying those ideas throughout the division's operations

---

[9] T. Howard Kelly, "Why General Edwards Was Sent Home," *New McClure's* (November 1928): 54. Kelly was a private and NCO in the 103rd F.A. Regiment during the war. Pershing later wrote that the division "presented a very creditable appearance, the officers seemed alert and military . . . the personnel looked strong and vigorous." It is interesting that Pershing credited Traub, the West Point graduate and long-term Regular who commanded of the 51st Brigade, for these characteristics. Pershing, *My Experiences*, 1: 233; and Coffman, *War to End All Wars*, 147.

[10] Edwards replied that he had been "misunderstood or misrepresented in every case." See Commander-in-Chief to Major General Clarence R. Edwards, Subject: Pessimism, 15 December 1917, and attached correspondence, Box 22, Edwards Papers, MHS.

had more to do with the organizational troubles within and without the division than to slow doctrinal adjustment.

Even before the division arrived in France, Edwards had been summoned to Europe along with other new division commanders to begin his own period of education and training, almost all of it with Allied units. After arriving in September, Edwards spent more than a month with various French and British divisions along the Western Front – including the veteran 51st (Highland) and 16th (Irish) Divisions of the BEF. Although some senior officers, such as Brigadier General Robert Alexander (who later commanded the 77th Division), left their tours criticizing the way Allied units deviated from traditional American doctrine, especially regarding the use of modern automatic weapons and artillery, Edwards readily appreciated the necessity of such differences.[11]

As the 26th Division began the training schedule developed by GHQ in mid-November, Edwards wrote letters to the commanders of the Highland and Irish Divisions detailing what he thought most valuable from his visits with them. Although other AEF officers thought trench weapons wrongly had supplanted the essential preeminence of the rifle and bayonet, Edwards wrote that throughout the Allied divisions, "the sense of proportion in the use of the various arms seems to me good." He appreciated their "reliance" on the machine gun and complimented their "use of artillery," which he found "excellent." He then admitted that nothing "made such an impression on me in my visit . . . as the machine gun barrage."[12]

A few weeks later, Edwards showed he was determined to act on these ideas. After discussing with Traub how the British army corps employed machine guns, he wrote, "if the use of the machine gun is so necessary in a corps, think what it is for a division. I am going to pay much attention to turning out all the machine guns of the division with that object in view

---

[11] Alexander seems to have visited many of the same Allied divisions as Edwards, even though Alexander made his visits months later. For Alexander's assessment of the Allied forces, see Robert Alexander, *Memories of the World War, 1917–1918* (New York: Macmillan, 1931), 32–3.

[12] Edwards to Maj. Gen. G. M. Harper, C.G. of 51st Highland Division, 17 November 1917, Box 22, Edwards Papers, MHS. It is interesting that in this same letter, Edwards made complimentary comments about Pershing and his GHQ staff, writing that Pershing had a "gigantic task and is doing splendidly. . . . He is broad and capable, and the heads of his various departments are as capable officers as we have in the army." He claimed that he was "delighted" with AEF GHQ – strange words from a man who was soon criticized for disloyalty, bad-mouthing superiors, and a defeatist attitude.

and to use them for direct covering of the whole front of the division, as well as the flanks."[13] Edwards may have become so enamored with his firepower ideas that he ran afoul of the guardians of official AEF doctrine in the GHQ training section, when he supposedly ridiculed them at a corps-level meeting regarding "training matters."[14] Although Edwards may have struggled to adequately train his unit to employ all its firepower, he certainly understood its importance.

Between November and January, the division followed the GHQ training schedule that placed the unit under French Army tutelage while insisting that it remain devoted to approved American ideas and methods – especially regarding the rifle and the bayonet.[15] Yet, as with the 1st Division that preceded it, the Yankee Division's infantry units began what one unit history called "intensive training for trench warfare." Two French infantry regiments gave their American counterparts "daily instruction...in grenade throwing, machine gun and automatic rifle practice, Stokes Mortar and 37mm guns, and in formations of approach and attack." Most of this training was done on the newly constructed "model system of fire, cover, and support trenches" that accommodated an entire battalion at a time.[16] In late January, Edwards finally got some of his machine-gun units to practice the massed barrages he was so impressed with in the Allied units. During these months, the artillery received their French pieces and conducted fire training at a separate training facility hundreds of miles away at Camp Coetquidan in Brittany. Like the infantry, the gunners learned the skills and methods essential to limited set-piece attacks – especially collective map-based barrages.[17]

---

[13] Edwards to Brig. Gen. P. E. Traub, (51st Brigade), 2 January 1918, Box 22, Edwards Papers, MHS.

[14] Malin Craig, Liggett's chief of staff in the I Corps, reported that during his first meeting with Edwards at a conference at Neufchateau, with Liggett and others from inside and outside of the 26th Division in attendance, Edwards openly ridiculed Colonels Fiske, Upton, and Malone – then the senior officers of training section at GHQ. Confidential Memorandum from Malin Craig to Drum, 8 December 1920, Personal File of H.A. Drum, "Copies of Reports, Letters, etc. of the Twenty-Sixth Division," Box 14, Drum Papers, USAMHI.

[15] Training Section, General Staff, "Program of Training for the 26th Division," 13 October 1917, Box 25, Edwards Papers, MHS.

[16] "Summary History of the Twenty-Sixth Division," p. 3, n.d., Folder 11.4, Box 6, 26th Division Historical File, RG 120, NA.

[17] HQ 102nd Infantry, C.O. to C.G., 26th Division, Subject: Report of Machine Gun Instruction, 26th Division, 2 February 1918, Box 22, Edwards Papers, MHS; "History of the Fifty-First Field Artillery Brigade," n.d., Folder 11.4, Box 57, 26th Division Historical File, RG 120, NA.

At the end of January, the division was finally gathered together and sent into the trenches in the Chemin des Dames area for a month of front-line trench-warfare training under the tactical control of French commanders. But, already, inspectors and at least one brigade commander had identified a litany of problems that hinted at slack discipline and sloppy leadership on the part of officers: units "paid no attention" to approved training schedules; instruction was "perfunctory in character"; some 250-man companies mustered just half their strength for training sessions; "some company commanders remained in quarters or offices" while the men trained; general discipline was "poor"; "nothing has been done toward training any unit larger than a company"; close-order drill was rated "poor"; officers had received "no instruction in giving commands"; "there had been no target practice"; "no proper effort... to prepare ranges"; "no training in open warfare...no company or battalion problems have been prepared or executed.... No instruction in use of gas masks.... The instruction did not, in the average, cover six hours a day. On Saturdays nothing is done beyond inspection"; and one regiment had just received its 37mm guns and was still without its Stokes mortars.[18]

Although some of these problems were the fault of officers within the division, others were caused by GHQ. During this period, weapons and equipment shortages were endemic throughout the AEF and were more likely a failure of GHQ than any divisional officer. GHQ also detailed hundreds of divisional soldiers shortly after their arrival in France – including as many as six infantry companies at one time – to do "Line of Communications work" (later called Service of Supply) due to a lack of labor troops in the AEF. Even the AEF official history admits that for many weeks, training "was considerably hampered" by these details.[19] Many of the Guardsmen must have bristled at such uninspiring work, and they may have suspected that Pershing would not have used Regulars in this way.[20] Whatever the perceptions, the decision hindered the development of the AEF's second combat division.

Another factor working against the 26th Division was the heavy turnover of officers, including regimental commanders. Although the

---

[18] "Extract from Report of Tactical Inspection 26th Division, December 10–13 1917," Folder 56.2, Box 48, 26th Division Historical File, RG 120, NA. The origin of this report is unknown, but the extract was sent from the C.G., 52nd Brigade, Brig. Gen. Cole, to the commander of the 103rd Infantry.

[19] USAWW, 3: 594.

[20] Pershing did, in fact, detail some Regulars to work on the Line of Communications, including a number of troops from the 2nd Division.

division retained stability in its division and brigade commanders (with only one change between August 1917 and October 1918), below that level many officers were removed and replaced. When the commander of the French 162nd Regiment reported on the Yankee Division's progress in training, he claimed that "one may surely lay many of the errors in the training...to the non-continuity of commanders."[21] At least two of the four infantry regimental commanders, as well as the division's chief of staff, were changed before the division ever went into the trenches. Of potentially greater trouble was the rate of change of more junior officers, who were forced to attend numerous staff and specialty schools while their platoons, companies, and battalions had to train without them.[22]

In January, just before the division entered the trenches, it was assigned to Hunter Liggett's new I Army Corps, which was to monitor training and administrative matters. Throughout the month, Liggett grew increasingly displeased with Edwards for his tendency to show up late for meetings or miss them altogether. He was even more concerned by the weak leadership and poor discipline Edwards allowed in the division. When corps inspectors monitored unit training, they often found the troops standing around and getting little accomplished. What was done, was done poorly.[23] One inspector returned from a visit to some of the division's machine-gun units – supposedly one of Edwards' emphasis items – with a scathing report: they knew "nothing about indirect fire," and the officers did not even know how to compute firing data.[24]

Apparently, these specific problems were quickly solved when Edwards responded by initiating a short period of "intensive training" under the watchful eye of a trusted colonel, John H. Parker, who was named both the 102nd Infantry Regiment commander and the new Division Machine Gun Officer.[25] In early February, Parker reported that the divisional machine-gun teams knew how to lay their guns, compute barrage data, and fire "strictly" according to the timetable. To prove their competence, he drove

---

[21] Col. Bertrand, Commanding 162nd Regiment of Infantry to the Colonel Commanding the Infantry of the 69th Div., 3 January 1918, Box 22, Edwards Papers, MHS.

[22] "Summary History of the Twenty Sixth Division," p. 3., n.d., Folder 11.4, Box 6, 26th Division Historical File, RG 120, NA.

[23] Stackpole Diary, pp. 2–4.

[24] Ibid., p. 8.

[25] Parker was a Regular officer of long service and had been an active and somewhat controversial machine-gun expert in the prewar Army. See the many references to him in David A. Armstrong, *Bullets and Bureaucrats: The Machine Gun and the United States Army, 1861–1916* (Westport, Conn.: Greenwood Press, 1982).

his car under the barrage, got out, and walked around underneath it.[26] Nevertheless, the critical reports proved to some senior AEF officers that Edwards could not be trusted with the division, while officers in the 26th grew increasingly sure that the AEF high command held a unique grudge against the first Guard division in France.

Possibly the only man in the AEF who understood what was going on was Hunter Liggett, who believed that *both* parties were correct. He knew that many Regular AEF officers, including some on his own staff, were biased against Edwards and the Yankee Division, and he told his aide that "he wanted to end the prejudice of his staff" against them. He admitted that Edwards was very popular within the division, and that the unit's morale was "excellent." But, he also understood that Edwards had serious problems. He thought Edwards was "not sound from a military point of view," was dishonest, did not consistently obey orders, and did not inspect his units and troops enough. Most important, he did not think Edwards could handle the division properly in combat. Finally, Liggett believed Edwards' popularity was gained by "political methods," and he was sure that "an organization held together by this sort of thing was not so strong as one supported by excellence of training and discipline." Liggett considered relieving him but deferred doing so for a host of reasons.[27]

Despite the training problems and command controversies, the 26th Division joined its supervisory French unit in the front trenches along the Chemin des Dames, near the town of Soissons, in early February. It was the first time the entire division – infantry, artillery, and support troops – had ever trained together. Although members of GHQ treated this period of training as a necessary evil that interrupted the path to proficiency in open warfare, officers in the division considered it a "finishing course of practical instruction." As with the other divisions, this period of training

---

[26] C.O., 102nd Infantry, to C. G., 26th Division, Subject: Report of Machine Gun Instruction, 26th Division, 2 February 1918, Box 22, Edwards Papers, MHS.

[27] Stackpole Diary, pp. 20–21, 29, 38, 42–3, 53, 58. Liggett declined to relieve Edwards because he, as a major general of a temporary corps command, did not feel he had the authority to relieve another major general commanding a permanent unit like a division. He also was suspicious of the bias of his own corps staff – especially Malin Craig, his chief of staff, and Stuart Heintzelman – although there is no evidence that he took any action other than reminding them to be objective. Liggett decided to wait until "some definite and conclusive evidence of incompetency has developed in current operations." He advised Pershing of his concerns about Edwards, and although Pershing agreed, he also decided not to relieve him. I am not aware of a single instance in which a corps commander relieved a division commander. Those decisions appear to have remained the prerogative of Pershing.

immersed American units into French methods and confirmed the realities of the modern battlefield. Under the tactical command and "minute personal instruction" of the French, the division learned the finer points of trench warfare.[28] For his part, Edwards continued to stress to others the importance of the machine guns, calling them a "great factor of strength" and "a vital power."[29]

The division's record in the trenches was mixed. After a couple of weeks in the line, a GHQ inspector wrote a critical report of the division's performance. He claimed some unit commanders had insufficient control of their men; platoon leaders were hard to find; units had poor liaison with those next to them; the trenches were dirty, wet, and insecure; and there was an "absence of initiative, alertness, or activity." He did remark that some units were much better than others and that the artillery was good. Yet, he concluded by writing:

the personnel of the 26th Division may receive some instruction as individuals while in the sector of the XI Army Corps, but they are receiving no training in the sense of teamwork and coordination.... the time spent in this sector as a divided organization is lost insofar as systematic training is concerned.... the command is losing considerably in the way of absorbing habits of sanitary regularity and carelessness as to military activity and morale; and in the suppression of the initiative and organization of positions, and their desire for quiet along the front.[30]

As expected, many found Edwards' leadership to be especially lacking. Malin Craig, Liggett's chief of staff, insisted that during eight days of "continuous inspection of all the units of the Division" by himself and the corps commander, they noticed that Edwards did not once visit any of his units, including his brigade command posts.[31] Liggett was also dissatisfied with Edwards' reaction to various orders regarding the training of staff officers with the French. At one point, Liggett supposedly told Edwards that the "trouble with him was that he never obeyed his orders or made

---

[28] "Summary History of the Twenty Sixth Division," p. 4., n.d., Folder 11.4, Box 6, 26th Division Historical File, RG 120, NA.

[29] See Edwards endorsement to Liggett attached to C.O., 102nd Infantry to C.G., 26th Division, Subject: Report of Machine Gun Instruction, 26th Division, 2 February 1918, Box 22, Edwards Papers, MHS.

[30] GHQ, AEF, Report of Inspection of 26th Division, 27 February 1918, *USAWW*, 3: 600–602.

[31] Confidential Memorandum from Malin Craig to Drum, 8 December 1920, Personal File of H.A. Drum, "Copies of Reports, Letters, etc. of the Twenty-Sixth Division," Box 14, Drum Papers, USAMHI.

his officers obey theirs."[32] Such interactions furthered the impression in the minds of senior officers that Edwards was providing poor leadership in his already suspect Guard division.

Other evidence offers a less gloomy picture. On more than one occasion, American elements drove off small German raids without suffering any significant loss. On 23 February, within three weeks of entering the lines, volunteers from the 101st Infantry took part in a raid of their own, covered by an American rolling barrage, and brought back twenty-four prisoners, including two officers. This may have been the first successful American raid of the war. It is interesting that Pershing's official communiqué of the next day trumpeted this raid, stressing that the "Americans employed rifles exclusively and were commended for their work therewith."[33] Other regiments soon carried out raids of their own. Despite the problems identified by the GHQ inspector, French commanders at many levels were impressed by the division.[34] Even Pershing admitted that although the French corps commander, General Louis de Maud'huy, thought most of the division's senior officers needed more experience (although Traub impressed him a good deal) and that the unit had too many sick soldiers (perhaps a sign of poor discipline), he also "spoke with considerable enthusiasm of the men and officers of the 26th Division ... and especially praised their conduct of trench raids."[35] By mid-March, the division practically held the sector by itself and was prepared to leave the trenches and begin its month of open-warfare training.

The last units of the Yankee Division left the trenches on 21 March, the day that the first German Spring offensive began. By the time the 26th Division had marched to its training area, the German attack had destroyed the British Fifth Army and caused a crisis within the Allied high command. In response, Pershing agreed to send the 26th Division

---

[32] Stackpole Diary, p. 157. Evidence in some unit histories and his own undeniable popularity with the officers and men of the division suggest that Edwards must have spent some time with his troops at the front. However, his visits may have been filled more with glad-handing than professional inspection.

[33] "Extracts from General Pershing's Cabled Communiqués Relating to the Twenty-Sixth Division," n.d., Box 25, Edwards Papers, MHS. The communiqué stated that the American volunteers joined with French infantry in this raid, whereas other sources claimed this was the first of the division's all-American raids.

[34] "Summary History of the Twenty-Sixth Division," p. 4., n.d., Folder 11.4, Box 6, 26th Division Historical File, RG 120, NA; Gen. Capdepont to Edwards, 17 March 1918, Box 22, Edwards Papers, MHS.

[35] Pershing, *My Experiences*, 1: 340; General Maud'huy to Edwards, February 1918, Box 22, Edwards Papers, MHS. During its six weeks in the front lines as part of the French XI Army Corps, the 26th Division suffered 404 casualties.

immediately back into the trenches. He ordered it to head east and relieve the 1st Division, which was then holding a relatively quiet sector of the front on the south face of the St. Mihiel salient. This allowed the Regulars to do a little more open-warfare training before entering an active part of the line. By 3 April, the 26th Division was back in the front trenches, opposing hostile German forces, but this time they were on their own. Although it had not completed the GHQ training plan, it had received nearly all the formal training it was going to get.

Like the other three pioneer AEF divisions, the 26th had trained primarily for trench warfare. It had never engaged in any brigade- or division-wide maneuvers and could not have known much about waging open warfare. Despite Pershing's fear that too much interaction with Allied forces would weaken commitment to "American methods," the 26th Division had done practically all of its training with and under Allied instructors. Although some evidence indicates that it was struggling – the division's movement out of the Chemin des Dames sector was widely criticized as how a relief was *not* to be done – the 26th nevertheless gained an appreciation of the doctrine and methods that Allied forces had painfully learned over the previous three years.[36] The challenge would be to put those ideas and techniques to use while overcoming the internal and external handicaps that were working against it.

Holding the Front Lines, April–June 1918

While the 1st Division ran through another open-warfare maneuver and prepared to enter the front near Cantigny, the Yankee Division settled into muddy trenches that proved to be its new home for the next three months. Due to the need to withdraw other French units to help stop the first two German offensives of 1918, Edwards was forced to spread his units across an 18-kilometer front. Unfortunately, the division not only had to hold this terribly long sector but also had to do so under General Augustin Gerard of the French Eighth Army, who thought little of the latest defense-in-depth tactics and ordered Edwards to pack half of his front-line units into the most forward positions. Edwards protested strongly that Gerard's

---

[36] Although many sources discussed the problems with the 26th Division's move from the Chemin des Dames to replace the 1st Division near Seicheprey, none did so as harshly as Malin Craig. He called the move "the most disgraceful case of mismanagement and inefficiency that I have ever seen in the Army." Confidential Memorandum from Malin Craig to Drum, 8 December 1920, Personal File of H. A. Drum, "Copies of Reports, Letters, etc. of the Twenty-Sixth Division," Box 14, Drum Papers, USAMHI.

orders were unsound and dangerous, but they were not changed.[37] The twin requirements of having to spread the entire division across the long front while keeping whole companies in front-line trenches placed the Yankee Division in a difficult position. Beyond endangering the most forward companies, the policies also reduced the division's opportunity to have some units continue training while others held the front lines, as Bullard did with the 1st Division. During the three months the division spent under such conditions, it experienced a few operational successes and one notable failure but proved unable to develop its combat skills in anything but trench warfare.

Although officially designated as a "quiet" sector, the division's area immediately proved to be active and dangerous. An average of thirteen hundred artillery rounds were fired each day, even when no raids or minor attacks were being made. The division suffered more than two thousand casualties in this sector, even though it never attempted to advance the front lines.[38] Much of this was due to the increased activity of the division itself, as it continued the aggressive patrolling operations carried on by the 1st Division before it.

More than seven hundred of the casualties occurred during two German raids launched during the division's first few weeks in the sector. Between 10 and 13 April, the 104th Infantry joined with French forces on the western flank of the sector in resisting a series of heavy enemy raids. The French corps commander, General Passaga, was so pleased with the American reaction – which yielded no Allied prisoners, caused heavy enemy losses, and actually captured thirty-six German attackers – that he passed out 117 medals, cited the regiment in his general orders, and decorated its colors with the Croix de Guerre – making the 104th Infantry Regiment the first American unit in history to receive foreign decoration.[39] Instead of issuing congratulations and American medals, Pershing sent Colonel Fox Conner to investigate the incident. Conner reported that while the men apparently fought like tigers, the unit's overall handling of

37 Although the 1st Division's service in the line near Seicheprey occurred under the command of General Debeney of the French First Army, an officer more in agreement with the latest tactical developments and much admired by Bullard, changes in command sectors brought the 26th Division under the control of the French Eighth Army. Edwards to General Passaga, 6 April 1918, Box 22, Edwards Papers, MHS; and Millett, *The General*, 355.
38 "Summarized History," Folder 11.4, Box 6, 26th Division Historical File, RG 120, NA.
39 "Summary History of the Twenty-Sixth Division," n.d., p. 5, Folder 11.4, Box 6, 26th Division Historical File, RG 120, NA.

the sporadic fighting and even its overall discipline and organizational efficiency showed much room for improvement.[40]

Of much more consequence for the division was the substantial German raid carried out between 21 and 22 April on the easternmost flank of the sector, near the town of Seicheprey. Five weeks before the 1st Division attack at Cantigny, the fight at Seicheprey was the first major battle of the AEF. Unlike Cantigny, it was only a defensive fight for the AEF, and it was perceived to be a defeat.

In the heavy early-morning fog, twenty-eight hundred German soldiers, led by a number of special stormtroop units, followed a dense artillery barrage, crashed through the most forward American infantry companies, and drove nearly a kilometer into the American lines. The attack thoroughly disrupted communications within the 26th Division, forcing Traub and Edwards to struggle throughout the day and following night to develop a coherent counterattack while operating in a haze of confusion and ignorance. The counterattack was delayed, then summarily canceled by the attacking battalion commander who thought his force was not ready. By the time American troops advanced the next morning, the Germans were gone.[41]

The 26th Division suffered more than 650 casualties, including about 180 prisoners, making it the costliest American engagement of the war thus far.[42] Although Edwards insisted the Germans suffered worse (they later admitted to six hundred losses), GHQ was not convinced. It treated the event as an embarrassing defeat and sent inspectors to discover what went wrong. As during the previous raid, communications proved a weak spot, especially at the company and battalion echelons; the infantry failed to adequately prepare its positions for defense and did not maintain liaison with the French on the right; and the artillery reaction was somewhat slow. For those looking for evidence of problems within the division, the fight at Seicheprey seemed to offer sufficient material.

But, for those who looked closer, there was much to the Yankee Division's credit. Again, all indications were that the men fought bravely and generally well. If the artillery was late in starting and often out of touch with the infantry battalions, it maintained good communications with

[40] *USAWW*, 3: 611–12.

[41] For a narrative account, see Coffman, *War to End All Wars*, 148–9; Taylor, *New England in France*, 121–31.

[42] The breakdown of the American losses was 80 killed, 195 wounded, 216 gassed, and about 190 missing. "Casualties on Dates of April 20th and April 21st," n.d., Box 22, Edwards Papers, MHS. For Edwards' report, see *USAWW*, 3: 613.

higher infantry commands and made up for its tardiness by firing some twenty-five thousand rounds in the 24-hour period.[43] Even Pershing's inspector admitted these points and stressed that certain company and battalion officers seemed to have done a superb job against a vastly superior enemy. The inspector emphasized, as did General Passaga, that the German attack was "carefully planned and well executed" and that the division probably did well to inflict as many casualties on the attackers as it did.[44] Liggett, who at first thought the fight a disaster, later conceded to Edwards that "after talking with you and with Gen. Passaga...the 26th did well all around."[45]

The remaining months in the line saw nothing as sensational as the Seicheprey fight, but the division did repel a number of smaller German raids while successfully carrying out at least one raid itself. This raid, of three hundred volunteers from the 101st Infantry, was well organized and thoroughly supported by machine guns, engineer troops, aircraft, and all the divisional artillery, which fired heavy rolling and box barrages.[46] The raid was successful enough to earn a response from the army commander, General Gerard, who congratulated the division on an operation "as well planned as it was energetically conducted."[47]

When the division left the sector at the end of June, it went with a record and reputation as mixed as those it brought in. Inspectors identified problems in the division's organization, discipline, administration, and coordination.[48] Senior AEF commanders and staff officers continued to distrust and dislike Edwards. And, regardless of the stiff resistance of its

---

[43] The 102nd F.A. alone fired nearly fourteen thousand rounds. C.O., 102nd F.A. to C.G., 26th Division, Subject: Report of Action, April 20–21, 1918, 26 April 1918, Folder 33.6 Box 25, 26th Division Historical File, RG 120, NA; Taylor, *New England in France*, 131.

[44] Stackpole Diary, p. 75. See also Memorandum for Assistant Chief of Staff, G-3, Subject: Report on 26th Division Affair of April 20th, 24 April 1918, Box 14, Edwards Papers, MHS.

[45] Liggett to Edwards, 24 April 1918, Box 22, Edwards Papers, MHS. These assessments eventually received more support from German documents supposedly captured after the St. Mihiel attack in September. In those documents, German officers admitted that although their forces gained all objectives in the raid, the resistance met and the losses suffered were "far in excess of anything that he had expected, and he was obliged to look upon the operation as a failure." "History of the 51st Infantry Brigade," n.d., p. 6, 26th Division Boxes, World War I Survey Collection, USAMHI.

[46] HQ 26th Division, Field Orders No. 38, 28 May 1918, Folder 32.1, Box 13, 26th Division Historical File, RG 120, NA.

[47] Gerard to Edwards, 8 June 1918, Box 22, Edwards Papers, MHS.

[48] Even the division staff admitted that the units still demonstrated poor sanitation, sloppy care of weapons and supplies, and little improvement of the defensive positions. See HQ 26th Division, Bulletin No. 105, 6 May 1918, Box 22, Edwards Papers, MHS.

men during the Seicheprey attack, the division had suffered severely in a supposedly "quiet" sector. However, its actual operational record showed that the division had done fairly well in a long, hard, inglorious tour in an increasingly active sector. Although some in the AEF may have been displeased with the 26th, the French seemed satisfied. Gerard sent the division off with high compliments for its stiff resistance of the numerous German raids, and Passaga issued general orders praising the division for its "splendid" performance throughout the tour at the front.[49] Of course, all of the mistakes and the successes had been made under trench-warfare conditions. Although the officers of the division hoped the unit was heading back to a training area to rest, refit, and continue where its training left off, GHQ ordered it to move directly from the supposedly quiet sector near Seicheprey to relieve the worn-out 2nd Division in its undeniably active sector near Belleau Wood.

The Aisne-Marne Offensive, 18–25 July 1918

The 26th Division moved out of the Seicheprey sector on 28 June and immediately headed west toward Château-Thierry. By 10 July, it had relieved the 2nd Division and was holding the dangerous *Pas Fini* sector. Although it became a part of General Degoutte's French Sixth Army, it finally entered an operational American corps – Liggett's I Corps – holding the sector with the 167th French Division on the left and the Yankee Division on the right. If the division's officers were glad to be in an American corps, the I Corps staff was not happy to again deal with the 26th because it reported continued evidence of sloppiness and poor discipline. Malin Craig claimed that while entering the front lines, the men "openly and continuously violated" orders against daylight movement and that Edwards did not set up his command post where the corps directed.[50] It was the start of a rocky campaign, in which the Yankee Division's mistakes and weaknesses were magnified and its accomplishments and adaptations diminished.

After four days of typical sector duty, without the benefit of any deep trenches or good dugouts along the lengthy 10-kilometer division front,

[49] French XXXII Army Corps, General Orders, 27 June 1918, Box 22, Edwards Papers, MHS; French Eighth Army, Service Memorandum, 17 June 1918, Box 22, Edwards Papers, MHS.
[50] Confidential Memorandum from Malin Craig to Drum, 8 December 1920, Personal File of H. A. Drum, "Copies of Reports, Letters, etc. of the Twenty-Sixth Division," Box 14, Drum Papers, USAMHI.

the division fought off attacks made in support of the German Army's final offensive of the war between 15 and 17 July. This success resulted in large part from the tremendous depth of the American defensive position, which extended back many kilometers. Nevertheless, during the first week in the sector, the division suffered more than one thousand casualties. These losses, when added to those from the Seicheprey sector and the lack of replacements, meant that the Yankee Division entered its first major offensive significantly under-strength in its infantry and machine-gun units and tired from five months of nearly uninterrupted duty in the front lines.

On the afternoon of 17 July, Liggett called Edwards to his command post and announced that the corps was to attack the following morning as part of Foch's giant Aisne-Marne Offensive. During the conference, Liggett's aide suspected that Edwards "did not seem to grasp his responsibilities in the matter or to have a clear idea of his mission." An anxious Edwards probed Liggett "for advice and suggestions," and the corps commander told him only "not to crowd men too much in the front line . . . and not to let the attack run away beyond the objective."[51]

The official corps attack order arrived at Edwards' HQ at 2215 hours, and it directed an attack by only Cole's 52nd Brigade at 0435 the next morning. Although the Yankee infantry was to jump-off at the same minute as the 1st and 2nd Divisions to the north near Soissons, it had an entirely different mission. While the Regular divisions in Mangin's Tenth Army were to break through the enemy line, the 52nd Brigade, on the far southern flank of the main offensive, was only to make a limited advance of about 2 kilometers (see Map 12). Liggett directed that it strictly regulate its progress to that of the French 167th Division, ordered to advance on its left.[52]

Edwards' attack plan, issued just after midnight, stressed the need to keep abreast of the French to the left. In accordance with army and corps orders, no preliminary artillery fire was allowed, but Edwards did direct the artillery brigade – now commanded by Brigadier General Dwight W. Aultman – to fire a strong rolling barrage in front of the attacking infantry. Although only one infantry brigade attacked, elements from all three artillery regiments were to support the assault, a decision necessitated

[51] Stackpole Diary, p. 146.
[52] HQ 26th Division, "Report of Operations," 7 August 1918, Folder 33.6, Box 25, 26th Division Historical File, RG 120, NA; HQ I Army Corps, Field Orders No. 9, 17 July 1918, Folder 32.1, Box 15, I Army Corps Historical File, RG 120, NA.

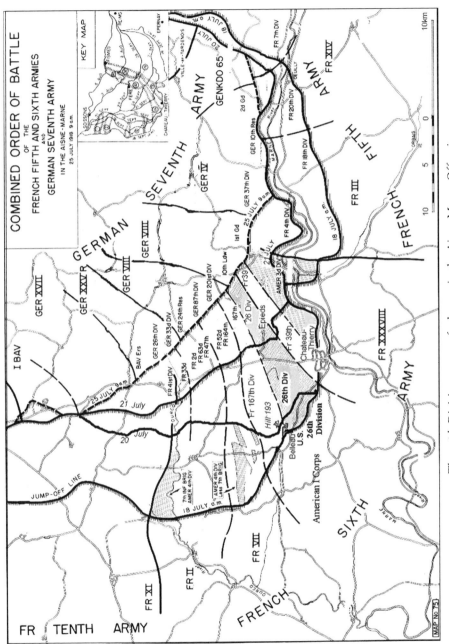

MAP 12: The 26th Division sector of advance in the Aisne-Marne Offensive.

by the lack of any divisional artillery augmentation, except one battery of 220mm trench mortars.[53] Of more significance, Edwards carried through on his plan to support his attacking infantry with heavy machine-gun fire. While some machine-gun teams were to advance with the attacking infantry, others – including some from the 51st Brigade on the right of the sector – were to fire supporting barrages during the attack. This was an important tactical development, one many AEF divisions would not make use of until September and October.[54]

Although the 26th had been in the sector for days, fully expecting to eventually make an attack, it proved unprepared to deliver the assault on time. Only one of its three attacking infantry battalions was able to jump-off at 0435 hours. Although that unit successfully advanced behind what the commander called "a perfect barrage" and seized its objective by 0540, even it had to advance without special tools, supplies, and its supporting machine-gun teams, which did not hit the jump-off line on time. Many of the troops even lacked full canteens of water.[55] The other battalions did not reach the jump-off line before H hour and they missed the barrage.

Although the disorganization in the attacking brigade shows the unit's organizational problems, the reaction of the regimental and brigade commanders to these initial problems proved the extent to which they appreciated the need for firepower to cover the attack. Whereas some commanders in similar situations simply ordered late-arriving troops to immediately attack and try to "catch up" to the barrage, Cole asked his regimental commanders when the battalions would be ready to attack, then arranged for the supporting artillery and machine guns to refire their barrages at the second start time. Eventually, some 3 hours after the original H hour, the other two battalions advanced and took their objectives without difficulty.[56]

One battalion demonstrated its enthusiasm, and its lack of discipline, by chasing a number of enemy troops up Hill 193, an elevation in the

---

[53] For some reason, most of the artillery orders and fire plans throughout this first major offensive are no longer in the division records. Nevertheless, the general nature of the artillery support, as well as some details, can be reconstructed from the division field orders and the operation reports from the infantry and artillery units.

[54] HQ 26th Division, Field Orders No. 51, 18 July 1918, 0030 hours, Folder 32.1, Box 13, 26th Division Historical File, RG 120, NA.

[55] "Report of the Part Taken by the 3rd Bn. 103 Inf. in the Action of 18–24 July Incl.," n.d. Folder 33.6, Box 47, 26th Division Historical File, RG 120, NA.

[56] C.G., 52nd Infantry Brigade to C.G., 26th Division, "Report of action taken by this Brigade from 18–24 July '18," 3 August 1918, Folder 33.6, Box 37, 26th Division Historical File, RG 120, NA.

French sector to the north. When local commanders realized where they were, they withdrew, leaving the important hill – then weakly defended – in German hands. That hill was one of the main objectives of the French 167th Division that day, and the Frenchmen failed to take it. That evening, the enemy fire from Hill 193 was so intense that one Yankee battalion actually withdrew from its new line – another sign of poor discipline, respect for firepower, or both.[57] Casualties were not severe, but commanders reported that they were heavier than necessary because the men bunched up too much. Nevertheless, the division had taken its objectives and kept abreast of the French on the left. That day, Malin Craig reported to GHQ "everything lovely," and General Degoutte visited Liggett to thank him for "the successful performances of the Americans engaged."[58] Despite the difficulties, the Yankee Division's first real attack had to be considered a modest success.

That night, Liggett ordered the attacks to continue at 0400 the next morning, again with "particular attention being paid to regulating the advance of each unit by the progress of the unit on its left."[59] Edwards issued his own orders, this time to both brigades, laying out a series of three "successive objectives" and directing that "the advance will be made from objective to objective, with brigades side by side." The orders warned units to stop and reorganize on each objective, using great care to "keep the troops well in hand."[60] Both the corps and division orders describe an attack limited in objective and more in line with prevailing trench- than open-warfare ideals. Again lacking artillery augmentation, Edwards arranged for each light-gun regiment to support one infantry brigade and for the howitzers to spread their fire over both brigade attack sectors. However, because the French 167th proved unable to take Hill 193 at any time on 19 July, Edwards' units simply held their lines throughout the day to stay in line.

At 1120 on 20 July, Liggett ordered both his divisions to attack at 1500 hours that afternoon. The 26th Division was to take a first objective about 2 kilometers to the front, then push on to a second objective about

---

[57] Cole insisted that had the objective not been limited, his battalion could have taken all of Hill 193 that day. Ibid.

[58] Stackpole Diary, p. 147.

[59] HQ I Army Corps, Field Orders No. 11, 18 July 1918, 2240 hours, Folder 32.1, Box 15, I Army Corps Historical File, RG 120, NA.

[60] HQ 26th Division, Field Orders No. 52, 18 July 1918, 1600 hours, Folder 32.1, Box 13, 26th Division Historical File, RG 120, NA; HQ 26th Division, Field Orders No. 53, 19 July 1918, 0030 hours, Folder 32.1, Box 13, 26th Division Historical File, RG 120, NA.

3 kilometers farther. The corps artillery preparation was to begin at 1330
hours to soften up the enemy defenses and knock out enemy artillery.
Edwards issued his attack plan at 1400 hours, simply calling for both
brigades to attack and for the artillery to carry out a prearranged fire
plan that incorporated a period of preliminary fire and then a rolling
barrage that advanced at the extraordinary rate of about 100 meters every
2 minutes. Unlike in the first attack, no machine-gun barrage was specified
in the division orders. However, both brigade commanders incorporated
overhead machine-gun barrages into their attack plans. As before, the
division was to advance in line with the units on its flanks.[61]

Despite the artillery preparation and the covering artillery and
machine-gun barrages, the attacks that afternoon met heavy resistance.
Losses were heavy. Although the units in the center took the first objectives, aided by strong supporting fire from their machine guns and 37mm
pieces, those on the flanks struggled to advance and could not hold the
positions they took. Both flanks ran into galling fire from adjacent sectors,
as the 167th Division again failed to take Hill 193 on the left, while the
French 39th Division did not advance at all on the right. Some units struggled as they advanced straight through dense woods, even though Liggett
had warned Edwards to send his men around them. One report claimed
that Edwards sent his men into the woods because he did not want to make
them march any more than necessary, further confirmation to the corps
staff that Edwards babied his men and was a poor tactician as well.[62]

There were other reasons for the limited gains of that day. Tactically,
the troops attempted to move forward in the standard linear waves regularly used on the training ground. Often, this led not only to heavy
casualties in the ranks but also to the loss of the junior officers and NCOs

[61] The length of the artillery preparation before this attack remains unclear. The division
field orders directed the artillery fire to begin at 1330 hours, in accordance with corps
orders, but because the division plan was not published until 1400 hours, this probably
did not happen. Cole reported an hour of preliminary fire, whereas Shelton, on the right,
reported just 15 minutes. HQ 26th Division, Field Orders No. 55, 20 July 1918, 1400
hours, Folder 32.1, Box 13, 26th Division Historical File, RG 120, NA; HQ I Army
Corps, Field Orders No. 15, 20 July 1918, 1120 hours, Folder 32.1, Box 15, I Army
Corps Historical File, RG 120, NA.
[62] Cole insisted his northern regiment actually gained all its objectives that day but could
not retain them due to the lack of the French 167th Division to advance on the left. Other
sources suggest the 104th Infantry hardly advanced at all. Either way, the troops ended
the day where they began. C.G., 52nd Infantry Brigade to C.G., 26th Division, "Report
of action taken by this Brigade from 18–24 July '18," 3 August 1918, Folder 33.6, Box
37, 26th Division Historical File, RG 120, NA; Stackpole Diary, p. 151; ABMC, *26th
Division Summary of Operations in the World War* (Washington, D.C.: GPO, 1944), 14.

that held the small units together. Lieutenant Russell A. Harmon, of the 104th Infantry, later reported that "men everywhere were falling so fast, that I saw immediately that the smooth line always taught for waves in advancing was affording a beautiful target." Harmon reported that he quickly "forged well into the front wave and broke up the alignment and made the wave a rugged filtering echelon, after which my losses depreciated more than was expected."[63] Lieutenant W. E. Barnett, of the same regiment, identified the same problem, and he also shifted from "wave formation" to a system of "short rushes of a few yards at a time, lying down flat in between rushes."[64] In those units that lost their leaders early on, attacks generally broke down before the changes in formation could take effect. Even when the changes were made, the damage had already been done; Lieutenant Barnett noticed that his platoon lost thirty of its forty-two men in its initial advance. He also reported that the tactical changes, so necessary for saving lives, complicated troop control and led to a breakdown in lateral liaison.[65]

Many company and battalion commanders reported that liaison and communications were breaking down all over, particularly in the 52nd Brigade. Even before the attack of 20 July, many small-unit leaders were not given maps, clear objectives, or time to prepare the assault. During the attacks, they had trouble communicating with each other, with senior commanders, and with the artillery. Apparently, commanders relied exclusively on runners, and they died in droves. Midway through the attack, senior commanders lost control of their units, which limited their use of artillery due to the fear of shooting into the leading ranks. On the right of the sector, Brigadier General Shelton, who replaced Traub on the eve of the battle, made the only decision that seemed to offer any chance of success; after the advance had broken down completely, he ordered his troops to dig in while he arranged for artillery fire to shell the enemy lines, not just immediately before the next attack, but throughout the entire night.[66]

---

[63] "Report of 2nd Lt. Russell A. Harmon, Comdg. Co. A, 104th Inf., Operations July 20 to July 25, 1918," Folder 33.6, Box 52, 26th Division Historical File, RG 120, NA.

[64] "Report of 1st Lt. W.E. Barnett, Comdg. 4th Platoon, Co. B, 104th Inf., Operations of period from July 18 to July 25, 1918," Folder 33.6, Box 52, 26th Division Historical File, RG 120, NA.

[65] Ibid.

[66] "Report of Brigadier General George H. Shelton, Comdg., 51st Inf. Brig. Operation of Period 18 July to 25 July 1918," 6 August 1918, Folder 33.6, Box 35, 26th Division Historical File, RG 120, NA.

Convinced that the Germans were making a rapid withdrawal from the Marne and only covering their retreat with a weak rear guard, senior Allied commanders were displeased with the slowness of the attack, particularly with that of the Yankee Division. During visits to Edwards' HQ, Liggett learned that his division commander could not tell him exactly where the infantry units were or how far they had gone. Edwards complained that he had suffered thousands of losses and that his boys "were all tired out." When Degoutte visited Liggett, even he "showed much disappointment at the failure of the 26th to get its objective."[67] Neither of the senior commanders appeared convinced that insufficient artillery augmentation or the lack of progress by the adjacent French divisions was a sufficient excuse for the short advance.

They therefore ordered attacks to continue at daylight the next morning. Despite the evidence of stronger than expected resistance that day, the orders directed that the attack shift into more of a pursuit. It is significant that this was the first corps plan that gave any hint of open-warfare sentiment. Each division was to race forward as fast as possible, without waiting for the advance of adjacent divisions. The attack was to "push forward at all costs" and reach a line about 5 to 7 kilometers ahead.[68] While Edwards' orders confirmed the sense of urgency in the corps orders and the need for the division to press forward regardless of the advances by neighboring divisions, he reaffirmed prior instructions that his infantry were to advance on a step-by-step basis, successively from objective to objective, maintaining close internal liaison. Of greater significance, his field orders included no discussion of the fire-support arrangements except the standard note that each brigade would be supported by one regiment of 75mm guns and about half of the 155s.[69]

Whatever the specific fire-support arrangements may have been, they were not used because the German rear guard pulled out that night. At dawn the next morning, the infantry found no significant enemy resistance and both brigades advanced rapidly, passing the Soissons to Château-Thierry highway some 6 kilometers away by noon. Optimistically, Degoutte and Liggett determined to harry the enemy withdrawal for at least another 12 kilometers.

---

[67] Stackpole Diary, pp. 151–2.

[68] HQ I Army Corps, Field Orders No. 17, 20 July, 2000 hours, and Field Orders No. 18, 20 July, 2330 hours, both in Folder 32.1, Box 15, I Army Corps Historical File, RG 120, NA.

[69] HQ 26th Division, Field Orders No. 57, 21 July 1918, 0315 hours, Folder 32.1, Box 13, 26th Division Historical File, RG 120, NA.

But, just as the senior commanders were raising their expectations that afternoon, the leading troops began to meet enemy fire near the towns of Trugny and Epieds. Colonel Parker, the regimental commander of the 102nd Infantry, raced ahead of his troops to make a personal reconnaissance of the enemy rear guard, and what he found was discouraging. He saw not a simple rear guard but rather a real enemy line of defense called the *Berta* Line (i.e., one of four such lines between the Marne and Aisne Rivers). Further investigation by "strong patrols" proved "the extent and character" of the enemy line and, that evening, Parker sent back word warning that a "strong artillery preparation" was absolutely necessary before making any further attacks.[70] Unfortunately, Edwards had just received a call from the corps HQ directing that the attack continue throughout the night and gain a line more than 10 kilometers farther by daylight.[71] Edwards issued orders claiming "the moment for the supreme test has arrived" and directing the attack to be pushed "without delay and cessation."[72] Attacks were attempted, apparently without any significant artillery support whatsoever. Although some units made it into Epieds, they were forced back in the early evening.

The evening attacks failed because they were uncoordinated with each other and unsupported by the divisional artillery. Both problems were the result of the continued breakdown in liaison and communication during the day's deep advance. Artillery commanders chaffed at not being able to support their infantry. Aultman reported "great difficulty . . . in giving immediate support to the Infantry, due to the lack of information as to the exact location of our own lines."[73] But, the disorganization within the division went beyond mere communications and impacted troop control. One staff officer who visited the front of Cole's brigade reported to Liggett that "the confusion in the 52nd Brigade was hopeless," with "stragglers and trophy hunters all over the place."[74] After four days of battle and an advance of about 10 kilometers, elements of the division, especially in the 52nd Brigade, were coming apart.

---

[70] "Report of Colonel John H. Parker, 102nd Infantry," 4 August 1918, Folder 33.6, Box 44, 26th Division Historical File, RG 120, NA.

[71] HQ 26th Division, "Report of Operations," 7 August 1918, Folder 33.6, Box 25, 26th Division Historical File, RG 120, NA.

[72] HQ 26th Division, Field Orders No. 58, 21 July 1918, 1725 hours, Folder 32.1, Box 13, 26th Division Historical File, RG 120, NA.

[73] C.G. 51st F.A. Brigade to C.G. 26th Division, Subject: Report of Operations from July 18th to August 4th, 1918, 7 August 1918, Folder 33.6, Box 59, 26th Division Historical File, RG 120, NA.

[74] Stackpole Diary, p. 153.

Despite these signs of trouble, Liggett issued orders at 2240 hours that were sure to make matters worse. Apparently unaware of the strong resistance then facing the leading infantry, he declared that the enemy was retiring "all along the front." He admonished each unit to press the attack "without cessation" throughout the night in order to "make the enemy's retreat a rout." Cavalry was being sent forward in the hope that it could "at the proper time . . . intercept and disorganize the enemy's communications." These orders, clearly based on the spirit of the U.S. Army's aggressive prewar doctrine, demonstrated how out of touch the senior command and staffs were with the realities of the battle. Liggett further complicated events when he ordered that after the all-night attacks, the 52nd Brigade was to slide to the left and take over the sector of the worn-out French 167th Division. The 51st Brigade was to take over the entire sector of the 26th Division. Both American brigades were then to immediately resume the attack.[75] The corps sector was narrowing considerably, and the small 167th Division (with about a third of the infantry in an AEF division) surely needed relief, but Liggett's demand that this maneuver be made at dawn, after an all-night attack during which the divisions were to advance without concern for lateral liaison, seems stunningly unwise.

As one might have expected, these orders led to considerable confusion. Edwards' staff successfully passed the word along to Shelton, who quickly shifted troops to his left to take over the entire division sector before pressing a dawn attack. But, by the time Cole got the word, his brigade was already carrying out an early-morning attack from his existing sector. Units became intermingled. Edwards quickly informed Liggett of the confusion, and the latter then canceled the sector changes.

Despite all this confusion, both American brigades attacked the *Berta* Line that morning but with weak artillery support. Aided by machine-gun barrages, some troops passed Trugny and entered Epieds, but almost all withdrew due to enemy fire and the desire to arrange "further artillery preparation."[76] A second attempt was made at 1500 hours, and one young officer reported that he had received "ample assurance that the machine guns previously encountered in the morning had been wiped

75 HQ I Army Corps, Field Orders No. 19, 21 July 1918, 2240 hours, Folder 32.1, Box 15, I Army Corps Historical File, RG 120, NA.

76 HQ 26th Division, "Report of Operations," 7 August 1918, Folder 33.6, Box 25, 26th Division Historical File, RG 120, NA.

out."[77] However, any such assurance was wishful thinking. The hastily arranged shelling and thin rolling barrages from such guns as were available did not neutralize the resistance. Although a few gains were held on the far right thanks to some courageous flanking maneuvers around the more isolated enemy strong points, little headway was made on the left. Apparently, some kind of more organized effort was necessary.

That afternoon, Edwards convinced Liggett to try a different kind of attack.[78] Instead of a general advance along the entire corps front, each division was to pick just one regiment to attack after an intense 10-minute artillery preparation and behind a rolling barrage concentrated on the narrow front. This regiment was to penetrate what Liggett hoped to be a "shell of resistance" and then "spread out to the right and left, taking the remaining portions of the enemy line in flank and reverse."[79] Other divisional units were to support this penetration on its flanks. The only limit on the maneuver was that each regiment was ordered to stay within its own divisional sector. Edwards ordered Colonel Edward L. Logan's 101st Infantry, in the right sector, to carry out the attack, and he ordered Aultman to "immediately form a plan of action for the artillery" that gave special attention to the town of Epieds and the woods immediately south of it. Also, 10 minutes before the attack, his gunners were to "lay a violent fire of destruction" on the zone of attack.[80]

Throughout the night, Aultman's guns fired on the enemy lines and then following what Edwards called a "thorough artillery preparation,"

---

[77] "Report of 1st Lt. Howard W. Robbins, 1st Battalion, 104th Inf., Operations of Period July 18 to July 25, 1918," Folder 33.6, Box 52, 26th Division Historical File, RG 120, NA.

[78] Edwards insinuated in his operations report that this operational idea was his brainchild, and Taylor's divisional history, written by a division operations officer, clearly credits Edwards for the new approach. Edwards reported to Liggett, "Our experience in the rush forward had shown the futility, without undue losses, of attempting a head-on attack of Epieds and Trugny. . . . I therefore determined to throw a wedge on the road through the Bois de Trugny." See HQ 26th Division, "Report of Operations," 7 August 1918, Folder 33.6, Box 25, 26th Division Historical File, RG 120, NA; and Taylor, *New England in France*, 195–6.

[79] Liggett may have tried a new tactic, but he still maintained the hope of decisive results: "It should be impressed upon all officers and soldiers that a wonderful opportunity for inflicting a crushing defeat on the enemy of four years standing lies before us and can be secured by the aggressive action which the united spirit of the Allies expects of every soldier of liberty." HQ I Army Corps, Field Orders No. 20, 22 July 1918, 1945 hours, Folder 32.1, Box 15, I Army Corps Historical File, RG 120, NA.

[80] HQ 26th Division, Field Orders No. 59, 22 July 1918, 2250 hours, Folder 32.1, Box 13, 26th Division Historical File, RG 120, NA.

the 101st Infantry surged forward.[81] It gained more than a kilometer that morning before being stopped by enemy fire. It held that forward line into the afternoon, then decided to withdraw to allow more artillery support. The *Berta* Line may not have been as strong as the famous *Kriemhilde Stellung* of the Meuse-Argonne, but it proved much thicker than a "shell of resistance."

Another reason for the limited success of the attack was the failure of the other regiments to join the fight. They were exhausted, depleted, and thoroughly disorganized. They desperately wanted to be relieved. When Liggett visited various brigade and regimental headquarters, he saw demoralized commanders who were obviously disturbed by the high casualty rates.[82] They were also upset at the lack of support for their troops. One regimental commander angrily "urged artillery aid on machine guns," and Aultman told Liggett it was "useless to put men up against machines." He insisted that "machine-gun nests must be destroyed by guns."[83] These assertions warned Liggett that the division was not just physically exhausted and organizationally disorganized but was becoming doctrinally heretical as well. Liggett responded by reiterating the importance of having infantry use flanking rather than direct attacks on machine guns. The Yankee commanders probably thought Liggett missed their point – that certain enemy positions simply could not be taken by infantry maneuvers but rather needed to be deluged with firepower.

That night, Liggett ordered the 52nd Brigade to be relieved by the 58th Brigade of the 28th Division. Edwards was to use the fresh brigade, as well as his own 51st Brigade, in a new attack at 0405 hours the next morning. Shortly after learning of the attack, Edwards called Liggett to ask "permission to postpone the attack for more artillery preparation." Liggett denied the request, claiming that nothing he had seen in his visit to the front convinced him to modify his conclusions regarding the proper approach to overcoming machine guns.[84]

---

[81] HQ 26th Division, "Report of Operations," 7 August 1918, Folder 33.6, Box 25, 26th Division Historical File, RG 120, NA.

[82] HQ I Army Corps to C.G., First Army, AEF, 2 August 1918, Box 29, Edwards Papers, MHS.

[83] Stackpole Diary, p. 155.

[84] It is fair to note that although Liggett's order for this attack called for only a 10-minute preliminary bombardment, other aspects of the order show a marked increase in the emphasis on artillery support. The order directed the 26th Division to "concentrate and use all" of its "available artillery." The division was to cover the infantry advance with a "normal barrage" and push some individual 75mm guns forward to knock out

Despite Liggett's continued faith in infantry tactics, commanders in the 26th Division attempted to make a more substantial use of artillery. Before learning of his brigade's relief, Cole arranged for a 3-hour-long preparation prior to the attack he expected to make the next morning, and Shelton made similar plans for his brigade. Aultman later reported that the division finally was able to develop a "formal artillery plan" for the expected attack on the morning of 24 July.[85]

However, early the next morning before the attack began, word arrived that the German troops to the front had withdrawn. As on 21 July, the infantry were ordered forward to catch up with the enemy, and resistance was so light that Edwards ordered his motorized machine-gun battalion to drive forward in its cars to regain contact. Troops from both the 58th and 51st Brigades advanced for nearly 9 kilometers before meeting significant enemy fire in front of the next prepared German withdrawal position, called the *Caesar* Line.[86]

Again, just as the troops were running into serious resistance, army and corps commanders were dreaming of even bigger gains. Liggett ordered the attack to continue through the night and demanded that the infantry push past the town of Sergy by 0200 on 25 July.[87] That meant an advance of about 10 kilometers beyond the *Caesar* Line. Although the orders were passed along by Edwards, no major effort was made to assault the new German line by the worn-out troops. They dug in that night and were relieved by the American 42nd Division the following day.

During its fifteen-day service in the I Corps, the Yankee Division suffered a total of 4,857 casualties and had an additional 1,200 men

machine-gun nests. It also stated that "the Corps Artillery will assist the attack and will use every available piece of artillery for this purpose." If nothing else, the tone was markedly different. HQ I Army Corps, Field Orders No. 22, 23 July, 1900 hours, Folder 32.1, Box 15, I Army Corps Historical File, RG 120, NA; Stackpole Diary, p. 156.

[85] C.G. 51st F.A. Brigade to C.G. 26th Division, Subject: Report of Operations from July 18th to August 4th, 1918, 7 August 1918, Folder 33.6, Box 59, 26th Division Historical File, RG 120, NA. See also C.G., 52nd Infantry Brigade to C.G., 26th Division, "Report of action taken by this Brigade from 18–24 July '18," 3 August 1918, Folder 33.6, Box 37, 26th Division Historical File, RG 120, NA.

[86] For the men of the 56th Brigade, under Maj. Gen. William Weigel, this was a campaign of great endurance. They marched constantly for two days and nights just to get to the 26th Division's front lines, without any food except for their emergency rations, which had been consumed early in the movement. Under such conditions, the men began the day's attack. HQ 26th Division, "Report of Operations," 7 August 1918, Folder 33.6, Box 25, 26th Division, RG 120, NA.

[87] HQ I Army Corps, Field Orders No. 24, 24 July 1918, Folder 32.1, Box 15, I Army Corps Historical File, RG 120, NA.

evacuated for illness or exhaustion.[88] At that price, it advanced about 18 kilometers but captured just 250 prisoners, three field pieces, and three large mortars.[89] Although Edwards seemed proud of his division's accomplishments, others were not. Liggett and the corps staff criticized the disorganization, lack of liaison, and unnecessary losses. They even accused Cole's brigade of getting "lost" for days during the advance. Too often, the undisciplined infantry made unauthorized withdrawals from forward objectives due to enemy fire. Malin Craig thought the 26th performed "very badly" and others suggested it was time to relieve some of the division's senior officers.[90] Although most of the criticism was accurate, some of it applied equally to the attacks of the 1st and 2nd Divisions to the north, each of which suffered heavier losses than the Yankee Division.

Despite all the division's troubles, it had done reasonably well for a unit in its first major attack. Unlike the 1st and 2nd Divisions, the 26th never received any large-scale maneuver training before this battle, so this was the first time the officers had to advance, maintain liaison, communicate, and fight all at the same time. The division started on a huge 10-kilometer front and had to make a number of difficult direction changes as it advanced through a sector that shrank to a width of less than 2 kilometers. Often, its neighbors failed to advance as ordered and for the first half of the battle, the division was ordered to stay in line with them. The I Corps often directed difficult if not impossible advances and maneuvers and twice attempted to change the sector assignments before revoking the orders. Tactically, the division had problems similar to those of the 1st and 2nd Divisions near Soissons – infantry advanced in long lines or bunched together, machine-gun nests were rushed rather than outflanked, and units failed to maintain coordinated attacks and had great difficulty arranging adequate artillery support. But, it had also shown a willingness and an ability to use massed machine-gun fire to support infantry attacks and even to employ "accompanying batteries" of light artillery – tactics

---

[88] The 56th Brigade, serving in the 26th Division for about two days, also suffered 149 casualties. The numbers of killed and wounded represented more than 17 percent of the division's authorized strength. Counting those sick, the division lost more than 21 percent of its authorized strength, and the casualty rates in some infantry regiments approached 50 percent. ABMC, *American Armies*, 103.

[89] Taylor claimed the division captured twenty-one guns and seven *minnenwerfers*, but I could find no documentary substantiation of those figures. The totals cited come from Edwards' operations report. Taylor, *New England in France*, 208.

[90] Confidential Memorandum from Malin Craig to Drum, 8 December 1920, Personal File of H.A. Drum, "Copies of Reports, Letters, etc. of the Twenty-Sixth Division," Box 14, Drum Papers, USAMHI.

conspicuously absent in the attacks of the more highly regarded Regular divisions near Soissons.[91]

Commanders throughout the Yankee Division knew that they and their men made too many mistakes that cost lives and that improvements needed to be made. Despite his poor reputation throughout the AEF, Edwards' operations report on the Aisne-Marne Offensive demonstrated an impressive awareness of his division's problems and the possible solutions. Edwards reported that "the greatest difficulty" in gaining objectives was overcoming "the cleverly and ingeniously placed machine-gun nests." Edwards' solution was that "whenever time will allow," small "specifically developed" reconnaissance teams were to advance and locate the enemy guns. Then, instead of simply insisting it was the job of "self-reliant infantry" to neutralize the machine guns, Edwards suggested that "the 155's are the best agency" to knock them out. Another "excellent" option "to destroy and neutralize these nests" was the heavy Newton–Stokes trench mortars of the artillery brigade. The third option was – not surprisingly for Edwards – a resort to one's own heavy machine guns, which could saturate the enemy area "from 3,000 yards with a hail" of bullets. He then offered the necessary disclaimer that "it goes without saying that wherever possible machine guns must be flanked out by infiltration from both sides," and he claimed that "this method was constantly used by battalion and regimental commanders."[92]

Edwards was rightly concerned about the amount of firepower his infantry could immediately bring to bear on the enemy, and he was especially dissatisfied with the automatic rifle that the AEF provided his men. He reported that the losses suffered by his Chauchat men were "abnormal" and he warned that the weapon "since this battle, is an unpopular arm...due to the excessive casualties."[93] Edwards knew his

[91] Aultman reported that the accompanying batteries were not successful when pushed too far forward and used in close-up, direct-fire missions. Better results were achieved when the pieces were used from a range of about 2,000 meters and controlled with forward observation. C.G. 51st F.A. Brigade to C.G. 26th Division, Subject: Report of Operations from July 18th to August 4th, 1918, 7 August 1918, Folder 33.6, Box 59, 26th Division Historical File, RG 120, NA.

[92] Edwards reminded his readers that his divisional trench mortar battery did not receive its large 6-inch Newton–Stokes mortars until after the battle, but he was sure they would be useful in the future. HQ 26th Division, "Report of Operations," 7 August 1918, Folder 33.6, Box 25, 26th Division, RG 120, NA.

[93] Edwards thought the reason for the high casualty rates among the Chauchat men were due to the need to use it at close range, the need for the barrel to be polished into a gleaming silver condition in order to keep it working, and the German soldier's emphasis on knocking out the weapon.

men also disliked the weapon because it had a short range, was relatively inaccurate, and jammed with terrible regularity. Summerall identified similar problems in his division after Soissons. Like Summerall, Edwards had heard of the impressive features of the BAR, and he hoped there were enough of them on hand "to arm his division immediately with these rifles." He then reiterated, "I cannot too strongly urge that course . . . and I recommend a slightly greater proportion of Brownings than the present Chauchat equipment."[94] Edwards wanted the best automatic weapons available, and he wanted more of them.

Regarding the artillery, Edwards praised his gunners but admitted that at times his infantry commanders could not locate their front lines accurately enough to allow close artillery support. He stressed that the job of the divisional artillery was "solely to protect and permit the advance of the infantry," and his regular use of rolling barrages during the battle showed that he meant it. He thought his gunners were hampered by "too few gas shells" and recommended that "the proportion should be much greater hereafter, even in open warfare." He asserted that gas "can be effectively used against machine-gun nests where the proper interval elapses between the preparation and the assault," and he called for "a much greater allowance of gas shells of all calibres for counter battery work of the Corps Artillery, as one of the best agents in the neutralization of opposing batteries."[95] In his understanding of the power of chemical weapons, as with his appreciation of the machine gun, Edwards proved ahead of many senior officers in the AEF.

Although the 26th Division never received any tanks to assist in its advance, Edwards commented on that weapon too. He claimed that on "several occasions in the eight day advance" he was convinced "that we could get through with tanks easily and save lives." He called for four tanks to be given to each infantry battalion and insisted that "the use of tanks . . . is the solution for overcoming the German machine gun tactics if we ever expect a clean march through." Edwards also noted the importance of the Air Service in the battle and claimed that he needed more of it in the future.[96]

Finally, Edwards closed by stating, "the most important thing . . . that confronts a division commander is the answer to the question: 'Where is

[94] HQ 26th Division, "Report of Operations," 7 August 1918, Folder 33.6, Box 25, 26th Division Historical File, RG 120, NA.
[95] Ibid.
[96] Ibid.

my infantry?' . . . this information is essential for the Divisional Artillery to perform its role." He reported that brigade and regimental commanders were reluctant to use the artillery unless the infantry line was "definitely known." He thought runners were not the answer and cited the casualty list of runners to prove it. Although he claimed that "scientific men" told him that "a wireless telephone is the answer," until he possessed that technology, he wanted enough telephone wire for each infantry battalion to have as many as eight communication lines in concurrent use.[97]

Most of Edwards' assessments of the recent battle were accurate, and most of his suggestions were sound. Some were on the cutting edge of tactical and technological changes then underway. He certainly did not seem mired in the constraints of prewar American doctrine; he wrote nothing about the power of the rifle and bayonet and many of his ideas suggested he would lean increasingly on modern firepower and other emerging weapons technologies to make successful attacks in the future. Although few other reports from Yankee Division officers dealt with these topics in such depth and detail, those that offered commentary were uniformly in agreement with Edwards' conclusions. They stressed the need for more and better firepower employment, increasingly flexible infantry formations, and the importance of having sufficient time to properly coordinate attacks with limited objectives.[98] The division seemed to have learned a number of important lessons; whether it could apply those lessons during the strain of battle, and whether senior American officers would ever acknowledge Edwards' assessments, remained open questions.

[97] Ibid. For more evidence of Edwards' interest in the radio, see his endorsement of Col. John H. Parker to C.G., AEF (through C.G. 26th Div.), 16 August 1918, Box 22, Edwards Papers, MHS.

[98] See "Report of 1st Lt. W.E. Barnett, Comdg. 4th Platoon, Co. B, 104th Inf., Operations of period from July 18 to July 25, 1918," Folder 33.6, Box 52, 26th Division Historical File, RG 120, NA; "Report of Colonel John H. Parker, 102nd Infantry," 4 August 1918, Folder 33.6, Box 44, 26th Division Historical File, RG 120, NA; C.G., 52nd Inf. Brigade to C.G., 26th Division, "Report of action taken by this Brigade from 18–24 July '18," 3 August 1918, Folder 33.6, Box 37, 26th Division Historical File, RG 120, NA.

5

The 26th "Yankee" Division

Doctrine, Demoralization, and Disintegration

After the long march back through its attack sector, the Yankee Division spent the next two weeks in corps reserve, where it finally had time to rest and refit. On 11 August, it entrained to the Chatillon training area where it at last began to train for a "war of movement." For the first time, one unit history could claim that "the methods of open warfare dominated all study and drill."[1] Units practiced communicating while moving and working with aircraft. During this two-week period of training, a number of poorly trained enlisted replacements arrived (practically the last ones the division received during the war), and they had to be integrated into units and brought up to standards. At the same time, the division had to yield twenty-three officers and seventy-two precious NCOs for duty as instructors back in the United States. Nevertheless, the division finally conducted a couple of full-division maneuvers. On 27 August, it began its move back to the front lines to take part in the St. Mihiel attack.[2]

The St. Mihiel Attack, 12–13 September 1918

The Yankee Division ultimately played a more prominent role in the St. Mihiel attack than anyone expected. During its initial advance over

[1] Taylor, *New England in France*, 211.
[2] During August, when the 26th Division was undergoing its last phase of intensive training and preparing for the American First Army's first major attack, Liggett grew increasingly dissatisfied with Edwards' performance as a division commander. Liggett's aide wrote that the corps commander was ready to tell Pershing that Edwards was "absolutely untrustworthy" and that even during those critical days, he was taking "promiscuous leaves to Paris." Stackpole Diary, p. 185.

difficult terrain, it outpaced one veteran French division and kept pace with another. It then finished the battle with an impressive night-time advance that closed the salient from further enemy escape. The division captured thousands of German troops, while its own losses were light. It showed an improved ability to advance against enemy resistance, maneuver around machine guns, maintain liaison and communications, and employ its firepower. Yet, the division received little credit for its accomplishments at St. Mihiel.

On 8 September, the division took over a 4-kilometer-wide front on the western side of the St. Mihiel salient, joining the U.S. V Corps, commanded by Edwards' West Point classmate, Major General George H. Cameron. The 26th was on the southern flank of the V Corps with the French 15th Colonial Division on its left and the French 2nd Dismounted Cavalry Division, of the French II Colonial Army Corps, on its right. To the left of the French 15th Division was a brigade from the American 4th Division, but its role in the attack was minimal. The 26th Division was, therefore, the only American division with any significant role in the attack of the western face, which was considered the less important of the two simultaneous attacks (see Map 5 in Chapter 3).

The mission of the V Corps was to drive into the salient and swing toward its left to finish the advance facing the new German line at the base of the old salient. The attack was to move through the wooded elevation called the Heights of the Meuse. The enemy positions to be taken were formidable, based on the new "Hindenburg Line" formula, with wide trenches, deep traverses, and concrete emplacements. General Cameron called it a "very comprehensive and complete system of defense."[3]

Shortly after entering the sector, Cameron asked Edwards to offer his thoughts on the only remaining controversy in the First Army attack plan – how long should the artillery preparation be? Should it be as long as 22 hours or omitted altogether? Edwards' answer clearly reflected the appreciation of firepower gained in the Aisne-Marne Offensive. Edwards wrote that he "would like to have the 22 hours first suggested." He insisted "it should not be less than 14 hours." He claimed the Germans had too many installations that needed to be "neutralized" and that it was wise in such "unknown conditions . . . to upset the equilibrium of the Boche in every way before assaulting, tire him and disturb him and to make him

---

[3] HQ V Army Corps, "Special Report of Recent Operations in the Reduction of the Saint Mihiel Salient," 25 September 1918, Folder 33.6, Box 28, V Army Corps Historical File, RG 120, NA.

get his breath through a gas mask [*sic*]."[4] Although Pershing settled on a 4-hour preparation for the main attack, Cameron, who had commanded the 4th Division in its attacks during the Aisne-Marne Offensive, secured approval to add 3 hours of artillery fire before his attack. Although all guns would begin to fire at 0100 hours, the V Corps attack would not occur until 0800, 3 hours after the attack on the south face.[5]

Edwards' attack plan placed Cole's brigade on the left and Shelton's on the right, but while Cole was to put his regiments abreast, Shelton was to stack the 102nd Regiment behind the 101st. Army and corps orders specified a two-day attack, with the first-day's objective about 6 kilometers to the front. Edwards added two intermediate objectives, each with a 30-minute halt to keep the infantry better organized and closer to the artillery. The rate of advance was 100 meters every 4 minutes, half the rate of some of the attacks in the Aisne-Marne Offensive. After gaining the day's objective, the troops were to dig in and prepare to beat back counterattacks.[6]

Each of the four assaulting battalions was augmented with its own machine-gun company, a platoon of 37mm guns, a platoon of Stokes mortars, a section of "Gas and Flame" troops from the 1st Gas Regiment, and a section of 75mm guns. Battalions in the second line each advanced with another machine-gun company. The lead battalion also had teams of engineers with wire cutters and bangalore tubes to help get through any uncut wire and assist moving the field pieces forward. Infantry units were encouraged to assist neighboring units that were held up "even though it may take them slightly beyond their zones of action for the time being."[7]

The supporting fire plan was much more comprehensive than anything the division had used before. The 51st Field Artillery Brigade, now commanded by Colonel Otto W. B. Farr, was heavily augmented, giving it a total of 108 75mm guns, 48 155mm howitzers, a few batteries of 220mm

---

[4] Edwards to Cameron, 9 September 1918, Personal File of H. A. Drum, "Copies of Reports, Letters, etc. of the Twenty-Sixth Division," Box 14, Drum Papers, USAMHI.

[5] Cameron claimed that at the preattack conference with Pershing, he insisted on having "several hours of observed daylight fire" on the enemy strong points near Les Eparges and Les Combres to "blow the top off of these two places and capture them without fail." He proudly noted that General Blondlat, commander of the French II Colonial Corps to his right, smiled in agreement. Pershing acquiesced. "The Operations of the 26th Division at St. Mihiel," 29 January 1922, Folder 33.6, Box 25, 26th Division Historical File, RG 120, NA.

[6] HQ 26th Division, Field Orders No. 77, 11 September 1918, 1330 hours, Folder 32.1, Box 13, 26th Division Historical File, RG 120, NA.

[7] Ibid.

and 270mm howitzers, and a battery of 240mm trench mortars. These pieces took part in the three phases of the fire plan – the preparation, the attack, and the "postbarrage" period.

During the preparation, all firing was to be on prearranged targets, many of them located by recent aircraft photographs. Certain pieces were designated to cut a number of gaps in the enemy's massive belts of wire. Wisely, the 155s were prohibited from firing on the sector's only good road, the Grande Tranchée de Calonne. The preparation also included two pauses – a 5-minute break at H minus 3 hours and a 10-minute break at H minus 1 hour – during which gas concentrations were to be fired on trenches and troop locations. These would catch some defenders racing out of their dugouts and help "train" others to react more slowly when the attack finally came.[8]

To cover the infantry assault, the light artillery was to fire a rolling barrage that continued for about 4 hours. The rolling barrage nearly covered the entire first-day's advance because almost all of the guns could reach the first-day's objective from their starting positions. Unlike most rolling barrages, Colonel Farr adjusted the rate of advance "to secure proper concentrations on really dangerous points, and to avoid wasted fire on unoccupied ground." Sometimes the rate was to accelerate and at other times it was to linger on "vital points," but the overall rate corresponded to that of the infantry. In addition, the howitzers were to fire "progressive concentrations in advance of the barrage on enemy organizations and suspected organizations."[9] To ease the flow of traffic, some light guns were to begin moving forward at H plus 3 hours, but no heavy pieces were to move until 10 hours after the attack began. During the attack, each artillery regiment was assigned to support a specific infantry unit, and the guns were subject to special requests from infantry commanders. Two battalions of howitzers were equipped with wireless equipment and designated to work with the observation balloons and aircraft to hit "fugitive targets."[10] Although Edwards' order did not specify any

---

[8] The pauses in the artillery preparation also allowed a brief period of sound ranging to locate enemy batteries that might retaliate. HQ 51st FA Brigade, Operations Order No. 272, 10 September 1918, Folder 32.12, Box 57, 26th Division Historical File, RG 120, NA.

[9] C.O., 51st F.A. Brigade to C.G., 26th Division, Subject: Report of Operation during September 12–13, 1918, Folder 33.6, Box 59, 26th Division Historical File, RG 120, NA.

[10] HQ 51st F.A. Brigade, Operations Order No. 272, 10 September 1918, Folder 32.12, Box 57, 26th Division Historical File, RG 120, NA.

machine-gun barrages, reports show that these were arranged by subordinate commanders.

At 0800 hours on 12 September, 3 hours after the I and IV Army
Corps attacked the southern face of the salient, the lead Yankee battalions jumped-off behind their own rolling barrage. On the left, troops
from Cole's brigade met some resistance but were able to overcome it
while staying close to the barrage. On the right, Shelton's brigade made
progress too, but the thick underbrush and occasional enemy machine
guns caused the troops to fall behind the barrage and become increasingly disorganized.[11]

The disorganization was increased by the new tactics the infantry used
to overcome the few strong points that survived the artillery fire. Instead
of neat lines advancing in frontal waves, troops from both brigades relied
more on small, thin columns that adjusted their shape and direction to
the nature of the terrain and the enemy resistance. They also apparently
relied on their auxiliary weapons much more than their rifles. Although
these changes enabled the advance to continue, they led to considerable
intermingling between the battalions, and they slowed down the advance
considerably.

By 1300 hours, the troops had only advanced between 3 and 4 kilometers. Cole's brigade was considerably slowed by fire from the French sector
to the left, where the 15th Division was making even slower progress. By
late afternoon, its attack essentially ended for the day after an advance
of about 4 kilometers. When the 101st Infantry hit the second intermediate objective, it was so disorganized that Edwards authorized Shelton to
have the 102nd "leap-frog" it to continue the advance. That change was
completed by 1600 hours, and the 102nd – under the command of Hiram
A. Bearss, a Marine Corps colonel – pushed on to the first-day's objective
by 1900 hours. By then, major changes in the shape of the battle were
underway.[12]

[11] C.G., 26th Division to C. in C., First Army, Subject: Observations on operations for
reduction of St. Mihiel Salient, 20 September 1918, Folder 33.6, Box 25, 26th Division
Historical File, RG 120, NA.

[12] Ibid. "Report of Operations in Connection with Reduction of St. Mihiel Salient," 7 Octo-
ber 1918, Folder 33.6, Box 25, 26th Division Historical File, RG 120, NA; C.G., 51st Inf.
Brig. to C.G., 26th Division, Subject: Report of Operation – St. Mihiel, September 12–13,
1918, 23 September 1918, in "History of the 51st Infantry Brigade," n.d., 26th Division
Boxes, World War I Survey Collection, USAMHI; "Report of Brig. Gen. Charles H. Cole,
Comdg. 52nd Inf. Brigade. Operations from 11 Sept. 18 to 15 Sept. 18," Folder 33.6,
Box 37, 26th Division Historical File, RG 120, NA.

On the afternoon of the first day, senior commanders began to intervene in the 26th Division's fight. Concerned by what he called "the slow, timid progress" of the French 15th Division of the left, Cameron ordered Edwards to adjust his attack to take over a significant part of the French division's sector.[13] But before Edwards' units could make these changes, Cameron called with a second, more urgent demand – one that came from Pershing himself. In response to the deep advance of the 1st Division to the south and to reports that the Germans were attempting a full withdrawal of the salient, Pershing ordered Cameron to send the 26th Division toward Vigneulles, where it was to meet up with Summerall's troops and close the salient. This was not simply an acceleration of the existing plan but rather a significant change in the direction, rate, and nature of the attack.[14]

Cameron called Edwards and gave him Pershing's order to "reach Hattonchatel by daylight" in order to "bag the artillery" still at the tip of the salient. Cameron told him that, except for the French 2nd Dismounted Cavalry Division on Edwards' immediate right, "none of the divisions of the 2nd Colonial Army Corps have done anything but nibble and in consequence the [German] field artillery has not been withdrawn." Perhaps aware that this was Edwards' best opportunity to prove wrong both his and the Guard's detractors, Cameron closed his message by writing, "This is your chance, old man. Go do it.... Try to beat the 1st Division in the race and clean up."[15]

Faced with the opportunity to make a name for himself, prove the competence of his beloved division, and outperform Pershing's favorite Regular division, Edwards moved swiftly and boldly. He ordered Shelton immediately to send Bearss and the 102nd Infantry "right down the Calonne road," toward Hattonchatel and Vigneulles. He knew none of his artillery, including even the so-called accompanying artillery, had yet advanced successfully through the obstacles in No Man's Land, so the attack would

[13] "Extract from the statement of Major General George H. Cameron, Commanding the Fifth Corps in the St. Mihiel Operation," Folder 33.6, Box 28, V Army Corps Historical File, RG 120, NA.

[14] Pershing's orders obviated Cameron's most recent directive to swing to the left to take over territory in the 15th Division's sector, forced the division to attack straight through what had been the French 2nd Dismounted Cavalry Division's sector on the right, and turned a very structured two-day advance into a rapid one-day pursuit. HQ V Army Corps, Operations Instruction, Folder 32.11, Box 17, 26th Division Historical File, RG 120, NA.

[15] HQ 26th Division, "Extracts from Journal of Operations," 12 September 1918, Box 29, Edwards Papers, MHS.

be made by unsupported infantry. This did not dissuade him. With an urgency still palpable today, Edwards told Shelton that Pershing said "it is a race between the 1st Division and the 26th Division... it is a test between us and the 1st Division.... Get it out to the men that it is a race between us... and we will be the first division there."[16]

Edwards proved correct. Within 2 hours of Cameron's order, Bearss had his regiment well on its way down the Grande Tranchée de Calonne road toward Vigneulles, with advanced and flank guards protecting the main column and machine-gun teams ready to set up and support the advance with fire if necessary. No fire was needed. The German defenses were thoroughly broken by nightfall, and the 102nd Infantry marched 9 kilometers straight through what had recently been deep defensive positions. Bearss' troops set up road blocks at all intersections of the main road, took hundreds of prisoners along the way, and entered Vigneulles before 0300 hours the next morning – well ahead of the lead troops from the 1st Division. Bearss then sent patrols out in numerous directions, taking the towns of Hattonville, Creue, and Heudicourt, the latter another 7 kilometers to the south. The regiment ultimately gathered more than one thousand prisoners. It was an audacious and impressive achievement, and the column suffered just four casualties during the advance.[17] By dawn on 13 September, the battle was over for the 26th Division.

As after the Aisne-Marne fighting, Edwards was proud of his unit's performance. In less than 24 hours, his men had advanced more than 12 kilometers (some as many as 19) and captured about twenty-five hundred prisoners, as well as dozens of enemy guns. The division suffered just 479 total casualties, with very few killed or severely wounded. Probably Edwards' proudest accomplishment was that his unit had beaten Summerall's 1st Division in the race to Vigneulles.[18]

The 26th Division also showed that it had made significant improvements from its bloody efforts of July. Yet, Edwards still made little mention

[16] Ibid.
[17] C.G., 26th Division to C. in C., 1st Army, Subject: Observations on operations for reduction of St. Mihiel Salient, 20 September 1918, Folder 33.6, Box 25, 26th Division Historical File, RG 120, NA; C.G., 51st Inf. Brig. to C.G., 26th Division, Subject: Report of Operation – St. Mihiel, September 12–13, 1918, 23 September 1918 in "History of the 51st Infantry Brigade," n.d., 26th Division Boxes, World War I Survey Collection, USAMHI; C.O., 102nd Infantry to C.G., 26th Division, Subject: Report of Operations Sept. 12–23, 1918, 19 September 1918, Folder 33.6, Box 39, 26th Division Historical File, RG 120, NA.
[18] The 26th suffered less than 2 percent casualties in the attack. ABMC, American Armies, 165.

of the rifle and bayonet. He stressed that the 37mm guns, machine guns, and mortars gave his battalion commanders "a very powerful means for the reduction of machine gun nests." He admitted that the 75mm accompanying guns could not get through No Man's Land in time to help the advance, but he thought they would be of assistance in future battles. He noted that the 37mm guns "were used to much better advantage" than during the Aisne-Marne Offensive and that they were crucial to the advance. The mortars of the attached "Gas and Flame" troops from the AEF's 1st Gas Regiment also "assisted very materially" in knocking out machine-gun nests. He claimed that "too much training cannot be given platoons in maneuvering while attempting to reduce machine gun nests," and he suggested that such attacks were "essentially a series of platoon attacks supported by the 37mm, Stokes mortar, machine gun, and smoke and thermite detachments." In sum, "there was a great deal of improvement in the maneuver of platoons."[19]

Edwards' comments flowed naturally from the reports of his subordinate commanders. Cole reported that his troops relied on overhead fire from the 37mm guns and used the combined fire of rifle grenades and automatic rifles to help the infantry take machine-gun nests.[20] Shelton related that his infantry ran into enough resistance that, "according to instructions given," it shifted from lines to small columns and, finally, into "small combat groups." These groups pushed forward,

largely by infiltration, helping each other where they could.... parts of the line were held up for considerable time by machine guns nests, but through the advance of other parts, these were successfully flanked and driven back or captured and the ultimate advance of the parts held up thus assured. The advance in this way prevented serious casualties and in the end hastened the advance of the whole line.

Shelton did admit that such tactics resulted in the "practical disorganization" of the battalion" but that seemed a small price to pay for reducing casualties.[21]

[19] C.G., 26th Division to C. in C., First Army, Subject: Observations on operations for reduction of St. Mihiel Salient, 20 September 1918, Folder 33.6, Box 25, 26th Division Historical File, RG 120, NA.

[20] "Report of Brig. Gen. Charles H. Cole, Comdg. 52nd Inf. Brigade. Operations from 11 Sept. 18 to 15 Sept. 18," Folder 33.6, Box 37, 26th Division Historical File, RG 120, NA.

[21] C.G., 51st Inf. Brig. to C.G., 26th Division, Subject: Report of Operation – St. Mihiel, September 12–13, 1918, 23 September 1918, in "History of the 51st Infantry Brigade," n.d., 26th Division Boxes, World War I Survey Collection, USAMHI.

As for the artillery support, results were mixed. By all accounts, the value of the artillery support suffered from the rolling barrage's excessive rate of advance. Cole's brigade was able to keep with it for only about 2 hours, and Shelton's troops lost it long before that. Edwards stated that he did not like a "uniform rate of advance" throughout a corps or even a division front because the terrain often varied so widely.[22] When the infantry fell too far behind the barrage, the enemy machine-gunners had time to set up and slow the advance further. Colonel Farr suggested that in future attacks through wooded country, the barrage should never move faster than 100 meters in 6 minutes.

Apparently, infantry–artillery liaison was much improved but not yet good enough to slow or stop a rolling barrage that was racing away from the assault troops. Farr reported that some of the artillery liaison groups with the leading infantry battalions "kept up an almost constant flow of information during the progress of the infantry behind the barrage."[23] More than once during the attack, the artillery knocked out machine guns holding up the advance due to direct requests from infantry commanders. After the completion of the rolling barrage, the artillery successfully responded to two different requests from Cole to shell certain areas for 30 and 60 minutes to weaken enemy resistance. But, one regimental commander admitted that "lack of liaison with forward infantry elements rendered effective use" of his artillery impossible because the rainy weather prevented good observation and a lack of wire restricted telephone communications.[24] Furthermore, the division took many hours to get any of its light guns forward and did not even attempt to move the 155mm pieces until the following day. Had they needed the support of those pieces at the end of the engagement, no support could have been provided.

[22] C.G., 26th Division to C. in C., First Army, Subject: Observations on operations for reduction of St. Mihiel Salient, 20 September 1918, Folder 33.6, Box 25, 26th Division Historical File, RG 120, NA.

[23] C.O., 51st F.A. Brigade to C.G. 26th Division, Subject: Report of Operation during September 12–13, 1918, Folder 33.6, Box 59, 26th Division Historical File, RG 120, NA.

[24] "Report of Lt. Col. Robert E. Goodwin, Comdg., 101st Field Artillery. Operations for period from Sept. 8 to Sept. 13," Folder 33.6, Box 60, 26th Division Historical File, RG 120, NA. See also "Report of Lieut. Colonel J.F.J. Herbert, Commanding 102nd Field Artillery. Operations of Period 10 September 18 to 14 September 18," Folder 33.6, Box 61, 26th Division Historical File, RG 120, NA; "Report of Colonel P. D. Glassford, Comdg. 103rd Field Artillery. Operations of Period 9 Sept. 18 to 14 Sept. 18," Folder 33.6, Box 62, 26th Division Historical File, RG 120, NA.

Some commanders offered other evidence – noticeably absent in the report Edwards forwarded to his superiors – that the division still suffered from administrative and logistical problems that limited the implementation of its doctrinal ideals, especially regarding its desire to rely more heavily on firepower. Cole reported that despite the emphasis placed on such weapons, his unit could not secure sufficient rifle and hand grenades, discharger cups for the rifle grenades, and ammunition for the mortars and 37mm guns. Cole suspected that road congestion, often caused by faulty staff work and poor road discipline, was to blame in most cases. He also admitted not getting enough wire to maintain telephone communications with his forward units, forcing them to rely on runners. One artillery commander noted the sloppy staff work that ordered his twenty-four–gun regiment to carry out a fire plan built for a thirty-six–gun unit. The same colonel claimed it was "impossible" to get any of the gas and smoke shells called for in the plan.[25] Some of these problems may have been aggravated or even caused by poor staff work in the V Corps, the First Army, or GHQ, but the fact remains that the division certainly failed to solve them before the battle.

The 26th Division finished the St. Mihiel in a curious position. Members of the division thought it had done exceptionally well, eventually gaining all objectives at light cost, while demonstrating its improved tactical prowess. But, some senior officers in the AEF still discounted the division's quality. Few could deny the impressive performance of Bearss' regiment, but they isolated that achievement from the rest of the division's operations. Pershing praised the night march of the 102nd Infantry but also mentioned that up to that point, the attack against the salient's western face was "not so satisfactory."[26] Cameron did the same thing but more explicitly. After agreeing that just "one regiment" of the 26th Division "acquitted itself with distinction," Cameron reported that

the discipline of some units is very poor and a great improvement in this regard is to be insisted upon . . . the straggling of American units on the move is very great and it is believed this is due to lack of discipline on the part of company officers. . . . There was considerable straggling in the captured area during this

[25] "Report of Lieut. Colonel J.F.J. Herbert, Commanding 102nd Field Artillery. Operations of Period 10 September 18 to 14 September 18," Folder 33.6, Box 61, 26th Division Historical File, RG 120, NA. "Report of Brig. Gen. Charles H. Cole, Comdg. 52nd Inf. Brigade. Operations from 11 Sept. 18 to 15 Sept. 18," Folder 33.6, Box 37, 26th Division Historical File, RG 120, NA.

[26] Pershing, *My Experiences*, 2: 269. See also Marshall, *Memoirs*, 145.

operation by the 26th Division. . . . It is noted that at times orders are not obeyed with the alacrity so necessary to complete military success."[27]

Cameron's displeasure with the 26th Division in no way extended to the doctrinal and operational adjustments the unit made at St. Mihiel. In his report on the battle, the corps commander affirmed a heavy reliance on firepower in the attack: "Machine gun nests . . . may best be put out of action by the following system: the minute the infantry line is held up in its advance by a located machine-gun nest the artillery must be informed at once; the infantry stay in place until it is put out. . . . As a rule machine gun nests are so close together laterally that the flanking out of a single nest is very frequently impossible by infantry alone."[28] Doctrinally and operationally, Cameron agreed with Edwards and the rest of the Yankee Division.

Although the specific details behind Cameron's criticisms remain undisclosed (as do any private motivations Cameron may have had), his fault-finding verified the negative sentiments held by many throughout the AEF. Later that month, when the 26th Division was withdrawn from his corps, Cameron found enough wrong in the unit to tell Liggett that he was glad to be rid of the Yankee Division. In one harsh outburst, Cameron claimed it "was rotten because the spirit emanating from his friend and room-mate Clarence [Edwards] was rotten."[29] These senior commanders were sure that Edwards was disloyal and untrustworthy, was not getting the most out of this division, and his inability to instill discipline was reducing its effectiveness, regardless of its tactical improvements. Yet, despite their displeasure with Edwards and their fear that he was destroying what should have been a good unit, he escaped relief for another five weeks. Although the division may have suffered from certain aspects of his leadership, it would ironically be his belated relief during the division's final battle that sent the division into a downward spiral of demoralization and ineffectiveness.

---

[27] Cameron never specified which orders he thought the 26th Division was slow in executing, but he probably was referring to his orders sending Cole's brigade forward to the Army objective and through the sector of the French division on the left. HQ V Army Corps, Special Report of Recent Operations in the Reduction of the Saint Mihiel Salient, 25 September 1918, Folder 33.6, Box 28, V Army Corps Historical File, RG 120, NA.

[28] Ibid.

[29] Stackpole Diary, p. 220.

The Meuse-Argonne Offensive, 14 October–11 November 1918

After the close of the battle, when the American First Army moved to the Meuse-Argonne to begin its final and greatest offensive, the Yankee Division moved into the new front lines along the *Michel Stellung* at the base of the old St. Mihiel salient. Ten days later, when the First Army jumped-off on 26 September, two battalions from the 26th Division began a costly day-long diversionary attack on the towns of Riaville and Marchville. Six days later, when the 1st and 2nd Divisions were heading back onto crucial battlefields near Exermont and Blanc Mont, and the 77th Division was earning fame by grinding its way through the Argonne Forest, Edwards' men were successfully carrying out another well-organized but costly and unnoticed raid on the German lines. Only on 8 October did GHQ order the 26th Division out of the front lines and direct it to join the Meuse-Argonne Offensive – and even then only as part of the French XVII Army Corps operating on the Heights of the Meuse, east of that river.

Despite the small size of the operations along the *Michel Stellung*, the division suffered heavily during its three weeks there. With the German Army expecting an attack toward Metz, the sector never assumed the "quiet" form it had before the attack of 12 September. The Yankee Division suffered hundreds of casualties and continued to be worn down mentally and emotionally.[30] Sickness began to spread as well. Losses were especially heavy in officers, and the division continued to suffer from a serious lack of replacements. By early October, the 51st Infantry Brigade had just less than 60 percent of its authorized number of officers, and many battalions were well below 50 percent. One battalion was commanded by a second lieutenant, its ranking officer. Other divisions had experienced similar problems *after* hard battles (e.g., the 1st and 2nd after Soissons) but never on the eve of entering one. Shelton notified his superiors that "the whole situation is so fraught with danger that I beg to urge some action looking to the immediate replacement, in part at least, of the officers in the higher company grades now absent."[31] But, none were sent.

---

[30] Between 17 September and 9 October, the division suffered 799 casualties. ABMC, *26th Division Summary of Operations*, 48.

[31] C.G., 51st Infantry Brigade to C.G., 26th Division, 5 October 1918, quoted in "History of the 51st Infantry Brigade," n.d., 26th Division Boxes, World War I Survey Collection, USAMHI.

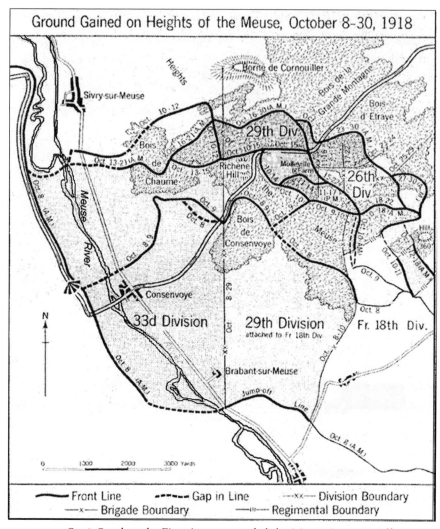

Ground Gained on Heights of the Meuse, October 8-30, 1918

—— Front Line ▪▪▪▪▪ Gap in Line ⋯×× Division Boundary
—×— Brigade Boundary —ɪɪɪ— Regimental Boundary

MAP 13: On 8 October, the First Army expanded the Meuse-Argonne Offensive by attacking east of the Meuse River. On 15 October, the 26th Division entered the lines there and a week later made its last significant attack of the war.

By 14 October, the Yankee Division – already worn out and depleted – entered the inferno of the front lines east of the Meuse (see Map 13).[32]

---

[32] The division had not yet solved some of its most basic operational problems either and was apparently plagued by serious communications troubles. See HQ 26th Division, Instructions Nos. 108 and 109, 21 October 1918, Personal File of H.A. Drum, "Copies

Pershing had expanded his First Army offensive east of the river on 8 October to clear out the German artillery that pounded his infantry from the Heights of the Meuse, but after gaining about 4 kilometers in the first assault, the offensive stalled. The conditions there were even worse than those along the *Michel Stellung*, and casualties quickly mounted while sickness and disease spread throughout the division. Psychiatric cases soon increased dramatically as well. On 15 October, troops from the 104th Infantry were fed into the French 18th Division to take part in a small attack. Despite the support of sixteen tanks, the only time Yankee Division troops worked with tanks in the entire war, the attack gained nothing. By 18 October, the division had command of its own sector of the front, and Major General Henri Claudel, the French corps commander, ordered it to continue the offensive by joining with the American 29th Division on its left in a short assault on a series of wooded hills.

Edwards' plan for this attack represented the culmination of his division's doctrinal development during the war. As parts of two regiments from the 29th Division drove to the east, units from the 26th were to carry out a converging two-phase attack that seized the hills to its front. One battalion, facing east, was to drive forward about 700 meters to an intermediate objective, where it was to stop for 40 minutes and re-form. Before advancing farther, that unit was to signal a second attack battalion to its right, then facing north, to join in the attack to the main objective, another half kilometer away. If all went well, a support battalion would pass through these units and drive about another kilometer forward to take and hold woods called the Belleu Bois.[33]

More than any other attack by the Yankee Division during the war, this assault was based on the highly coordinated use of firepower to gain the objectives. Each attacking battalion was augmented with 37mm guns, Stokes mortars, teams from the 1st Gas Regiment, and a company of machine guns. Even though the assaulting battalions came from the 101st Infantry, the 37mm guns and Stokes mortars of the 102nd Infantry were added to the attacking force, as were nearly all the division's machine guns. While some machine guns advanced with the infantry, others took up firing positions to shoot barrages all across the front and flank of the assault zone. All the guns of the artillery brigade, augmented with an

of Reports, Letters, etc. of the Twenty-Sixth Division," Box 14, Drum Papers, USAMHI; Dennis J. Vetock, *Lessons Learned: A History of US Army Lesson Learning* (Carlisle Barracks, Penn.: U.S. Army Military History Institute, 1988), 47–9.

33 HQ 26th Division, Field Orders No. 92, 21 October 1918, 0100 hours, Folder 32.1, Box 13, 26th Division Historical File, RG 120, NA.

additional regiment and a number of corps guns, were to fire a 45-minute preparation into the attack zone before the assault. Then the infantry, advancing in small columns through the woods, was to closely follow the slowest rolling barrage yet used – advancing 100 meters every 10 minutes. Each battalion had a liaison team from its supporting artillery regiment, and one battalion of 75mm guns was ready to deviate from its prepared fire plan to meet any special call from the infantry. Because all divisional artillery was employed in the attack made from only the far left of the division sector, the artillery of neighboring units was called on to fire diversionary barrages that also provided some protection against an enemy counterattack.[34] This assault, like so many AEF attacks, more resembled a limited, set-piece assault based on firepower than the ambitious open-warfare attacks so often written about by Pershing and other GHQ officers.

But, before this plan was carried out, two significant events occurred – one that hinted at the continuing disciplinary problems within the division and another that made those problems much worse in the short term. First, on the morning of 19 October, a number of enlisted men met some German troops in No Man's Land, but instead of fighting them, they had a conversation. When Edwards received the report of this meeting later in the day, he apparently considered the event to be more of an interesting, impromptu intelligence-gathering operation than a dangerous case of fraternization with the enemy, and he forwarded the report to Liggett, the new First Army commander. Liggett shot back a strongly worded note condemning such behavior and demanding that Edwards ensure that no more fraternization occurred in his unit.[35] For many in the AEF leadership, this was just another example of the loose ship Edwards ran and of the poor discipline and lack of fighting spirit throughout the unit.

The next day, 20 October, the other major event occurred – Edwards received a note from Pershing's chief of staff, General James W.

---

[34] Ibid. 51st F.A. Brigade, Plan of Employment, 19 October 1918, Folder 32.1, Box 58, 26th Division Historical File, RG 120, NA.

[35] In a letter on 20 October, Liggett warned Edwards that "this constitutes a flagrant case of the most insidious and dangerous propaganda we have yet run up against, its intent being to weaken the fighting determination of our men. . . . take the most rigorous measures at once to stop it. . . . suppress it absolutely." Liggett to Edwards, 20 October 1918, "In the Matter of Major General Clarence R. Edwards, N.A." 7 May 1919, Binder 1-f, Box 8, RG 200, NA; Edwards to the Adjutant General of the Army, 19 March 1919, Box 22, Edwards Papers, MHS.

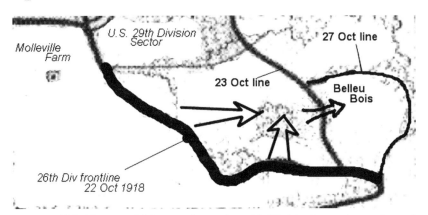

MAP 14: This blowup of Map 13 shows the 26th Division's attack to take and hold the Belleu Bois.

McAndrew, ordering him to leave the division and return to the United States as part of an exchange of senior officers. Despite the proximity of the events, the connection between the fraternization incident and Edwards' relief remains unclear. Pershing had long been displeased with Edwards, and it is possible the events were coincidental. Whatever the immediate purpose, Pershing stripped the division of its leader on the eve of battle, and the belated change seems to have caused more harm than good.[36] Edwards was shortly instructed to retain command until his replacement, Brigadier General Frank E. Bamford, arrived from the 1st Division to replace him. But that did not occur until 24 October.

Under these adverse conditions, the division began its last major battle. After a powerful artillery preparation, which included phosgene shells, the infantry drove through the wooded hills and took its objectives. According to plan, the infantry then pushed on and took its "exploitation" objective of the Belleu Bois (see Map 14). Losses were light and for a while it looked

[36] Edwards' relief was made official in GHQ, AEF, Special Orders No. 293, 20 October 1918, which accompanied the letter from McAndrew. Whether all of this was done so quickly after the fraternization incident is unclear. Col. Walter S. Grant, a First Army staff officer, later claimed to have a telegram from GHQ to First Army dated 19 October announcing the impending relief of Edwards and the appointment of Bamford to the command. The file on Edwards' relief certainly included plenty of material on the fraternization incident, as well as on other negative events such as the Seicheprey raid. See "In the Matter of Major General Clarence R. Edwards, N.A." 7 May 1919, Binder 1-f, Box 8, RG 200, NA; Walter S. Grant to Hugh A. Drum, 4 February 1921, Personal File of H. A. Drum, "Copies of Reports, Letters, etc. of the Twenty-Sixth Division," Box 14, Drum Papers, USAMHI.

as though the division was going to overcome its internal difficulties. Claudel quickly issued a glowing letter of congratulations to Edwards, announcing that "The reputation of your Division has long since preceded it here.... In a few hours, as in a maneuver, it realized all the objectives to which it had been assigned in the difficult region of woods.... The operation testifies assuredly of superior instruction, flexibility and will."[37] But then the problems began to surface.

In response to heavy enemy artillery fire that evening, the leading battalion commander withdrew his lines from the Belleu Bois without approval from any senior officer. That night, Edwards ordered the attack to continue again the next morning, with essentially the same fire-support arrangements. The only change was that the 102nd Infantry would also attack and take Hill 360 to its front, which dominated the Yankee lines. On 24 October, this attack succeeded in taking Belleu Bois again and in pushing back the Germans near Hill 360, but four strong counterattacks forced them to yield most of the gains. The next day, the division attacked again, this time with Bamford in command, but it made no permanent advance. Shelton reported that in these attacks, "The resistance here was from machine-gun nests believed to be in concrete emplacements which our artillery fire yesterday wholly failed in destroying. In my judgment these positions cannot be taken except after very heavy and continued destructive artillery preparation by the heaviest calibers."[38] As after previous attacks, the division's senior officers saw firepower, or the lack of it, as the determining element.

On 26 October, the division prepared its last major attack of the war. Like those of the previous days, it was an explicitly set-piece attack. As the division operations report stated, "The rate of advance, provision for mopping up parties, resistance to possible enemy counter-attacks, consolidation of the conquered positions, and the establishment of liaison groups as required, were all embodied in the provisions of the field order." All the auxiliary weapons were incorporated into the attack, including massed machine-gun barrages. Bamford also secured an additional twenty 155mm guns, as well as thirty-five mortars ranging from 190mm to 280mm. After a 60-minute preparation and a 20-minute standing barrage from all guns in the division and corps, troops from both regiments in the 51st Brigade

---

[37] Maj. Gen. Claudel to Edwards, 24 October 1918, Box 22, Edwards Papers, MHS; ABMC, *26th Division Summary of Operations*, 55.

[38] Shelton is quoted in Taylor, *New England in France*, 258. "Report of Operations, 26th Division, October 23d–26th, 1918," Folder 33.6, Box 25, 26th Division Historical File, RG 120, NA.

were to follow a slow rolling barrage about a kilometer forward, stop, dig in, and prepare to meet counterattacks. This attack, on 27 October, finally succeeded in taking and holding the Belleu Bois, but Hill 360 remained in German hands.[39] Although the division remained in the line and followed up German withdrawals between 7 and 11 November, the attack of 27 October was its last major effort of the war. That assault was only partially successful and casualties were heavy. All told, the division suffered about thirty-eight hundred casualties to move the line just a couple of kilometers between 14 and 27 October.[40]

The cause of the division's operational inadequacies during the fighting east of the Meuse have much more to do with the division's organizational problems and the difficulties of the tasks assigned them than any doctrinal or tactical failures. The Yankee Division continued to issue attack orders that maximized firepower and relied on the latest developments in infantry tactics. Near Belleu Bois, the division needed only to execute a strong assault that was more like a giant trench raid than any decisive breakthrough based on open warfare. Rather, the operational problems reflected the moral and physical breakdown within the division, a breakdown that probably began in late September, continued throughout mid-October, and then exploded in the final weeks of the war after Pershing relieved Edwards.

Shelton, a highly regarded Regular officer, had warned on 5 October that unless the division received some officer replacements, severe problems would occur. GHQ never sent any officers, or other enlisted troops for that matter, yet it kept the division in the front line or moving from one front to another from early September until the Armistice on 11 November.

Discipline and morale began to break down and the disease rate skyrocketed. The division's sanitary report for October counted 1,506 men being treated for wounds and another 1,441 for gas or "suspected gas" casualties, sometimes a euphemism for malingering. But, it also listed

---

39 "Report of Operations, 26th Division, October 23d–26th, 1918," Folder 33.6, Box 25, 26th Division Historical File, RG 120, NA; HQ 26th Division, Field Orders No. 96, 26 October 1918, 1530 hours, Folder 32.1, Box 13, 26th Division Historical File, RG 120, NA.

40 Many of these casualties were simply the result of having four infantry regiments in the front lines of an extraordinarily active sector for two weeks. Still, the thirty-eight hundred casualties meant a combat loss of about 14 percent of the division's authorized strength. But, the 26th was already well below strength when it entered the battle, and the records suggest about 90 percent of these losses were in the infantry and machine-gun units. ABMC, *26th Division Summary of Operations*, 63.

181 troops being treated for injuries due to "accidents" and some 3,631
sick with a variety of illnesses. The report detailed the living conditions
that contributed to these latter statistics, and it painted the picture of a
division in a pathetic physical and emotional state. The report noted that
the men had been in nothing but shelter tents for the entire month, with
the forward infantry in shell holes. In the lines, there was "No drainage.
No sewerage. All waste disposed of by burial in shell holes dug for the
purpose. Manure is piled away from picket lines." Even behind the lines,
there were "No baths. No delousing plants. No sanitary appliances."
Throughout the sector, "Water is contaminated and is ordered boiled or
chlorinated. Such treatment has been impossible for parts of the front
line where troops have been under constant heavy fire, and the men have
used untreated water from any source, i.e., shell holes, puddles, etc. This
accounts for the considerable number of cases of diarrhea." Although the
"food supply has been ample, of good quality and variety and well prepared... men in front lines in active combat have had only one meal a day,
necessarily. Transportation to the front lines has been almost impossible
on account of the destructive fire.... Men's clothing is in filthy condition,
is badly worn and busted and is of too thin and poor quality for the work
and the season. The command is 99% infested with lice; is filthy, bod-
ily; needing bathing and delousing, and fresh underclothing and in many
cases new uniforms and shoes." The surgeon recommended the division
be rested "as soon as the military situation will permit." It summarized:
"The physical condition of the men of the command is below normal,
vitality is lowered, resistance to infections almost nothing and many men
are, for the first time, exhausted nervously."[41]

This last comment was cause for special concern. Between 12 and
21 October – *prior to* the battle for Belleu Bois – ninety-three new psychological cases emerged. After the battle, the rate of collapse increased, with
more than ninety new cases in just the three-day period ending 30 October.
The total since joining the French XVII Corps came to 223 cases, including
13 officers and 39 NCOs. Lieutenant Harry Steckel, the division psychi-
atrist, reported that the recent casualties convinced him that even "the
best material" was breaking under the constant pressures and dangers
of "the hardest kind of warfare." He warned it was "an human impossibility for the troops to continue to stand the terrible stress and strain,
through which they have recently gone, without becoming permanently

[41] Sanitary Report, 26th Division, October 1918, Box 22, Edwards Papers, MHS.

incapacitated for efficient front line work."[42] On 1 November, the division surgeon, Colonel R. S. Porter, reported that the poor physical, mental, and emotional health of the troops had "*greatly* lowered fighting efficiency."[43]

Although these reports might be dismissed as the oversensitive musings of noncombat officers, the comments of the division inspector, Colonel H. P. Hobbs, who also served as a regimental commander, cannot. At the end of October, Hobbs inspected the infantry regiments and issued a grave report. He claimed officers admitted their soldiers were "shell shy," "all in," and "mentally and physically exhausted," while he himself noted that the enlisted men appeared to be in "a depressed state of mind and suffering from both nervous and physical fatigue." Many were "sick with constant coughing." He reported that morale was "very low due to the continued exposure to bad weather, to hard fighting, to continued exposure to shell and machine-gun fire, and to lack of rest," and he stated that he believed that the infantry, especially in the 101st and 102nd Regiments, "was not in condition for even defensive operations." He warned that "the 51st Infantry Brigade is in a state of mind and body to break into panic on slight provocation."[44] Even if one concludes that these reports were exaggerated, as some did at the time, it seems that the condition of the Yankee Division in mid and late October provides sufficient explanation for the operational failures despite the unit's doctrinal and tactical improvements.[45]

[42] 102nd Field Hospital, Memorandum for Division Surgeon, 26th Division, 24 October 1918, Box 22, Edwards Papers, MHS; 102nd Field Hospital, Memorandum for Division Surgeon, 26th Division, 30 October 1918, Box 22, Edwards Papers, MHS.

[43] Emphasis in original. See Office of the Division Surgeon, Memorandum to the Chief of Staff, 26th Division, 1 November 1918, Box 22, Edwards Papers, MHS.

[44] Colonel H. P. Hobbs, 101st Infantry to CG, 51st Inf. Brigade, Subject: Inspector's report on morale, 6 November 1918, in "History of the 51st Infantry Brigade," n.d., 26th Division Boxes, World War I Survey Collection, USAMHI.

[45] Hobbs' report was so dire that Shelton protested it and demanded a formal explanation from him. Hobbs then described how he arrived at his conclusion and asked that he "be not misjudged and considered a calamity howler." He then claimed, a week after his first report, that "the few days of comparative rest that the men have had has brought about a very marked change in spirit. The morale is again high and officer and men are cheerful and look upon the bright side of things." Quite possibly, he was exaggerating in both instances. That was the conclusion of the First Army Inspector General, who looked into the matter for Liggett. He wrote that he was "convinced that the above report [i.e., Hobbs' initial one] is greatly exaggerated. There is no danger of panic. The degree of exhaustion is not now as stated. The sickness is not as serious as is indicated in the report. . . . The fact remains that the morale of the division is low. This is unquestionably due to indiscreet conversations about the hardships endured by the division, on the part of officers in the presence of, and to, enlisted men. This evidently came from the top

Two points seem clear regarding this breakdown in the 26th Division. First, it was well underway by mid-October, when the division began its last major offensive. Second, it accelerated after Edwards' untimely relief. For all his many faults, Edwards was extraordinarily popular among the officers and men of the Yankee Division. He regularly referred to them as his "stout-hearted lads" and they nicknamed him "Daddy." The officers and men of the division were profoundly affected by Edwards' relief. One officer described the condition of the unit at the end of the war to Edwards' former aide:

I haven't written you or the General as to the effects of the cessation of hostilities. As far as the infantry in the lines was concerned it was the most terrible and awful moment that I have ever known. The men were all in, absolutely all gone. They had no brains nor feeling left – those that were still there. From the infantry there wasn't a sound. They just quit benumbed.... They simply sat down where they were and continued to stare. They didn't know enough to care whether it was over or not.... They were not in the best of shape when the General left and they had held up until then on his account, by their nerve. After he went and Logan went and Hume went, they were dazed. They felt that someone had put something over on them. They were told that they were not tired but only yellow.... They went forward like whipped curs. They went forward because they were driven, without heart and lifeless.... They were just all gone.... The men remembered the General's request to them to "carry on" after he left. They tried. But when animals have been called "nice doggie" and coaxed and put through their tricks by kindness they can't understand what it means to be called a yellow dog.[46]

and the belief that the men are tired out has been encouraged by officers all down the line." However, he admitted, "the division is badly in need of replacements, especially among the officers." Walter Grant then recommended a series of command changes, subsequently approved by Liggett, that would have moved both Shelton and Cole to other brigades. As a point of comparison, the report included information on the 32nd Division, originally composed of Guard units from Wisconsin. The 32nd had also fought for a long time in the Meuse-Argonne, but although its battle casualties were every bit as severe as those of the 26th Division, their report added: "Every man completely outfitted with new or good as new clothing throughout." Memorandum for Chief of Staff, HQ First Army, Subject: Extract from Inspector's Report, 5 November 1918, in "History of the 51st Infantry Brigade," n.d., 26th Division Boxes, World War I Survey Collection, USAMHI.

[46] Charles A. Stevens to Major John W. Hayatt, 19 December 1918, Box 22, Edwards Papers, MHS. Another captain wrote Edwards directly, stating that "every man loves, admires, and respects their former Commanding General. We knew that in you we had a friend." Captain Blinn Francis Yates to Edwards, 17 January 1919, Box 22, Edwards Papers, MHS. Another wrote that Edwards was "beyond a doubt loved by one and all; Pershing, etc. can never compare with the grand old man...his leaving was the biggest loss the Division had." Daniel L. Pendergast to Edwards, 19 February 1919, Box 22, Edwards Papers, MHS. Many wanted Edwards to run for governor after the war.

Unlike commanders such as Robert Bullard, who explicitly strove to develop the 1st Division into a finely tuned machine that would "work independently of the quality of the man that turns the crank," Edwards did just the opposite. Whether unwittingly or not, he made himself the center and symbol of the unit. He encouraged his men to take criticism of the division, or even of the division commander himself, personally. He fostered dissension and distrust of higher authority and while commiserating with his officers and men, he earned their devotion at the expense of others.

Liggett was right – despite the division's doctrinal improvements and tactical adaptations, its previously high morale was built largely on a shaky foundation established by Edwards, not on "excellence of training and discipline." The division did not always receive fair treatment, but the persecution complex nurtured by Edwards was certain to bear bad fruit. The division had problems in discipline and organization that seem never to have been solved, and some of them, when combined with the division's poor treatment by GHQ, contributed to the breakdown. Pershing's belated relief of Edwards was the last straw. The division saw it as the fulfillment of the conspiracy Edwards had so often discussed. Discipline and morale crumbled, and no combination of doctrinal, tactical, and technical adaptations could compensate for that breakdown, especially in the difficult environment along the Heights of the Meuse.[47]

Conclusions

The 26th Division was surrounded by controversy from the day its already unpopular commander finagled overseas shipping for his division

---

[47] Taylor asserted this when he wrote, "The separation of General Edwards from his command, under the circumstances, appeared to many as the culminating incident in a long campaign." *New England in France*, 252. However, Pershing also relieved the first commanders of both the 1st and 2nd Divisions, Generals Sibert and Bundy, respectively (though earlier on in the war), and those units showed no signs of such a loss in morale. Bamford added fuel to the fire by relieving Col. Logan, another popular figure who had commanded the 101st Infantry since leaving Boston, within two days of taking command. He fired him for "lack of decision, force and aggressiveness in the performance of his military duty." Bamford added that "It has always been difficult to overcome his inertia, and lack of prompt obedience of orders is constitutional with him." These were extraordinary accusations from such a new commander. Before the end of the war, Bamford relieved a number of other Guard officers, including Brig. Gen. Cole and Col. Hume, who led the 104th Infantry. All were reinstated after the armistice. Bamford, however, was replaced on 16 November 1918 by Maj. Gen. Harry C. Hale, who had trained and brought to France in September 1918 the 84th Division but never saw battle with it. Division Commander to C.G., First Army, Subject: Relief of Colonel Edward L. Logan, 101st Infantry, HQ 26th Division, 26 October 1918, Box 22, Edwards Papers, MHS.

of suspect National Guardsman. Nevertheless, the 26th Division showed
signs of adaptation and improvement, particularly in doctrine and combat
method. It learned many of the same lessons as the best AEF divisions –
using more open formations; relying on flanking and infiltration tactics;
and maximizing its available firepower with saturation bombardments,
rolling artillery barrages, direct and indirect overhead machine-gun support, and fire from all of the other infantry auxiliary weapons. However,
the division's ability to put its doctrinal and operational adaptations into
practice on the battlefield did not uniformly improve during the war. After
reaching a high point in mid-September, the division became less effective,
thanks to a host of internal and external factors.

Edwards appears to have run a loose and undisciplined organization,
based more on personality and emotion than on professionalism and technical competence. Although he gained the love and admiration of his officers and men, he apparently did so in part at the expense of more senior
officers, superior commands, and the AEF in general. The 26th Division
occasionally showed signs of poor discipline in its sloppy encampments,
disorganized marches, inadequate supply system, and weak communications arrangements. These failures probably contributed to higher rates of
sickness and disease, to units entering battle without sufficient supplies or
ammunition, and to difficulty communicating during combat. At times,
the infantry units may not have demonstrated the kind of aggressiveness that enabled the best AEF divisions to destroy enemy units and earn
impressive reputations. Despite this, the division did achieve some operational successes. Yet, when Pershing replaced Edwards, the heartbroken
men were convinced it was the fulfillment of a plot by Regular Army
officers to embarrass them, their commander, and the entire National
Guard.[48]

The allegations were not without foundation. From the start, Pershing
and his staff disliked Edwards – and, by extension, his division. GHQ
inspectors made a number of reports critical of the division, and Pershing
allowed it to languish for almost five months in the muddy front trenches
of inglorious "quiet sectors" that were, actually, far from peaceful.
Pershing's censure of the division after the Seicheprey fight was unjus-
tified, given the number of casualties it inflicted on the Germans, and he
did not ensure that the division received any of the large-unit maneuver

[48] Edwards' relief remained highly controversial long after the war ended, generating a
congressional investigation and long-term hostility against the Regular Army throughout
New England.

training he claimed was so important before its first battle. The division's hard fighting during the Aisne-Marne Offensive also brought more criticism than praise. At St. Mihiel, the division never got the recognition it deserved for its audacious operations on the first evening. Then, the division was not only left out of the start of the Meuse-Argonne, but instead of being placed in reserve – as was done with the 1st and 2nd Divisions – it was also given the undignified task of holding the line near St. Mihiel and making a costly diversionary attack. After holding the line there for weeks, suffering casualties and losing men to illness, it received no replacements. This trend continued during its grueling operations on the Heights of the Meuse in late October, when thousands of vacancies in the combat units went unfilled. While the AEF was running short of replacements in October, GHQ sent other units (particularly the 1st and 2nd Divisions) large groups of fresh officers and men.[49] Then, at the start of the division's final series of partially successful limited-objective attacks, Pershing relieved Edwards, and from that point, the division's combat ability – regardless of its previous successes and important tactical adaptations – decreased markedly until the end of the war.

The Yankee Division continued to maximize firepower employment and increase the flexibility of its infantry tactics. But, in the end, as so often throughout the war, the 26th Division's internal and external organizational problems overshadowed the unit's doctrinal and operational developments.

---

[49] During the war, the 26th Division suffered 13,664 killed and wounded but received just 14,411 replacements. In comparison, the 1st Division suffered 22,320 casualties but received 30,206 replacements, and the 2nd Division lost 23,235 casualties but gained 35,343 replacements. Even among Guard and National Army divisions, the Yankee Division fared badly. The 42nd Division received 17,235 replacements although it lost 14,683 men, the 32nd Division gained 20,140 men while losing just 13,261 men, and the 77th Division received 12,728 replacements to fill its 10,194 combat losses. See the tables in ABMC, *American Armies and Battlefields*, pp. 515–17.

6

The 2nd Division

Bloody Lessons in "Open Warfare"

The 2nd Division may not have been the first American division in France, the first to enter training, or the first to meet the enemy in battle, but by November 1918, its combat record gave it the right to be considered the best American division of the war. During its five major offensive operations, the 2nd consistently advanced farther and faster than neighboring units and, by the end of the war, it had taken more enemy prisoners and captured more enemy guns than any other American division. Although senior commanders often gave it challenging missions, the 2nd Division ultimately succeeded in taking every major objective assigned.[1] However, the 2nd Division paid a high price for its operational success; it suffered more casualties than any other AEF division.[2]

Although the division's first engagements were deemed successes, many of those assaults proved that it had much to learn about combat on the First World War battlefield. More clearly than any of the other pioneer divisions, the 2nd went into its first battles seemingly committed to fight in a manner consistent with the official doctrinal pronouncements of senior

---

[1] The division's 12,026 German prisoners represented an astounding 19 percent of the entire AEF total of 63,079. The 2nd took more prisoners than the combined totals of the next two divisions, the 1st and the 89th, and as many as the combined total of the bottom sixteen American divisions. The 2nd Division also captured 343 artillery pieces, about a quarter of the AEF total during the war, and as many as the next three divisions combined. The entire American First Army took just 911 in the St. Mihiel and Meuse-Argonne campaigns. ABMC, *American Armies*, 513–15; Ayres, *War with Germany*, 110–12; John A. Lejeune, *The Reminiscences of a Marine* (Philadelphia: Dorrance and Co., 1930), 445.

[2] Its casualty total of 23,235 represented almost 10 percent of all AEF casualties and equaled the combined casualty figure for the bottom nine divisions. ABMC, *American Armies*, 513–15.

AEF leaders. Yet, the division's adaptations and innovations made during and after those first bloody battles proved equally apparent. Leaders at all levels within the division soon eschewed any notion of self-reliant infantry and stiff linear formations. They quickly learned to maximize firepower, to coordinate it with the infantry, and to attack with flexible formations and the latest infantry tactics. In some cases, they even employed techniques that deviated not only from the spirit but also from the letter of instructions from senior commanders. These risks paid off and were significant factors in the division's operational successes late in the war.

Training in the United States and France, August 1917–May 1918

Like the 1st Division, the 2nd Division proudly carried the designation of Regular, but it too was more Regular in name than in reality. Each of its combat regiments contained a majority of troops in their first year of military service and in some units, 90 percent of the men had been in military service less than a year.[3] However, again like the 1st Division (but unlike many of the Guard divisions), all of its battalion, regiment, and brigade commanders were professional officers of long-term service. Its three successive division commanders, Omar Bundy, James G. Harbord, and John A. Lejeune (a U.S. Marine Corps major general), were all distinguished officers. Although Bundy exerted little influence on operations before leaving the division, Harbord and Lejeune were both strong commanders who nevertheless showed different doctrinal and operational tendencies. Harbord, Pershing's protégé and former chief of staff, proved thoroughly committed to official AEF doctrine, while Lejeune demonstrated an impressive ability to adjust preconceived ideas and methods to the reality of the battlefield.

The 2nd Division was unique in two other important ways. First, whereas all other divisions were created in part in the United States and sent abroad, the 2nd Division was created in France in September 1917.

---

[3] The major combat units of the division were the 3rd Infantry Brigade, with the 9th and 23rd Infantry Regiments; the 4th Marine Brigade, with the 5th and 6th Marine Regiments; and the 2nd Field Artillery Brigade, with the 12th and 15th F.A. Regiments (75mm) and the 17th F.A. Regiment (155mm howitzers). Of the four infantry regiments, the percentages of first-year troops were the 5th Marines, 66 percent; the 6th Marines, 93 percent; the 9th Infantry, 88 percent; and in the 23rd Infantry, 90 percent. In the 17th F.A., 90 percent of the troops had been in uniform fewer than twelve months; in the 15th F.A., the total was 87 percent; and in the 12th F.A., the total was 84 percent. Oliver J. Spaulding and John W. Wright, *The Second Division, American Expeditionary Force in France, 1917–1919* (New York: Hillman Press, 1937), 6–7.

Some of its units were already in France at that time and others were shipped over during the remaining months of the year. While the division command waited for the units from the United States, its infantry split its time training for combat, guarding AEF installations, and doing manual labor for the Line of Communications. Second, the division was the only one in the AEF that had a brigade of Marines as one of its two infantry brigades. Half of that brigade, the 5th Marine Regiment, had traveled to France in the initial AEF contingent with units of the 1st Division in July and trained with those troops until ordered to join the newly created 2nd Division in September. The other Marine regiment, the 6th Marines, was created in the United States and joined the division over the next few months. Although this half Marine–half Army split-service organization could have been a source of contention and strife within the division (and occasionally was), for the most part the divisional leadership apparently forged a sense of divisional allegiance and good-natured rivalry that yielded more positives than negatives from the unique organization.

The division's unique features contributed to its inconsistent level of training during its first months. A number of its infantry companies arrived in France during the summer of 1917, and although some of them became among the best trained in the AEF, others spent weeks doing labor instead of training. But, other infantry companies did not join the division and begin training until January 1918. Although GHQ gave the division a detailed training plan in October 1917, only a few units were able to follow it to any significant extent.[4] When staff officers from GHQ visited the division in January, they noted that some units had made excellent progress but others "were entirely untrained." Although some companies and battalions were in good shape, no brigade-level training "of any sort" had begun due to the dispersal of the units. The inspectors, colonels Harold B. Fiske and Paul B. Malone, stressed three important conclusions. The division had "excellent personnel" and was well led, it had "some well instructed companies" and others whose training was just beginning, and those units that were well trained had received plenty of "trench warfare training."[5]

---

[4] GHQ, AEF, "Program of Training for the 2d Division," Report of G-5, Folder 56.7, Box 249, Commander in Chief Reports, RG 120, NA.

[5] Memorandum for Chief of Staff from Training Section, GHQ, Subject: Tactical inspection and future training of the 2nd Division, 30 January 1918, Folder 56.2, Box 33, 2nd Division Historical File, RG 120, NA. See also Memorandum for Chief, Training Section,

The division's training began in earnest only in mid-January, when most of the units, less the artillery, finally arrived at the division training area near Bourmont in Lorraine. GHQ issued a completely revised training schedule in early February, specifying a new three-month training regimen for the division. The division was to complete a month of "small-unit training" by mid-March, spend its second month in front-line trenches with French units, and then move back to a training area for four weeks of large-unit exercises and maneuvers in open warfare.[6] The artillery regiments were to complete their firing training at Valdahon, join the division at the front trenches during the second month, and then take part in the open-warfare training. The program was designed to ensure that the division was ready to fight both in the trenches and out in the open. But, as with the training of nearly all other AEF units, the program was not fully accomplished.

The training regimen went well enough during the first period, although it was of necessity based primarily on developing only trench-warfare skills. Along with continued marching drill, target shooting, and bayonet practice, the troops learned how to throw grenades and carry out short assaults from mock trench systems. Although most of the training occurred under the leadership of the division's American officers, it was supervised by more than a dozen French officers who offered advice and supervision.[7] The influence of the French officers was particularly marked at the artillery camp, where they dominated the instruction of the gunners, basing all training on "French methods of firing."[8] The artillery brigade commander, Brigadier General George L. Irwin, admitted that the French officers were "officers of experience, devoted to their profession, and eager to render every assistance to their allies," but he also noted that "the long period of stationary trench warfare" had left them with "a very

---

GHQ, Subject: Visit to 2nd Division, 9 January 1918, Folder 56.2, Box 33, 2nd Division Historical File, RG 120, NA.

[6] Spaulding and Wright, *Second Division*, 8.

[7] Even the training that was supposed to focus on open-warfare skills tended to deal more with marching and deploying units for battle than with offensive tactics or attack techniques. See the report of one such "Open Warfare Exercise" in Chief of Staff, I Army Corps to C.G., 2nd Division, Subject: Exercises of February 20th, 1918, 28 February 1918, Folder 56.2, Box 33, 2nd Division Historical File, RG 120, NA. For one Marine's account of this training, see George B. Clark, ed., *His Time in Hell: A Texas Marine in France: The World War I Memoir of Warren R. Jackson* (Novato, Calif.: Presidio Press, 2001), 36–44.

[8] "History of the 12th Field Artillery," Folder 11.4, Box 4, 2nd Division Historical File, RG 120, NA.

palpable disregard of the methods necessary in a war of movement."[9]
The gunners closed this phase of training by firing a brigade-level exercise
done completely "under trench warfare assumptions," including typical
defensive barrages and a rolling barrage "according to a prearranged
scheme."[10] Few open-warfare skills were learned by the American gunners at Valdahon or by the infantry near Bourmont, but they learned well
the skills required to fight in and around the trenches.

In mid-March, the infantry and machine-gunners began the second
phase of training by joining French units in front-line trenches just north
of St. Mihiel. However, the neat schedule of slowly feeding each battalion,
regiment, and brigade into the trenches under firm French tactical command, as well as the overall length of the division's stay at the front, were
thrown off by the German Spring offensives. Shortly after the artillery
battalions joined French artillery regiments for training at the front in
late March, French units were pulled out to stop the German advances.
By 1 April, the regimental commanders received command of their own
sectors, and shortly after that, each brigade controlled a sector. Instead
of leaving the trenches in mid-April to begin the month of open-warfare
training, as the GHQ schedule directed, the division soon assumed command of its own sector and held it until 12 May. During this period, the
division was able, as was the 1st Division before it, to continue some
small-unit training for those troops not actually holding the front lines.[11]

By all accounts, the division did well in this phase of training. One
future division commander wrote that the weeks in the trenches were "of
very great value" to the division's development.[12] Unit histories note that
during this baptism by fire, the troops "learned a great deal about position
warfare," including carrying out patrols and repelling enemy raids.[13] The
local French commander complimented the infantry for the way it seized
control of No Man's Land with an aggressive schedule of patrols and
raids. On 14 April, the 9th Infantry successfully resisted a strong raid
by more than four hundred enemy soldiers, including stormtroop units,

[9] George L. Irwin, "Notes on the Training and Handling of Divisional Artillery in France,"
   Field Artillery Journal 9 (November–December 1919): 489.
[10] William D. Bickham and William E. Burr, "Second Field Artillery Brigade History,"
   pp. 2–3, n.d., Folder 11.4, Box 4, 2nd Division Historical File, RG 120, NA.
[11] Spaulding and Wright, *Second Division*, 18–30; Commander-in-chief to Chief of the
   French Mission, Subject: Training of 2nd Division, 16 May 1918, Folder 50.4, Box 32,
   2nd Division Historical File, RG 120, NA.
[12] Lejeune, *Reminiscences*, 291.
[13] Bickham and Burr, "Second Field Artillery Brigade History," pp. 4–7, n.d., Folder 11.4,
   Box 4, 2nd Division Historical File, RG 120, NA.

taking eleven Germans prisoner and killing nearly seventy of the attackers. Pershing sent his "warmest congratulations" for the resistance on that day.[14] He later claimed that the local French corps commander spoke highly of the 2nd Division and that the commander of the French Second Army told him that "without a doubt, it was then as efficient as any of his French divisions."[15] Yet, this was true only concerning trench warfare. Like other U.S. divisions, the 2nd had done practically no training for open warfare on the modern battlefield. That was to be the focus of the third and final period of training.

Although the third period of training was supposed to last at least four weeks, the crisis of the German offensives and the desire to get American units ready for unsupervised service on more active fronts abbreviated the schedule. When the 2nd Division moved into its training area, GHQ gave it a training schedule that called for "a minimum of six days' training" in open-warfare exercises and maneuvers, a quarter of the initial amount. It is interesting that a GHQ memorandum to the head of the French Mission admitted that while Pershing's staff was confident that the smaller units were in excellent shape, there were still "some questions as to the efficiency of the Division's Command," and those questions needed to be answered by having GHQ monitor the command's handling of these final large-unit maneuvers.[16] The training included "command exercises" (i.e., with unit commanders but no troops); regimental- and brigade-level maneuvers; and at least one division-sized attack, complete with artillery preparations, infantry assaults, and preparations to meet an expected counterattack. The chief indication that these were "open-warfare" maneuvers was the lack of any rolling barrage to cover the advance.[17] No records describe how well the division did in these maneuvers, but the fact that Pershing relieved no senior commanders suggests that the division performed satisfactorily.

Immediately after the conclusion of these maneuvers, the division received orders to relieve the 1st Division near Cantigny. But, before

[14] Pershing to C.G., 2nd Division, 14 April 1918, in *The Ninth U. S. Infantry in the World War* (n.p., n.d.), 2–5. Total AEF losses in this raid were fourteen killed, fifty wounded, fifty-two gassed, and twenty-eight missing. *USAWW*, 3: 512–13. The division suffered 881 casualties during its four-week stay along the St. Mihiel salient. ABMC, *American Armies*, 165.

[15] Pershing, *My Experiences*, 1: 381–2; 2: 48.

[16] Commander-in-chief to Chief of the French Mission, Subject: Training of 2nd Division, 16 May 1918, Folder 50.4, Box 32, 2nd Division Historical File, RG 120, NA.

[17] Ibid.; Lejeune, *Reminiscences*, 291; Bickham and Burr, "Second Field Artillery Brigade History," pp. 4–7, n.d., Folder 11.4, Box 4, 2nd Division Historical File, RG 120, NA.

those orders were executed, GHQ gave the 2nd Division a new mission. On 27 May, the third German Spring offensive had broken through the French lines along the Chemin des Dames, and within two days, the stormtroopers had penetrated to a depth of 25 kilometers on a front of 70 kilometers. Pershing turned the 2nd Division over to Marshal Foch, who ordered it to speed toward Château-Thierry to help plug the hole in the lines. The division's training period was over.

The 2nd Division completed roughly sixteen weeks of training, but only one was in any way devoted to teaching the skills and methods considered most important by the AEF leadership. That one week of training dedicated to open warfare may have been more than the 26th Division received before its first major engagement, but it was substantially less than GHQ thought necessary to ensure proficiency. The division may have known how to advance, communicate, and use its weaponry, but that was true only during the stable environment and limited attacks associated with trench warfare. It had done little to ensure that it could carry out the kind of deep, decisive attacks on open terrain envisioned by GHQ. Of equal importance, some commanders had not adjusted their prewar doctrinal ideas that formed the basis of those visions.[18]

Belleau Wood and Vaux, June–July 1918

The 2nd Division's first major engagement occurred at Belleau Wood, a 3-kilometer long and 1-kilometer wide kidney-shaped forest about 10 kilometers west of Château-Thierry. The brutal struggle for that small but densely overgrown patch of woods quickly became, and has remained ever since, one of the most celebrated AEF battles of the entire war. Yet,

---

[18] As the fighting in and around Belleau Wood demonstrated, many officers in the 2nd Division, including some new brigade and regimental commanders, were committed to initiate open warfare on the Western Front. However, one document shows that the division commander, Omar Bundy, may have had a better understanding of the challenges of doing so. In mid-May, Hugh A. Drum, then a staff officer in the operations section of GHQ, submitted a memorandum to Fox Conner, the GHQ operations chief, on the appropriateness of the AEF's large "square division." Drum included comments from a number of division commanders, including Bundy, who stated, "Since on the western front open warfare will occur only in periods, followed by long periods of trench warfare, the ideal organization is that best suited for offensive trench warfare." But, Bundy was not a forceful commander and he exerted little influence on the fighting at Belleau Wood. He left the division in July. In his report, Drum concurred with Bundy and recommended retaining the big four-infantry-regiment division, partially because "In some cases the enemy's deployment may be so dense that the old time shoulder to shoulder function will be required." Drum to Assistant Chief of Staff, G-3, 18 May 1918, *USAWW*, 2: 406–12.

for all its fame, the battle was neither particularly well fought by the troops nor well managed by senior officers. Many times during the three-week fight, both the attack plans developed by senior officers and the tactics employed by the junior officers and men showed that they all had much to learn – and much to unlearn. Initial attacks by weakly supported infantry in rigid linear formations ended in disaster. However, by the end of the battle, the division had demonstrated two important characteristics. First, the Marines and soldiers who fought in and around the wood showed a toughness and determination that impressed all who monitored the battle, especially the French and Germans. Second, some of the division's later attacks showed significant improvement in both planning and execution, particularly in the use of overwhelming firepower. Then, a week after the victorious conclusion to the fighting in Belleau Wood, the division demonstrated even more impressive planning and operational abilities by carrying out a nearly perfect attack on the village of Vaux. Thus, although this series of engagements in June and July began with a futile bloodbath of inexperienced Marines in the wheat fields west of Belleau Wood, it ended with well-orchestrated combined arms attacks that annihilated enemy garrisons with relatively little cost in American life.[19]

On 31 May 1918, as thousands of panicked civilians evacuated Paris in response to the rapid German advances of the previous four days, units of the 2nd Division hurried east to begin their first major battle. The following day, two of the infantry regiments established a long line of resistance blocking the Château-Thierry to Paris highway. Even then, only fragments of broken French divisions remained between that line and the onrushing Germans. On 2 June, as the rest of the 2nd Division entered the sector, German attacks drove many of the remaining French troops through the American lines. Despondent French soldiers told the fresh Doughboys and Marines, "*la guerre est fini,*" and at least one retreating French officer ordered American troops to withdraw. A Marine major quickly countermanded the order. By the next afternoon, the division's four infantry regiments were holding a 20-kilometer-wide front, with machine-gun and artillery units in position to support them.[20]

---

[19] For a thorough examination of the French reaction to Belleau Wood, see Robert B. Bruce, *A Fraternity of Arms: America and France in the Great War* (Lawrence: University Press of Kansas, 2003), p. 217.

[20] American troops commonly retorted that the war was "*pas finie*" as long as they were still in it, and the sector soon became known as the *Pas Fini* sector. Spaulding and Wright, *Second Division*, 40–41.

What appeared to be shaping into a defensive stand to save Paris soon turned into an opportunity for the division to make its first major attack. Although American troops suffered from sporadic enemy small-arms and artillery fire during these first days of June, and the Marine brigade repelled at least one strong attack on 3 June, the approaching German divisions stopped before running headlong into the American line.[21] On 5 June, the commander of the French XXI Corps, General Joseph Degoutte, felt confident enough to order the 2nd Division and the French 167th Division on its left to make short advances on the following day to seize better defensive ground. With the exception of small trench raids and the 1st Division's limited attack at Cantigny, these were the first AEF offensive actions of the war.

Senior officers in both the German and American armies recognized the importance of these initial clashes. Believing the optimistic promises of naval officers in the *Kriegsmarine*, many German officers had never expected American troops to get to France. After AEF troops began arriving, army officers told their men that the inexperienced Americans would prove no match for the Kaiser's battle-tested veterans. When General Erich Ludendorff, the de facto head of the German Army, learned that AEF units were opposing his forces near Château-Thierry, he ordered that they be "hit particularly hard."[22] He knew any American success would further damage the faltering morale of his own troops and revive the flagging Allies. The commander of one German division opposite the 2nd Division at Belleau Wood was more explicit, announcing:

Should the Americans on our front even temporarily gain the upper hand, it would have a most unfavorable effect for us as regards the morale of the Allies and the duration of the war. In the fighting that now confronts us, we are not concerned with the occupation or non-occupation of this or that unimportant wood or village, but with the question as to whether the Anglo-American propaganda that the American Army is equal to or even superior to the German, will be successful.[23]

Senior officers in the 2nd Division were equally concerned about the moral dimension of the fight. Bundy stated flatly that "effects on both American and German morale and prestige . . . make imperative the

---

[21] The division suffered 546 casualties between 1 and 5 June, even though it made no attacks. On 4 June, the commander of the German IV Reserve Corps, opposite the 2nd Division, ordered his front-line divisions to temporarily assume a defensive posture. See ABMC, *American Armies*, 103.

[22] Ludendorff quoted in Smythe, *Pershing*, 139.

[23] ABMC, *American Armies*, 49.

James G. Harbord, commander of the Marine Brigade at Belleau Wood and of the 2nd Division at Soissons, before assuming command of the Services of Supply in July 1918.

occupation of the Bois de Belleau."[24] Harbord, the Army general who commanded the Marines throughout June and exerted the most influence over the battle, later claimed that "every man in the Marine Brigade realized that America was on trial as to the courage and fighting quality of her sons." He agreed with the opposing division commander that "more than the Bois de Belleau was at stake...it was a struggle for psychological mastery."[25] Such conditions might have been expected to encourage senior American officers to ensure that all attacks were planned and executed in a manner almost certain to achieve success, but other forces, including prewar doctrinal convictions, exerted negative influences on the campaign.

[24] "Journal of Activities of the 2nd Division from May 31st to June 30th," Folder 33.3, Box 13, 2nd Division Historical File, RG 120, NA.
[25] Harbord, *American Army*, 296, 300.

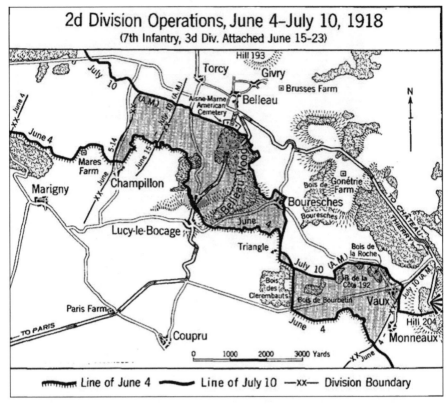

MAP 15: Operations of the 2nd Division in and around Belleau Wood.

In accordance with Degoutte's directive of 5 June, Harbord ordered his leftmost battalion to advance about a kilometer and take a small elevation named Hill 142, just west of Belleau Wood (see Map 15). The battalion to its right was to make a slight advance to maintain its connection with that unit. Both moves were required to keep the division abreast of the French 167th Division on the left, which was to advance its entire line a short distance.[26] The terrain was generally open, few trenches existed for troops on either side, and units were generally dispersed on exceptionally wide frontages. To officers such as Harbord, it must have seemed like ideal conditions to put into practice the official AEF doctrine of warfare.

Harbord, a devoted disciple of the official open-warfare doctrine, arranged little fire support for the initial attack. Six batteries of 75mm

[26] HQ 4th Brigade, Field Orders No. 1, in "Diary Containing Field Orders and Instructions," p. 7, Folder 33.5, Box 79, 2nd Division Historical File, RG 120, NA.

guns and two batteries of 155mm howitzers were available for the operation – about one fifth of the divisional artillery at the time, which was augmented by two regiments of French light guns and two battalions of howitzers. More significant than the numbers of guns was the manner in which they were used. The artillery orders plainly stated that "there will not be any preparation properly speaking, so as not to attrack [*sic*] the attention of the enemy." A little "raking fire" was authorized on Hill 142 during the preceding night, but only by the light guns. Even during the attack itself, the big howitzers only fired interdiction missions deep behind the enemy lines. For 5 minutes immediately preceding the infantry assault, the light guns were to place "a violent annihilating fire" on the objective, but that fire was to shift to more distant targets the minute the Marines jumped-off.[27] No rolling barrage was to cover the advance. Instead, one artillery regiment was detailed to provide any additional support requested by Harbord. Although Harbord's orders directed two machine-gun companies to join the attack, he made no mention of them firing in support of the advance.

The attack began promptly at 0345 hours on 6 June, and by 0700, the assault companies had taken their objectives, captured more than a dozen prisoners, and were consolidating their new positions. Although the battalion commanders reported they had met "heavy artillery and rifle fire" and suffered "quite a number" of casualties, enthusiastic congratulations were soon zipping through the phone wires to the appropriate regimental and battalion commanders. This first attack was treated as a major success, with the regimental and brigade commanders bragging that their men had "advanced faster than the French."[28] But, the formations and tactics used left much to be desired. One Marine claimed that the assault companies had advanced in "a beautiful deployment, lines all dressed and guiding true."[29] They had apparently made the advance in fine linear waves and executed the final assault with little more than

---

[27] William Chamberlaine, "Report of Operations, 2d Field Artillery Brigade, 2d Division, During Month of June, 1918," p. 16, 10 September 1919, Folder 33.6, Box 78, 2nd Division Historical File, RG 120, NA; HQ 2nd F.A. Brigade, Orders No. 1, 5 June 1918, U.S. Army, 2nd Division, *Records of the Second Division (Regular)*, (Washington, D.C.: Army War College, 1924), vol. 9 (hereafter *RSD*). See HQ 4th Brigade, Field Orders No. 1, in "Diary Containing Field Orders and Instructions," p. 7, Folder 33.5, Box 79, 2nd Division Historical File, RG 120, NA.

[28] "Diary Containing Field Orders and Instructions," p. 8, Folder 33.5, Box 79, 2nd Division Historical File, RG 120, NA.

[29] Robert B. Asprey, *At Belleau Wood* (New York: Putnam's Sons, 1965; reprint, Denton, Tex.: University of North Texas Press, 1996), 145.

their own rifle fire, the point of the bayonet, and a good deal of courage. Some even pushed well beyond the objective and had to move back to the correct position. The Marines took Hill 142 but suffered heavy casualties.[30]

Before Harbord had received the final casualty figure for the morning attack, he issued orders for a follow-up attack that afternoon to seize Belleau Wood, situated directly in front of his brigade. Degoutte's original order had directed the division to take the wood "as soon as possible" after making the morning advance, and the 2nd wasted no time in attempting to do so.[31] In a rare instance of intervention during the battle, Bundy instructed Harbord to make the second attack at 1700 hours that afternoon. Harbord quickly issued his orders at 1400 hours, directing four Marine battalions to attack in two phases: the first to seize the wood and the second to take the town of Bouresches just southeast of the wood.[32]

For this attack – more than twice the size of the morning advance and likely to be much more difficult – Harbord allocated *even less artillery support*. Although a few more guns were included in the fire plan, they were only to provide "interdiction and harassing fires in the zone to be attacked" and place some fire "on the points where it is possible that there are nests of machine guns."[33] The attack orders contained no details regarding the rates of fire during the preparation and no mention of any heavy barrage during the infantry attack. Again, a rolling barrage was conspicuously absent, as was any mention of supporting fire from the brigade's machine guns, mortars, and 37mm guns.

---

[30] Maj. Gen. John A. Lejeune, the future commander of the division, later wrote that the morning attack was made with "very little artillery support and in the face of a withering machine gun fire" and led to "very heavy casualties." Lejeune, *Reminiscences*, 293. One division history claims that the morning attack led to as many as four hundred casualties and the capture of just twenty enemy soldiers. Spaulding and Wright, *Second Division*, 49.

[31] HQ French XXI Corps, General Operations Order, 5 June 1918, *USAWW*, 4: 143.

[32] Throughout the fighting around Belleau Wood, Bundy and the division staff performed more like an administrative clearinghouse than a command and planning center. On 5 June, they issued Field Orders No. 8, which organized the division positions in the sector but gave no details regarding the upcoming attacks. The next official written orders issued by the division, Field Orders No. 9, were issued on 30 June for the assault on Vaux. Apparently, the real combat planning and commanding was left to the brigades. See *RSD*, vol. 1; HQ 4th Brigade, Field Orders No. 2, in "Diary Containing Field Orders and Instructions," p. 9, Folder 33.5, Box 79, 2nd Division Historical File, RG 120, NA.

[33] HQ 2nd F.A. Brigade, Field Orders No. 3, 6 June 1918, 1400 hours, *USAWW*, 4: 363.

The lack of firepower in the attack plan appears to have been intentional, a product of the official AEF doctrine that minimized its importance and exaggerated the capabilities of "self-reliant infantry." Harbord later claimed that he thought Belleau Wood was only lightly held by the enemy and that he wanted his men to make "a surprise attack" that was "not preceded by any unusual artillery activity." With the absence of deep trenches, the uncertainty regarding the strength and dispositions of the enemy, and nearly a kilometer of wheat fields between the opposing forces, it must have seemed like open-warfare conditions to Harbord. He was mistaken. After the morning attack, chances of surprising the enemy were small, and as he later admitted, "the Bois proved to be very occupied, with many machine gun nests, in positions well chosen among giant boulders."[34]

Although the lack of artillery support was a major weakness of the attack plan, the attacking infantry units did their share to add to the tragedy. At H hour, they formed up, as one observer reported, "in beautiful deployment in beautiful line" and began a long, slow march through the wheat fields toward Belleau Wood.[35] Few men from Major Benjamin S. Berry's battalion made it. Halfway across the wheat field, German machine guns and rifles opened up on the long straight lines and mowed them down. Berry's regimental commander, Colonel Wendell Neville, reported that most of the battalion was probably killed or wounded. To the right, where the distance between the American lines and the wood was much shorter, Major Berton W. Sibley's battalion made it into the southern edge of the wood before being stopped by enemy fire. He soon reported that enemy machine guns "had done a lot of damage," losses were "heavy," and he was "unable to advance" any farther. His regimental commander, Lieutenant Colonel Harry Lee, told Harbord that it

---

[34] Harbord, *American Army*, 289–92. Despite Harbord's postwar explanation that the French had informed him that Belleau Wood was "unoccupied," Marine patrols had just confirmed that the wood was held by the enemy, and their report supposedly was forwarded to Harbord and to the division HQ, which even included a note to that effect in the day's entry in the journal of operations. See Millett, *In Many a Strife: General Gerald C. Thomas and the U.S. Marine Corps, 1917–1956* (Annapolis: Naval Institute Press, 1993), 37; and Asprey, *Belleau Wood*, 157–63. Spaulding and Wright claim that as many as a thousand German troops, with machine guns and trench mortars, were holding the wood on 6 June. *Second Division*, 53.

[35] "Diary Containing Field Orders and Instructions," p. 11, Folder 33.5, Box 79, 2nd Division Historical File, RG 120, NA.

seemed "impossible to attack hostile gun positions without artillery."[36]
That is exactly what had been attempted that day in both attacks, and
the results were horrific – 1,087 Marine casualties – while only shattered
fragments of the battalions made it into the wood.

Few histories note that troops from the 3rd Brigade also made hastily
organized attacks on 6 June and that they achieved little more than the
Marines. The 23rd Infantry was directed to assault the German line with
two battalions at 1700 hours in support of the 4th Brigade's simultaneous attack on Belleau Wood. Although the attack was to be supported
by machine guns, mortars, and 37mm guns (an improvement over the
Marine attack), time constraints prevented the attacking battalions from
arranging such support before the attack had to be launched. A regimental
staff officer later admitted that the attack plan made "no arrangements"
whatsoever for artillery support, even though the infantry had to advance
over a "rolling wheat field." He noted that, in the end, "little, if any, supporting fire" of any sort aided the attack and the results were predictable:
"enemy machine gunners opened fire from the front and flanks, inflicting
heavy casualties and halting the attack." Apparently, Harbord was not
alone in attempting to implement the AEF's official open-warfare doctrine
on 6 June.[37]

Back at Belleau Wood, Harbord ordered Sibley to halt all attacks
during that first night, but by the next morning, Sibley's Marines were
trying to work their way forward again. They made little headway on
7 June and even less on the following morning. Harbord tried to get
some mortars to the assault troops and arranged some artillery fire on
the wood, but these efforts were too little, too late, and poorly coordinated. Months later, Major General John A. Lejeune, the innovative
and firepower-conscious Marine who took command of the division
in late July, wrote a critical report on the division's operations in and
around Belleau Wood. In it, he claimed that all the attacks between 6 and
8 June were attempted essentially "without artillery preparation." Lejeune
condemned such tactics, caustically emphasizing that "little progress was
made" and that "the reckless courage of the foot soldier with his rifle
and bayonet could not overcome machine guns, well-protected in rocky

---

[36] Ibid., p. 14, Folder 33.5, Box 79, 2nd Division Historical File, RG 120, NA. The smaller
secondary attack on Bouresches was successful, although casualties were severe in that
assault as well.

[37] Infantry School, U. S. Army, *Infantry in Battle* (Washington, D.C.: The Infantry School
Press, 1934), 294–96.

nests."[38] Although Lejeune was not assigned to the division during June, as the senior Marine Corps officer in the AEF, he took special note of the 4th Brigade's operations and visited the unit during the battle. He was impressed by the courage and fierceness of the Marines but not by the unsupported manner in which they were ordered to attack. Despite what looked like open-warfare conditions, Belleau Wood was apparently no place to make attacks based on supposedly "self-reliant infantry."[39]

By midday of 8 June, reports from numerous small-unit commanders and observers were painting just such a picture for Harbord. Berry's battalion was practically destroyed, Sibley's unit had suffered severe casualties and was stuck on an unidentified line in the southern part of the wood, untold numbers of enemy machine guns dominated the forest and the open ground surrounding it, and additional attacks were reported to be "impossible without further preparation."[40] Even the staff of the French XXI Corps knew different methods were needed, and they issued orders directing that future attacks be "conducted methodically, by means of successive minor operations, making the utmost use of artillery and reducing the employment of infantry to the minimum."[41] Although contrary to AEF doctrine, this was good advice.

On 8 June, Brigadier General William Chamberlaine, the artillery brigade commander, visited Harbord and proposed just such an attack. He suggested that for the first time, Belleau Wood be "systematically covered by artillery fire preparatory to another attack."[42] To Harbord's credit, he agreed. He quickly directed the preparation of detailed plans for a set-piece attack on 10 June and ordered Sibley to withdraw what was left of his battalion to an identifiable line at the southern edge of the wood, thus giving the artillery "a free hand" in neutralizing the strong German

[38] John A. Lejeune, "Summary of Battle of Château-Thierry, May 31st to July 10th, 1918," *RSD*, vol. 6.

[39] Pershing nevertheless seemed impressed enough with the 4th Brigade's operations of these first days, sending Bundy a telegram complimenting Harbord and his Marines "for the splendid conduct of the attack," which he considered to be "a magnificent example of American courage and dash." He was less impressed with Bundy's involvement in the battle, as his subsequent relief showed. See "Diary Containing Field Orders and Instructions," p. 26, Folder 33.5, Box 79, 2nd Division Historical File, RG 120, NA.

[40] "Diary Containing Field Orders and Instructions," pp. 16–22, Folder 33.5, Box 79, 2nd Division Historical File, RG 120, NA.

[41] HQ XXI Corps, Order, 7 June 1918, *USAWW*, 4: 403.

[42] Brig. Gen. Chamberlaine, "Report of Operations," p. 16, 10 September 1919, Folder 33.6, Box 78, 2nd Division Historical File, RG 120, NA.

defenses. Finally, Harbord was going to rely on the trench-warfare methods the division spent so much of its training period learning.

Harbord had Chamberlaine create a fire plan that organized the fire of all 160 guns in the sector in support of a single battalion attack to seize the southern half of the wood. Starting at dawn on 9 June and continuing throughout that night, all the guns were to maintain a heavy rate of fire on the wood and the surrounding area. Harbord told one regimental commander he expected this fire to "obliterate any enemy organizations" in the wood.[43] The next morning, for a full hour before the infantry assault, all the guns were to fire at a maximum rate on suspected and known enemy strong points in and around the forest. Both light guns and heavy howitzers were to pound the entire wood while other 155s hit support targets in the rear. Then, for the first time in the battle, the light guns were to shift to a dense rolling barrage to cover the attacking Marines. The barrage moved fast, advancing 100 meters every 2 minutes, but finally the infantry would attack with at least some coordinated artillery support. To help isolate the German garrison in the wood, Harbord ordered twelve machine guns to form a massed battery in the town of Bouresches, from where they could pour their fire along the eastern flank of the wood to box in the defenders. This was the first time the division incorporated machine-gun fire into an attack plan.[44]

At 0330 on 10 June, all the guns of the 2nd Division quickened their fire to their maximum rate, drenching Belleau Wood with artillery shells. One hour later, the rolling barrage began and a battalion from the 6th Marines followed it through the southern half of the wood. A few minutes into the attack, the battalion commander, Major John H. Hughes, reported, "Artillery barrage working beautifully" and that, unlike the attacks of the previous days, the enemy machine guns were generally silent. He soon reported that he had taken his objective "without opposition" (although he had accidentally stopped well short of it). Hughes praised the work of the artillery, which he claimed had "blown the Bois de Belleau to mince meat."[45] The destruction was the result of the twenty-eight thousand rounds from the 75mm guns and twelve thousand from the howitzers that

[43] "Diary Containing Field Orders and Instructions," p. 24, Folder 33.5, Box 79, 2nd Division Historical File, RG 120, NA.
[44] HQ 4th Brigade, Field Orders No. 3, 9 June 1918, 1830 hours, "Diary Containing Field Orders and Instructions," pp. 28–9, Folder 33.5, Box 79, 2nd Division Historical File, RG 120, NA.
[45] "Diary Containing Field Orders and Instructions," p. 30, Folder 33.5, Box 79, 2nd Division Historical File, RG 120, NA.

were sent into the wood during the previous 24 hours. Total American losses during the attack amounted to just eight killed and twenty-four wounded. By relying on detailed planning and heavy firepower, a single battalion of Harbord's men did more in just a few hours and at a fraction of the human cost than more than two battalions had been able to do in two full days.

Harbord quickly arranged for an assault on the rest of Belleau Wood to be made the next morning, using a similar scheme of attack. While Hughes' battalion held its line in the southern portion of the wood, a battalion from the 5th Marines was to drive eastward, join up with Hughes' men, and take the northern half. If the German defenses were facing south to meet Hughes' unit, the attacking battalion would drive in their flank and wipe them out. Harbord charged Chamberlaine with creating a similar fire plan for the new assault. Although the artillery maintained the intense hour-long preliminary bombardment and the rolling barrage, two other factors were to work against the new fire plan. First, unlike the attack for 10 June, the attack of the following day did not have a full day of destructive fire before the attack. Harbord could not wait another day because the French Army was threatening to remove much of his supporting artillery, and he apparently wanted to complete the seizure of the wood before he lost the extra guns. Perhaps of greater importance was that Chamberlaine had to plan on firing into woods half-filled with Marines. The exact position of Hughes' battalion became increasingly uncertain (i.e., he had stopped not only short of his objective but also of the main German line in the woods), and Chamberlaine had to build in a safe margin of error when firing the preparatory bombardment and barrage.

The flank attack of 11 June, although much more successful than the attacks of 6, 7, and 8 June, was much more difficult than the fighting of the previous day. The assault battalion, commanded by Lieutenant Colonel Frederick M. Wise, advanced through enemy fire across the bloody wheat field of 6 June and drove into the wood. But, as it worked through the forest, it ran into a number of enemy machine-gun nests hidden in the wood's gigantic boulders and felled trees. They had survived all the artillery fire and caused at least two hundred casualties in the attack force. Using automatic rifles and even some Stokes mortars, the Marines advanced but failed to swing north when in the wood. They eventually reached the eastern edge of the wood, taking an impressive total of four hundred German prisoners and thirty machine guns along the way, but they did not completely clear out the northern half of the wood. Observers also noticed that the machine-gun barrage decimated whole groups of German troops moving into and out of the wood. Nevertheless, despite initial reports that the entire wood was captured, a number of mutually supporting enemy strong points remained in the northern section of Belleau Wood.[46]

The following day, an impatient Harbord held a conference with regimental and battalion commanders to discuss options for rooting out the remaining German resistance. Although unaware of the exact location of his own lines and of the extent of the enemy resistance still in the wood, Wise still claimed that his unit could take the rest of the wood if he received sufficient artillery support. Harbord ordered Wise to attack that afternoon at 1700 hours, and he arranged for an hour and a half of fire from a few guns of the 12th Field Artillery. As he had done at the start of the battle, Harbord again underestimated the strength of the remaining German positions. An hour of preparatory fire by a few batteries of light guns could not provide enough support for an attack in the dense growth and rugged terrain in the north of the wood.

At 1630 hours, an hour into the preliminary artillery fire, Wise reported that the preparation was not having the desired effect. With the full agreement of his artillery liaison officer, Wise concluded that the fire of the 75s was "entirely too light" and that it was not knocking out the machine-gun nests. Fearing that his unit was "going to have a little bit of trouble" because the attack area was "entirely too large for the number of guns assigned," Wise requested an extra hour of artillery fire before the infantry attack. Harbord granted the request but even that extension proved inadequate.[47] At H hour, Wise's battalion attacked and slowly worked its way to the north end of the wood, meeting much machine-gun fire along the way and suffering heavy casualties. Wise reported his men had to use mortars and rifle grenades to destroy enemy strong points and that enemy artillery caused heavy losses. Although some reports claimed that the wood was "completely cleaned out of enemy detachments," it seems

---

[46] Wise initially reported that his men had gone all the way to the northeast section of the wood but, due to misdirection in the dense forest, they had veered to the south, leaving most of the northern portion untouched. Wise unwittingly gave Harbord inaccurate information regarding his success, leading Harbord and Bundy to conclude erroneously that the entire wood was taken. They reported this supposed success to Pershing, who even issued an official press release announcing the capture of the wood. When all of this was eventually sorted out later in the month, Wise lost his command and was transferred out of the division, only to rejoin it after the battle of Soissons. See Asprey, Belleau Wood, 255–65.

[47] "Diary Containing Field Orders and Instructions," pp. 39–40, Folder 33.5, Box 79, 2nd Division Historical File, RG 120, NA.

that this was not the case. Wise's battalion was so weakened that it could not adequately mop up the attack area or stop groups of German troops from infiltrating the wood.[48] Determined to deny their fledgling enemy a complete victory, senior German commanders ordered hundreds of troops to filter back into the wood after dark, and within a few days, they had established a huge machine-gun nest in the far northwest corner.

The firepower-based attacks between 10 and 12 June had not yet completely cleared the enemy from Belleau Wood, but they had been much more successful than the open-warfare–based infantry attacks of the first three days. Lejeune's report on the battle seized on this very fact, claiming that a comparison of the "little progress" made during the initial attacks with the successes of the later efforts showed that "the need for artillery in the attack" was "strikingly obvious."[49] The report might have added that ample use of automatic rifles, mortars, rifle grenades, and machine guns had also proven helpful, but his appreciation of the crucial role of artillery support was an important element of the doctrinal learning process within the division.

If those lessons were clear enough later, they were apparently not so clear then, at least not to Harbord. Between 13 and 24 June, he directed a number of small attacks on the remaining German machine-gun nest, and each was made without sufficient artillery support – and some were attempted without any artillery support at all.[50] Despite intelligence

---

[48] Journal of Operations, 12 June 1918, *RSD*, vol. 6. Asprey concludes that Wise's battalion did not even reach the far northern edge of the wood. Other sources indicate they did but could not hold such an extended line. In either case, the result was the same. Over the next few days, the Germans maintained and even increased their presence in the northern tip of the wood. See Asprey, *Belleau Wood*, 278–84.

[49] Lejeune, "Summary of Battle of Château-Thierry," *RSD*, vol. 6.

[50] The 4th Brigade, augmented by fresh companies from the 7th Infantry of the 3rd Division between 17 and 21 June, made at least two such attacks between 20 and 23 June. Before the second attack by the 7th Infantry, on 21 June, the attacking battalion commander told Harbord he needed one thousand hand grenades and five hundred rifle grenades to have any chance of success. Then, in a pointed confidential message to Harbord, he warned that "Orders have been issued for an attack tomorrow morning" but "under the conditions noted I do not believe any attack without a heavy artillery fire preceding can move the guns from the woods. They are all emplaced and strongly held. The woods is almost a thicket [*sic*] and the throwing of troops into the woods is filtering away men with nothing gained." He recommended withdrawing the two most forward companies and "that a heavy artillery fire" precede the attack. He warned again, "I can assure you that the orders to attack will stand as given, but it cannot succeed. This is only my individual expression and has not reached the ears of any one else . . . please consider this . . . the two Stokes won't even worry the German Machine Guns." Harbord did hastily order a short preliminary bombardment and even a rolling barrage, but the attack failed nonetheless.

reports that estimated the Germans had stuffed as many as two hundred soldiers and fifteen machine guns into the strong point, Harbord refused to order another firepower-based set-piece attack. When he sent Major Maurice E. Shearers' tired battalion back into the wood on 21 June, Harbord explicitly stated that he thought it was "not practicable to withdraw again and give further artillery preparation." With the enemy's aggressive policy of reinfiltrating the wood and the necessity of withdrawing the Marines to a clearly identifiable line behind their current positions before any new saturation bombardment, Harbord probably did not want to take the risk that the Germans would simply follow up the Marine withdrawal and take control of more of the wood. But, still convinced of the "great power" of the rifle, Harbord also believed his infantry could do the job on their own. He told Shearer that "by judicious use of sharpshooting snipers," he should be able to eliminate the remaining enemy position "without much expenditure of men." The only other specific advice he offered was a dangerous frontal attack supported by whatever infantry weapons could be brought to bear: "With the sniping . . . you should be endeavoring to get the machine gun nests surrounded so you can rush them when ready."[51] Shearer attempted such an attack on the evening of 23 June and it failed terribly. The battalion suffered heavy losses and one company was reportedly "almost wiped out." The next morning, Shearer boldly told Harbord that "infantry alone cannot dislodge enemy [machine] guns."[52] The division leadership had underestimated the importance of firepower and overestimated the power of unsupported riflemen one more time in Belleau Wood. Thankfully, it proved to be the last time.

On 24 June, Harbord returned to the same methods used so successfully two weeks before. He held a conference with all infantry and artillery commanders, and they settled on another firepower-based set-piece attack. Shearers' battalion was directed to withdraw to an identifiable line to the south by 0300 hours the next morning, after which the artillery was "free to fire" on any points to the north. From that hour, the artillery was to begin shelling the woods heavily enough to prevent any enemy movement. After this methodical 13-hour bombardment by both light and heavy artillery, all the guns were to fire for another hour at their maximum rate,

The battalion commander described the artillery fire as "light in volume and ineffective." See "Diary Containing Field Orders and Instructions," pp. 51–2, Folder 33.5, Box 79, 2nd Division Historical File, RG 120, NA; and Asprey, *Belleau Wood*, 310.
[51] "Diary Containing Field Orders and Instructions," pp. 54–5, Folder 33.5, Box 79, 2nd Division Historical File, RG 120, NA.
[52] Ibid.

then shift to a rolling barrage that advanced 100 meters every 3 minutes. At 1700 hours, Shearers' Marines were to follow the barrage to the north edge of the wood and ensure that no resistance remained.

The strong artillery preparation and combined infantry–artillery attack of 25 June finally eliminated the remaining German positions in the northern tip of Belleau Wood. The Marines reported meeting "very little machine gun fire" and worked their way to the far edge of the forest, rooting out all enemy troops that survived the barrage. Although the mopping up continued into the morning of 26 June, Shearers' unit suffered just 123 casualties in the attack. They captured more than three hundred enemy troops and nineteen machine guns and reported "considerable" German dead on the forest floor. A later report prepared by the division staff admitted that, as during the attacks of 10–12 June, this final assault demonstrated the necessity of maximizing firepower during the attack.[53]

The successful attack of 25 June closed the 4th Brigade's battle for Belleau Wood, but it did not end the 2nd Division's active operations in the *Pas Fini* sector. On 1 July, the 3rd Brigade carried out an attack of its own against German positions in and around the village of Vaux, on the far right of the division sector. Although the 3rd Brigade played a minor role in the operations of June, its attack on Vaux proved that it had not missed the division's dearly bought lessons regarding the importance of accurate information on the enemy, knowledge of the attack zone, well-understood attack plans, and, especially, massive firepower.

Unlike Harbord's hurried and simplistic orders at the start of the fighting near Belleau Wood, the division staff took many days to plan the attack on Vaux. They made extensive use of a mountain of information gathered by Colonel Arthur L. Conger, a former member of Pershing's staff who had recently become the division's new intelligence officer. Conger was both a fine linguist and an experienced campaigner, having headed a crack intelligence-gathering unit during the Philippine War. After joining the 2nd Division, he collected information from infantry patrols, secured aircraft photographs of the town, and personally interviewed numerous former residents of the village to create a dossier on the town that offered all the information required to develop a meticulous set-piece attack plan. The

---

[53] Lejeune, "Summary of the Battle of Château-Thierry," *RSD*, vol. 6. HQ 2nd Division, "Report of Operations," 25 June 1918, *RSD*, vol. 6. Asprey gives higher casualty figures on both sides for this operation, claiming Shearers' unit suffered about 250 casualties and that the Germans lost 450 men. See Asprey, *Belleau Wood*, 322.

location, design, and strength of every building, cellar, enemy strong point, machine-gun nest, trench mortar emplacement, sentry post, supply route, and billeting location was identified on intelligence maps. The attack planners had all the information they needed to prepare a devastating attack plan, and they proved willing and able to put this information to good use.[54]

With the assistance of the division's new artillery brigade commander, Albert J. Bowley, the division planners created a fire-support plan that overwhelmed the German defenses. The plan choreographed the fire of every gun in the division sector that could reach the town or its surrounding area. For 12 hours before the infantry assault, the fire from sixty-six light guns, thirty-six heavy howitzers, and a number of large trench mortars was directed at a target area less than 2 kilometers wide and 2 kilometers deep. During the final 3 hours of the preparation, guns from the 15th Field Artillery were to fire six thousand rounds of persistent mustard gas along a line just north of the town to seal it off from German reinforcement and to increase losses among any enemy evacuees. During the final hour before the infantry advance, the rate of fire was to increase dramatically. Three minutes before H hour, half the 75mm guns were to shift to a box barrage around the town while the other half began a standing barrage just in front of the American lines. At H hour, the standing barrage was to begin rolling forward 100 meters every 2 minutes through the first half of the town, then slow to 3 minutes for each 100 meters through the northern half of the attack zone.[55]

Following that rolling barrage were to be just two battalions from the 3rd Brigade, about the same number of troops that first attacked Belleau Wood on that bloody day of 6 June. But, at Vaux, each battalion was augmented with dedicated machine-gun and engineer companies and each smaller unit had its own specific mission. Some were to follow the barrage straight through the town in about 30 minutes, establish a new line on the far side, and prepare it for immediate defense. A few units were to mop up resistance in the village itself, while others wiped out the various strong points in and around it. Somewhat like the 1st Division attack at Cantigny, these assault teams had rehearsed their tasks before the battle, thanks to the wealth of intelligence provided by Conger. After rolling

---

[54] For details on the planning of the Vaux attack, see *USAWW*, 4: 636–44; and Spaulding and Wright, *Second Division*, 74–5. For Conger's background, see Nenninger, *Leavenworth Schools*, 96.

[55] HQ 2nd Division, Field Orders No. 9, 30 June 1918, *USAWW*, 4: 641–3.

forward past the final objective, the artillery barrage was to stand for an additional 90 minutes to protect the attackers during the consolidation phase.[56]

The attack plan did not limit itself to coordinating just the artillery and infantry. Five French flying squadrons and three observation balloons were to assist in the battle by gaining air supremacy, keeping senior commanders aware of the attack's progress, and directing artillery fire. Two platoons of machine guns were to support the attack with "long-range firing" under the direct command of Brigadier General Edward M. Lewis, the commander of the 3rd Brigade, who was charged with "the conduct of the attack."[57] Although not mentioned in divisional or brigade plans, the attack orders of the two regimental commanders show that the 37mm guns and Stokes mortars were included in the attack plan as well. Furthermore, each rifleman was ordered to carry two hand grenades and other infantrymen were designated to carry either ten hand grenades or fifteen rifle grenades.[58] It seems that few officers in the 2nd Division were still concerned about the supposed "great power" of the rifle or the inherent dominance of open warfare. The plan represented an admittedly small but superbly detailed set-piece operation, based thoroughly on the latest methods and techniques of trench warfare. And it worked amazingly well.

At 1800 hours on 1 July, after the completion of the preliminary bombardment, the American infantry attacked and took Vaux without any significant difficulty. Lewis reported that the attack plan was "carried out to the letter" and all the evidence supports his claim.[59] Early the next morning, German forces attempted a counterattack supported by artillery and gas, but it was easily repulsed. When the casualty reports were finalized, the magnitude of the victory became even more clear. The 2nd Division suffered 328 casualties, with just 47 deaths and a high percentage of slightly wounded; the opposing German division reported that it lost 254 killed, 162 wounded, and 510 missing (nearly all were captured) – a total of 926 casualties.[60]

The artillerymen were proud of their own contribution to the Vaux attack, and the reports of the infantrymen proved such pride was fully

---

[56] Ibid.
[57] Ibid.
[58] See HQ 9th Infantry, Field Orders No. 15, and HQ 23rd Infantry, Field Orders No. 43, *USAWW*, 4: 652–6.
[59] HQ 3rd Brigade, "Special Operations Report," 2 July 1918, *USAWW*, 4: 674.
[60] Spaulding and Wright, *Second Division*, 78. Asprey claims that German losses were even higher – more than twelve hundred. Asprey, *Belleau Wood*, 336.

justified. One battalion commander reported that "the destructive fire of the artillery and divisional medium trench mortars was most excellent and far beyond our greatest expectations."[61] The commander of the other attacking battalion simply stated that the artillery fire was "perfect."[62] Lewis admitted that the artillery preparation was "most thorough and complete and contributed in large measure to the success of the operations." He also praised the attack's planners, noting the connections between the superb use of firepower, the orderly infantry assault, and the detailed planning effort that led to both.

Although the attack proved that the division possessed the will and skill to plan and execute a superb artillery fire plan, the actions of the infantry were also noteworthy. Like the artillery, they too were able to carry out their portions of the plan practically to the letter. The infantry battalion commanders reported that when enemy machine guns were encountered, and a number were, the assault troops immediately resorted to their own machine guns to fight fire with fire as other troops carrying grenades worked to the flanks to destroy enemy strong points. Some infantry, machine-gunners, and engineers set up the new line of defense without incident while others carried out the plans for rooting the enemy out of the cellars just as they had rehearsed before the battle. Telephone communications to the rear were established within an hour and a half of the initial assault, and the wounded were expeditiously handled. All this was even more impressive when one considers that the French division on the immediate right, attacking at the same time, failed to take its objective that day.

The differences between the division's handling of its first attacks at Belleau Wood and the successful seizure of Vaux were obvious. On 6 June and even later, the division seemed intent on attempting to fight according to the official open-warfare doctrine. Both brigades made unsupported frontal attacks without detailed plans or orders. The infantrymen tried to advance in linear formations more suitable to the drilling ground than the battlefield. And, perhaps of most significance, the first attacks exaggerated the offensive power of the infantry and underestimated the value of supporting firepower – especially artillery but often of other modern

---

[61] 2nd Battalion, 9th Infantry, "Special Operations Report," 3 July 1918, *USAWW*, 4: 668. See also "Report of 2d Battalion, 9th Infantry, Taking of Vaux at 6 pm," 1 July 1918, Folder 33.6, Box 57, 2nd Division Historical File, RG 120, NA.

[62] C.O., 3rd Battalion, 23rd Infantry to C.O., 23rd Infantry, 7 July 1918, *USAWW*, 4: 672.

weapons as well. Such attacks not only failed to gain their objectives, they also contributed to the division's casualty total of about eight thousand men during its forty days in the *Pas Fini* sector.[63] The 2nd Division faced many serious handicaps during the June fighting, such as a lack of accurate maps, an insufficiency of gas shells, thorough enemy air supremacy, and the natural difficulties of fighting in a dense forest against determined defenders in strong positions. But, the division's own failings were severe enough in their own right.

However, in the 4th Brigade's most successful attacks – particularly the final one of 25 June – and in the 3rd Brigade's assault of Vaux, the 2nd Division displayed two important improvements. First, the division proved capable of planning and executing the kind of limited, firepower-based, set-piece attacks for which most of its training had prepared it. Second, and of equal importance, the division demonstrated a willingness – more slowly in Harbord's brigade, to be sure – to adapt its methods to the realities of the modern battlefield. By the end of June, the division had dismissed any notion of self-reliant infantry and open warfare and implemented the much-maligned Allied doctrine so closely associated with trench warfare. Lejeune later wrote that during the final attacks on Belleau Wood and Vaux, "both brigades had found themselves," and he closed his report on those operations by describing the division's doctrinal development this way: "Again was decisively shown the great importance of artillery to infantry. Infantry alone, without material, makes little or no progress. If the enemy combines personnel and material, we must do the same or lose the game. This lesson was well impressed on the 2d Division at this time."[64]

Although the division's losses were heavy, its eventual use of firepower enabled it to inflict severe losses on the defending German units. During its forty days in the sector, the 2nd Division effectively crippled four of the ten different German divisions that it faced and earned high marks

---

[63] ABMC, *American Armies*, 103. One divisional report counted approximately ninety-seven hundred total casualties, but that unofficial figure probably included those wounded so slightly that they were immediately returned to duty, those wounded twice, and possibly noncombat losses such as those sick. Overall, the division suffered about 28 percent casualties in the sector, although it received hundreds of replacements during those weeks as well. See 2nd Division Commander to Assistant Chief of Staff, AEF, Subject: Operations Information, 30 December 1918, Divisional Skeleton Histories, Entry 443, RG 120, NA.

[64] Lejeune, "Summary of the Battle of Château-Thierry," *RSD*, vol. 6; Lejeune, *Reminiscences*, 295.

from some senior German officers.[65] The opposing German corps staff issued an intelligence report that praised the aggressiveness of the American infantry and noted that, overall, "the American 2nd Division may be considered as a very good division, if not even an attack [i.e., elite stormtroop] unit."[66] During these battles, the 2nd Division's soldiers and Marines ultimately showed that they possessed the courage, knowledge, and ability to successfully carry out the kind of limited set-piece attacks generally associated with trench warfare. Their ability to fight out in the open remained untested.

The Aisne-Marne Offensive, 18–19 July 1918

After being replaced by the 26th Division on 10 July, the 2nd Division shifted into corps reserve as it waited for orders to move to a quiet rest area to clean up, absorb replacements, re-equip, and continue training. However, by 16 July, it received unexpected orders to move north immediately and join Mangin's French Tenth Army. Harbord, who had taken command of the division on the previous day, yielded it to the control of the French supply and transportation system and sped north in his command car to report in at Mangin's headquarters. He learned just how imminent the upcoming operation was when he discovered that the Tenth Army commander had already moved to his advanced combat command post.[67]

---

[65] The German Army rotated their regiments and divisions through the front lines much more quickly than the French or Americans in this battle. Although comprehensive casualty figures for the German side are unavailable, many infantry units appear to have suffered crippling losses. For example, on 5 June, the 461st Infantry Regiment of the German 237th Division had about 1,000 soldiers, but a week later it could muster just 9 officers and 149 men. The 197th Division reported two thousand casualties in the first week of June alone. The 40th Infantry Regiment of the 28th Division suffered nearly eight hundred casualties during 10–12 June – when the 2nd Division carried out its first series of attacks preceded by massive artillery fire. See Millett, *In Many a Strife*, 44; and Asprey, *Belleau Wood*, 301.

[66] German IV Reserve Corps, Intelligence Report, 17 June 1918, *USAWW*, 4: 607. Spaulding and Wright, *Second Division*, 94; Smythe, *Pershing*, 140.

[67] Pershing had grown increasingly dissatisfied with Bundy, who provided little leadership during the fighting at Belleau Wood. The AEF commander visited the 2nd Division HQ during the first days of the fighting at Belleau Wood. By 9 June, despite hearing Foch talk of the division's "splendid showing," Pershing wrote in his diary, "Gen Bundy disappoints me. He lacks the grasp. I shall relieve him at the first opportunity." Entry for 9 June 1918, Pershing Diary, LOC. Pershing relieved Bundy by briefly promoting him to command the new American VI Army Corps, then sending him back to the United States. Lejeune replaced Harbord at the head of the 4th Brigade, but he did not assume command until

Although its leaders did not know it at the time, the division was finally going to take part in a battle that was designed to inaugurate just the kind of open-warfare conditions Pershing and the GHQ had written and spoke so much about. Pershing had authorized the French high command to add the 2nd Division to the spearhead of the Aisne-Marne Offensive of 18 July, where it joined the U.S. 1st Division and the French Army's 1st Moroccan Division in the French XX Corps, located just southwest of Soissons.

When Harbord finally received a copy of the French army and corps attack orders, barely 24 hours before the battle, he did not even know whether his division would arrive at its jump-off positions in time. With the combat regiments at the mercy of the French transportation and supply systems, Harbord, Bowley, and the division chief of staff, Colonel Preston Brown, quickly prepared the division attack order. The detailed instructions from the army and corps plans left few important decisions to the division leadership. The division was to attack along a front of 3 kilometers at 0435 hours on 18 July, as the southernmost division in the XX Corps. Its main objective for the first day was the town of Vierzy, more than 7 kilometers away, but the attack was to be pushed without cessation past the Soissons to Château-Thierry highway, if possible. The 1st Moroccan Division was on its left and the French 38th Division, of the French XXX Corps, was on its right. One of the four infantry regiments, the 6th Marines, was designated as part of the corps reserve and was therefore unavailable for the initial attack. The division was to be augmented by one regiment of French light guns, and although a rolling barrage was ordered, all other artillery preparation was prohibited to ensure complete surprise. To compensate for the lack of artillery fire, the division was to be aided by forty-eight Schneider tanks.[68]

Harbord's attack order identified three successive objectives for the first day, each being a north-south line approximately 3, 5, and 7 kilometers, respectively, from the jump-off. He naturally divided the attack in three phases. On the left, the 5th Marines were to spread two battalions across the entire 4th Brigade sector. On the right, the 3rd Brigade was to place its regiments abreast. Both brigades were to advance at the rapid rate of

immediately after the battle of Soissons (i.e., Brig. Gen. Wendell C. Neville, USMC, led it during the battle). Brig. Gen. Hanson Ely, who had led the 1st Division attack at Cantigny in May, replaced Lewis in the 3rd Brigade. Lewis took command of the new 30th Division. Journal of Operations, 15–17 July 1918, *RSD*, vol. 6; and Harbord, *Leaves from a War Diary* (New York: Dodd, Mead, 1925), 318.
[68] Harbord, *American Army*, 323–6; Spaulding and Wright, *Second Division*, 108; and French XX Corps, Operations Order No. 227, 16 July 1918, *USAWW*, 5: 290–2.

100 meters every 2 minutes all the way to the main objective, and the two halts at the intermediate objectives were to be "short." The attack order did not even specify exactly how short, but judging from the artillery fire plan, the pauses lasted no more than 20 minutes. The infantry was to begin the attack heading slightly north of east, then had to turn to the southeast to reach its final two objectives.

One indication that the attack was supposed to be a more traditional open-warfare engagement was Harbord's note on the supplies and weapons to be carried by the infantry. Unlike at Vaux, when some infantry were designated to fight exclusively with grenades and rifle grenades, these orders merely directed that every man be given two days' rations and 120 rounds of rifle ammunition. The only mention of machine guns was a note that a few were to be added to the special liaison teams working on the division flanks. The orders never directed any machine-gun barrages nor did they discuss the use of the mortars or 37mm guns.[69] More than any other AEF attack of the war, this battle became a test of the offensive power of the rifle and bayonet.

Bowley's fire-support plan was heavily influenced by the corps orders and the number of guns available to him. He had just over 100 guns to cover an attack 3 kilometers wide and more than 7 kilometers deep. The distance of the final objective meant that the rolling barrage could not cover more than the first half of the advance, another sign that the division would finally be waging some form of open warfare. During the latter half of the attack, all artillery support would have to be coordinated "on the fly" between battalion and regimental commanders. Bowley issued a memorandum describing how his subordinate commanders were to assist the advance after the conclusion of the rolling barrage. He assigned each regiment of 75mm guns to an infantry brigade (e.g., the 12th Field Artillery supported the Marines and the 15th Artillery was to assist the 3rd Brigade), and each was to be prepared to advance immediately after completing the initial barrage. The howitzers of the 17th Artillery, which could fire farther than the light guns, were only to advance upon his orders. Bowley's instructions stressed the importance of getting the batteries forward quickly, finding good advanced firing positions, and maintaining contact with senior commanders. However, he made no mention of the critical challenge of ensuring communications with the assaulting infantry battalions, and that was where the artillery fire would be needed most.[70]

---

[69] HQ 2nd Division, Field Orders No. 15, 17 July 1918, 0430 hours, *USAWW*, 5: 328–9.
[70] HQ 2nd F.A. Brigade, Operations Memorandum No. 1, 17 July 1918, *RSD*, vol. 2.

While Harbord and Bowley finalized their orders, the regimental commanders struggled to get their units to the proper jump-off positions. Throughout 17 July and the following night, the infantry marched practically nonstop in a tremendous thunderstorm beside roads completely jammed by trucks, tanks, ammunition caissons, and horse-carts. For most of the men who attacked at 0435 on 18 July, the last meal they had eaten was on the evening of 16 July, before they began the long trip to the Tenth Army. Although the 9th Infantry arrived at its attack positions with a few minutes to spare, the 23rd Infantry had to run the final kilometers to get to its jump-off line by 0435 hours, and the 5th Marines reached theirs only *after* the rolling barrage had started. In some instances, these units did not have liaison with one another even at the start. None of the officers had seen the terrain and few got maps. All weapons but the rifles carried by the troops were tied up in traffic, as was most of the telephone equipment, and few soldiers even got the required amount of ammunition. One regimental commander reported that "it seemed futile to hope that any attack under the circumstances could be a success."[71] Two factors turned this inauspicious beginning from an almost certain failure into a dramatic but costly victory: the completeness of the surprise achieved against a tired enemy in hastily prepared positions and the willingness of the reckless American infantry to press the attack, even under such terrible conditions.[72]

Promptly at 0435 hours on 18 July, the artillery barrage started and the infantry pressed forward behind it (see Map 3 in Chapter 2). Because of the traffic jams behind the lines, most of the supporting tanks were late, and they joined the attack with the advancing support battalions. Yet, within an hour or so, all three infantry regiments had advanced 3 kilometers against light resistance and reached the first objective. Hundreds of German troops – caught off guard in poor defensive positions, overwhelmed by the speed and weight of the advance, and suffering from deteriorating morale – were captured. Casualty rates during this initial phase were relatively low among the attacking units, thanks to a surprised and unprepared enemy, the presence of the rolling barrage, the help of those tanks that got far enough forward, and the aggressiveness

---

[71] C.O., 23rd Infantry to C.G., 3rd Brigade, "Report of Operations, July 17–18–19, 1918," 21 July 1918, Folder 33.6, Box 70, 2nd Division Historical File, RG 120, NA.

[72] Col. LaRoy Upton to Brig. Gen. Hanson Ely, Field Message, 0540 hours, *RSD*, vol. 4; 18 July 1918, HQ 3rd Brigade, "Report of Action of 3rd Brigade, June 1st to July 15th/18," 16 August 1918, *RSD*, vol. 7; Johnson and Hillman, *Soissons*, 58–71.

of the American soldiers and Marines. However, the rest of the day was much more difficult.[73]

After hitting the first objective, the American infantry companies were supposed to turn to the southeast to stay within the division sector. A few stayed on course, but most either turned too much or too little and veered into other sectors. Units became increasingly intermingled. Enemy resistance also stiffened markedly in mid-morning, just when the 75mm guns reached the limit of their range, discontinued the barrage, and began displacing forward. On the far right, the leading troops from the 23rd Infantry Regiment made the best time, reportedly hitting the second objective by 0700 hours and approaching the third, near the town of Vierzy, by 0930 hours. Their advance may have been aided somewhat by the fire of a battalion from the 15th Field Artillery, which had moved into forward firing positions sometime after 0800 hours, but there was little coordination between the firing batteries and assault companies. The 9th Infantry in the center and the 5th Marines on the left both had to fight through more resistance, and some Marines swerved so far into the Moroccan sector that they met up with troops from the 1st Division. Despite these troubles, by noon the leading troops of the 2nd Division had also reached the main objective, making the 2nd the first division to gain that line. Its scattered infantry units spent the next 6 hours consolidating the new line and mopping up the conquered area.

Reports of the countless small infantry attacks during the advance describe some troops attempting to take machine guns by envelopment and making use of the terrain. But, these efforts were flawed in execution and too often, many of the other weaknesses shown by the infantry of the 1st Division were demonstrated as well: too much recklessness and unnecessary exposure to fire, advance and attack formations too rigid and too dense, and insufficient attention to reducing enemy resistance by firepower. They certainly had trouble communicating with supporting forces to the rear, especially the artillery. Colonel Leroy S. Upton, the commander of the 9th Infantry, admitted that in his sector "there was absolutely no control on artillery by the troops in line or by commanders."[74] Instead,

---

[73] C.O., 23rd Infantry to C.G., 3rd Brigade, "Report of Operations, July 17–18–19, 1918," 21 July 1918, Folder 33.6, Box 70, 2nd Division Historical File, RG 120, NA; 2nd Battalion, 5th Marine Regiment, "Report of Second Attack made NE of Vierzy on 18th-19th of July, 1918," 23 July 1918, Folder 33.6, Box 88, 2nd Division Historical File, RG 120, NA; and Holger H. Herwig, *The First World War: Germany and Austria-Hungary 1914–1918* (London: Arnold, 1997), 417–18.

[74] Col. L. S. Upton, 9th Infantry, "Report on Battle of Beaurepaire Farm," 18 July 1918, Folder 33.6, Box 59, 2nd Division Historical File, RG 120, NA.

battalion and regimental commanders relied on the sheer weight of unsupported riflemen to push the advance, and they prematurely pushed support and reserve companies into the front lines. As a result, all three regiments suffered much heavier losses and greater disorganization in these later advances, in large part because of tactical problems but also because the American infantry surged well ahead of the French divisions on both flanks. For most of the day, the 2nd Division's infantrymen were in a salient of their own making – sometimes 2 kilometers deep – and they suffered heavily from enemy flanking fire from the neighboring sectors.[75]

When word of the 2nd Division's achievement reached the army and corps commanders, they sensed that a breakthrough was imminent. Disregarding its high losses and disorganization, they ordered the division to make additional attacks immediately and sent cavalry into its sector to exploit any further successes. In compliance with these orders, at 1330 hours, Harbord directed that his leading regiments attack to push the line past the town of Hartennes, situated 5 kilometers beyond the current front line.[76]

Due to the difficulty of getting Harbord's order forward and reorganizing the assault units, the attack was not made until after 1900 hours. Even then, as Brigadier General Hanson Ely, the 3rd Brigade commander, admitted, it was "launched in a rather ragged manner."[77] The order specified no details for fire support except the simple phrase that "the attack will be supported by the 2nd Field Artillery Brigade."[78] But, the only mention of friendly artillery fire by an infantry commander in an after-action report came from Major R. S. Keyser of the 5th Marines, who specifically noted that his battalion attacked *without any artillery support at all*. The assault was assisted by about fifteen tanks and, thanks in large part to this help, the infantry pushed the line forward about 2 more kilometers before darkness and increasing enemy resistance forced the exhausted, depleted, and thoroughly disorganized infantry to stop for the night. Casualties in all three regiments were severe, losses from straggling

[75] C.O., 23rd Infantry to C.G., 3rd Brigade, "Report of Operations, July 17–18–19, 1918," 21 July 1918, Folder 33.6, Box 70, 2nd Division Historical File, RG 120, NA; 2nd Battalion, 5th Marine Regiment, "Report of Second Attack made NE of Vierzy on 18th–19th of July, 1918," 23 July 1918, Folder 33.6, Box 88, 2nd Division Historical File, RG 120, NA; Col. L. S. Upton, 9th Infantry, "Report on Battle of Beaurepaire Farm," 18 July 1918, Folder 33.6, Box 29, 2nd Division Historical File, RG 120, NA.

[76] Division Commander to C.G., 3rd Brigade, 18 July 1918, 1330 hours, *USAWW*, 5: 333.

[77] C.G., 3rd Brigade to C.G., 2nd Division, Subject: Report of Operations Third Brigade July 17th to 21st, in the attack of Twentieth Army Corps 'X' French Army," 27 July 1918, *RSD*, vol. 7.

[78] Ibid.

(both intentional and unintentional) were sometimes even greater, and all were disorganized: the 9th Infantry could positively account for just four hundred men from the three thousand that began the attack; the 23rd Infantry reported it had lost more than half its officers and men; and losses in the 5th Marines were equally heavy.[79] Yet, the speed and depth of the day's advance, as well as the thousands of German prisoners then streaming to the rear, emboldened the army and corps commanders.

Still convinced that a breakthrough was at hand, at 0200 hours on 19 July, the corps commander ordered Harbord to make another attack at 0400. Because he believed that his three forward regiments were exhausted, Harbord secured, or simply appropriated, the use of the 6th Marine Regiment from the corps reserve for the attack.[80] He also knew that this unit was well behind the front lines and could not get to the attack position for several hours, so he ordered the assault to begin at 0700. Harbord also directed an hour of artillery preparation before the attack but, in accordance with his ideas of open warfare, he ordered no rolling barrage. The infantrymen would have to work their own way forward.[81]

The 6th Marines advanced to the jump-off line through heavy enemy artillery fire that both slowed its progress and caused many casualties. When the Marines finally began the attack, sometime after 0800 hours, all friendly artillery support had long since stopped, and the advance was made across flat, open wheat fields and in the face of heavy enemy machine-gun and artillery fire. Apparently, the division was either unwilling or unable to coordinate better fire support for the attack. Some accounts report that as the Marines advanced through the foxholes of the existing front line, the well-dug-in infantrymen of the 9th and 23rd Regiments pleaded with them to get down and take cover. As their comrades had done near Belleau Wood, most marched straight into the tempest of enemy fire. Aided by a few tanks, they managed to push the line

---

[79] Col. Upton to Brig. Gen. Ely, Field Message, 19 July 1918, *RSD*, vol. 4; 2nd Battalion, 5th Marine Regiment, "Report of Second Attack made NE of Vierzy on 18th–19th of July, 1918," 23 July 1918, Folder 33.6, Box 88, 2nd Division Historical File, RG 120, NA.

[80] There are no records to show that the XX Corps commander released the 6th Marines for the morning attack, but Harbord was never sanctioned for using it either. See Johnson and Hillman, *Soissons*, 104.

[81] C.G., 2nd Division to C.G., XX Army Corps, 19 July 1918, in *RSD*, vol. 6; and Spaulding and Wright, *Second Division*, 108.

forward almost 2 more kilometers before being stopped just a few hundred meters short of the Soissons to Château-Thierry highway. However, they took very few enemy prisoners and their own losses were horrific. One Marine sergeant later wrote that the enemy fire of this day was "a thousand times worse" than that met on 6 June.[82] Of the 2,450 Marines that began the operation, about 1,300 became casualties in a few hours. Even so, by late morning, Allied artillery was shelling the road, closing one of the main supply arteries of the German divisions along the Marne. Having achieved one of the main goals of Mangin's entire offensive, Harbord convinced the French corps commander to replace his exhausted, disorganized, and depleted division with a fresh unit.[83]

After making three distinct attacks in just over 24 hours, the 2nd Division's part in the Aisne-Marne Offensive was over. No other Allied division had gone so far, so fast, or achieved so much in such a short period. It had driven the enemy lines back nearly 11 kilometers, captured about three thousand enemy soldiers and seventy-five artillery pieces, and brought a critical enemy supply artery under close artillery fire. But, the price paid for this achievement was substantial: the division suffered 4,319 casualties, nearly all of them infantrymen.[84]

In the days and weeks following the Aisne-Marne Offensive, the division's officers had to come to grips with the unit's performance in the recent battle. Although most reports expressed great pride at the division's accomplishments, they did not avoid the harsh realities of the tremendous casualty rates or the serious problems in maintaining liaison, communication, and organization during the attack. As most commanders noted, the conditions under which the division entered the battle caused many of the problems. The troops were exhausted, hungry, and thirsty when they jumped-off in the initial assault. Officers had no chance to survey the attack sectors and few company commanders received maps. Nearly

---

[82] Sergeant William Scanlon is quoted in Johnson and Hillman, *Soissons*, 108.

[83] "A Brief History of the Sixth Regiment, USMC," n.d., Folder 11.4, Box 90, 2nd Division Historical File, RG 120, NA; and C.G., 2nd Division to C.G., XX Army Corps, 19 July 1918, in *RSD*, vol. 6. The artillery brigade stayed a few more days, supporting attacks by the relieving French 58th Colonial Division. That unit attacked on 20 July but, after briefly pushing its line across the Soissons to Château-Thierry highway, it was thrown back to its jump-off line with heavy losses.

[84] The losses in killed and wounded represented about 15 percent of the division's authorized strength but about 25 percent of the two infantry brigades. C.G., 2nd Division to Asst. Chief of Staff, G-3, GHQ, Subject: Operations Information, 30 December 1918, Folder 33.6, Box 31, 2nd Division Historical File, RG 120, NA.

all the division's machine guns, mortars, grenades, and 37mm guns were lost in the chaos of the French army and corps rear areas. Most of its telephones, wire, flares, and other communications equipment also failed to arrive before the attack began. Even rifle ammunition was in short supply. Some assault battalions did not have liaison with adjacent units when they jumped-off, and none had any chance to ensure coordination with their supporting artillery forces. Most attacked without even seeing a written field order. All of these problems resulted from the difficulties of inter-Allied relationships and can be put on the account of the French army and corps staffs, whose desire to ensure surprise directly led to the confusion. American commanders were justifiably proud of their unit's performance after a start under such conditions; at that point in the war, few Allied divisions would have pressed an attack with so many handicaps.

Once the battle began, the American units proved willing to carry on the fight but unable to retain sufficient control over the attack. Due to unfamiliarity with the terrain, little experience in such maneuvers, and increasingly severe enemy fire, infantry companies veered off course, entered neighboring sectors, and intermingled with other units. Furthermore, as Ely laconically reported after the battle, "liaison was unsatisfactory."[85] Most units did not know where their neighbors were and a few did not even know where they were. Progress reports to regimental, brigade, and divisional command posters were so rare and inadequate that senior commanders were completely unable to coordinate attacks or provide proper support. In the absence of news from the front, they often pushed more and more support companies into the assault line, giving enemy machine-gunners and artillery more and more targets. Of particular importance, Ely reported that the confusion regarding the conditions and location of the assault companies made close artillery support impossible; commanders were unwilling to risk shooting into their own men.[86]

The related issues of communication within the division (generally called "liaison" at the time) and the coordination of artillery support (indeed, of all available fire support) proved to be the salient lessons of the battle – as future attack plans and battle management would show.

---

[85] C.G., 3rd Brigade to C.G., 2nd Division, Subject: "Report of Operations Third Brigade July 17th to 21st, in the attack of Twentieth Army Corps 'X' French Army," 27 July 1918, *RSD*, vol. 7.

[86] Ibid. See also L. S. Upton, 9th Infantry, "Report on Battle of Beaurepaire Farm," 18 July 1918, Folder 33.6, Box 59, 2nd Division Historical File, RG 120, NA.

Although the 2nd Division was in many ways hamstrung by the French command's desire to ensure secrecy at all costs, its inability to maintain any reasonably effective method of communication or to provide its infantry with any semblance of adequate fire support after the first few hours of the first morning also reflected the doctrinal leanings of divisional leadership. Communications among the attacking infantry, the supporting artillery, and all levels of command up to the division headquarters were not maintained in part because officers failed to appreciate both how difficult it was to maintain them during the attack and how essential it was that close communication be maintained. As a result, at countless decision points during the battle, officers ranging from lieutenants to generals ordered and executed continued attacks at the expense of maintaining communications. Such attacks were ordered and attempted in the face of evidence that existing communications were so abysmal that the assault units could not possibly coordinate artillery support. Nor could subordinate commanders reply that such attack orders, if executed without fire support, were tantamount to suicide. Similarly, and possibly of greater negative effect on the assault companies, officers continuously underestimated the critical importance of fire support and repeatedly ordered attacks without sufficient covering fire.

The attack of the 6th Marines on the second morning demonstrates this very point. Harbord had been ordered to attack at 0400. He took the minor risk of delaying the assault 3 hours to allow the Marines time to get to the jump-off (he could hardly have done otherwise), but neither he nor anyone else exhibited enough concern for the necessary fire support to ensure that it was both adequate in amount and sufficiently coordinated with the infantry to actually assist the assault. Apparently, the time necessary to ensure such support would have delayed the attack further and this neither Harbord nor any subordinate commander was willing to accept. So, the 6th Marines attacked without any fire support, with poor communications to the rear, and were mauled by the enemy fire.

The industrialized battlefield of 1918 – so different from the human-centered environment envisioned in official AEF doctrine – was a harsh teacher, but the division did learn. Its first battles had been different kinds of engagements; some, like the attacks of 6 June and 19 July, were hastily ordered, energetically executed, but poorly supported, and these led to small gains and terrific casualties. The other kind of battle – such as the attacks of 10, 11, 12, and especially 25 June in Belleau Wood; of 1 July at Vaux; and, to a much lesser extent, the first few hours of

18 July – led to successful gains, lower casualties, and heavy enemy losses. The challenge for the division leadership, if they proved willing to make doctrinal adjustment, was to engineer its remaining battles so that they would conform more to the latter type – the limited, set-piece attack based on heavy firepower.

Changes in the divisional leadership helped speed this development along. Fewer than ten days after the battle of Soissons, Pershing ordered Harbord to give up his command and take control of the AEF's chaotic logistical organization, the Services of Supply. On 28 July, John A. Lejeune took over command of the division, after having assumed command of the Marine brigade just three days before. Harbord had commanded the division for only two weeks and, except for the painful lessons learned under his leadership at Belleau Wood and Soissons, his legacy in the division was soon overshadowed by the innovative Marine.

Lejeune was a professional Marine Corps officer of long service, but his time as a student at the Army War College gave him a close affiliation with the U.S. Army.[87] He began the war in Washington but joined the AEF in mid-1918. During a brief tour as a brigade commander in the 32nd Division in early July, he served just long enough in the front trenches while his unit trained with the French to gain an appreciation for their doctrinal sentiments and operational methods.[88] As the senior Marine in the AEF, he aspired to command the 4th Brigade and visited the unit during its grueling struggle in Belleau Wood.[89]

Under his leadership, the 2nd Division worked hard to improve infantry tactics, the ability to provide fire support, and the communication capability necessary to coordinate all elements during the attack. Equally

---

[87] Lejeune knew many prominent Army officers, including a number of division and brigade commanders, and was close to some senior officers at GHQ. When Harbord announced to the division staff that Lejeune was to be his replacement, Ely knew Lejeune well enough to say, "I have known General Lejeune for years and I know of no one I would rather have succeed General Harbord." Lejeune, *Reminiscences*, 286.

[88] During his tour at the front with the 64th Brigade, Lejeune had lengthy discussions with a Colonel Morvaux, the commander of a French infantry regiment, who served as his "counsellor [sic], adviser and instructor." Lejeune claims that during the "hours" of conversation between the two, "I found myself becoming skilled in understanding his accounts of his war experiences and in comprehending their application to the tactical questions which they were intended to illustrate." Lejeune, *Reminiscences*, 274.

[89] Ultimately, Lejeune had hoped to convince Pershing to combine two Marine brigades in an exclusively Marine division, which he would have commanded, but Pershing denied this request. See Merrill L. Bartlett, *Lejeune: A Marine's Life, 1867–1942* (Annapolis: Naval Institute Press, 1991), 68–9.

important was the doctrinal shift made by Lejeune and his subordinate commanders, especially Bowley of the artillery brigade, that encouraged officers throughout the 2nd Division to do all they could to make future attacks, including those with deep objectives, more like the set-piece attacks that proved so successful, regardless of official AEF policies and practices. The division's performance in its three final battles showed that it had learned a great deal in its bloody early engagements.

7

The 2nd Division

The Rise of Set-Piece Battle

When Lejeune assumed command of the division in late July, he discovered that it was short about seven thousand officers and men. GHQ simply had not been able to send replacements as fast as the division was losing men in battle. Yet, by the start of August, dozens of officers and thousands of men were flooding the division, and veterans began the difficult job of teaching the replacements the important lessons learned at such great cost. That GHQ sent so many replacements so quickly was a sign of its satisfaction with the division's performance in battle. Divisions that did not meet GHQ expectations were chronically undermanned, while those deemed successful, such as the 1st and 2nd Divisions, were always restored to their full strength. No doubt this unwritten policy in turn contributed to the continued high performance of these two fine divisions and others like them. The other reason the division quickly received so many replacements was that GHQ wanted it to be ready to play a crucial role in the new American First Army's first great attack, the reduction of the St. Mihiel salient in September. But, before that fight, the division had much work to do to improve its battlefield performance.

Retraining and Reorganizing, August 1918

After a few days of rest and reconstitution behind the lines of the French Tenth Army in late July, the division moved to the Lorraine area, directly south of the St. Mihiel salient. There, it began to gather and train the thousands of replacements needed to fill its ranks. However, in early August, the division was unexpectedly ordered back into quiet trenches on the south face of the St. Mihiel salient due to the shortage of Allied divisions.

John A. Lejeune, USMC, commander of the 2nd Division at St. Mihiel, Blanc Mont Ridge, and the Meuse-Argonne.

The 1st Division, which suffered even more punishment at Soissons, went into line next to it.

Lejeune did not allow the return to the front line to distract his units from the training – and retraining – that he believed was crucial to battle-field success. As Summerall did with the 1st Division, Lejeune ordered that his combat regiments continue training for all units except those infantry battalions holding the most forward trenches. Infantrymen fired rifles, automatic weapons, rifle grenades, 37mm guns, and mortars on ranges behind the lines, and small units worked on the fire and maneuver tactics necessary to take machine-gun nests with the fewest casualties. Bowley drove the artillery regiments equally hard, training his officers and men to quickly identify new firing positions, set up the pieces, and rapidly compute and deliver accurate fire. He also stressed the need to maintain constant communication with superior officers and, more important, with the infantry they were supporting.[1]

[1] HQ 3rd Brigade, Memorandum, 9 August 1918, *RSD*, vol. 2; Lejeune, *Reminiscences*, 306; and Spaulding and Wright, *Second Division*, 137.

In mid-August, the division yielded the front trenches to the 82nd Division and moved to a dedicated training area behind the lines where it focused on large-unit exercises. The division fell under the administrative control of Hunter Liggett's I Corps, and Liggett told Lejeune that AEF operations in the Aisne-Marne Offensive had proved that "the question of liaison" deserved "very careful attention" in all division training.[2] At first, the infantry battalions practiced delivering assaults while maintaining communications with commanders in the rear, then entire regiments and brigades did similar exercises. Although many officers described this training as additional preparation for open warfare, the infantry uniformly practiced advancing "close up" behind an "imaginary barrage" in its mock assaults.[3] During the last two days of August, the whole division took part in a giant maneuver that many officers later referred to as a "rehearsal" for the upcoming attack near St. Mihiel.[4] The division had to advance about 10 kilometers, overcoming strong points along the way and maintaining unit cohesion and communications even through woods. The advance was made at a timed rate of 100 meters every 3 minutes to an intermediate objective, then at a slower rate to the final objective. Company and battalion commanders had to react to "special situations" given them by umpires, who then graded the responses. Strangely, the I Corps staff officers who designed the exercise determined that to make the maneuver a real test of open-warfare conditions, commanders were to use "all means of communication . . . except the telephone," a device apparently still considered by some to be only a facet of trench warfare.[5]

Such thinking reflected the traditionalism and anti-trench-warfare sentiment still prevalent in the AEF senior staffs. They envisioned open-warfare engagements not only as attacks based on lightly supported riflemen but as attacks controlled by a constant stream of runners (including

---

[2] C.G., I Army Corps to C.G., 2nd Division, Subject: Training, 24 August 1918, Folder 56, Box 33, 2nd Division Historical File, RG 120, NA.

[3] Paul B. Malone, "The Need for an Infantry School," n.d., Malone Folder, Box 122, JJP Papers, LOC.

[4] Lejeune later commented on this important training period: "From daylight to dark, these preparations for battle continued unceasingly." He claimed that the final division maneuver "simulated actual battle conditions as nearly as possible." Lejeune, *Reminiscences*, 306.

[5] Bickham and Burr, "Second Field Artillery Brigade History," Folder 11.4, Box 4, 2nd Division Historical File, RG 120, NA. See also HQ 2nd Division, Memorandum, 29 August 1918, Folder 56, Box 33, 2nd Division Historical File, RG 120, NA; HQ 3rd Brigade, "Report of Operations, Third Brigade, September 17th, 1918," *RSD*, vol. 7.

men on horseback) to and from senior commanders, much as was done during the nineteenth century. To them, the limitations of phone lines made telephone technology an exclusive element of trench warfare. But, in fact, the most successful divisions made extensive use of telephones during the attack – and any other means of communication necessary – to speed the flow of communications. The challenge during more mobile warfare was not to fight without high-tech communications equipment (just because it was a challenge to set up and maintain or because it often "went out,") but also to do whatever was necessary to increase the reliability of the communications system, including the telephone lines, which were the most rapid means of transmitting crucial information.

Shortly after the full-division maneuver, Bowley attempted to improve communication and coordination between the artillery and the infantry of the 2nd Division by implementing a new "plan of liaison" based primarily on telephones, not runners. According to the plan, the headquarters of both the division and the artillery brigade, which were usually co-located, would maintain "advance message centers" much closer to the front lines. Multiple telephone lines were to connect each advanced site to the other and to the headquarters in the rear. Bowley linked these new centers to a revamped system of forward artillery liaison teams, which were located with each infantry command and with each artillery regiment. Although the telephone lines were the approved means of communications, liaison teams with the attacking infantry battalions were advised to use the few early-model "wireless" sets when they needed to make urgent contact with the artillery regiment commanders. Runners could be used but only as a last resort.[6] In each of the division's following battles, it proved increasingly able to communicate while it fought.

The St. Mihiel Attack, 12–16 September 1918

In early September, the 2nd Division began the move toward its jump-off positions on the south face of the St. Mihiel salient. The approach to the attack sector contrasted sharply with the tortuous march toward the Soissons battlefield in July. Although all movements were made at night, they were completed sufficiently in advance of the attack to allow junior officers to examine the upcoming battlefield in person and by map. The men were well fed and rested and were provided with all their weapons

---

[6] HQ 2nd F.A. Brigade, Memorandum, September 1918, Folders 50.4–56.3, Box 79, 2nd Division Historical File, RG 120, NA.

and plenty of ammunition. Although many of the units that jumped-off on 18 July were still undermanned due to the losses from the fighting in June, by 12 September all the regiments were not only filled, some were over-manned. On the eve of battle, the division reported it had 1,030 officers and 28,600 men, a surplus of 60 officers and 1,400 enlisted troops.[7]

The attack plans for the St. Mihiel battle were also dramatically different from those of the Aisne-Marne Offensive. Although Pershing, like Mangin, still hoped to surprise the enemy and make deep advances during the two-day assault, the infantry was certain to be given more support than it had in the July fighting. Not only had the First Army gathered a massive collection of artillery, tanks, and aircraft, but the attack plans, particularly the division plans, also promised to use this material in a more controlled fashion that showed an appreciation for the benefits of the set-piece attack.

Army orders placed the 2nd Division on the far left of Liggett's I Corps, with the 5th Division on its right and the 89th Division of the American IV Corps on its left (see Map 5 in Chapter 3). Starting with a frontage of about 3 kilometers, the division was supposed to make three rapid attacks in about 24 hours. In the initial assault, the division was to push in about 5 kilometers to the "first-phase" objective, where it could halt and reorganize. After about an hour's rest, the division was to advance 3 more kilometers to the "first-day" objective, where it was to stop for the night. The I Corps plan called for a rolling barrage during the first phase (moving 100 meters every 4 minutes) but none in the second – no doubt presuming that the infantry would be beyond the effective range of the light artillery. During that second phase of the battle, as the division sector widened to 4 kilometers, the infantry was to rely on its own firepower and the support of whatever remained from the sixty-three tanks assigned to the division for the initial attack. In addition, the infantry was to be aided by a number of accompanying artillery pieces, per Pershing's *Combat Instructions*, with an entire battalion of the division's light guns broken up and given to each attacking infantry brigade. Considering the strength of the defensive positions being attacked, this was a very aggressive plan. But, if the first day was a success, the next morning the division was to make a very short attack to reach the "army objective," then stop and consolidate its gains.[8]

The I Corps' plan included somewhat confusing orders that betrayed a muddled understanding of the nature of the attack. The massive use of artillery in the first phase (i.e., more than 750 guns supported the I Corps alone), the concern over the enemy wire entanglements (called "the greatest obstacle to rapid progression" in the corps orders), and the strict regulation of the infantry advance to the rate of the rolling barrage were all typical aspects of trench warfare.[9] This was, after all, merely a giant, limited-objective, set-piece attack. However, other comments show the evidence of the AEF's developing doctrine of open warfare. The leading infantry units were instructed to locate and penetrate "lanes of least resistance" for "out-flanking" enemy strong points. The orders also directed the infantry to "vigorously" exploit any successes – somewhat confusing orders for an infantry instructed to hug the rolling barrage and stay within the prescribed limits of the attack phases. Finally, the requirement that each division break up artillery batteries and attach them to the attack infantry battalions as "forward guns" also showed an open-warfare bias.[10]

The army and corps staffs may have been confused about the kind of battle they intended to fight, but the 2nd Division was not. Under Lejeune's guidance, the divisional, brigade, and regimental plans transformed the corps orders into as much of a set-piece attack as possible, even going so far as to subtly dismiss the spirit of certain instructions regarding the employment of artillery. The division attack plans, prepared days before the attack, were extraordinarily detailed and totaled thirty-three pages.[11] They placed the two regiments of the 3rd Brigade in the front to make the assault and the two Marine regiments behind them in support. During the 4-hour preparatory bombardment, teams of infantrymen and engineers

[8] HQ I Army Corps, Field Orders No. 49, 8 September 1918, Folder 32.1, Box 14, I Corps Historical File, RG 120, NA.

[9] Ibid.

[10] Ibid. See also Brig. Gen. Wm. M. Cruikshank, Chief of Artillery, I Corps, "Lecture on Explanation of Plan of Artillery for First Corps for St. Mihiel Operations of September 12th, 1918, and Meuse-Argonne Offensive of September 26th, 1918," 20 January 1918, Box 22, Edwards Papers, MHS.

[11] Most of the details of the attack were included in the division's Tentative Plan of Attack, produced on 8 September. The actual field orders for the attack were much briefer and were issued on 10 September. See C.G., 2nd Division to C.G., I Army Corps, Subject: Tentative Plan of Attack, 8 September 1918, *RSD*, vol. 1; HQ 2nd Division, Field Orders No. 27, 10 September 1918, *RSD*, vol. 1; and Lejeune, *Reminiscences*, 322–3.

were to work forward and cut lanes in the enemy wire. At H hour, the assault battalions, each with attached machine-gun, mortar, 37mm, engineer, and signal units, were to drive forward to an intermediate divisional objective, then to the corps and army objectives per the corps orders. Infantry battalions were to "leap-frog" each other at the intermediate objectives, if necessary.

Far from solely relying on the American soldier's "well known natural characteristics of individual initiative, rapidity of decision, resolute daring and driving power" (as the I Corps plan stated), brigade and regimental commanders developed intricate plans for the attack and capture of various enemy strong points and defensive positions.[12] To improve communications during the attack, Ely even selected and announced the expected locations of seven successive forward locations for his HQ. Commanders were to keep attack formations thin and flexible and to rely on "hugging the barrage," as well as small infiltration and out-flanking maneuvers, to keep casualties to a minimum. Before the battle, brigade commanders gathered the officers of all the machine-gun, mortar, and 37mm-gun units to give them "definite and detailed instructions" for maximizing the use of such weapons during the attack.[13] All infantrymen were to carry hand and rifle grenades, as well as 220 rounds of ammunition. The attack orders included an entire annex to describe the important role of machine guns during the operation. Some were designated to fire overhead barrages at the start of the attack, while others were to advance with the assault battalions and provide fire support as the attack progressed. In sum, the division's detailed plans showed that the attack was to be a highly organized advance that relied on the controlled use of as much firepower as possible to get to, take, and hold the enemy positions.[14]

---

[12] The quote comes from the "Battle Instructions" attached to HQ I Army Corps, Field Orders No. 85, 28 October 1918, Folder 32.1, Box 14, I Army Corps Historical File, RG 120, NA.

[13] HQ 3rd Brigade, "Supplementary Report on Operations Third Brigade – September 10th to 18th incl.," 22 September 1918, Folder 33.6, Box 44, 2nd Division Historical File, RG 120, NA. See also C.G., 3rd Brigade to C.G., 2nd Division, Subject: Plans for carrying out "Tentative Plan of Attack" of 2nd Division, 9 September 1918, and HQ 3rd Brigade, Operations Memorandum No. 4, 10 September 1918, both in *RSD*, vol. 2.

[14] See Lejeune, *Reminiscences*, 317. Although the attack plan showed the determination to use all firepower available, it made no reference to the possible use of aircraft to provide fire support. The division had learned the hard way near Belleau Wood and Soissons that attack aircraft could cause great difficulties for troops in the open. But, even though the division had the dedicated support of an entire squadron of eighteen aircraft from the airbase at Toul, the division's plan confined all aerial missions to observation, reconnaissance, and some air superiority work. See C.G., 2nd Division to C.G., I Army

The 2nd Division most clearly demonstrated its desire to employ massive, coordinated firepower in its use of artillery. Although the corps plan called for a rolling barrage during the first phase of the attack and the use of accompanying guns under infantry control in the latter open-warfare phases, the 2nd Division used its artillery differently. The artillery brigade was augmented by two French regiments of light guns and a third of 155mm howitzers, giving it a total of 120 75mm pieces and 60 heavy howitzers. As many as ten batteries of heavy corps and army guns supported the division with counterbattery and other fire. The 2nd Division plan followed the corps orders by prohibiting any special fire before the artillery preparation and by directing a rolling barrage at the approved rate to the first-phase objective. From that point on, the corps expected the attacks to be made according to GHQ's latest "open-warfare" principles, with infantry supported by accompanying artillery. But, Lejeune and Bowley decided that they wanted to maintain barrage fire as long as possible. They ordered a standing barrage to be maintained for about 2 hours at the first-phase line while the infantry regrouped and prepared for the second phase, and then ordered a *second* rolling barrage to cover the advance all the way to the first-day objective. All the while, the heavy howitzers were to fire concentrations in advance of the light guns.[15]

The division's determination to continue use of the rolling barrage in the latter phase of the attack was a significant development. The reliance on such a distinctive feature of trench warfare signaled the division leadership's desire to fight a controlled, set-piece attack in order to ensure its infantry had the most fire support possible. The plan was risky for two reasons. First, it was difficult to arrange. Although the two French regiments of 75mm guns could fire a special Model D shell, which extended their range to 11 kilometers, the American light guns had to advance during the attack, set up in forward firing positions, and pick up the second barrage from those spots. Bowley ordered one battalion of each

Corps, Subject: Tentative Plan of Attack, 8 September 1918, *RSD*, vol. 1; C.G., 3rd Brigade to C.G., 2nd Division, Subject: Report of Action of 3rd Brigade in the Battle of Thiaucourt, 17 September 1918, Folder 33.6, Box 46, 2nd Division Historical File, RG 120, NA.

[15] The initial fire plan even included instructions for the rolling barrage to be fired in the short attack to be made on the morning of the second day. See 2nd F.A. Brigade, Operations Order No. 1, 9 September 1918, Folder 32.12, Box 78, 2nd Division Historical File, RG 120, NA; Capt. Erwin Davis, "Operations Report and History of the 2nd Field Artillery Brigade," n.d., Folder 11.4, Box 77, 2nd Division Historical File, RG 120, NA; and HQ I Army Corps, Field Orders No. 49, 8 September 1918, Folder 32.1, Box 14, I Corps Historical File, RG 120, NA.

American light-gun regiment to be "hitched and ready to advance" behind the infantry after the attack started, and he detailed engineers and supply teams to accompany them.[16] While the other 75mm guns fired the first barrage, these guns were to advance and prepare to join the French guns in the second barrage. While en route to the forward barrage-firing positions, these guns were technically available for emergency requests from the attacking infantry commanders. But, their main mission was to extend the rolling barrage and then to fire a 30-minute standing barrage in front of the infantry's final first-day objective. The second reason such a plan was risky was that it seems to have been contrary to both the corps' attack orders as well as official AEF doctrine. Pershing, GHQ, and probably the I Corps staff all expected the divisions to use accompanying guns in open warfare, not employ unending rolling barrages to extend the zone of trench warfare. Yet, the divisional attack orders, and especially its fire-support plan, show that it was trying to fight a very different kind of battle than GHQ envisioned – one based on a doctrine that understood massive firepower and detailed coordination to be the *sine qua non* of battlefield success.[17]

At 0500 hours on 12 September, after 4 hours of intense artillery bombardment on the German lines, the 9th and 23rd Infantry Regiments began the attack. Like most American units attacking the southern face of the salient that morning, they met and overcame weak enemy resistance. Smoke concentrations fired by certain light batteries combined with a heavy mist to conceal the infantry advance. The Doughboys followed closely behind the 75mm-gun barrage, outflanked the few strong points that resisted, and took their successive objectives right on time. Even without much assistance from the tanks, which could not keep up with the infantry due to mud and traffic, the lead battalions reached the first-phase line by 1000 hours, where units reorganized and support battalions moved into the assault position for the next phase. By 1030 hours, the advanced artillery battalions were set up and ready to support the second phase of the attack. Promptly at 1100 hours, the attack continued behind the second rolling barrage, which was arranged to escort the infantry to the first-day objective. Thirty minutes later, when the protective standing barrage in front of the new infantry lines concluded, patrols found

---

[16] 2nd F.A. Brigade, Operations Order No. 1, 9 September 1918, Folder 32.12, Box 78, 2nd Division Historical File, RG 120, NA.

[17] Ibid. Davis, "Operations Report and History of the 2nd Field Artillery Brigade," n.d., Folder 11.4, Box 77, 2nd Division Historical File, RG 120, NA.

enemy resistance so weak that the lead battalions pushed on the remaining distance to the second-day objective by about 1400 hours.[18]

In less than 9 hours, the division had advanced more than 8 kilometers over strongly fortified enemy positions and captured well over three thousand prisoners and more than ninety guns. For all this, the divisions suffered only light casualties – probably fewer than five hundred during the attack, even though the division pulled ahead of both divisions on its flanks (as it had at Soissons) – and held a salient for more than 24 hours after its final advance on the first day. Whereas other divisions had achieved their victories only against weak enemy forces anxious to withdraw, the 2nd Division ran into one of the only significant German counterattacks of the operation, and the Americans meted out much more punishment than they took. No division at St. Mihiel did more fighting than the 2nd Division, and none did as much damage to the enemy.[19]

Unlike some American divisions, such as the 1st and 26th, the 2nd Division was not relieved on the second day of the battle. It stayed in line until 16 September, made a number of short advances in the intervening days to bring its lines as close as possible to the enemy's new main line of resistance, and successfully fought off a number of local enemy counterattacks. While the division suffered losses until it was finally withdrawn, it conducted major operations only on the first day of the battle.[20]

---

[18] Both Ely and Lejeune agreed that the tanks were of little help in this attack because they were unable to keep up. See C.G., 3rd Brigade to C.G., 2nd Division, Subject: Report of Action of 3rd Brigade in the Battle of Thiaucourt, 17 September 1918, Folder 33.6, Box 46, 2nd Division Historical File, RG 120, NA, and HQ 2nd Division, "Report of Operations Second Division – 12–16 September, 1918," 16 September 1918, *RSD*, vol. 6. Also see C.G., 2nd Division to C.G., I Army Corps, Subject: Report of Operations – September 12, 1918, 13 September 1918, Folder 33.6, Box 30, 2nd Division Historical File, RG 120, NA.

[19] Lejeune reported that casualty rates were very low and that "the great majority" were "slightly wounded." Ely reported just 369 casualties in his entire brigade, which made the assault. By the time the division left the sector on 16 September, it had suffered a total of 1,477 losses. Figures for the number of guns taken vary from 92 to 120. C.G., 2nd Division to C.G., I Army Corps, Subject: Report of Operations – September 12, 1918, 13 September 1918, Folder 33.6, Box 30, 2nd Division Historical File, RG 120, NA. See also HQ 2nd Division, "Report of Operations Second Division – 12–16 September, 1918," 16 September 1918, *RSD*, vol. 6; Lejeune, *Reminiscences*, 330; and ABMC, *American Armies*, 165.

[20] Some of these small advances were costly. In accordance with corps orders, on 14 September, Lejeune ordered both Marine regiments (having relieved the Army infantry the previous night) to send out large "patrols" to advance the outpost line toward the enemy's main line of resistance. These patrols eventually ran into an enemy counterattack and a

As expected, the unit commanders were thrilled by the performance of their men, and their operations reports confirm that the division was willing and able to plan and execute such a large set-piece attack. By all accounts, the infantry made significant improvements over their previous operations. Instead of dense, rigid formations, the assault companies attacked with two widely separated waves of skirmishers followed by small, staggered columns of riflemen. The automatic riflemen advanced with the leading infantry and the machine guns regularly fired to aid the attack. The infantry took strong points by deluging them with fire from the machine guns, 37mm guns, and mortars, while men with automatic rifles and rifle grenades worked around the flanks. In many cases, the enemy positions were destroyed before they were fully enveloped. In a rare admission of the relative value of the infantry weapons, Colonel George W. Stuart of the 9th Infantry reported that "there was small opportunity for the use of the rifle," and although the auxiliary weapons had trouble keeping up with the rapid advance, the infantry relied on those that got forward to overcome any significant resistance.[21] Neville wanted his Marines to rely even more on the auxiliary weapons in future battles. Ely closed his report by claiming "the 'rehearsal' of this battle beforehand in the Divisional problem and the carefully prepared plans of the Division saved many lives and the whole movement was carried out almost exactly as planned and in some respects better than in the 'rehearsal' in the back area."[22] Such comments were a ringing endorsement of the set-piece attack.

The infantry was even more impressed with the artillery support during most of the attack. Stuart reported that artillery fire was "excellent," and

---

nasty battle ensued. The lines were advanced but only against heavy enemy machine-gun and artillery fire, and as many as five hundred casualties resulted from this hastily prepared and supposedly "minor" operation. The only evidence of fire support comes from Lejeune's memoir, in which he remembered observing "the effect of the concentrated fire of our regiment of 155's" on the enemy positions during the advance. See Lejeune, *Reminiscences*, 332; HQ 2nd Division, Field Orders No. 28, 14 September, 1620 hours, *RSD*, vol. 1.

[21] C.O. 9th Infantry to C.G., 3rd Brigade, Subject: Report of Operations of the Ninth Infantry, U.S.A., from Sept. 12–15th, 1918, 23 September 1918, Folder 33.6, Box 63, 2nd Division Historical File, RG 120, NA.

[22] C.G., 3rd Brigade to C.G., 2nd Division, Subject: Report of Action of 3rd Brigade in the Battle of Thiaucourt, 17 September 1918, Folder 33.6, Box 46, 2nd Division Historical File, RG 120, NA. See also HQ 2nd Division, "Report of Operations Second Division – 12–16 September, 1918," 16 September 1918, *RSD*, vol. 6; HQ 4th Brigade, "Ops Rept of 4th Brigade, Marines. Period covered September 12–15, '18," 17 September 1918, *RSD*, vol. 6.

the commander of the 23rd Infantry, Colonel Edward R. Stone, claimed that it was "all that could be asked for."[23] Ely called it "very effective," noting that enemy command posts as well as "many Machine Gun nests and trenches" were knocked out, while German artillery fire "was feeble."[24] Possibly the most important compliment came from a young private, who agreed that "it was the best artillery support our infantry had had up until this time and saved lots of casualties."[25] At the other end of the chain of command, Lejeune officially reported that "the barrage was well laid and closely followed by the infantry" and noted that the two forward 75mm battalions "rendered effective support" in the second phase of the attack. He made no mention of them firing a rolling barrage instead of being broken up into accompanying guns.[26]

However, in his report to Lejeune, Bowley took the corps artillery plan to task for directing that he break up his command. He stated that he had technically placed the required number of light guns under Ely's control during the first phase of the assault but then claimed that his plan to ultimately use them to extend the rolling barrage gave the assaulting infantry brigade "the immediate support of two regiments of 75's, instead of one battalion as ordered." He believed that "the methods followed in this Division will always give the Infantry far better support than where individual batteries or battalions are placed under the Infantry Commander's orders."[27] In other words, Bowley had more faith in the centralized trench-warfare formula than the AEF's official open-warfare methods, and others shared this attitude.[28]

[23] For Stuart's report, see C.O. 9th Infantry to C.G., 3rd Brigade, Subject: Report of Operations of the Ninth Infantry, U.S.A., from Sept. 12–15th, 1918, pursuant to Memo, 2nd Div., 20 Sept. 1918, 23 September 1918, Folder 33.6, Box 63, 2nd Division Historical File, RG 120, NA; and HQ 23rd Infantry Regiment, "Report of Operations, Sept. 12–15, 1918, 23rd Infantry," Folder 33.6, Box 73, 2nd Division Historical File, RG 120, NA.

[24] For Ely's initial report, see C.G., 3rd Brigade to C.G., 2nd Division, Subject: Report of Action of 3rd Brigade in the Battle of Thiaucourt, 17 September 1918, Folder 33.6, Box 46, 2nd Division Historical File, RG 120, NA.

[25] Carl Andrew Brannen, *Over There: A Marine in the Great War* (College Station: Texas A&M University Press, 1996), 41.

[26] HQ 2nd Division, "Report of Operations Second Division – 12–16 September, 1918," 16 September 1918, *RSD*, vol. 6.

[27] HQ 2nd F.A. Brigade, "Attachment to Report on Operations, 2nd F.A. Brigade, Sept. 12–15," 17 September 1918, Folder 33.6, Box 14, 2nd Division Historical File, RG 120, NA.

[28] Brig. Gen. Wendell C. Neville, of the Marine brigade, wrote much the same thing in his report of the battle. C.G., 4th Brigade to C.G., 2nd Division, 23 September 1918, *RSD*, vol. 7.

Lejeune later admitted that he and Bowley both "strongly believed that the artillery should be utilized to the limit of its capacity in order that victory might be achieved with the smallest possible loss of life among our assaulting troops." To some in the AEF, such a comment was a veiled challenge to the artillerymen to be courageous enough to risk almost certain death by operating individual guns in the most forward lines. But, this was not the case with Lejeune and Bowley, who were convinced that, regardless of official pronouncements on the supposed superiority of open-warfare methods, the rolling barrage was the most reliable form of heavy fire support for the infantry. Lejeune boasted of the "lavish...use of shell" in his division and claimed that his infantry also "had learned that in order to" succeed and survive, "it was necessary to follow the rolling barrage closely, or to 'lean on it' as they expressed it, even to the extent of suffering a few casualties."[29] They would use this tactic again and again later in the war and eventually receive official criticism from the AEF Inspector General for failing to use open-warfare methods.

Although all unit commanders were pleased with the division's performance at St. Mihiel, they also reported on areas of weakness. The chief problem noted by the infantry commanders was the lack of artillery support at the end of the first day, when the set-piece portion of the attack had concluded. Late in the afternoon of the first day, the 9th Infantry was hit by a strong counterattack supported by enemy machine guns and artillery. The infantry had to fight off attacks for 3 hours without any artillery support at all, suffering a significant portion of the day's total casualties. Stuart admitted that his unit had "lost liaison with our artillery" until about 1830 hours, when guns from the 15th Field Artillery finally opened up in close support, suppressing enemy fire and finally crushing the counterattack.[30] On the left of the sector, the 23rd Infantry also lacked artillery support in the afternoon – Stone reported that from 1400 to 1900 hours, liaison between his men and the artillery simply "did not exist" – and his leading companies withdrew slightly to a reverse slope to reduce exposure.[31]

Although Ely believed the liaison failures resulted from internal communications problems in the artillery brigade, that was only part of the problem. The tremendous physical obstacles among the German positions

[29] Lejeune, *Reminiscences*, 383.
[30] C.O. 9th Infantry to C.G., 3rd Brigade, Subject: Report of Operations of the Ninth Infantry, U.S.A., from Sept. 12–15th, 1918, pursuant to Memo, 2nd Div., 20 Sept. 1918, 23 September 1918, Folder 33.6, Box 63, 2nd Division Historical File, RG 120, NA.
[31] HQ 23rd Infantry Regiment, "Report of Operations, Sept. 12–15, 1918, 23rd Infantry," Folder 33.6, Box 73, 2nd Division Historical File, RG 120, NA.

combined with heavy rain to make forward displacement of even the light guns a slow and difficult task. Only a third of the 155mm pieces moved forward at all on the first day. After setting up in forward firing positions, most batteries struggled to establish their communications lines back to the rear and, more important, forward to the infantry regiments. Even the artillery liaison teams with the infantry units often could not locate much less communicate with the forward batteries. But, infantry reports also noted that by late morning on the first day, even *their* telephones could not keep up with the advance. The assaulting battalions had to rely on runners to communicate with their regiments, while the regiments also used runners and occasionally the wireless to talk with the brigade HQ. These communications problems led to considerable doubt in the minds of battery commanders as to the location of the infantry's front lines – an absolutely essential piece of information before any close support could be provided. Lejeune verified these problems in his report of the battle: "The apparent failure of a lack of artillery support during the afternoon of September 12th was due to the rapid advance of the infantry, and to the failure of obtaining prompt telephone connections. Artillery was in positions to give prompt support but hesitated in doing so due to lack of exact knowledge of the infantry front line positions."[32]

The lesson for the 2nd Division was clear. The artillery support, and indeed the whole attack, was well executed during the set-piece portion. But, after an advance of 9 kilometers, communications and fire support began to break down. The successes as well as the failures reinforced the desire throughout the division to improve liaison within the division and to fight even more highly coordinated, limited-objective, set-piece battles.[33]

---

[32] HQ 2nd Division, "Report of Operations Second Division – 12–16 September, 1918," 16 September 1918, *RSD*, vol. 6.

[33] On 27 September, Bowley issued new instructions to improve liaison between the infantry and the artillery. First, he stated that it was henceforth the "the duty of the 75m/m regimental and battalion commanders to establish telephone communications forward with the infantry they support" and no longer to wait for the infantry to initiate liaison with them. At the other end of the line, artillery liaison officers with infantry units were to take three couriers, a motorcycle, a bicycle, and a horse, and those with the assaulting battalions were to take double of everything. They were to know the locations of all artillery HQs and firing batteries and to ensure that they had telephone contact with them. Instead of simply providing advice regarding artillery support, the arranging of "quick support in an emergency" was to be "their primary duty." See HQ 2nd F.A. Brigade, Memorandum, Subject: Liaison Between Infantry and Artillery: General System of Artillery Support," 27 September 1918, Folder 32.11, Box 16, 2nd Division Historical File, RG 120, NA.

Blanc Mont Ridge, 2–10 October 1918

By 21 September, the division had moved to a rest area near Toul, where it awaited word of its assignment in the upcoming Meuse-Argonne Offensive. Within a few days, in response to an urgent request by Foch, Pershing agreed to send the veteran 2nd Division, along with the partially trained 36th Division, to the French Fourth Army to aid its advance on the immediate left flank of the American First Army. By the end of the month, Lejeune had reported to the Fourth Army commander, General Henri Gouraud, and learned that the French advance was stalled about 4 kilometers in front of the German main line of resistance, which sat on an elevation called Blanc Mont Ridge. Gouraud explained to Lejeune that he needed to take the ridge to get the Fourth Army's advance moving again. The Frenchman claimed that Blanc Mont, the high point of the ridge and the chief observation site in that sector of the Hindenburg Line, was "essential to the Germans if they wished to maintain their line in the Champagne." If the ridge could be taken and held, Gouraud was sure the Germans would evacuate the entire line and "fall back to the Aisne, a distance of 30 kilometers."[34]

The problem for Gouraud was that he did not believe any of his French divisions possessed the size, strength, or aggressiveness to carry out the mission. According to Lejeune, Gouraud admitted his divisions were "worn out" and that it was "doubtful" they were "equal to accomplishing this difficult task."[35] Indeed, Blanc Mont was so strongly defended that it was chosen as the observation post for the Kaiser when he came to the front to personally observe the German Army's last great offensive near Reims in July. Some French officers supposedly claimed the ridge would never be taken by direct assault.[36]

At the time, Lejeune was concerned about rumors that the French were considering breaking up the 2nd Division and using its brigades to reinforce French units already in line. Seeing an opportunity to avoid this, Lejeune told Gouraud, "If you do not divide the Second Division, but put it in line as a unit on a narrow front, I am confident that it will be able to take Blanc Mont Ridge, advance beyond it, and hold its position there."[37] Although it is possible to read too much into Lejeune's wording,

---

[34] Gen. Gouraud quoted in "Notes on Blanc Mont," Folder 33.2, Box 28, 2nd Division Historical File, RG 120, NA. See also U.S. Army, General Staff, Historical Branch, "Blanc Mont (Meuse-Argonne-Champagne)," Monograph No. 9, April 1920, USAMHI.

[35] Lejeune, *Reminiscences*, 342.

[36] Brannen, *Over There*, 101.

[37] Lejeune, *Reminiscences*, 342.

his offer was consistent with his commitment to carry out a limited, set-piece attack, not a breakthrough into the open. The French high command accepted Lejeune's offer and the stage was set for what may have been the division's greatest accomplishment, as well as its most bitter battle.

During the last days of September, the 2nd Division moved toward the front lines while the division staff developed what ultimately proved to be its most ingenious attack plan of the war. The original plan was rather ordinary, although thoroughly based on trench-warfare principles and methods, calling for a frontal attack on the ridge by the Marine brigade on 2 October. The division secured the dedicated support of a total of 120 light guns and 72 heavy pieces, as well as a number of tanks. According to corps orders, the artillery preparation proper was to be very short – just 5 minutes of all guns firing at their maximum rate. However, all the guns were to carry out a series of intense fire missions throughout the previous night to weaken enemy defenses and morale. This fire was to decrease slowly in the early morning hours, then stop entirely before the intense 5-minute hurricane bombardment began. Then, the light guns were to shift to a rolling barrage, advancing 100 meters every 4 minutes, while the heavy pieces maintained a standing barrage on the enemy's main line on the ridge until lifting at the last moment. The entire Fourth Army was to join in the attack at the same time, but the 2nd Division was the spearhead of the offensive.[38]

Then, one day before the attack, Lejeune did something very unusual: he successfully pressed for the assault to be postponed a day to help ensure its success. In his memoirs, Lejeune explained his reasons for the postponement, and all were directly or indirectly related to his desire to fight a firepower-based, set-piece attack. First, he noted that some of the artillery might not have been able to get in position in time to support the assault. Second, he not only wanted to be absolutely sure all the artillery was in place, he also thought it necessary to allow his gunners, as well as the attacking infantry, "to have a look at the terrain during the day-light hours" before carrying out their missions. Finally, Lejeune noted that during the extra day, his infantry could be sure to clear all enemy outposts and machine guns from the immediate front of the jump-off line to ensure that the assaulting columns got off to a good start. Lejeune believed it was absolutely essential for "the assaulting troops to follow the

---

[38] French XXI Army Corps, General Operations Order No. 3703/3, 2 October 1918, Folder 32.12, Box 17, 2nd Division Historical File, RG 120, NA; HQ 2nd Division, Field Orders No. 35, 2 October 1918, *RSD*, vol. 1.

artillery barrage closely" during the attack.[39] Although a day's postponement of a major attack for such reasons may seem insignificant today, it
was an all-too-rare event in 1918, and it showed the division commander's
determination to ensure that his unit was ready to carry out the attack
according to the plan, especially regarding its reliance on firepower.

The next day, 2 October, brought further changes, this time to the
attack plan itself. As the American infantry cleaned out the area in front
of its jump-off trenches, the commander of the French XXI Corps, Major
General Stanislas Naulin, informed Lejeune that a recent attack by the
French division on the immediate right had created a small bulge into
the German lines, which might be useful in the coming assault. Naulin
suggested one possible change to the attack plan but Lejeune quickly
rejected it, in part because it "would not be feasible to utilize the artillery
rolling barrage" in the proposed maneuver.[40]

After discussing the issue with his senior officers, Lejeune settled on a
plan that maximized use of the recent change in the line without sacrificing
any fire support. The Marine brigade's attack was to go as planned. But,
the 3rd Brigade was to join the assault from jump-off positions nearly 2
kilometers to the east so that it would make a converging oblique attack
on the ridge. This attack also enabled the division to avoid and cut off a
number of likely enemy strong points. The triangle-shaped area between
the two attacks was to be "cleaned up" by support and reserve troops
after the day's objective was secured (see Map 16).[41]

The new plan demanded that the artillery brigade fire two completely
separate rolling barrages, one in front of each brigade, and the angular
advance of the 3rd Brigade was certain to challenge the technical skill
of its supporting gunners. The use of such a complicated, converging fire
plan demonstrated the division's willingness to subordinate maneuver to
firepower, as did Lejeune's order demanding that each assaulting brigade
remain "strictly" within its own attack sector until both brigades came
abreast on the top of the ridge.[42] The rolling barrages were to lead the
infantry to the first objective on the main ridge, then shift into a lengthy
standing barrage while both brigades linked up and reorganized. Then,
the barrage was to roll forward again at the same rate to escort small combat patrols for about another kilometer, where artillery fire was to stand

[39] Lejeune, Reminiscences, 345.
[40] Ibid.
[41] HQ 2nd Division, Field Orders No. 35, 2 October 1918, RSD, vol. 1; and Lejeune,
    Reminiscences, 349.
[42] HQ 2nd Division, Field Orders No. 35, 2 October 1918, RSD, vol. 1.

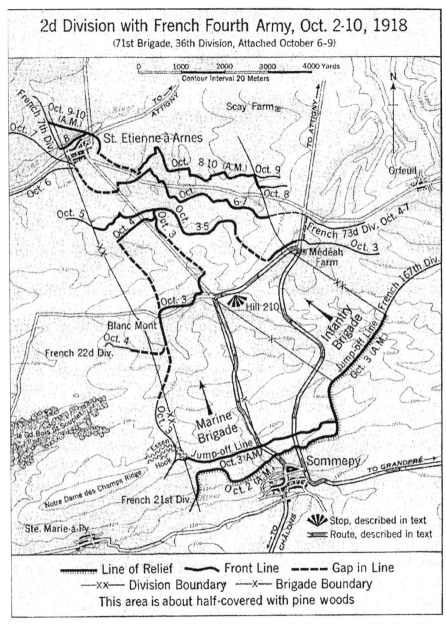

2d Division with French Fourth Army, Oct. 2-10, 1918
(71st Brigade, 36th Division, Attached October 6-9)

0   1000   2000   3000   4000 Yards

Contour Interval 20 Meters

N

Scay Farm

Oct. 9-10 (A.M.)

French 7th Div.

Oct. 7

Oct. 8

St. Etienne-à-Arnes

TO ATTIGNY

River

Oct. 6

Oct. 5

Oct. 4

Oct. 3

Oct. 8-10 (A.M.)

Oct. 9

Oct. 8

Oct. 6-7

Oct. 3-5

TO ATTIGNY

Orfeuil

French 73d Div. Oct. 4-7

Oct. 3

Médéah Farm

French 167th Div.

Hill 210

Infantry Brigade

Jump-off Line

Oct. 3 (A.M.)

Blanc Mont

Oct. 4

French 22d Div.

Oct. 3

Oct. 3

le Gd Bois St. Souplet

Essen Hook

Marine Brigade

Jump-off Line

Oct. 3 (A.M.)

Sommepy

TO GRANDPRÉ

Notre Dame des Champs Ridge

French 21st Div.

Oct. 2 (A.M.)

River

Ste. Marie-à-Py

TO CHÂLONS

⚜ Stop, described in text
═══ Route, described in text

━━━━ Line of Relief   ⌐━ Front Line   ━ ━ ━ Gap in Line
━xx━ Division Boundary   ━x━ Brigade Boundary
This area is about half-covered with pine woods

MAP 16: The 2nd Division's seizure of Blanc Mont Ridge as part of the French Fourth Army was one of the greatest achievements of any division in the war.

still again while the new gains were consolidated. During this advance, the heavy guns and howitzers were to fire intense concentrations 400 meters ahead of the rolling barrage, while other light guns filled the attack zone with smoke shell to obscure enemy visibility. No 75mm pieces were dispersed among the infantry battalions as accompanying guns, but two battalions were prepared to advance early in the attack to provide closer and deeper fire support. Regarding its emphasis on heavy fire support, the attack plan was based on an emerging formula developed more from Allied trench-warfare practices than any American beliefs in open warfare.[43]

Each infantry brigade was to attack with its regiments in column. The 9th Infantry was to lead on the right and the 6th Marines on the left. The 23rd Infantry and 5th Marines were to follow in support. Each assaulting regiment was to advance with machine-gun support, as well as twenty-four French tanks. Because the 3rd Brigade began closer to the ridge, the plan called for it to reach the objective first and immediately place heavy machine-gun fire into the flank and rear of the German troops opposing the Marines on the left. When the lead battalions of both brigades were on the objective, support companies were to push out patrols 1 kilometer to the front, while the rest of the force transformed the crest into the 2nd Division's new main line of resistance.[44]

The four infantry regiments went into this battle with one organizational change that demonstrates the continued doctrinal shift within the division. By the fall of 1918, each French infantry unit withdrew a small percentage of men prior to battle and kept them in the rear to ensure that a cadre of experienced troops was available to reconstitute the unit after the engagement. But, the practice also showed the division staff's understanding of the role of the infantry on the Great War battlefield. Divisions did not take objectives by weight of manpower but rather by the deliberate coordination of firepower with the agile movements of small combat groups. Excess infantry thrown into any battle simply led to more casualties. On 29 September, Lejeune issued a memorandum instituting such a practice in the 2nd Division. Henceforth, before going into action, the commanders of the infantry regiments and machine-gun battalions were to send 20 percent of their officers and men, "taken pro-rata" from all ranks, to the division staff. The memorandum explained that the lucky

---

[43] Ibid.
[44] HQ 2nd Division, Field Orders No. 35, 2 October 1918, 2300 hours, *RSD*, vol. 1; and HQ 3rd Brigade, Field Orders No. 37, 2 October 1918, 1130 hours, *RSD*, vol. 2.

officers and men would be used to guard equipment, serve as litter bearers, handle stragglers and prisoners, and bury the dead, but the real reasons for the change were those that led the French to institute the practice many months before. Lejeune's order was a recognition that he wanted his infantry formations to be thin, that his attacks were based more on firepower than manpower, and that he needed to ensure the survival of some of his best men.[45]

Despite some confusion created by the inability of French guides to get the 3rd Brigade into position well before the attack, the failure of the French division on the immediate left to clear out their jump-off positions, and late issuance of orders by the French XXI Corps, the American attack went off as planned at 0550 hours on 3 October. On the right, Ely's brigade followed its barrage closely all the way up the ridge, taking its initial objective by 0840 hours. Along the way, the 9th and 23rd Regiments essentially destroyed the German 410th Infantry, which reported 810 casualties on that day. Ely soon reported his men took the ridge "without serious loss" and had good liaison with the Marines on his left and the French 167th Division on his right.[46] Neville's Marine brigade also took its objective that morning but did so without any support at all from the French 21st Division on its left flank, which failed to advance. The leading battalions of the 6th Marines had pressed on nonetheless, adjusting their formations and maneuvers to avoid the galling fire from German machine guns on the left. They also took their objectives on schedule and reported that "during the advance our losses were light." Partly this was the result of a quick-thinking battalion commander of the supporting 5th Marine Regiment, who "immediately" sent an assault force – complete with 37mm guns, machine guns, and tanks – that reduced the enemy fire and eventually eliminated a strong German position holding up the French to the left.[47] After reorganizing on the ridge, the Marine and infantry brigades sent out the required patrols to the front behind the second rolling barrage and began consolidating their gains. The patrols pushed the line beyond the

---

[45] HQ 2nd Division, Memorandum, 29 September 1918, *RSD*, vol. 1. See also Millett, *In Many a Strife*, 61.

[46] "Messages Sent and Received (and Incidents) – Blanc Mont," Folder 32.16, Box 48, 2nd Division Historical File, RG 120, NA. See also Spaulding and Wright, *Second Division*, 173–4.

[47] HQ 4th Brigade, "Operations Report, 4th Brigade, Marines, October 1st-10th, 1918," *RSD*, vol. 7; and Ronald J. Brown, *A Few Good Men: The Fighting Fifth Marines: A History of the USMC's Most Decorated Regiment* (Novato, Calif.: Presidio Press, 2001), 66.

ridge to the final objective and, by late morning, the division had driven a
salient about 4 kilometers into one of the toughest German positions on
the Western Front.

The seizure of Blanc Mont Ridge was one of the greatest achievements
of the 2nd Division, or any AEF division, during the war. Fully aware
of the tremendous strength of the enemy position, Gouraud and Pétain
heaped praise on Lejeune and his division. The Fourth Army commander
reported that the division's attack was "brilliant," and he recommended
that the unit be cited in special orders. Pétain went further; not only did
he cite the division in special orders, but he also appointed Lejeune a
Commander of the French Legion of Honor and called the attack "the
greatest single achievement of the 1918 campaign."[48]

The division succeeded because it developed attack plans and carried
out assaults in accordance with a combat doctrine that in many ways differed from the open-warfare sentiments promulgated by Pershing and his
GHQ. In fact, the assault at Blanc Mont resembled just the kind of limited-
objective, firepower-based, set-piece attacks Pershing so often derided. To
be sure, the 2nd Division expected its infantry to fight its way forward,
to maneuver intelligently, and to take enemy strong points by envelopment. But, the division stressed the absolute necessity of basing even these
infantry attacks on as much firepower as possible. The infantry relied
heavily on the fire of automatic rifles, machine guns, mortars, and 37mm
guns. Lejeune knew, if Pershing did not, that the concept of "self-reliant
infantry" was meaningless in nearly all offensive operations. During 2nd
Division attacks, rolling barrages escorted the infantry to clearly defined
and limited objectives, and heavy standing barrages gave protection during the consolidation phase. If Pétain's pithy phrase, "Artillery conquers,
Infantry occupies," was an exaggeration, Lejeune knew it was more valid
than official AEF doctrine admitted.

The taking of Blanc Mont Ridge showed how skilled the division was at
preparing and delivering set-piece attacks. Its infantry did not simply rush
forward in dense waves expecting to shoot and bayonet its way forward.
The reports of defending German officers, always sure to mention the presence of tanks and overwhelming numbers, repeatedly noted that attacking Americans made excellent use of the terrain; outflanked, enveloped,
and annihilated the German positions; and extensively employed machine
guns. They also noted that the American infantry quickly stopped and

---

[48] Gen. Gouraud is quoted in Lejeune, *Reminiscences*, 365. Coffman quotes Pétain in *War
to End All Wars*, 284.

consolidated its new line on the ridge instead of racing wildly down the rear slope.[49] The division also demonstrated its ability to coordinate these infantry attacks with massed artillery support. German reports testified that the intensity of the preliminary bombardment "reached terrific proportions," interrupted all telephonic communication, knocked out half their machine guns, and caused as much as 25 percent losses in some companies.[50] American reports confirm this assessment. Ely wrote that his supporting guns from the 15th Field Artillery "did excellent work." Even the old problem of infantry–artillery communication, of which Ely previously had been very critical, was solved to his satisfaction. He reported that "close liaison was established and maintained . . . infantry and artillery worked well together" and that "it is not believed that closer cooperation between infantry and artillery could have been obtained."[51] Neville likewise complimented the artillery support for the Marine brigade, reporting that his men "testified to the excellency of the rolling barrage and the accuracy of special fire."[52] Lejeune's men had justified his confidence in their ability to carry out even the most difficult set-piece attack. Unlike the fight at St. Mihiel, even German officers admitted that the American success was gained in the face of "a most extraordinary tenacious resistance."[53] But, if Lejeune thought his division had completed its mission, he soon learned otherwise.

French commanders trumpeted the success of the 2nd Division's morning assault all the way to Marshal Foch, who responded predictably. Naulin, the corps commander, proclaimed that Foch had "learned of the success of the XXI Corps and of the Second Division. . . . He orders that this success be exploited to the limit. All must press forward at once, without hesitation. The breach is made; the enemy must not be given time to

[49] See the many German reports included in Lieutenant Colonel Ernst Otto's monograph, "The Battle at Blanc Mont (October 2 to October 10, 1918)," n.d., File 33.6, Box 30, 2nd Division Historical File, RG 120, NA. Otto commanded German troops at Blanc Mont and after the war wrote a number of histories on the battle, paying particular attention to the German side. Some were even published in America. See *The Battle at Blanc Mont*, trans. Martin Lichtenburg (Annapolis: U.S. Naval Institute, 1930).

[50] From various reports quoted in Otto, "The Battle at Blanc Mont (October 2 to October 10, 1918)," n.d., File 33.6, Box 30, 2nd Division Historical File, RG 120, NA.

[51] C.G., 3rd Brigade to C.G., 2nd Division, Subject: Report of Operations October 1–8th, 1918, 13 October 1918, *RSD*, vol. 6.

[52] HQ 4th Brigade, "Operations Report, 4th Brigade, Marines, October 1st–10th, 1918," *RSD*, vol. 7. See also "Operations Second Division (Regular): October 1st to 10th, 1918," n.d., *RSD*, vol. 6.

[53] Otto, "The Battle at Blanc Mont (October 2 to October 10, 1918)," n.d., File 33.6, Box 30, 2nd Division Historical File, RG 120, NA.

repair it."[54] Before noon on 3 October, Naulin had ordered cavalry to enter the 2nd Division sector and be ready to "break through" at the appropriate moment.[55] That moment never came. Lejeune noted that in the late morning, the previously pessimistic but by then "exultantly optimistic" Naulin suggested that the 2nd Division make "a further advance" to the town of Machault, 10 kilometers from the current line. Lejeune reminded the corps commander that his left flank was wide open for a distance of 4 kilometers due to the inaction of the French division on the left, and he denied the request.[56]

Lejeune's response to Naulin and his continued reluctance to make additional attacks after the initial assault are further evidence of the doctrinal shift within the 2nd Division. Lejeune's messages during the battle show that he was concerned not only about the lack of support on his left flank but also about the amount of fire support available for another attack. He reported that his artillery was advancing but would not be "well forward" until the afternoon. He also warned that no further attacks could be made unless his artillery received much more ammunition than allowed by the current corps allotment. He also must have been concerned by the removal of twelve French batteries from his division to support the flagging French 21st Division on his left, which continued to make no progress.[57]

An hour after Lejeune denied Naulin's first request, the corps commander called back, this time "insisting" that the division attempt the deep drive to Machault. Lejeune, who was already making plans for a much smaller advance to push past the ridge, became indignant. He claimed that until his "flanks were supported by the advance of the troops on our left and right, it would be courting certain destruction to drive a thin wedge 14 kilometers deep into the enemy lines."[58] He threatened to appeal any such order to the Fourth Army commander, General Gouraud. Naulin soon backed down and asked only that Lejeune push his lines sufficiently

---

[54] HQ XXI Army Corps, Document No. 3715/3, 3 October 1918, Folder 32.7, Box 15, 2nd Division Historical File, RG 120, NA.

[55] Message from HQ, XXI Army Corps to HQ, 2nd Division, 3 October 1918, 1130 hours, "Messages Received During the Battle of Blanc Mont Ridge," Folder 32.16, Box 5, 2nd Division Historical File, RG 120, NA.

[56] Lejeune, *Reminiscences*, 352.

[57] "Messages Received During the Battle of Blanc Mont Ridge," Folder 32.16, Box 5, 2nd Division Historical File, RG 120, NA. See also Spaulding and Wright, *Second Division*, 177.

[58] Lejeune, *Reminiscences*, 353.

beyond the ridge to ensure the safety of the new line. This Lejeune agreed to do.

At 1400 hours, Lejeune issued his formal order. After announcing that the morning attack was "a complete success," he directed an advance to a new line just a couple of kilometers to the front. The method of attack was to be the same as that of the morning, with both brigades advancing together behind a rolling barrage. After taking the new line, patrols were to be sent out another kilometer. However, possibly in an attempt to buy more time for his units to prepare for the attack, Lejeune did not set the time for the attack but only warned that H hour would be announced later. Then, at 1500, after most of his artillery was in forward firing positions, he issued a message announcing the H hour and warning that the artillery preparation would be "only of five minutes duration."[59]

The 3rd Brigade had little trouble arranging the afternoon attack. After coordinating its artillery support, it passed the 23rd Infantry through the lines held by the 9th Infantry, and the assault battalions followed a new rolling barrage forward. Unfortunately, the 23rd Infantry was the only regiment to make any additional advance that afternoon. The French division on its right never moved. On the left, not only had the French 21st Division not yet advanced, but it had *lost* the ground that the detachment from the 5th Marines had taken for it that morning. For its part of the afternoon attack, Neville had initially ordered the 5th Marines to pass though the 6th Marines and make the assault, but because the 5th was so actively engaged on the left flank, Lejeune authorized the attack to be delayed until early the next morning when it would be better organized. Lejeune's decision made perfect sense for the 4th Brigade, but it left the 23rd Infantry to hold a long salient throughout the night, during which it was subjected to heavy enemy fire from all sides. But, this suffering was not in vain; that night, Gouraud called Lejeune and informed him that the Germans were slowly beginning the withdrawal he had expected.[60]

Early the next morning, the 5th Marines pushed the 4th Brigade line abreast of the 3rd Brigade, a few kilometers north of Blanc Mont Ridge. The ridge was securely in Allied hands and all that seemed necessary was

---

[59] Most likely, the short preparation was the result of limited ammunition in the forward firing positions. HQ 2nd Division, Memorandum, 3 October 1918, 1500, and HQ 2nd Division, Field Orders No. 36, 3 October 1918, 1400 hours, both in *RSD*, vol. 1.

[60] C.G., 3rd Brigade to C.G., 2nd Division, Subject: Report of Operations October 1–8th, 1918, 13 October 1918, *RSD*, vol. 6; W. C. Neville, "Operations Report, 4th Brigade Marines. Covering period 1st–10th October '18," *RSD*, vol. 6; and Lejeune, *Reminiscences*, 353–4.

for the 2nd Division to dig in against the heavy fire and counterattacks the Germans were hurling at it, while other units pressed forward to hassle the enemy's withdrawal. However, the 2nd Division had apparently been *too* successful. Its gain of more than 5 kilometers and capture of nearly two thousand prisoners enticed the French high command to prod it forward, despite the poor progress of the units on its flanks and the decreasing amount of artillery at its disposal.

On 4 October, Naulin ordered the 2nd Division to attack again toward Machault, still far in the distance. Lejeune issued orders for the continuation of the attack but again inserted what he called "the saving clause" that the actual jump-off time would be issued later, when he was more assured of greater French support on the flanks.[61] By mid-morning, the corps informed Lejeune that the French divisions had successfully advanced, so he set the attack time and ordered his division to press forward.

Once again, in contrast to open-warfare ideals, the details of the morning's attack orders show the division's desire to wage another set-piece battle with limited objectives. The infantry was to follow a new rolling barrage to its final objective just a couple of kilometers away, where it was to consolidate the new line behind a protective barrage of all available guns and howitzers. The orders even explained that the designated objective was "an approximate line only. The best position in the vicinity will be taken." To emphasize the extent to which this assault was built around the fire-support plan, the orders then directed the infantry commanders to "see the Artillery Barrage Table for their idea of where that line should be and for their final barrage line."[62] In a separate note to Ely, Lejeune reiterated this: "Warn your men to be careful not to go too far forward of the line prescribed in the order for the objective, as they will run into Bowley's barrage, which at that time will be at the limit of its range."[63] Such statements show how far the 2nd Division had come in its appreciation of firepower in the attack and in its repudiation of open warfare.

Even so, these attacks ran into heavy enemy fire almost immediately, not only from front and flanks but even from the left and right rear. Rightly convinced that the French had not advanced as announced, the

---

[61] HQ 2nd Division, Field Orders No. 36, 4 October 1918, 0600 hours, *RSD,* vol. 1. Another example of the "saving clause" appeared in a note he sent to Ely that morning. See HQ 2nd Division, Memorandum to General Ely, 4 October 1918, 1055 hours, *RSD,* vol. 1.

[62] HQ 2nd Division, Note to Field Orders 37, 4 October 1918, *RSD,* vol. 1; HQ 2nd F.A. Brigade, 4 October, Annex to Field Orders No. 37, *RSD,* vol. 1.

[63] HQ 2nd Division, Memorandum to Gen. Ely, 4 October 1918, 1055 hours, *RSD,* vol. 1.

regimental commanders called off the attacks and ordered their men to dig in again. But the fighting continued. During the day, the German high command sent all nearby reserves toward the 2nd Division and made a number of frantic counterattacks to beat it back. Even Ludendorff reportedly telephoned the local German army commander to insist that certain counterattacks be delivered. The Americans held, but they suffered much more than they had on the first day.[64]

After learning of the enemy resistance and the failed attacks of the two fresh French divisions on his flanks, Lejeune cancelled all attacks to his front. He decided that his division would make no further attempts to advance until it had wiped out the resistance on his flanks and rear. Much of the most damaging enemy fire during the attacks of 4 October had come from a large German strong point on the western edge of Blanc Mont Ridge, on and across the border with the neighboring division. In response, the Fourth Brigade and the divisional artillery developed a detailed plan to annihilate the strong point by the next morning. Throughout the night, the gunners pounded the enemy position. In the morning, they fired an intense 60-minute bombardment, followed by a rolling barrage that escorted the Marines into the strong point. Without losing a single man, the attackers captured the entire dazed garrison of more than two hundred men and seventy-five machine guns.[65]

Early the next morning, Naulin ordered the division to attack again, "as was the daily custom," according to Lejeune.[66] Lejeune issued the required orders, along with the now standard "saving clause," and also with equally important provisions that the infantry was to regulate "its advance with those of the division on the right and left."[67] Because the French were making no headway on the right of the 3rd Brigade and were still considerably behind it, the orders essentially kept Ely's troops in place. In case Ely may have misinterpreted Lejeune directions, Lejeune telephoned the brigade commander to tell him privately, "H hour will not be given."[68] On the left, the Marines followed up the successful

[64] Some sources suggest that this was the most costly day of the war for the division. "Operations Second Division (Regular): October 1st to 10th, 1918," n.d., *RSD*, vol. 6.

[65] HQ 4th Brigade, "Operations Report, 4th Brigade, Marines, October 1st–10th, 1918," *RSD*, vol. 6; "Messages Received During the Battle of Blanc Mont Ridge," Folder 32.16, Box 5, 2nd Division Historical File, RG 120, NA; and Spaulding and Wright, *Second Division*, 181.

[66] Lejeune, *Reminiscences*, 359.

[67] HQ 2nd Division, Field Orders No. 38, 5 October 1918, 0400 hours *RSD*, vol. 1.

[68] Lejeune is quoted in U.S. Army, General Staff, Historical Branch, "Blanc Mont (Meuse-Argonne-Champagne)," Monograph No. 9, April 1920, p. 6, USAMHI.

reduction of the machine-gun nest on Blanc Mont by making a short advance to come abreast of the 3rd Brigade. But, even this small advance was costly.

By this stage of the battle, corps orders for the 2nd Division to advance were superfluous for a host of reasons. First, the Germans had been carrying out a massive withdrawal since the evening of 3 October, and many French divisions to the west were meeting no resistance as they followed the German retreat to the northeast, eventually all the way to the Aisne. Second, the only place along the front of the Fourth Army where the Germans were strongly resisting was against the 2nd Division, which had drawn all the enemy attention initially and whose salient position posed the greatest threat to an orderly withdrawal. Third, Naulin did not need to order the Americans to attack because they were so hotly engaged with the enemy that they were fighting for their lives anyway.

In accordance with the latter condition, both brigade commanders carried out well-prepared local attacks on 6 October primarily to reduce positions from which the Germans were pouring fire into the American lines. After the small costly advance of the previous afternoon, the Marines and infantry made "elaborate and thorough" plans to wipe out a number of enemy strong points to its front and flanks.[69] All the divisional artillery had been advanced over the preceding nights, and it was to mass its fire in a series of intense 1-hour concentrations, then shift into a rolling barrage to cover a 1-kilometer advance of the infantry. The assaulting battalions of each brigade were to coordinate their attacks to seize and hold the new line. Within 3 hours on 6 October, the division had pushed the line forward successfully without major loss, and communications between the infantry and artillery were sufficiently close that a large enemy counterattack was "broken up by a special barrage which was laid within eight minutes after receipt of the request."[70]

During the night of 6–7 October, the 2nd Division was augmented by the fresh but only slightly trained infantry of the 71st Brigade from the 36th Division. By the morning of the seventh, the rookie soldiers from Texas and Oklahoma had relieved most of the veteran infantry of the 2nd Division. But, Lejeune ordered some infantry, as well as the machine-gun, mortar, and 37mm-gun teams, to remain in the line while the new brigade organized itself in front-line positions for the first time. In his memoirs, Lejeune wrote that the men of the 71st Brigade were "excellent,

---

[69] HQ 4th Brigade, "Operations Report, 4th Brigade, Marines, October 1st–10th, 1918," *RSD*, vol. 6.
[70] Ibid.

but entirely lacking in combat experience."[71] In fact, the 36th Division had been in France for only two months; had not come close to completing the program of training given it by GHQ; had not even spent a single day in quiet front-line trenches; and lacked much of its own artillery, engineer, and transportation units.

Not wanting to subject such unprepared men and units to the trials of combat in one of the hottest sectors of the Western Front, Lejeune hoped he could "accustom its officers and men to front line duty while brigaded with the experienced battalions of the 2nd Division before being called on for offensive operations." But, Naulin had other ideas. Apparently as ignorant of the differences between experienced and inexperienced troops as was Pershing, he told Lejeune that the brigade would take part in a general attack on the morning of 8 October and that he expected the new troops "would achieve a success equal to that gained by the 2nd Division" on 3 October. Lejeune protested, telling Naulin he was "expecting the impossible of untried troops" and that the brigade was not ready for such an attack. But, Naulin insisted.[72]

In accordance with Naulin's orders, Lejeune prepared attack plans for the 71st Brigade that were becoming standard operating procedure: After a short preliminary bombardment, the infantry was to fight its way forward with all of its auxiliary weapons under the protection of a rolling barrage to gain a relatively close, limited objective – in this case, about 2 kilometers away. But, the green troops were not ready for the challenge. After pushing forward about half a kilometer and taking a few machine-gun nests, the advance stalled when the troops lost the barrage. Losses were heavy; the brigade suffered more than a thousand casualties in the short advance. One of the remaining Marine battalions had the most successful advance of the day, pushing the division's left flank through the town of St. Etienne and consolidating a new line about 1 kilometer to the front. The following day was spent reorganizing the line, and during the night of 9–10 October, the rest of the 36th Division entered the sector and officially relieved the 2nd Division.[73] The next morning,

---

[71] Lejeune, *Reminiscences*, 360.

[72] Ibid., 361.

[73] One source claims the brigade suffered nearly 1,400 casualties, about 20 percent of the men engaged, but that might be high because the ABMC put the brigade's total losses from 7 to 10 October at 1,506. See ABMC, *American Armies*, 369, and U. S. Army, General Staff, Historical Branch, "Blanc Mont (Meuse-Argonne-Champagne)," Monograph No. 9, April 1920, p. 11, USAMHI. After the 36th Division relieved the 2nd, the 2nd F.A. Brigade had to remain with the 36th, which did not have its own artillery brigade with it.

the remaining German forces opposing the Fourth Army began a rapid withdrawal to Aisne.

During its more than eight days in line from 2 to 10 October, the 2nd Division drove a salient nearly 8 kilometers into the enemy lines. It captured thousands of enemy prisoners and dozens of artillery pieces. It also suffered 4,821 casualties. But, the advances, captures, and losses suffered were not equally distributed during the week of combat. Nearly all of the gains and captures came in the first 24 hours, while casualties during that period were relatively light. Then, during the next two days, as the division struggled to make any further advances or capture any more men and material, it suffered some of its heaviest losses of the war. Finally, as Lejeune brazenly resisted making continued general attacks over the next few days, elements of the division made a few more well-designed set-piece attacks that wiped out enemy strong points, captured more enemy soldiers, and made a few short but less costly advances. The division's ability to resist countless enemy counterattacks while regrouping in the face of extraordinary losses and coordinating new attacks such as that of 6 October was in many ways as impressive an achievement as its gains of the first day. Only the division's improvements in infantry tactics, firepower employment, and communications capability, along with its rare esprit de corps, could have enabled such a feat. Behind most of these adjustments, and helping to bind them together, was the division's doctrinal shift away from any theoretical form of open warfare and toward the firepower-based, set-piece operations associated with the best practices of trench warfare.

The Meuse-Argonne Offensive, 1–11 November 1918

During the last three weeks of October, the division pulled out of the Blanc Mont sector and moved to a training area to rest, refit, retrain, and absorb thousands of replacements. Although the war was entering its final month and the Germans were being driven back everywhere, it seems that most of those in the 2nd Division fully expected to fight again. Some troops showed their expectations by retaining the few BARs they had "borrowed" from men in the 36th Division. Senior commanders did their part by cramming in a short training schedule to keep the veterans sharp and to allow them the chance to pass along their knowledge to the new men. Any doubt about the division's future must have been cleared up by the benevolent attention paid on it by GHQ: At the same time that Pershing was announcing a seventy-five–man reduction in the size of

AEF infantry companies due to a shortage of trained men, GHQ filled all vacancies in the 2nd Division's infantry regiments. It also began officially issuing a number of the new BARs, at the rate of twenty-five per regiment. The signs were unmistakable – the division would fight at least one more battle.[74]

By the end of October, GHQ had moved the 2nd Division to the American First Army in the Meuse-Argonne and assigned it to Summerall's V Army Corps. The 2nd Division was to serve once again as the spearhead of a major offensive. On 1 November, the division was to drive a deep salient into the enemy positions and capture the last remaining German lines of resistance south of the Meuse River. The few men in the division who had survived the unit's previous spearhead assaults at Soissons and Blanc Mont certainly had cause for concern with the division's latest assignment. Furthermore, the German resistance opposing the V Corps had proven tenacious over the past month, and a number of American divisions had suffered heavy casualties while gaining little ground. But, the three crucial commanders in charge of this 2nd Division attack were all committed to ensuring that the operation succeed and at a minimal cost in lives. Specifically, all three commanders shared, in varying degrees, an appreciation of the critical role of firepower in the attack and were not going to be constrained by the limitations of official AEF doctrine.

The first of these officers was the division commander, Lejeune, who had proven his willingness to take extraordinary action when necessary to improve chances for success and avoid senseless losses. At the top of the chain of command sat Hunter Liggett, who had replaced Pershing as commander of the First Army in mid-October and promptly discontinued all major offensive operations to allow the army, corps, and divisions time to reorganize and develop a new plan of attack. For the upcoming attack, Liggett chose objectives that, although relatively deep, were all within range of the supporting artillery. Suspicious that previous attacks had suffered due to excessive restrictions on the use of heavy firepower in direct support of the infantry advance, the new army commander authorized two important innovations. He directed the "complete use of artillery" for the upcoming attack, freeing dozens of heavy guns and howitzers to

---

[74] In his memoirs, Lejeune takes credit for securing some of these replacements through his own efforts at GHQ. See Lejeune, *Reminiscences*, 372–3; Millett, *In Many a Strife*, 61; and "Inspection Reports of Armies, Divisions, and Corps, 1917–1919," Inspector General, GHQ/Administrations Staff, Entry 590, RG 120, NA.

support the infantry. He also ordered the army's bomber aircraft to no longer focus only on hitting enemy rear areas but rather to attack "hostile infantry and artillery in close cooperation" with the assaulting infantry.[75] The third important commander, the leader of the V Corps, may have been the most important of the three. With capable and well-led divisions such as the 2nd and 89th (under Major General William M. Wright) in his command and with the full support of Liggett, Charles Summerall created the most powerful and comprehensive American attack plan of the war.[76]

Summerall's field orders for the attack contained the crystal-clear directives that "fire superiority, rather than sheer man power, be the driving force of the attack" and that "the assault battalions must be covered by artillery and machine gun fire in all stages of the advance."[77] The remainder of the plan helped make those statements a reality. First, even though the army plan directed an infantry advance of nearly 9 kilometers on the first day, Summerall ensured that the supporting artillery from the army, corps, and divisional units could pound the ultimate objective before the attack and escort the infantry all the way to it during the assault with a thick rolling barrage. This meant the use of heavy long-range guns in direct support of the infantry and the gathering of sufficient quantities of the long-distance 1917 Model D shell for the 75mm guns. Second, Summerall was in full agreement with Liggett that the fire plan drench the enemy with various kinds of gas, especially on the enemy's artillery batteries and most powerful strong points. Third, Summerall gathered an unprecedented mass of guns to support the attack of the two divisions in his corps. Although the 1st and 42nd Divisions were in the reserve, Summerall ordered their artillery brigades to join that of the 2nd Division to support its attack and the brigades of other reserve divisions to support the 89th. When the dedicated corps and army batteries are included, each V Corps division advanced with the support of more than three hundred

---

[75] "Report of First Army," *USAWW*, 9: 367.

[76] The 89th Division was a National Army division that arrived in France in June 1918. It completed a month of trench-warfare training behind the lines and spent another month training in quiet trenches at the front before fighting reasonably well on the left flank of the 2nd Division in the St. Mihiel attack. After suffering nearly fifteen hundred casualties holding the newly active sector along the Michel Line for the next three weeks, the 89th joined Summerall's V Corps on 20 October. Its commander, Maj. Gen. Wright, had initially led the 35th Division and briefly commanded each of the III, V, and VII Corps before taking the 89th in early September and commanding it for the rest of the war. See William M. Wright, *Meuse-Argonne Diary: A Division Commander in World War I*, Robert H. Ferrell, ed. (Columbia: University of Missouri Press, 2004).

[77] HQ V Army Corps, Field Orders No. 101, 28 October 1918, *RSD*, vol. 1.

guns and howitzers. Summerall did much the same with the machine guns in his corps, ordering a massed barrage by hundreds of machine guns to cover the entire frontage of his attack. Lejeune noted that at least 255 machine guns supported the 2nd Division attack alone. Summerall also brought up batteries of powerful 6-inch Newton Mortars to ensure the assault met little resistance at the start.[78]

Summerall divided the supporting fire plan into four distinct phases: the period before the preliminary bombardment, the preliminary bombardment, the fire accompanying the infantry assault, and the support after the consolidation of the main objective. In the days immediately preceding the attack, Summerall ordered the artillery to begin preparing the attack zone. Making extensive use of the latest aerial photographs, American guns were to shoot gas and explosive rounds on important targets such as batteries, command posts, and transportation routes. The success of the British attacks in the summer and fall of 1918 was in large measure due to having used such preparation fire to win the counterbattery contest before the attack even started. Unlike before the initial First Army attack in September, the Americans had the time and opportunity to make a similar effort in late October. Occasionally, all guns were to open fire together on the enemy lines for a predetermined period in order to register the pieces without the enemy's knowledge. These programmed barrages also were intended to "train" enemy machine-gunners to emerge more slowly from their dugouts when the real rolling barrage passed over on the day of the attack. Such techniques were used in some of the most successful German and Allied attacks of 1918 and were on the cutting-edge of artillery tactics.

However, the real preliminary bombardment was to begin just 2 hours before the attack on 1 November. Summerall and the army planners were convinced that the intensity of the preparatory fire was more important than the duration, and the length of 2 hours was determined by the amount of ammunition available for the guns while firing at their maximum rate. During this period, the light guns were to hit enemy front lines and suspected troop concentrations while the heavy howitzers hit towns,

---

[78] HQ V Army Corps, Field Orders No. 101, 28 October 1918, *RSD*, vol. 1; HQ Artillery, V Army Corps, Operations Order No. 5, 29 October 1918, File 31.12, Box 17, V Army Corps Historical File, RG 120, NA; Rexmond Cochrane, *The Use of Gas in the Meuse-Argonne Campaign, September-November 1918,* Study No. 10, U.S. Army Chemical Corps Historical Studies: Gas Warfare in World War I (Army Chemical Center, Maryland, 1958), 4; Conrad H. Lanza, "The Artillery Support of the Infantry in the A.E.F.," *Field Artillery Journal* 26 (January–March 1936), 75; and Lejeune, *Reminiscences,* 384.

woods, strong points, and machine-gun nests. The guns with the longest range targeted enemy batteries to neutralize them before the attack, making extensive use of both persistent and nonpersistent gas. The brief but intense preliminary bombardment, known as a "hurricane" bombardment in the BEF, was also a key element in the German Spring offensives.[79]

Summerall believed that covering fire during the attack was even more important than the preliminary bombardment. His experience in the 1st Division, like Lejeune's in the 2nd, taught him that the density, thickness, and length of the rolling barrage was probably the single most important element in the attack. Summerall's barrage on 1 November was to be unique in three ways. First, because most of the counterbattery firing was to occur during the preliminary fire, nearly all the guns in the corps sector were available to join in the rolling barrage. Second, instead of simply adding the heavier pieces to the standard 75mm barrage or having them fire concentrations ahead of it, Summerall grouped all the pieces by size and ordered them to fire additional rolling barrages ahead of the light guns. This meant that when Lejeune's men jumped-off on 1 November, they closely followed a dense wall of high-explosive fire from the 75mm guns. Two hundred meters ahead of that barrage was to be a line of shrapnel and smoke rounds from other batteries of 75s to confuse and destroy troops caught out in the open. Three hundred meters ahead of that line was to be a rolling barrage from the 155mm howitzers. Finally, 500 meters ahead of the 155mm rounds was to be a layer of fire from the biggest guns available, including the massive 8-inch howitzers. Although some pieces were assigned to fire emergency counterbattery missions, they were ordered to join the appropriate barrage when not handling such requests. These barrages were to move forward together but not at a static rate. When covering infantry over open ground, the barrages were to advance 100 meters every 4 minutes; when firing on hills and slopes, they were to slow to 100 meters in 6 minutes; and when moving through woods, the barrages were to pound forward 100 meters in 8 minutes. To ensure that the infantry would have sufficient support at the end of the attack, the V Corps artillery plan issued a detailed schedule announcing when each artillery battalion was to move forward, what

---

[79] Charles P. Summerall, "Recent Operations from the Standpoint of Employment of Artillery with Particular Reference to Co-operation between the Infantry and the Artillery" (lecture given to the ACAS, 16 December 1918), Box 14, ACAS Files, Entry 371, RG 120, NA.

route it was to use, and to where it was to move. Without a doubt, it was the most centralized and complex fire plan the 2nd Division ever executed.[80]

Although the fire plan was the key element of the attack, the infantry had its duties as well, and these duties were clearly spelled out. The 4th Brigade was to make the main assault, with the 6th Marines on the left and the 5th Marines on the right. The attack plan included three clear phases, each with its own objective, as well as a rest for reorganization and the leap-frogging of tired units by fresh units, if necessary. At H hour, the Marines were to drive forward about 3 kilometers to the first objective and consolidate that line. Three hours after the initial jump-off, the attack was to push on to the second objective, another 3 kilometers to the front, and consolidate that line. At H plus 6 hours and 50 minutes, the Marines were to advance 3 more kilometers to the third and final objective, where they were to dig in, prepare the line for defense, and send out patrols. Beyond each objective, the rolling barrage was to shift into a standing barrage to provide protection. Certain units were tasked to prepare and execute detailed plans to take various enemy strong points. Some of these plans, such as the Marine attacks on the Bois l'Epasse and the town of Landres-et-St. Georges and the 23rd Infantry assault on the Bois de Hazois, became miniature set-piece attacks in their own right. Similarly, Lejeune directed the brigade commanders to "arrange in advance" even the mopping up of all captured areas, using specific teams from the "support and reserve battalions."[81] Far from relying solely on initiative, these plans sought to leave little to chance.

The corps and division plans both emphasized that throughout the attack, the infantry was to make "every possible use" of "machine guns, 37mm guns and Stokes mortars to assist the advance." Summerall's plan reiterated that "no effort must be spared to insure a vigorous, powerful attack supported by every available means of delivering fire." While the advance was to be controlled by the barrage and intermediate objectives, the infantry was to avoid dense formations and advance by outflanking, envelopment, and infiltration. It was to be assisted by one company of

[80] HQ Artillery, V Army Corps, Operations Order No. 5, 29 October 1918, File 32.12, Box 17, V Army Corps Historical File, RG 120, NA.

[81] HQ 2nd Division, "Tentative Plan for Attack," 25 October 1918, *RSD*, vol. 1. See also HQ 2nd Division, Field Orders No. 47, 26 October 1918, *RSD*, vol. 1; HQ V Army Corps, Field Orders No. 101, 28 October 1918, *RSD*, vol. 1.; HQ 2nd Division Memorandum No. 1, 26 October 1918, *RSD*, vol. 1; HQ 3rd Brigade, Operations Memorandum No. 24, 27 October 1918; and HQ 4th Brigade, Field Orders No. 32, n.d., RSD, vol. 2.

fifteen American-operated tanks, as well as a number of mortar crews from the 1st Gas Regiment. The infantry also was to make use of a new measure of flexibility in the attack, should it have trouble keeping up with the barrage. Instead of simply ordering the infantry to stay close to the barrage and hoping it could do so, Summerall included a provision that allowed each infantry battalion to recall its portion of the barrage "to some well established line to rest" until the infantry caught back up to it. For this reason, the barrage was to be "entirely under the control of the assault battalions."[82] Each battalion's artillery liaison team was to maintain communication with its supporting batteries throughout the assault to make this possible.

The centralized nature of the V Corps plan coordinated the attacks of the 2nd and 89th Divisions and provided a comprehensive fire plan, but it also seemed to leave the division commanders with few decisions to make except determining which units fulfilled which missions. However, Lejeune did make at least two important adjustments to the plan and tried unsuccessfully to make a third to conform the battle more to his liking. First, having learned that many recent AEF attacks failed when the attacking infantry ran into machine-gun fire even before it could close up on the rolling barrage, Lejeune added an ingenious modification to the fire plan. The corps plan called for the 75mm guns to shift to a standing barrage on the front German position 10 minutes before the attack was to begin. Lejeune ordered that barrage to fall instead at least 200 yards *in front* of the enemy front line so it would catch those machine-gunners trying to set up their pieces inside the starting line of the rolling barrage. The second change to corps plans was the refusal to use accompanying guns. The corps orders specified that "batteries or single guns" were to be detailed to the assaulting infantry battalions to knock out machine-gun nests, but Lejeune and Bowley did what they had done at St. Mihiel.[83] Two battalions of light guns were designated to advance early on in the attack, but they were never broken up and sent forward with individual infantry units. Finally, in an effort to prevent his division from being used in some misguided attempt to make unprepared and poorly supported attacks after completing the set-piece portion of the attack, Lejeune tried

---

[82] HQ V Army Corps, Field Orders No. 101, 28 October 1918, *RSD*, vol. 1. See also HQ 2nd Division, "Tentative Plan for Attack," 25 October 1918, *RSD*, vol. 1.

[83] HQ Artillery, V Army Corps, Operations Order No. 5, 29 October 1918, File 32.12, Box 17, V Army Corps Historical File, RG 120, NA.

to secure from Summerall an agreement to relieve the division "as soon as it took its [final] objective." Although Summerall told Lejeune that he was unwilling to even discuss such a question before the battle, the very request itself shows the level of Lejeune's commitment to fight a limited, set-piece battle.[84]

At 0530 hours on 1 November, the attack began (see Map 17). Throughout the assault, weeks of planning and, of equal importance, months of learning came to fruition. The infantry surged forward closely behind what became known as the "Summerall Barrage" and overcame all resistance from the broken and demoralized enemy. It reached each intermediate objective on time and, by afternoon, had completely consolidated the final objective and sent patrols out well to the front. The division captured at least thirteen hundred prisoners and seventy-five guns on the first day, while suffering light casualties.[85] It had broken through the last German lines of resistance south of the Meuse – the *Brunhilde* and *Freya Stellung* – and had secured a line from which American artillery could shell the important German railroad running west through Sedan. The remainder of the offensive became a pursuit of the German forces racing to establish a new defensive line across the Meuse. Many senior AEF officers rightly considered this the most successful American attack of the war.

The achievement of the 2nd Division and of the entire V Corps on 1 November resulted from a number of factors. Certainly, the deterioration of the German forces by this point in the war accounts for much of the success, as with the gains made by all Allied forces from July 1918 on. However, the fact that just two weeks prior to the November attack the German forces opposing the V Corps had met strong American attacks with stiff resistance, causing heavy losses and only small gains in the 42nd and 32nd Divisions, suggests other factors may have been at work. First, the planning process throughout the First Army, and especially the V Corps, contributed to the victory. Unlike so many previous operations, numerous conferences between senior commanders and staff officers

---

[84] Summerall, "Duty, Honor, Country," 118. See also Lejeune, *Reminiscences*, 381; C.O., 2nd F.A. Brigade to Chief of Staff, 2nd Division, Subject: Report of Operations during the Period November 1st to November 11th, *RSD*, vol. 8.

[85] Neville, whose Marine brigade led the attack, reported that his command lost about 5 percent of the men engaged on this day, and most of those were from shell fire. W. C. Neville, "Operations Report- 4th Brigade Marines. Covering period 24 Oct.–11 Nov. '18," *RSD*, vol. 6.

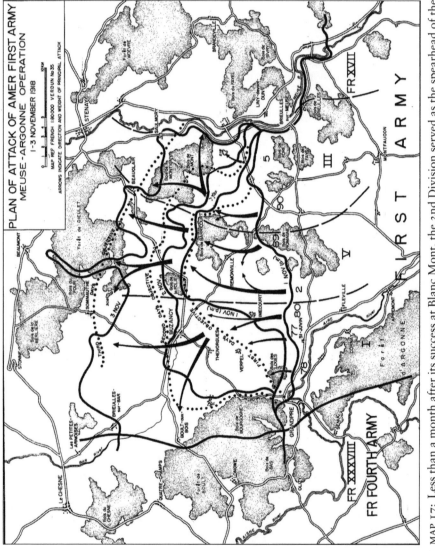

MAP 17: Less than a month after its success at Blanc Mont, the 2nd Division served as the spearhead of the American First Army's final and most successful major attack in the Meuse-Argonne on 1 November.

provided planners and the combatants the opportunity to develop a plan that was comprehensive, well understood, and entirely realistic.[86] Second, the plan produced by this process ordered a very detailed, limited-objective, set-piece attack by a rested, organized, and thoroughly prepared force. Third, the two divisions of the V Corps that did so well on 1 November were both veteran divisions that had prior experience planning and carrying out set-piece attacks. Finally, and possibly of greatest importance, the attack was openly based on the overwhelming use of firepower in every phase of the advance.

After the war, Summerall described the role of firepower in the V Corps attack and recalled the hostility he received when he first suggested such an approach as part of the Baker Mission in 1917: "The success of the assault depended upon the covering artillery fire to protect the infantry from the German machine guns and artillery at the beginning and as the line advanced. I planned to use every weapon to its maximum power.... This was the only place where the artillery approximated the strength which I had advocated at Paris for attack and the saving of the infantry was proved as well as the overwhelming of the enemy."[87]

In different ways, each of these factors – the emphasis on detailed planning and conferences, limited-objective and set-piece attacks, and overwhelming firepower – was related to the doctrinal shift taking place in

---

[86] For a discussion of the planning process in the V Corps and the 2nd Division, see Lejeune, *Reminiscences*, 377–9. After the war, Maj. Gen. George Cameron, who commanded the V Corps during the St. Mihiel and Meuse-Argonne Offensives (before being relieved in mid-October), claimed that Pershing only held one preattack conference throughout his entire tenure as commander of the First Army – when he solicited advice regarding the length of the artillery preparation before the St. Mihiel attack. If true, it means that Pershing never held a conference of his senior commanders before or during any phase of the Meuse-Argonne Offensive. See Cameron's statement in "The Operations of the 26th Division at St. Mihiel," p. 4, Folder 33.6, Box 25, 26th Division Historical File, RG 120, NA. This problem did not exist in Summerall's V Corps, but it may have remained a problem in Dickman's I Corps. Maj. Gen. George Duncan, the commander of the 82nd Division that fought in the I Corps from 7 to 31 October, wrote later, "Not once during the twenty-six days of the operations of this Division was I personally called upon by the Corps or Army Commander for an estimate of the situation in our front, or questioned as to the condition of the troops, or as to what could be reasonably expected of them; nor was I ever called into conference with Division Commanders on the right and left so that the plan of mutual support and cooperation would obtain its best development and brought into full accord.... At no time was I personally asked for my estimate of the situation in any attack that was ordered, or for my plan of execution." See George B. Duncan, "General Missions of the 82nd Division in the Meuse-Argonne," p. 13, 3 February 1919, Box 30, Edwards Papers, MHS.

[87] Summerall, "Duty, Honor, Country," 119–20.

various places throughout the AEF. Combat commanders were discarding the theoretical vision of open warfare and relying on a doctrinal framework and operational approach that were closer to the Allied version of trench warfare and much more in line with the capabilities of AEF combat forces.

Between 1 and 5 November, the 2nd Division carried out a series of innovative advances that brought it to the Meuse River, some 29 kilometers from its original jump-off line. During the initial attack, the division proved it had mastered the art of carrying out set-piece attacks based on massive power, even against a tenacious enemy in prepared positions. All infantry commanders testified to the accuracy and intensity of the fire support, and their reports confirm that what little resistance survived the artillery and machine-gun barrages was overcome by a skilled combination of fire and envelopment. One brigade commander reported that the "resistance of the enemy was shattered by the intensity and rapidity of the barrage," and a proud regimental commander insisted the attack "was marked by a brilliant coordination of arms, the artillery laying down an absolutely smothering barrage which the infantry followed closely."[88]

During the final three days of the drive to the Meuse, the 2nd Division faced conditions that most senior AEF officers thought were perfect for conducting open warfare, but the division's reaction betrayed its lack of faith in those anachronistic methods. When ordered by higher authority to continue the advance, the 2nd Division generally resorted to a unique combination of night marches and prearranged artillery support, including rolling barrages, to reduce casualties.[89] For example, on the afternoon of 3 November, the 23rd Infantry found itself facing a strong enemy rearguard position in the Bois de Belval. Instead of carrying out a hurried and

---

[88] C.G., 3rd Brigade to C.G., 2nd Division, Subject: Report of Operations, 16 November 1918, *RSD*, vol. 6; HQ 23rd Infantry, "Report of Operations, Nov. 1–11, 23d Infantry," 27 November 1918, *RSD*, vol. 7.

[89] I do not mean to suggest that the 2nd Division carried out a mistake-free advance to the Meuse. It did not. On 4 November, after successfully using the nighttime march technique the night before, the 3rd Brigade, then 6 kilometers ahead of the divisions on its flanks and with only one battalion of light guns in direct support, ran into a strong enemy line 2 kilometers south of Beaumont. The brand new brigade commander, Col. James C. Rhea (formerly the division chief of staff), claimed to have reported the situation to Lejeune and was soon ordered to advance anyway. Rhea reported that his command suffered nearly a thousand casualties in an attack that moved the line only 1 kilometer. Whether Lejeune made the decision to attack or received the order from a more senior commander is unknown. See 3rd Brigade to C.G., 2nd Division, Subject: Report of Operations, 16 November 1918, *RSD*, vol. 6; and Lejeune, *Reminiscences*, 394.

poorly supported daylight attack, Colonel Robert O. Van Horn, the regimental commander, coordinated with the 15th Field Artillery to support an evening advance that night. After shelling the woods for a while, the artillery fired a dense rolling barrage that extended just 200 yards to each side of the one road through the wood. Van Horn formed his regiment in a long column of twos, ordered heavy advance and flank guards to move out, and followed the barrage for a distance of 6 kilometers. Along the way, the flank guards captured two hundred unsuspecting enemy troops hiding in the woods. Using such innovative tactics, by the time the division reached the Meuse, it had taken a total of more than 1,700 prisoners, 105 artillery pieces, and 500 machine guns.[90]

Despite the successes of the November attack, staff officers at GHQ found much to criticize. GHQ observers reported to Major General Andre W. Brewster, the AEF Inspector General at GHQ, that the 2nd Division made no attempt to place accompanying guns in the infantry battalions. Brewster promptly forwarded the report to Summerall, along with a copy of Pershing's *Combat Instructions* and a pointed reminder of "the well-known desires of the Commander-in-Chief" on the issue. Brewster admitted it was "but fair to add that the results of yesterday in this Division go to show that the artillery satisfactorily supported their infantry," but he added that "perhaps if the artillery were used after the manner prescribed in *Combat Instructions* even better results would be obtained."[91] Brewster apparently did not consider the possibility that the 2nd Division's success may have been in part a result of the division's determination to use massed, prearranged barrages in lieu of sporadic, ad hoc fire from individual horsedrawn pieces.

The comments in GHQ's official analysis of the battle, entitled *Notes on Recent Operations No. 4*, provide more glaring evidence of the gap

[90] The division conducted one more attack after reaching the Meuse. On 10 November, apparently against the recommendations of Neville, Lejeune, and even Summerall, the First Army ordered the division to cross the river in the face of the enemy. It attempted to force two crossings but only one succeeded, and the casualties in that operation were severe. Between 1 and 11 November, the division suffered a total of 3,282 casualties. "Operations Report of the 2nd Division West of the Meuse November 1 to November 11, 1918, Inclusive," *RSD*, vol. 6; Col. R.O. Van Horn to C.G., 2nd Division, Subject: Report of Operations, 3rd Brigade from October 17, 1918, to 2nd November, 1918, 9 January 1919, *RSD*, vol. 6; C.G., 3rd Brigade to C.G., 2nd Division, Subject: Report of Operations, 16 November 1918, *RSD,* vol. 6; W.C. Neville, "Operations Report-4th Brigade Marines. Covering period 24 Oct.–11 Nov. '18," *RSD*, vol. 6; and C.O., 23rd Infantry to C.G., 2nd Division, 27 November 1918, *RSD*, vol. 7.
[91] Brewster to C.G., V Corps, 1 November 1918, Folder "Artillery," Entry 590, RG 120, NA.

that had developed between many of the best combat divisions and the senior staffs and commanders in the rear. The report stated:

The disadvantages of limited objectives were much in evidence. As soon as assigned objectives were reached there almost invariably followed an immediate relaxation of all effort. Ordinarily, by this time the hostile resistance was furnished only by small rear guards. Usually there was still some daylight left...also a great part of the division concerned was comparatively fresh. Under such circumstances pursuit to the limit of capacity of men and animals should have been the rule. But the assignment of limited objectives immediately ended all thought of further efforts.[92]

After criticizing one of the key elements of the successful V Corps attack – limited objectives – GHQ moved on to another – the reliance on massive firepower:

The criticism of previous operations that too little use was made of the rifle and of all the infantry weapons must be repeated...the infantryman does not use his rifle enough. He is too prone to leave the whole matter of fire superiority to the artillery. This is not in accordance with American tradition or doctrine, and deprives the infantryman of the most efficient single aid to his advance – the rifle.[93]

GHQ was right to encourage the infantryman to use his rifle; it was, after all, the only long-range weapon in the hands of the vast majority of attacking soldiers. But, GHQ apparently failed to appreciate the degree of firepower superiority required to make any significant advance against a skilled enemy without sustaining the kind of prohibitive losses the 2nd Division suffered on 6 June near Belleau Wood, on 19 July near Soissons, and on 4 October north of Blanc Mont. On each of those days, the infantrymen of the 2nd Division had plenty of rifles and most knew how to use them fairly well. Long before November, those riflemen knew – if more senior commanders and staff officers did not – that although their rifles were still useful, they were no longer the margin of victory on the modern battlefield. Whether such a belief accorded with "American tradition or doctrine" ceased to matter to those in the 2nd Division. The officers and men needed to find a way that allowed them to fight, advance, win, and live, and in so doing they helped create an unofficial but very real AEF way of war.

[92] GHQ, AEF, *Notes on Recent Operations No. 4* (Chaumont, France, 22 November 1918), 1.
[93] Ibid.

Conclusions

The history of the 2nd Division provides one of the finest examples of doctrinal and operational development in the AEF. After finishing a very abbreviated training regimen that better prepared the division to wage trench warfare than to engage the enemy in a fluid war of movement, the division nevertheless entered its first battle with the lingering effects of the official AEF doctrine. All attempts to make hurriedly prepared and poorly supported infantry attacks against enemy positions led to short gains and massive casualty rates. During the grinding battle to take Belleau Wood, the division learned, slowly and imperfectly, that it needed to plan and execute different kinds of attacks to be successful. By late June, and certainly by the 1 July attack on Vaux, the division showed it had the will and the skill to carry out limited, set-piece attacks based on massive firepower.

Fewer than three weeks later, in the Aisne-Marne Offensive near Soissons, the division showed that it may have had the courage and ferocity to drive an outnumbered and unprepared enemy from the field but also that it did not possess either the will or the ability to make well-coordinated, sufficiently supported attacks in an almost prototypical open-warfare environment. Over a number of weeks, it trained and retrained, and under the new leadership of John Lejeune, it began to formulate its own combat doctrine. Henceforth, it sought to make each of its remaining engagements into the kind of limited-objective, firepower-based, set-piece attacks that it believed it could execute successfully and at a modest cost in human life. At St. Mihiel, Blanc Mont Ridge, and the Meuse-Argonne, the 2nd Division did all it could to fight according to its own doctrine, even to the extent of employing unauthorized artillery tactics, resisting orders from superior commanders to make continued attacks, and asking for early relief from the battlefield. In the end, such methods helped produce the great irony in which the AEF's most productive division deviated the most from official AEF doctrine.

8

The 77th "Liberty" Division

Training for the Trenches and Fighting on the Vesle

The 77th Division, the first and most active of the draftee National Army divisions, had in many ways a remarkably different wartime experience than the 1st, 26th, and 2nd Divisions.[1] As with other National Army divisions, it had from the very beginning fewer officers and NCOs who had spent any time in either the Regular Army or the National Guard.[2] Possibly of more importance, the 77th accomplished most of its training in the United States and only ran through an abbreviated training regimen in France before being ordered into combat. This undoubtedly had an impact on the division's combat experience, probably by lowering its overall effectiveness but also by limiting the amount of exposure its men had to the AEF's official combat doctrine.

Among the most significant distinctions between the 77th Division and many other experienced divisions was that its longest serving commander, Major General Robert Alexander, seemed to adapt both his thinking and

---

[1] Different sources give various nicknames for the 77th Division. The division's official history, written by unit officers while still in France, calls it the "Liberty" Division, which matches the division's shoulder patch of a yellow silhouette of the Statue of Liberty on a blue background. However, the ABMC refers to it as the "Metropolitan" Division (and states that the 79th Division was given the "Liberty" moniker), while Laurence Stallings calls it the "Melting Pot" Division. All three make sense, and each may have been used but, considering the unit patch and the authority of the division's own officers, the term "Liberty" Division is the best. See J. O. Adler, ed., *History of the 77th Division: August 25th 1917–November 11th 1918* (New York: The 77th Division Association, 1919), 139.

[2] The primary combat units in the 77th Division were the 153rd Infantry Brigade, composed of the 305th and 306th Infantry Regiments; the 154th Infantry Brigade, with the 307th and 308th Infantry Regiments; and the 152nd Field Artillery Brigade, with the 304th, 305th, and 306th Field Artillery Regiments, the latter being the heavy howitzer unit.

his methods very little during the year he spent in Europe. A devoted adherent of prewar American combat doctrine, Alexander's faith in the rifle, bayonet, and infantry maneuver as the keys to battlefield success never wavered, nor did his reliance on a decentralized style of command that pushed the responsibility for operational planning down to his brigade, regimental, and battalion commanders. Alexander's traditional doctrinal views and his philosophy of command combined to inhibit the division's ability to make the kind of adjustments and adaptations seen in the AEF's best divisions.

Despite Alexander's weaknesses, the officers and men within the 77th Division, well below Alexander in rank and authority but much more involved in the day-to-day decisions and actions on the battlefield, seemed to learn some of the same lessons picked up in the more experienced AEF divisions, and they struggled to apply them. Fairly quickly, they became more cautious, and to the extent that they could, they demonstrated an increasing willingness to rely more on modern firepower than on traditional rifle power. In fact, some lessons, especially regarding caution while advancing, may have been learned too well. Although the 77th may not have become as adept as the best AEF divisions at preparing or carrying out set-piece attacks and at coordinating and employing heavy firepower, it did ultimately learn how to make limited attacks at reasonable cost.

Training in the United States, September 1917 to March 1918

Alone among the divisions in this study, the 77th Division underwent significant training in the United States prior to traveling to Europe. It also experienced much less training, of all sorts, after arriving there. Despite these differences, the 77th shared with the 1st, 26th, and 2nd Divisions the experience of training primarily for trench fighting rather than open warfare. In fact, it did almost no training to fight battles of maneuver in an open-warfare environment.

The War Department organized the 77th Division at Camp Upton on Long Island, New York, in August 1917 and appointed Major General J. Franklin Bell, the Philippine War veteran, as the first commander. Both the officer corps and enlisted ranks of the division were filled primarily with former civilians from New York City. The initial complement of officers was composed of graduates from the First Officers Training Camp at Plattsburg, New York; a number of men commissioned directly from civilian life (many based on previous attendance at the summer military

training camps during the 1915–1916 preparedness movement); and a
small cadre from the Regular Army.[3] The division received so few Regular
officers that Alexander claimed *all* officers outside of the division staff
were "officers of reserve." Even one of the crucial infantry regimental
command positions was held by a non-Regular. Alexander also claimed
that the division's officer contingent was filled with "the most important
younger business element of New York City," as well as other professional
men such as Major Charles Whittlesey, a Wall street lawyer; Captain
George McMurtry, a Harvard graduate and stockbroker; and Captain
Wardlaw Miles, an Ivy League English professor.[4]

The ranks of the 77th were filled by draftees from the urban masses
of the New York City area, along with a small contingent of Regular
Army NCOs.[5] As such, the Liberty Division took on the complex character of the city. Alexander bragged that forty-three languages and dialects
were spoken in the division (others noted that many troops spoke almost
no English) and claimed that the division represented "as heterogeneous
an assembly as could well be imagined."[6] Commanders even attempted
to employ common terminology to flesh out the combative spirit of the
urbanites, referring to small combat groups as "gangs." The division history insisted that between the officer and enlisted contingents, a "Who's
Who" of the division would have been "the most cosmopolitan com-
pendium ever compiled" because the unit contained representatives "of
every nationality and status of life."[7]

During September, the first increment of draftees began to flow into
the camp and were inducted into the division. Much of the first month

[3] Throughout the war, the U.S. Army commissioned about two hundred thousand officers.
Nearly half of these (48 percent) came from the officers training camps, a surprising
13 percent was commissioned directly from civilian life (many for technical, logistical,
and administrative work), 8 percent was commissioned from the ranks, 6 percent from
the National Guard, and just 3 percent from the Regular Army. Physicians accounted
for the remaining 21 percent. Ayres, *The War with Germany*, 21–2; U.S. Army, *Order of
Battle of the United States Land Forces in the World War* (Washington, D.C.: GPO, 1931–
1949; Center for Military History reprint, 1988), 2: 299. For more on the preparedness
movement and the presence of hundreds of businessmen at the summer training camps,
see James L. Abrahamson, *America Arms for a New Century: The Making of a Great
Military Power* (New York: Free Press, 1981), 132–4; and John Patrick Finnegan, *Against
the Specter of the Dragon: The Campaign for American Military Preparedness, 1914–1917*
(Westport, Conn.: Greenwood Press, 1974), 65–72.
[4] Robert Alexander, *Memories of the World War, 1917–1918* (New York: Macmillan, 1931),
106.
[5] *History of the 77th Division*, 139.
[6] Alexander, *Memories*, 108.
[7] *History of the 77th Division*, 13.

was spent accomplishing routine administrative matters, such as giving
the thousands of arriving men medical inspections and inoculations and
issuing uniforms and equipment. After about a week in the camp, the men
began physical conditioning and learning the fundamentals of close-order
parade drill. Although the infantry supposedly made "splendid progress"
in drill and marching with their Springfields, the new artillerymen had
to train with picks, shovels, and "wooden horses" due to a complete
lack of equipment and guns. By mid-October, as the first increment of
men was becoming somewhat proficient in the basics of military life –
what was then called "the school of the soldier" – large groups of new
draftees flooded the camp on a daily basis. These men quickly entered
into the training program. More junior officers from the "Second Training Camps" also arrived in November and December to help fill the division's officer quota. In addition to drilling the men throughout the day,
the officers attended lectures in the evening and held special classes for
the NCOs, many of whom had only distinguished themselves as NCO
material in the previous few weeks.[8]

As winter weather hit the camp, first turning it into a "sea of mud"
and then freezing the ground solid, the divisional engineers constructed
two important training areas that also represented the doctrinal differences separating Pershing and his GHQ from the more experienced Allied
forces: a life-size trench system and rifle ranges. Although it might have
been an accidental result of geographical requirements, the divisional
infantry training seems to have stumbled into a reasonable and realistic blend of the two styles of fighting. When target shooting started in
January, the infantry did its firing "from trenches in the standing, kneel-
ing, and prone positions, at stationary and disappearing targets," and the
men were told to work at getting off ten to fifteen aimed shots a minute. By
maintaining a commitment to proficiency with the rifle, still the primary
weapon in the hands of the division's twelve thousand infantrymen, but
focusing on its use in and around the trenches that dominated the fighting on the Western Front, the original infantrymen of the 77th Division
may have been rather well served.[9] At this time, the artillerymen finally
received one four-gun battery of 3-inch field pieces and began firing on
a small 3,000-yard range near the camp. While the gunners took turns
learning the basics of moving and firing their weapons, the training for
the rest of the combat troops got more involved.

[8] Ibid., 14.
[9] Ibid., 17.

The unit's official history describes the training during this period and shows that it continued to focus on trench-warfare scenarios, skills, and methods:

Maneuvers were held daily, and mimic battles waged in the new trench system which the Engineers had constructed. Some days it seemed like real warfare, with the huge tank, brought from England, lumbering over "No-Man's Land," machine guns in emplacements, and the infantry going "over the top," their bayonets flashing in the winter sun. The men began to realize what modern warfare meant and talked intelligently of "zero hour," "parapets," "communications trenches," and other technical terms.[10]

Conspicuously absent from these and all other descriptions of the divisional training at Camp Upton is any mention of the term "open warfare" and, more significant, evidence of any kind of training other than rifle target practice that might have prepared the division to fight particularly well out in the open.

One possible reason for this emphasis on trench warfare may have been that, as with the early training of the first American divisions in France, European instructors played a significant role in teaching the new officers and men of the 77th and in monitoring their progress. The 77th Division had its share of the eight hundred Allied officers and NCOs with Western Front experience who came to American training camps to improve and speed along American training.[11] The "French Mission" with the 77th conducted important training, especially with the artillerymen and the automatic riflemen. They also reported on its overall progress, leaving an intriguing record of the successes and weaknesses of the division's training for war. In late February, the head of the French Mission reported that his team of instructors had achieved "satisfactory results...considering the conditions under which they have had to conduct their work." But, he reported it was "striking to see that after four months of training the instruction of the men with regards to the specialties [i.e., auxiliaries] is only just beginning or in some cases non-existent." The reasons for this slow progress were clear: weapon "material" was "absolutely insufficient," especially in grenades, automatic rifles, artillery pieces, and communications equipment; the division lacked any school that focused on teaching the "intimate coordination of the use of the different weapons"; and the cold weather and frozen ground made it hard to work on field

[10] Ibid.
[11] Ayres, *The War with Germany*, 31–5.

fortifications.[12] As with the division history, the reports of French officers describe an emphasis on trench rather than open warfare. While bemoaning the lack of the kinds of weapons most necessary for trench fighting on the Western Front, they also made explicit references to the impressive growth in appreciation, if not yet skill, among division members for preparing for that kind of warfare. They wrote that the officers and men seemed "very much interested in the instruction given them and to get a clear idea of importance of the new armament in trench warfare, also of the new tactical formations."[13]

In mid-March, as the German Army was preparing to launch its first massive Spring offensive near St. Quentin, the 77th Division got ready to ship out for Europe. At the same time, the division commander who had organized, administered, and helped train the units, J. Franklin Bell, was removed from command for medical reasons and the senior brigade commander, Brigadier General Evan M. Johnson, took temporary command. Between late March and mid-April, most of the division sailed to England and then to France, where it disembarked as the first National Army division in Europe, and prepared to continue its training as part of Pershing's AEF. By all accounts, it had thus far learned almost nothing of open warfare, and while its theoretical basis for trench fighting was well laid and it had gained some skills for this kind of warfare, even that was necessarily proscribed by a lack of material, equipment, and weaponry.[14]

Training in France, May–August 1918

Due to the timing of its arrival and arrangements Pershing made with British officials so recently stung by the first two German Spring offensives, the 77th Division fell under British supervision for the first phase of its training in Europe. After exchanging its Springfields for shorter but equally reliable British Enfield rifles, the bulk of the division moved to its designated training area on 6 May to begin "a month's intensive training"

---

[12] The report noted that even this far into the training, one artillery regiment had just four guns, another only two, and the third had "no guns of the caliber they will use in the field." The division had only thirty automatic rifles spread out throughout all the different units and training schools. Captain Thibaud, Head of French Mission, to Brig. Gen. McDonald, Subject: General state of the instruction of specialties in 77th Division, 20 February 1918, Folder 50.9, Box 12, 77th Division Historical File, RG 120, NA.

[13] Ibid.

[14] *History of the 77th Division*, 19–20.

under the veteran British 39th Division.[15] At this time, Major General
George B. Duncan, formerly a brigade commander in the 1st Division,
took command of the division, bringing along with him his many months
of experience in training and commanding infantry, but nearly all of it in
trench warfare.

Whatever Duncan's doctrinal leanings, he took over the 77th just in
time to turn it over to British trainers intent on preparing the division for
warfare on the Western Front in their own way. The impact of these British
instructors appears to have been pervasive, and American accounts admit
that while they hated the British ration, when it came to combat training,
"American methods with which we were familiar were abandoned for
British methods" and that, in particular, "men absorbed British bayonet
drill and British combat methods." Although the AEF General Staff might
have been satisfied with British bayonet training, they were not impressed
with much else of the BEF's emerging style of fighting. Nevertheless, that
is what the 77th Division apparently learned. Officers and men not only
rehearsed the "practical side of warfare" during drills and maneuvers, but
they were also sent in small groups to the British front to see what life
was like in the front-line trenches. It is not surprising that the Americans
"seemed to have been most impressed by the vast amount of shelling."[16]
After just a few weeks of this training, the entire division, less its artillery,
began a three-day series of maneuvers on a British training ground, all
conducted on a life-size trench system.[17]

By mid-June, the infantry was sent into the front trenches in a quiet sector near the town of Baccarat in Lorraine. Although they said goodbye to
their British trainers (and were reissued American firearms), they immediately fell directly under the supervision of a French division that continued
to teach the Americans the important elements of living and fighting in the
trenches. On 24 June, they experienced their first heavy German attacks –
primarily a combined phosgene and mustard-gas bombardment – and suffered about 100 severe gas casualties. Apparently, most were due not to

---

[15] While in the United States, machine-gun training was conducted on a few old Colt guns,
but after joining the BEF for training, the men of the 77th had to switch to the British
Vickers gun. The machine-gunners later switched to the French Hotchkiss gun, which
they used in all combat operations. *History of the 77th Division*, 21; Henry W. Smith, *A
Story of the 305th Machine Gun Battalion* (New York: Modern Publishing, 1941), 16,
21.

[16] *History of the 77th Division*, 21–2.

[17] The unit histories all make clear that this training was all focused on trench warfare.
"The 77th Division," p. 1, Folder 11.4, Box 2, 77th Division Historical File, RG 120,
NA.

slowness in getting the mask on but rather in being too quick to take it off. Division officers were both critical of the skill their men exhibited as they responded to the attack and proud of their toughness. One officer admitted that "the inexperience of our troops and their lack of knowledge in the use of their weapons proved a serious handicap." But, that same report, as well as others, also stressed that while only one American died from gas exposure, twenty-five of the supposedly more experienced Frenchmen were killed in that manner.[18] The division soon learned the features and the importance of the elastic defense, but apparently practiced little of offensive warfare while the French retained command of the sector because patrols in No Man's Land were the "only really aggressive work in this area."[19]

After completing their introductory training at Camp Upton in late April, the artillery units embarked for Europe and arrived at their French training site at Camp Souge, France, in mid-May. Having left their few American guns on Long Island, the 304th and 305th Regiments finally received their complement of French 75mm guns and began serious combat training "as gun crews." Even then, no 155mm howitzers or horses were available for the 306th Regiment, so that unit continued to accomplish theoretical training, computation of firing data, and fake gun drills on mockup weapons. After two weeks of preliminary instruction, the light-gun crews began firing, and the division history stresses that they "learned the firing methods of position warfare," right down to including such variables as barometric pressure and powder temperature when computing firing data.[20] These units did not even receive their initial draft of horses – so crucial to any form of maneuver warfare – until the end of May. Finally, on 8 June, the 306th Regiment received its Schneider howitzers and, to catch up, began live-fire training just two days after first touching the weapons. Throughout June, the units improved their firing skills, shooting numerous rolling barrages and ultimately firing together as a brigade. All this training was done from prearranged, prepared positions, not the kind of firing expected in open warfare.[21]

---

[18] "Report on operations as a unit of a French or British Corps," HQ 154th Infantry Brigade, 17 December 1918, Folder 33.6, Box 17, 77th Division Historical File, RG 120, NA; and "Final report of gas attack," Division Gas Officer, 12 July 1918, Folder 63, Box 14, 77th Division Historical File, RG 120, NA.

[19] *History of the 77th Division*, 33–4.

[20] Ibid., 27–8.

[21] Although the artillery training of the 152nd Field Artillery Brigade may have been somewhat abbreviated, it did allow for lots of firing. The light-gun regiments fired nearly fifty

In mid-July, after an absence of four months, the artillery regiments finally rejoined the division near Baccarat and almost immediately, on 18 July, the French units were completely withdrawn, giving Duncan sole command of the sector.[22] Three days later, the division attempted the first minor raid of its own and patrols to seize enemy troops were increased.[23] Evidently, Duncan had his artillery do enough firing to become so dissatisfied with the commanders of both the 152nd Field Artillery Brigade and the 306th Regiment that he wanted to sack them. Although he could summarily remove the regimental commander, Duncan requested that GHQ send an investigator to confirm his suspicion that Brigadier General Thomas H. Rees, a career army engineer, was not qualified to command the artillery brigade. The inspector confirmed that Rees lacked sufficient knowledge of artillery and was too poor a leader to retain command. It is interesting that the inspector also confirmed that during the brigade's artillery training at Souge "no instruction seems to have been given in direct laying, a matter of great importance in the use of artillery as accompanying guns, for anti-tank work, and in the present approved organization of

thousand practice rounds and the 306th Regiment shot off more than six thousand of the large 155mm shells. In a statement that is as much an indictment of the anemic training of the prewar U.S. Army as a compliment to the wartime development of the AEF, one unit history noted that "in one month the brigade fired more ammunition than would be used in a year by the peace time army." "The 77th Division," p. 2, Folder 11.4, Box 2, 77th Division Historical File, RG 120, NA.

[22] The 305th Field Artillery joined the division on 10 July, the 306th on 12 July, and the 306th on 16 July. Memorandum from Commander-in-Chief, AEF, to C.G., 77th Division, Subject: Battle Participation, 20 March 1919, Box 2, Folder 11.4, 77th Division Historical File, RG 120, NA.

[23] The only 77th Division raid with any remaining documentation occurred on 21 July. It was a somewhat curious and failed effort to nab German troops in what George C. Marshall described as "a silent daylight raid." Apparently, a captain in the division came up with a plan to sneak a combat patrol of about fifty men into the German trenches by maneuvering through a wooded section that connected the two front lines. After successfully entering the German lines, the patrol was mauled by a superior German force. Less than half the raiding party returned to American lines. Marshall, shortly after joining the AEF General Staff, was sent to investigate the incident and he decided nothing worse than bad luck and inexperience were to blame for the failure. See Marshall, *Memoirs*, 121–3. More curious, though, was the lack of artillery support for the raid. A postwar report claims that the raid "was executed without artillery support, although data had been figured and the guns were laid in case artillery support should be required." Because no attack orders for the raid have been found and the captain leading the patrol was killed, details for the full plan of the raid and the reason why the artillery support was not called for remain a mystery. See HQ 305th Field Artillery Regiment, Memorandum for the C.G., 152 F.A. Brigade, 4 February 1919, Folder 11.2, Box 30, 77th Division Historical File, RG 120, NA.

the ground for defense."[24] Although it is difficult to imagine how these weaknesses could have become apparent while holding a quiet sector of the front in late July, the report did expose that the brigade's training focused almost exclusively on such trench-warfare skills as map shooting and barrage firing. Regardless of whether the problems cited by the inspector matched Duncan's original concerns, Duncan immediately agreed to GHQ's offer to send him Colonel Manus McCloskey, an experienced regimental commander in the 2nd Division's 2nd Field Artillery Brigade, as Rees's replacement.[25]

During the first week of August, after about six weeks in the trenches, the 77th Division was relieved from its position near Baccarat by the American 37th Division.[26] GHQ subsequently ordered the 77th Division to join the American III Corps, commanded by General Bullard, then fighting its way toward the Vesle River northeast of Château-Thierry. Within ten days, the division had replaced the worn-out American 4th Division, which had suffered heavy casualties while helping drive the Germans out of the giant salient between the Marne and the Vesle Rivers. At that point, the training period for the 77th Division had essentially concluded and the division, with one brief exception in late October, would spend the remaining weeks of the war either actively engaged against the enemy or moving from one hostile sector to another.

Yet, despite all the emphasis that AEF GHQ placed on open warfare, the 77th Division had done almost no training for it. Its early instruction at Camp Upton, heavily influenced by Allied instructors, stressed basic military training and trench-warfare skills. All the training in Europe, with the British near Ypres and with the French near Baccarat, had continued this emphasis. As for a commitment to open warfare and the skills necessary to wage it, the division had little to offer. After a number of months of training, the infantrymen probably were adequate marksmen, and a few of the Regular officers might have been devoted to or at least familiar

---

[24] "In the Matter of the Relief of Brigadier General Thomas H. Rees, 152nd Field Artillery Brigade," 21 May 1919, Binder 2-y, Box 8, RG 200, NA.

[25] McCloskey, who formerly commanded the 12th Field Artillery Regiment of 75mm guns, joined the 77th Division on 5 August 1918. Alexander noted that McCloskey was a Leavenworth honor graduate and described him as a "brilliant officer and an excellent gunner." Alexander, *Memories*, 103.

[26] While the division served in the Baccarat sector under the French VI Corps from 21 June to 4 August, it suffered a total of 375 casualties. ABMC, *American Armies*, 427.

with traditional army doctrine. Other than that, open-warfare skills and ideas could only have been picked up by reading pamphlets published by GHQ. The Liberty Division never had a single division-wide maneuver, and the infantry brigades completed no large-scale exercises to give its commanders at all levels practice in controlling their men and communicating while advancing and, more important, while attacking. The infantry and artillery units had little opportunity to work together and what chances they did have were in the stable environment of front-line trenches. Just how well the division would be able to perform in an active trench-warfare environment was still an open question, but no one should have even entertained the thought that the 77th Division was capable of carrying out combat operations in an open setting. Subsequent operations along the Vesle and Aisne Rivers in August and September proved this to be the case.

The Vesle-Aisne Offensive, August–September 1918

When the 77th Division took over a wide 6-kilometer front along the Vesle River in mid-August, it entered a sector almost as stable as the one it had just left near Baccarat, but one that was much more active. Not only did the infantry have to maintain a long front line in the exposed valley just south of the river, it also was ordered to maintain a few horribly exposed positions on the German side. By the end of its first week in the line, the division had suffered approximately fourteen hundred casualties and it had not even attempted a major attack.[27] The incessant artillery fire, frequent gas attacks, occasional enemy raids, lack of adequate trenches and dugouts, exposed infantry detachments, and a policy of aggressive patrolling all contributed to the high casualty figure. Soon, the men of the 77th Division were calling the sector "the Hell-hole Valley of the Vesle"; other Doughboys referred to it simply as "Death Valley."[28]

---

[27] The fourteen hundred casualties represented a loss of about 5 percent of the division's total strength.

[28] During most of this first week, the division was supported by the 4th F.A. Brigade of the 4th Division, which stayed in support until the 152nd F.A. Brigade arrived to replace it. The German gas shelling was so severe that the division suffered hundreds of gas casualties some nights, including 460 on the night of 16 August alone. While this might be a sign that gas discipline was lax in the unit, the fact that most casualties were from mustard-gas burns and not from poor use of the gas mask hints that the casualties were

The Germans had withdrawn to the defensive positions along the Vesle in early August, and the Allied pursuit to that line exposed serious differences between French and American commanders and weaknesses within American units. Robert Bullard, having gained an appreciation of the need for heavy firepower while commanding the 1st Division, repeatedly tried to convince General Jean Degoutte, the French Sixth Army commander, that the infantry in his new American III Corps did not have sufficient artillery support to press the Germans too firmly or even to expand the bridgeheads across the Vesle. They certainly lacked the resources necessary to drive forward 10 kilometers to the Aisne River beyond it, as Degoutte wished. More in agreement with the old French *offensive à outrance* school of thought than Pétain's conservative firepower-based beliefs, Degoutte continued to press his Allied troops forward. Two days before the 77th Division entered the line, Bullard was so concerned about senseless casualties that he ordered the 28th Division, on the right of the sector, to discontinue attempts to expand its bridgehead near Fismette. While maintaining the letter of Degoutte's order that contact with the enemy had to be maintained, Bullard told his divisions that only small infantry patrols, always well supported by artillery fire, should be sent out. And, he announced that any hostile fire whatsoever from the enemy was sufficient contact. When he later learned that even those minor patrols were suffering heavy casualties, he ordered a halt to them and he urged Degoutte to allow the 77th and 28th Divisions to withdraw their most advanced infantry positions – which suffered at least four hundred casualties a day in the two divisions – to more defensible terrain.[29] After Degoutte refused, Bullard went so far as to order the withdrawal

---

more a result of the severity of the shelling and the exposed positions of the infantry than bad training or poor discipline. *History of the 77th Division*, 40; ABMC, *American Armies*, 104; G-3 Journal, III Army Corps, Folder 33.0, Box 28, III Army Corps Historical File, RG 120, NA.

[29] Bullard was in part reacting to the strongly worded reports coming from local commanders like Colonel N. K. Averill, who led the 308th Infantry. Averill reported that his positions across the river were "untenable." No adequate bridge remained to keep the men supplied, making resupply and communications efforts with the detachment "almost impossible." The two forward companies had been decimated by heavy gas attacks, and he "urgently" requested to pull them back across the Vesle so he could hold the south bank in the same manner that the enemy held the northern one. He claimed that if his unit tried to hold out any longer, a whole battalion "will have been entirely sacrificed." C.O., 308th Infantry to C.G., 77th Division, Subject: Position of advance battalion in this zone, 16 August 1918, Folder 32.8, Box 8, 77th Division Historical File, RG 120, NA.

anyway, but Degoutte discovered and countermanded the directive. Within a matter of days, most of these exposed troops were annihilated by prepared German attacks.[30]

While both brigades of the 77th held positions in the front line, the senior commanders passed along tactical lessons learned the hard way by more experienced American divisions. Brigadier General Edmund Wittenmyer, the commander of the 153rd Brigade on the left of the sector, warned his troops that too often American soldiers had "advanced with insufficient intervals in their lines" and that "the tactical execution of the operations by the platoon and company commanders has not been up to the required standard." He stressed that "machine guns must not be attacked frontally, but should be enveloped" and that whenever troops ran into strong points, they were to press forward between them and attack them from the flank or rear, covering the advance with the fire of "automatic arms" throughout. He also advised them that "considerable use" had been "made of the Stokes mortars and 37mm in the recent operations."[31] Although these instructions certainly represented important elements for waging open warfare (and warfare in the trenches, for that matter), they included no references to the power of the rifle or the importance of the bayonet.

After Bullard gave his divisions permission to discontinue the patrolling that did little but add to the growing casualty lists, the 77th planned a number of small attacks against specific enemy positions that poured fire into its most forward units. On the evening of 21 August, a company from the 308th Regiment seized a tannery that held a German machine-gun nest. The tannery was taken after an artillery preparation so heavy that one account claimed the facility was "obliterated" by the concentrated fire from an entire regiment of 155mm howitzers.[32] The attackers met little opposition.

Possibly in retaliation for this attack, early the next morning the Germans executed a much larger assault on the few American positions

---

[30] Bullard gives an admittedly embittered description of this sad series of events, calling Degoutte's plans to use his "so-called bridgeheads" entirely "hopeless." The 77th Division's positions were hit on 22 August and those of the 28th Division were wiped out five days later. See Bullard, *Personalities and Reminiscences*, 231–8. See also HQ 77th Division, Memorandum to Infantry, Brigade and Regimental Commanders, 19 August 1918, USAWW, 6: 172; and Millett, *The General*, 385–8.

[31] HQ 153rd Infantry Brigade, Field Orders No. 5, 16 August 1918, Folder 32.1, Box 15, 77th Division Historical File, RG 120, NA.

[32] "The 77th Division," p. 5, Folder 11.4, Box 2, 77th Division Historical File, RG 120, NA.

on their side of the river. The well-supported attack caused heavy losses in the exposed companies and drove the survivors across the river. Even though the division leadership had pressed hard to evacuate these exposed positions, it apparently felt its units should not stand for being summarily forced out of them, and counterattacks were initiated that afternoon to retake some of the lost ground. The next morning, the 77th made additional counterattacks, retaking more of the remaining lost ground. Further local attacks were made on subsequent days. No battle plans remain (if they were ever developed) to show what tactics the division used in these counterattacks, but numerous division and corps reports do mention that the attacks had artillery support, some stressing "heavy artillery preparation" and others mentioning the use of an accompanying "barrage."[33] The only hints regarding the success of these attacks are that most of the ground was retaken – but only after a number of attacks over many days, suggesting that while the division may have had some understanding of the importance of using firepower, even in hasty counterattacks, it is unclear how effective it was in coordinating its efforts.

While the troops were engaged in this series of minor battles, the division experienced an important shift in its leadership. Duncan was relieved from command for medical reasons and Evan Johnson was again placed in temporary command.[34] Although Johnson led the division only until Robert Alexander assumed command about ten days later, he ordered it to carry out two significant local attacks on the morning of 27 August. The first attack, against the village of Bazoches on the division's left, was made

---

[33] The III Corps journal of operations states that the guns throughout the corps were "extremely active" during these days, supposedly firing twenty-two thousand 75mm shells and more than three thousand rounds from the 155s. Operations Report, 2000 hours 21 August to 2000 hours 22 August, 77th Division, 23 August 1918; and Operations Report, 22 August to 23 August, 77th Division, 24 August 1918, *USAWW*, 6: 173–4; G-3 Journal, III Army Corps, Folder 33.0, Box 28, III Army Corps Historical File, RG 120, NA.

[34] Johnson assumed temporary command between 16 and 19 August; reports differ as to the exact date. The nature of Duncan's medical problems remains unclear. Some reports suggest that he was suspected of having syphilis. After originally being ordered to return to the United States, Duncan secured a second medical examination on 18 September 1918. This medical board determined that there was "sufficient changes in the manifestations" of his condition to warrant that he be given "two weeks leave for rest and recuperation," ordered to undergo another reexamination in six months, and returned to field duty in France. He assumed command of the 82nd Division on 4 October and led that division throughout its heavy fighting in the Meuse-Argonne campaign and to the end of the war. "In the Matter of the Relief of Major General George B. Duncan, 77th Division," 18 May 1919. in Binder 1-e, Box 8, RG 200, NA.

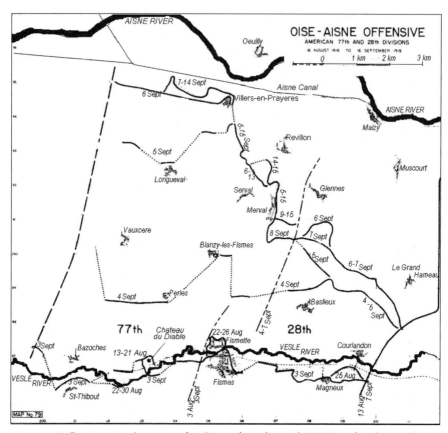

MAP 18: Between 12 August and 3 September, the 77th Division fought a series of small but violent engagements along the Vesle River. From 4 to 16 September, the division advanced to and fought along a German defensive position just south of the Aisne River.

by elements of the 306th Infantry. The second, against the aptly named Château du Diable, was made by units from the 307th Infantry, holding the right sector (see Map 18). Neither attack was ultimately successful, but each failed for different reasons and showed distinct characteristics of the division and its limited capabilities.

The two attacks occurred almost simultaneously, but the assault of Bazoches was the primary effort. A draft plan for an attack on the town, dated 18 August and prepared under Duncan's supervision, showed an impressive awareness of the need to mass firepower to support the attack by combining most of the divisional artillery, trench mortars, thermite projectors, and machine guns.[35] The plan also stressed the importance of repelling the German counterattacks certain to follow the attack and emphasized that a thorough mopping up of the town was crucial to success. Although the final draft of this plan has not been found, the supporting artillery plan, issued by General McCloskey, suggests that the final plan differed little from the draft.

For its part, McCloskey's fire-support plan was a thorough and detailed effort to pound the village before the attack, neutralize the enemy during the assault, and protect the infantry throughout the operation. Guns from all three artillery regiments supported the attack, and they fired a combination of smoke, high-explosive, and shrapnel rounds. After a slow pounding of the town by the 155s throughout the previous day and night, the attack was to follow an intense 2-minute preparation. One regiment of 75s then fired a rolling barrage to escort the attackers into and through the village, while the other guns fired concentrations in and around it. Covered by this fire, the assault troops, probably numbering about three hundred infantrymen and machine-gunners, were to enter the town from the left flank, set up machine guns on its far corners, and systematically mop up the town from north to south. The total advance would be less than 1 kilometer.[36]

Although the plans were thorough, the execution was not, and the attack failed primarily due to an inability to carry out the two specific missions stressed in Duncan's draft order – mopping up and resisting counterattacks. On the morning of 27 August, the infantry advanced behind the barrage and took Bazoches without appreciable difficulty or significant losses. However, by the admission of the assaulting officers, the green Doughboys failed to thoroughly mop up the town – often simply throwing grenades into the buildings and neglecting to kill or capture the enemy hiding in cellars and dugouts. They also failed to root out small groups hiding just outside of the town or to prepare adequately to resist counterattacks. Shortly after taking the town, the enemy counterattacked – supported by artillery and trench mortar fire – and wiped out the machine guns set up on the town's corners. At the same time, enemy troops emerged from

---

[35] Thermite was an explosive agent made of aluminum powder and a metal oxide. It was fired into enemy positions by mortar-like projectors, and its explosion threw a wide circle of glowing white-hot liquid. In the AEF, it was often fired by chemical-warfare troops, especially those of the 1st Gas Regiment.

[36] HQ 152nd Field Artillery Brigade, Memorandum No. 117 and Operations No. 25, 1400 hours, 26 August 1918, Folder 33.6, Box 17, 77th Division Historical File, RG 120, NA.

their dugouts, helping to destroy or drive out the American contingent. The attacking companies suffered 25 killed or wounded and another 133 missing.[37]

Although the attack ended in failure and heavy losses, all accounts show that this was the result of inexperienced execution, primarily in the mopping up and consolidation phases. The actual assault of the town was generally successful, thanks in large part to the strength of the artillery support. One lieutenant reported that "the artillery fire and barrage appeared to have successfully prepared the way" for a successful operation. Colonel George Vidmer, the commander of the 306th Infantry, admitted as much when he reported that "Owing to the ease with which our troops penetrated into the village with practically no casualties, a proper mopping up of the town should have ensured the success of the operation."[38] This appears to have been the most significant failure.

However, some reports indicate that the supporting artillery fire was not all it should have been. Two officers claimed that although the rolling barrage and other fire in the town was fine, some guns may have placed their standing barrages farther from the town than called for in the plan. This left too many enemy machine guns untouched and gave less protection to the men holding the town. The response to the German counterattack also exposed a lack of infantry–artillery coordination.

The commander of the attacking battalion also identified two important failings. Whereas the 1st Division attack on Cantigny was made by three reinforced battalions and that of the 2nd Division at Vaux by two battalions, also well supported by machine guns and engineers, the 77th tried to seize, mop up, and hold Bazoches with an attacking force of about one third of a battalion. The battalion commander reported that he would need "one whole battalion to clean up Bazoches and get rid of machine guns" and at least one additional company "to follow up" and "clean up the place properly." He then added, "There are so many machine gun nests on hill opposite us that it is an artillery job to clean up that place."[39] It was an important lesson that each American division

[37] The attacking units thus suffered about 50 percent casualties. The attacking regiment submitted three different reports on the battle; see HQ 307th Infantry Regiment, "Report of Operations Against Bazoches, August 27, 1918," "Attack by Our Troops Upon Bazoches," and "Report of Attack on Bazoches," all attached, Folder 33.6, Box 23, 77th Division Historical File, RG 120, NA.

[38] Ibid.

[39] Report of C.O., 2nd Battalion, 306th Infantry, 1130 hours, 27 August 1918, Folder 33.6, Box 17, 77th Division Historical File, RG 120, NA.

seemed to learn only by personal experience; although good infantrymen could outflank and knock out isolated enemy machine guns, groups of well-sighted enemy guns, in sufficient quantities, required a heavy hand from the supporting firepower available. Although the division proved capable of silencing these guns during the assault, it failed to neutralize them during the counterattack.

The Bazoches attack seems to have miscarried despite a good plan and a promising start, but the attack against the Château du Diable was flawed from the outset. Although the Bazoches assault was at least ten days in the making, Johnson ordered the 307th Infantry to draw up an attack plan to advance about 1 kilometer only one day before the attack. Johnson's order also warned that "In making your plans you will not be able to count on artillery support, as our brigade artillery has been temporarily turned over to the 153rd Brigade" [for the attack on Bazoches].[40] At a conference that afternoon, the unfortunate battalion commander designated to plan and make the attack – having just taken over a sector of the front line the night before – asserted "he did not feel it was possible" to make an adequate reconnaissance and draw up detailed plans for an attack the next morning and asked to push the attack back at least a day. He also commented negatively on the lack of artillery support, which he confirmed "would not be available."[41] Nevertheless, Johnson ordered the attack to go as scheduled, only telling the attackers that they could request artillery if they needed it and that it would respond if it could.

At 0415 hours, three companies of infantry and supporting machine-gun teams moved out and immediately ran into enemy fire. They quickly stopped their advance and called for artillery fire from the 305th Field Artillery Regiment, then busy firing at targets for the Bazoches attack, which began at the same time. The 305th apparently diverted one battery to meet the urgent need of the men attacking the Château du Diable. After 15 minutes of "normal barrage" by this battery, four more batteries joined in for another 15 minutes of general barrage fire.[42] Although the attacking troops appear to have made a valiant effort to advance when this ad hoc artillery fire ended, they again ran into heavy German

---

[40] HQ, 154th Brigade, Memorandum to C.O., 307th Infantry, 26 August 1918, Folder 33.6, Box 23, 77th Division Historical File, RG 120, NA.

[41] HQ 307th Infantry Regiment, "Report of Operations Against Bazoches, August 27, 1918," "Attack by Our Troops Upon Bazoches," and "Report of Attack on Bazoches," all attached, Folder 33.6, Box 23, 77th Division Historical File, RG 120, NA.

[42] C.G., 77th Division, to C.G., III Army Corps, Subject: Report of Action, 30 August 1918, Folder 33.6, Box 9, 77th Division Historical File, RG 120, NA.

Robert Alexander, commander of the 77th Division along the Vesle and Meuse-
Argonne.

artillery and machine-gun fire. The American attack broke down, units
were intermingled and thrown off course, and eventually all surviving
attackers worked their way back to their starting positions. As many as
149 were killed, wounded, or missing.[43]

The Bazoches attack may have shown inadequacies in the skills of the
division's inexperienced troops, but that attack at least demonstrated an
apparent awareness of the need to mass artillery fire and to coordinate
that fire with careful infantry maneuvers. The attack on the Château du
Diable called even this into question. Johnson's effort to belatedly add an
additional attack while the division was busy trying to carry out a highly
detailed and meticulously planned assault probably threw off both operations. The secondary attack, ordered without any organized preliminary
fire or rolling barrage and made against strong defensive positions, seems
to have had almost no chance of success. The diversion of twenty guns
from the Bazoches fire plan (i.e., almost one third of the guns involved)
while that attack was still underway probably allowed numerous German
machine-gunners surrounding that town to remain in position and pour
their fire into the American troops during the counterattack.

On the day that these two attacks failed – in fact, while they were failing – Alexander arrived at the division headquarters to assume command.
After standing aside while Johnson presided over the final moments of his

---

[43] C.O., 307th Infantry, to C.G., 77th Division, Subject: Report of Attack of 27th August
1918, 31 August 1918, Folder 33.6, Box 17, 77th Division Historical File, RG 120, NA.

broken attacks, he stepped in, sent Johnson back to his brigade, and began his attempts to make the 77th Division his own. His doctrinal tradition-alism and bellicosity came through in his first order, sent out the very afternoon he joined the division. Although the previous division leader-ship had spent weeks trying to convince the corps and army commanders that exposed infantry positions should be given up to preserve manpower, Alexander announced that it was "indispensable that such footings as we have north of the Vesle must be maintained at all hazards" because the bridgeheads might be needed "within 24 hours."[44] Such news must have been a shock to many in the division. Also, although Bullard condemned the overly aggressive manner in which Degoutte used his infantry, Alexan-der admired Degoutte, who was, in his estimation, one of the few French commanders who "maintained the tactical doctrine which all experience has shown to be the true one."[45]

Whatever Alexander's failings, they were not due to a lack of experience either in prewar operations or while in Europe before the summer of 1918. The son of a circuit court judge in Baltimore, Alexander read law for two years at a Maryland firm before passing the bar himself. Then, in 1886, at the age of twenty-two, he enlisted in the Army for unknown reasons. After three years in the ranks, he earned a commission in the Infantry and subsequently served in Puerto Rico during the Spanish–American War, on the islands of Leyte and Samar during the Philippine War, and in Mexico during the Punitive Expedition. Although not a West Pointer (one of the few to command an AEF division), he was a graduate of two Leaven-worth courses – the School of the Line and the Army Staff College.[46] In November 1917, Alexander joined the AEF and served as the Inspector General of the Lines of Communication. Like other senior officers, he spent some time touring the front as the guest of British divisions but, somewhat like Pershing, he appears to have been more of a critic than a student. He saw much that he disliked, particularly the BEF's growing affinity for massive artillery support and heavy use of the new "auxiliary" weapons – automatic rifles, machine guns, mortars, grenades, and 37mm guns. After commanding a replacement division well behind the lines and

---

[44] HQ 77th Division to Commanding Generals, 153rd and 154th Brigades, 1630 hours, 27 August 1918, *USAWW*, 6: 177.

[45] Alexander, *Memories*, 55. Compare Alexander's admiration of Degoutte with the more critical perspective offered by Bullard in *Personalities and Reminiscences*, 231–8.

[46] Alexander apparently did not graduate from college. All the other commanders of the 1st, 2nd, 26th, and 77th Divisions were West Pointers, except John Lejeune, who graduated from the Naval Academy in 1888.

briefly leading an infantry brigade in the 32nd Division, Alexander moved to the 77th Division and commanded it for the remainder of the war.[47]

In two important ways, Alexander shaped the way the Liberty Division fought. Despite an apparent awareness of the very limited experience and skill of his officers and men, and in the face of hard fighting and heavy casualties, Alexander maintained his faith in official AEF combat doctrine. He spoke and wrote regularly of the importance of training and fighting according to open-warfare principles, decried what he called the "trench warfare cult," stressed the significance of the rifle and bayonet, and favored mobility and maneuver over massed firepower.[48] More important, to the extent that he influenced the division's combat operations, he generally attempted to have it fight according to his and GHQ's traditional doctrinal views, with only minor adaptations.

Beyond Alexander's doctrinal commitments, another crucial factor that influenced the way the division fought and the way its men attempted to adapt to the realities of battle was the division commander's style of command. Alexander demonstrated a remarkable willingness to push responsibility for battle planning, tactical schemes, and especially the control and employment of firepower down the chain of command – not just to his division staff but also to his brigade and regimental commanders. Although the advantages of such a decentralized style of command may be readily apparent to modern readers, it brought significant challenges to divisions in the Great War. Because only Alexander commanded both infantry and artillery units, his decentralized approach forced the subordinate infantry and artillery brigade and regimental commanders to rely on cooperation and teamwork rather than command authority. In a highly trained division, with reliable communication capability and substantial experience working together as a unit, this kind of flexibility might have been an asset. But, for the 77th Division from August to November 1918, it led to a general dispersal of the division's firepower, complicated all efforts to mass firepower for complex fire-support missions, and contributed to a reliance on ad hoc firepower employment. During the division's three-week battle to drive through the Argonne forest, it faced many other unique challenges that further complicated efforts to mass firepower. Nevertheless, to the extent that they could, the men and junior officers in the division seem to have chosen to fight their own way, advancing cautiously, minimizing casualties, and maximizing firepower.

[47] Alexander, *Memories*, 32–3; and *History of the 77th Division*, 161–2.
[48] Alexander, *Memories*, 2–3.

As the new 77th Division commander, Alexander submitted reports on the failed attacks of 27 August to III Corps. In these reports, especially regarding the attack on the Château du Diable, he showed a tendency that he repeated throughout the war to blame all failure not on a lack of firepower – as Summerall, Lejeune, or Edwards might have done – or even on poor infantry–artillery coordination, but simply on a flawed scheme of infantry maneuver. Completely neglecting the inadequate fire support in the secondary attack, Alexander claimed the failure occurred because the troops "apparently made a direct attack upon a very strongly forti-fied machine gun nest, advancing in regular formation with no apparent attempts for outflanking the position." He claimed that a smaller force might have "suffered less casualties" and would have "stood a better chance of filtering into the position and overcome the defense."[49] One sees in these words shades of Harbord's suggested tactics that failed so mis-erably at Belleau Wood in June (i.e., tactics that Alexander later claimed to have further proved the continued relevance of the rifle).[50] Alexan-der completely neglected what the battalion and regimental commanders had seen as early as their preattack conference – that the attack needed more and better planned fire support to succeed. Yet, Alexander's focus on the infantry as the key was consistent with his doctrinal convictions, as expressed so often in his memoirs with statements such as "The infantry soldier, using intelligently the fire power of his rifle, is still, as always since the introduction of firearms, the dominant factor of victory. . . . In war, the machine, while it may assist the man, can never replace him."[51]

After submitting the reports, Alexander ordered that each unit begin an intensive ten-day period of training, to begin on 31 August. The infantry regiments were to focus their instruction on small-unit drills and exer-cises, beginning with the smallest combat groups – called "gangs" in the

[49] Alexander's opinion was similar to that of Johnson, who apparently thought the time allowed to prepare the attack was sufficient, that the attack plan was "well drawn," and that such an attack could be adequately executed with the ad hoc support of just a few guns made partially available to the attacking battalion commander "in case he should call for its action." See Johnson's endorsement of the regimental commander's report in C.O., 307th Infantry, to C.G., 77th Division, Subject: Report of Attack of 27th August 1918, 31 August 1918, Folder 33.6, Box 17, 77th Division Historical File, RG 120, NA; and C.G., 77th Division, to C.G., III Army Corps, Subject: Report of Action, 30 August 1918, Folder 33.6, Box 9, 77th Division Historical File, RG 120, NA.

[50] Alexander claimed that during the 2nd Division's operations at Belleau Wood, "the infantry rifle was again to demonstrate the fact that, when properly employed, it is still as powerful a factor in battle as it has ever been." Alexander, *Memories*, 61–2.

[51] Alexander, *Memories*, 44–5.

77th – and progressing through platoons, companies, and battalions. The latter two organizations were to carry out full terrain exercises as well. This training probably was an effort to improve the division's open-warfare skills, and it did emphasize the importance of coordinating the use of machine guns, mortars, and 37mm guns with rifles – which is somewhat surprising considering Alexander's disdain for those "auxiliaries."[52] But, the training program had two problems: First, it never scheduled any maneuvers for units larger than a battalion; and, second, the training never was completed.[53] Just a couple of days into the schedule, the division had to follow up a German withdrawal, turning its attention from training back to fighting.

In early September, as General Mangin's French Tenth Army to the west slowly drove back the German lines, the III Corps made preparations to follow up an expected enemy withdrawal from the Vesle. By the afternoon of 3 September, signs of a withdrawal were so evident that Alexander ordered "strong patrols" to head out immediately to take the high ground north of the river. No artillery support was directed. If the patrols succeeded, full battalions were to follow. Alexander also told his brigadiers to send their "best and most aggressive officers" on the patrols, and if they followed with a battalion, to pick a commander "who knows his business."[54] Such comments suggest that Alexander was not uniformly confident in the training and capabilities of his battalion commanders. It is interesting that while Alexander focused his attention on aggressive, unsupported infantry patrols, subordinate commanders in the 307th Infantry and 305th Field Artillery apparently arranged for a rolling barrage to cover the advance up the ridges north of the river.[55] As would be the case in many 77th Division attacks, it was up to the lower-ranking officers to ensure adequate fire support for their infantry advances.

---

[52] While the coordination of these more firepower-intensive weapons in infantry operations was becoming accepted practice even in the AEF by this point in the war, Alexander had repeatedly criticized the tendency to spend too much time training what he called "the auxiliaries" or "specialists" – men who fought with grenades, mortars, 37mm guns, and machine guns. He contended that "the importance claimed for these auxiliaries had grown to absurd proportions.... [T]he auxiliaries alone never yet won a war, nor will they ever, alone." Alexander, *Memories*, 16.

[53] Senior Instructor, Divisional School for the Combined Use of Infantry Arms, to C.G., 77th Division, 1 September 1918, Folder 50.9, Box 12, 77th Division Historical File, RG 120, NA.

[54] HQ 77th Division, Memorandum to Chief of Staff, 1755 hours, 3 September 1918, Folder 32.0, Box 4, 77th Division Historical File, RG 120, NA.

[55] HQ, 305th F.A. Regiment, Memorandum for the C.G., 152nd F.A. Brigade, 4 February 1919, Folder 11.2, Box 30, 77th Division Historical File, RG 120, NA.

Having found the Germans withdrawing to the Aisne, the patrols took their objectives. Alexander then ordered the entire division to cross the Vesle and, with the optimism that so often seemed to go hand in hand with traditional doctrine in the AEF, he directed that patrols "be pushed aggressively across the Aisne and establish themselves" on the heights north of that river.[56] Apparently, self-reliant infantrymen were to attempt this without any prearranged artillery fire. Over the next two days, Alexander repeatedly urged his infantry to get to and across the Aisne, even telling them to swim across if necessary![57] This was all completely unrealistic and seems to have been a result of Alexander wanting to see the inauguration of open warfare so badly that he dismissed all thoughts to the contrary. In fact, the Germans were merely shifting from one prepared defensive position to another. The 77th Division did not cross the Aisne during its remaining ten days in the sector, and no Allied division crossed the river in that sector until 11 October.[58]

The advance from the Vesle also showed two other important characteristics of the 77th. First, the infantrymen may have pursued the Germans aggressively but they did not do so efficiently. This was the division's first major effort to advance on fairly open terrain as an entire division, and the German rear guards and artillery made it an inhospitable exercise in on-the-job training. The advance started all right but became disorganized as it was pressed forward. Commanders had trouble controlling and coordinating the advances of their units and even more difficulty maintaining liaison laterally and up the chain of command. Troops occasionally strayed into neighboring sectors. Officers failed to accurately determine the coordinates of their front lines. These errors made any effort to cover the advance with artillery very difficult, though it apparently caused Bullard more distress than Alexander. Yet, the infantrymen did move reasonably fast, especially at the start of each day (i.e., about 4 kilometers each morning), moving ahead of both the French division on their left

---

[56] HQ 77th Division, Field Orders No. 26, 4 September 1918, *USAWW*, 6: 181–2.

[57] Alexander's overaggressiveness and sense of urgency were also encouraged by his belief in erroneous reports about other divisions, which fed his fear of not doing well as a new commander. In one order, he announced that the divisions on both flanks were already on the Aisne (they were not), and he exclaimed that "this division cannot afford to be left behind." C.G., 77th Division, Memorandum to Chief of Staff, 2245 hours, 4 September 1918, Folder 32.0, Box 4, 77th Division Historical File, RG 120, NA; HQ 77th Division, Memorandum to Commanding Generals, 153rd and 154th Infantry Brigades, 5 September 1918, *USAWW*, 6: 183.

[58] See the map of the entire Allied Aisne-Marne offensive included in ABMC, *American Armies*.

and the 28th Division on their right. Some groups went so fast that they moved right past German detachments, who then fired into their flanks and rear. It is not surprising that the infantry paid for this combination of aggressiveness and inexperience by suffering unnecessary casualties.[59]

A second feature of the advance was Alexander's tendency to push responsibility, especially for developing fire support for the attacks, down to his subordinates. On 5 September, he told his brigadiers that during the advance there would be no artillery fire on any targets south of the Aisne, "unless specially called for" by them.[60] Later that day, the commander of the U.S. 28th Division asked Alexander for assistance in taking a large hill called La Petite Montagne near the divisional boundary. Instead of directly taking a role in developing a joint plan, he simply told General Johnson, commanding the brigade on the right, that the 28th Division needed assistance in the attack, that he was to "cooperate to the fullest," and that he should "push forward vigorously" in whatever effort he determined to make.[61] Conspicuously absent was the offer of any artillery assistance, especially from the 155mm regiment, which Alexander kept under his personal control. In this way, Alexander demonstrated a failure to understand the necessity of fully utilizing all the heavy firepower under his control. As before, if the infantry was to have any fire support, it was up to the brigade and regimental commanders to provide it. During his advance, Johnson apparently preceded each attack of his brigade with a 30-minute artillery preparation and Wittenmyer used his guns to reduce strong points on 6 September.[62]

Nevertheless, by 7 September, the 153rd Brigade on the left had advanced nearly 10 kilometers and was on the Aisne, while the 154th had moved between 6 and 8 kilometers and had bent back its right flank to link up with its new neighboring division, the French 62nd, which replaced the 28th Division that day. On the morning of the 8th, Bullard directed the division to push its right brigade up to the Aisne. Alexander subsequently ordered Johnson to attack toward La Petite Montagne

---

[59] The number of casualties suffered during the advance from 4 to 6 September is unknown. For the ten-day period starting on 4 September, the division suffered more than seventeen hundred casualties. *History of the 77th Division*, 53; Bullard, *Personalities and Reminiscences*, 249–54; and Millett, *The General*, 389.

[60] HQ 77th Division, Memorandum to Commanding Generals, 153rd and 154th Infantry Brigades, 5 September 1918, *USAWW*, 6: 183.

[61] HQ 77th Division, Message for C.G., 154th Brigade, 1040 hours, 5 September 1918, *USAWW*, 6: 184.

[62] ABMC, *77th Division Summary of Operations in the World War* (Washington, D.C.: GPO, 1944), 15.

that evening in conjunction with the French 62nd, which was to advance and reduce a German strong point in the town of Glennes, also near the division boundary. This time, Alexander's order included provisions for a rolling barrage, though his plan for the brigade's 4-kilometer advance on a wide 4-kilometer front was impractical, including no halts for rest and reorganization nor any changes in the rate of advance. The rate of advance of 100 meters every 3 minutes was rather fast and was especially so considering both the nature of the attack (i.e., expected to move through the town of Revillon and up a large hill) and the condition of the division, which was tired after being in line almost a month and completely inexperienced in such attacks.[63] No preliminary fire preceded the attack, and there was no mention of any support from either the division machine guns or additional French guns. In fact, considering the width of the division front at this time – nearly 8 kilometers – it is likely that some of the division's 75mm guns were not within range to support the attack. Neither the French nor the American attack made any significant progress at all. Although no senior commander in or above the divisions apparently recognized it, both units had run into a highly organized defensive line well south of the Aisne that would not fall until 1 October.

Blaming the attack's lack of success on the failure of the French to take Glennes, from where Germans poured fire into the American flank, Alexander immediately ordered the 154th Brigade to prepare to attack again the next morning.[64] However, no attack occurred until a week later, on 14 September, when the 77th Division – by then under the command of the French XVI Corps of the French Fifth Army – played a supporting role in what was to be a major effort by the French V Corps to its right.

At first glance, Alexander's orders for the supporting attack seem to show significant development over previous attack plans. The attack was broken into three distinct phases and was thoroughly set piece in nature. After a 15-minute artillery preparation by all guns, most of the 75s shifted

---

[63] HQ 77th Division, Field Orders No. 27, 8 September 1918, Folder 32.0, Box 4, 77th Division Historical File, RG 120, NA.

[64] After the attack failed, Alexander ordered Wittenmyer to move over and temporarily replace Johnson as commander of the 154th Brigade because the latter was evacuated as a gas casualty and did not return to duty until 19 September. It is interesting that Alexander's memoir claims that Johnson had to be evacuated on 6 September, two days before this attack. Records show that Wittenmyer was not sent to lead the 154th until after the failed attack of the 8th, which suggests that the brigade was suffering some sort of crisis in command while Alexander was ordering it forward. Alexander, Memorandum for C.O., 154th Brigade, through Chief of Staff, 8 September, *USAWW*, 6: 187; Alexander, *Memories*, 129.

to a standing barrage to allow the infantry to close up on it, while twelve other guns concentrated on enemy strong points. Then, the barrage rolled forward 100 meters every 5 minutes (considerably slower than in Alexander's earlier attempt). All this was simply to allow one battalion of the 154th Brigade to slightly advance its right flank a few hundred meters, where it was to stop, reorganize, dig in, and await the advance of the French on the right. During the second phase, as American infantry waited for the French to come forward, the artillery was to maintain a standing barrage and hit targets on the German flank. When the French division on the immediate right came abreast, the third phase was to begin, and the infantry was to attack through Revillon and up La Petite Montagne. This time, 77th Division machine guns were also to fire barrages both before and during the attack.[65]

However, an examination of the translated copy of the orders he was given by General Deville, the new corps commander, shows that every significant feature of Alexander's plan was essentially copied from the translated version of corps orders.[66] The division order thus reveals little of Alexander's development as a tactician; what it does offer only confirms previously described characteristics, such as his tendency to allow subordinates to run the battle. After stating that the ultimate objectives for the advance were "dependent upon the success of the French on our right," Alexander told Wittenmyer that because "the Division Commander cannot be in a position where he can himself direct the movement," Wittenmyer had to be prepared to order his brigade forward for the third phase on his own if the French attacks progressed more quickly than expected. Alexander also demonstrated his traditional attitude by reminding the attackers that "the utmost aggressiveness be displayed and that any sign of weakening on the part of the opposition be immediately and fully exploited." This kind of unhelpful advice was out of place in a detailed set-piece attack.[67]

Although the battle began on time at 0515 hours on 14 September and the troops worked their way forward to the first phase objective by 0645, the plan began to unravel in mid-morning when the French

---

[65] HQ 77th Division, Field Orders No. 30, 2300 hours, 11 September 1918, *USAWW*, 6: 191.

[66] Compare Alexander's order with HQ XVI Army Corps, Special Order Number 1050, 11 September 1918, and Special Order 1051, 13 September 1918, Folder 32.7, Box 8, 77th Division Historical File, RG 120, NA.

[67] HQ 77th Division, Field Orders No. 30, 2300 hours, 11 September 1918, *USAWW*, 6: 191.

were slow in advancing toward Glennes. Records show that despite the slow progress of the French 62nd, at 0900 hours, the XVI Corps directed the 77th Division to initiate the third phase anyway and take La Petite Montagne.[68] In his memoirs, Alexander claimed credit for convincing his corps commander to allow him to press this attack because he thought "an advance promised no greater loss than was already falling upon us, and there was reasonable prospect that such an advance and its possible consequences would bring about a withdrawal of the enemy." If this is true, Alexander displayed an audacity that bordered on recklessness. He also snidely added that he hoped the French would at least follow even if they would not lead.[69]

Alexander's field messages for this attack are curious because they seem to give instructions that must have changed the prearranged nature of the third phase. He directed that a 10-minute period of "intensive fire" be put on a certain objective line, starting at 0935. The infantry was to begin the advance at that same time, apparently working its way forward by its own means. The artillery was then to shift its fire onto the crest of La Petite Montagne at 0945 and keep it there until ordered to stop.[70] Why he did not order a rolling barrage, having used one for the first phase of the operation, is unclear. This kind of artillery fire, jumping from one defensive line to the next while skipping the area between, had been discarded in favor of the rolling barrage by 1916 in most armies and seems out of place here.

In both his operations reports and memoirs, Alexander claimed his attack went well and that his troops advanced all the way to the objective before having to withdraw because French failures left them too exposed.[71] Other sources suggest that the attacks of the third phase were

[68] HQ 77th Division, Memorandum for Chief of Staff, 14 September 1918, Box 4, Folder 32.0, 77th Division Historical File, RG 120, NA; and HQ 77th Division, Memorandum, 4 September, *USAWW*, 6: 196.

[69] Several details of Alexander's account do not square with other official accounts or even with much of the message traffic during the battle, especially regarding the timing of certain events and the success of the division's attacks. Other accounts only corroborate that the corps eventually ordered the advance. Nevertheless, Alexander's claim to have requested permission to proceed with the third phase is significant. Alexander, *Memories*, 140–1.

[70] HQ 77th Division, Memorandum for Chief of Staff, 14 September 1918, Box 4, Folder 32.0, 77th Division Historical File, RG 120, NA; and HQ 77th Division, Memorandum, 14 September, *USAWW*, 6: 196.

[71] For a favorable interpretation of the attacks, see C.G., 77th Division, to C.G., XVI Army Corps, Subject: Operation of 14th September, 1918, 14 September 1918, Folder 33.6, Box 9, 77th Division Historical File, RG 120, NA; and Alexander, *Memories*, 142.

slow in starting, met stubborn resistance, and made only little progress.[72]
Either way, the end results were the same: the 77th suffered between
three hundred and five hundred casualties (out of perhaps two thousand
engaged) and moved the lines just a few hundred meters. The next day,
the division yielded the front trenches to an Italian division and moved to
the rear to rest and refit. Before leaving the sector, Alexander submitted an
operations report for the final attack and, as before, placed all the blame
for its ultimate failure on the poor performance of the French to the right.
Neither that report nor any other source suggests that he made a sincere
evaluation of his division's performance and how it might be improved in
future attacks.

After the 77th Division's nearly five-week stay in a very active sector,
during which it made a number of attacks and advances, the unit needed
all the rest it could get. Since entering the line in the second week of
August, it had suffered 4,623 battle casualties. After an unbroken thirty-
eight day stretch of combat in a sector with lots of enemy fire, continuous
gas shelling, and inadequate trenches and dugouts, all the officers and
men were thoroughly exhausted. When losses from sickness and straggling were added to the battle losses, the division was short more than
six thousand troops.[73] Despite this condition, the rest period was brief.
Within ten days, the division had moved to another sector, reentered the
front lines, and begun its greatest battle of the war: the struggle for the
Argonne forest.

Although Alexander's tactical beliefs developed little during his first
weeks as a division commander, some evidence indicates that his subordinates, especially the junior officers and men, did learn important lessons
in the Vesle-Aisne sector. The brigade commanders had to learn to control
not only their men but also the artillery that Alexander so often delegated

---

[72] For a more critical description of these attacks, see ABMC, *77th Division Summary*, 19–
21. Even Alexander's initial operations report, submitted immediately after the battle, as
well as his messages during the battle show evidence that the attacks did not start on time,
that they could not have received much aid from the initial 10-minute artillery barrage,
that the brigade commander was ordered to call "for such artillery support as he wants
on the points he desires it" (which means that no rolling barrage was underway), and that
the brigade commander was running the battle. Unfortunately, none of the regimental
or brigade reports have been found. See also Memorandum for Chief of Staff, HQ 77th
Division, 1015 hours, 14 September 1918, Folder 32.0, Box 4, 77th Division Historical
File, RG 120, NA; and Memorandum to C.G., 154th Infantry Brigade, 77th Division,
1030 hours, 14 September 1918, USAWW, 6: 197.

[73] The division suffered greater than 20 percent losses during this period. As usual, infantry
units suffered the highest casualty rates, many losing more than 30 percent of their
authorized strength. ABMC, *77th Division Summary*, 21.

directly to them. The attack on Bazoches showed a certain degree of appreciation for the use of firepower. When Alexander put the guns at their disposal in the advance to the Aisne, both brigadiers used the light guns to cover their advances. At the company and platoon level, the men learned how to stay alive, both in stabilized situations and in open attacks. After the division suffered an average of 177 casualties a day during the first week, the next two weeks saw daily losses drop to just 86. During the last two weeks, with the advance to the Aisne, rates jumped again to 134 a day as the men struggled to fight in more fluid conditions.[74] A more subtle change also may have shown itself in the final attacks of the 154th Brigade, when its battalions failed to take and hold its objectives but did not suffer the huge losses so common in unsuccessful advances.[75] Although some of this can be explained by tactical improvement in small units, it also hints that the junior officers and men may have been more cautious in their advances. In light of what happened in the Argonne, this conclusion must be considered.

[74] The division suffered 1,413 casualties from 10 to 17 August, 1,462 from 18 August to 3 September, and 1,736 from 4 to 16 September. ABMC, *77th Division Summary*, 21.
[75] Some reports of casualties for the 14 September attack put the figure as low as 319. C.G., 77th Division, to C.G., XVI Army Corps, Subject: Operation of 14th September, 1918, 14 September 1918, Folder 33.6, Box 9, 77th Division Historical File, RG 120, NA.

9

The 77th "Liberty" Division

Dogma, Delegation, and Discretion

Although Alexander ordered his division to begin a new training program on 19 September to improve small-unit tactics, events prevented any significant training. Within days of leaving the front lines, AEF GHQ ordered the 77th to join the First Army to take part in its giant Offensive scheduled to begin on 26 September. On 21 September, the division arrived in its position in the Argonne forest on the far left of the army front, becoming part of Hunter Liggett's I Corps. Two days later, as the men rested and prepared for another attack, the senior officers met to discuss the plan of attack and the division's role in it.[1]

The Argonne, 26 September–16 October 1918

As previously discussed (see Chapter 3), the First Army plan for the 26 September attack in the Meuse-Argonne was extraordinarily optimistic. The plan called for the three divisions in the center V Corps (i.e., the 91st, 37th, and 79th) to gain the "Corps Objective" by driving a 12-kilometer-deep salient into the German lines within the first few hours (see Map 19). By the end of the second day, the V Corps was to reach the "American Army Objective," a line some 22 kilometers from the starting position. The goals for the I Corps and III Corps were slightly more reasonable, especially on the far flanks of the attack. The original role given the 77th Division, although certain to be physically grueling due to the terrain, required relatively more modest advances. Although

---

[1] HQ 77th Division, Memorandum for G-3, 19 September, Folder 50.9, Box 12, 77th Division Historical File, RG 120, NA; Alexander, *Memories*, 169.

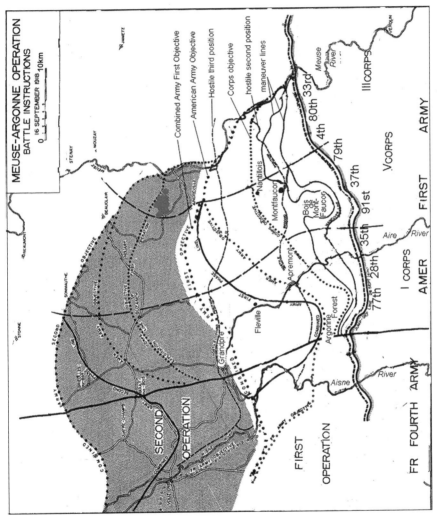

MAP 19: Plan for initial attack in the Meuse-Argonne on 26 September.

the 77th had to spread itself out across nearly 7 kilometers of front in the thick of the Argonne, the unit only had to drive forward 2 to 3 kilometers on the first morning to hit the "Corps Objective" and then another 3 to 5 kilometers more to hit the "American Army Objective" by nightfall.[2]

Many discussions of the Meuse-Argonne Offensive portray it as an unimaginative frontal attack, but the initial plan envisioned a number of important maneuvers to flank certain enemy positions and gain the objectives. In the center, the difficult seizure of Montfaucon was to be assisted by flanking attacks from divisions on both sides. Likewise, the 77th Division's mission in the Argonne was to be assisted by the deep advances of the 28th Division on the right and the French Fourth Army on the left. Those attacks were to drive up on both sides of the Argonne, outflank the defenders in the forest, and either capture them or force their withdrawal. The 77th was to push forward and keep enough pressure on the Germans to disrupt their reaction to the outflanking attacks on the edges of the forest. This plan was clearly laid out in the First Army, I Corps, and division plans, but its accomplishment took much longer than expected.[3]

More than anything else, the terrain of the Argonne promised to obstruct the advance of the 77th Division. Those who fought in it were careful not to leave the impression that the Argonne was just a large forest. Alexander described it as a "wooded mountain . . . extremely rugged with deep, scarped valleys cutting into the central mass, the whole covered by a thick, in some places impenetrable, forest, with dense undergrowth."[4] Its ridges and hills dominated the valleys of two rivers, the Aire to the east and the Aisne to the west. Many of the ravines that cut across the forest

---

[2] The First Army plan, which called for a deep penetration in the center, allowed for shorter intermediate objectives toward the flanks. Thus, the 35th Division, on the right flank of the I Corps, had to go nearly 10 kilometers in 4 hours just to hit the "Corps Objective," while the 77th had to go just 2 to 3 kilometers. While the 35th had to advance 15 kilometers to hit the "American Army Objective," the 77th had to go between just 5 and 8 kilometers. Only at the very end of the first phase of the First Army's attack, after the Argonne had been cleared, was the 77th supposed to make a rapid advance and catch up with the divisions in the center on the "Combined Army First Objective," after a total advance of nearly 20 kilometers. See the detailed campaign map in *USAWW*, 9: 81.

[3] HQ I Army Corps, Field Orders No. 57, 22 September 1918, Folder 32.1, Box 23, I Army Corps Historical File, RG 120, NA; and HQ 77th Division, Field Orders No. 43, 24 September 1918, 1930 hours, Folder 32.0, Box 4, 77th Division Historical File, RG 120, NA.

[4] Robert Alexander, "Operations of the 77th Division: From the Argonne to Sedan," in Adler, *History of the 77th Division: August 25th 1917–November 11, 1918* (New York: The 77th Division Association, 1919), 143.

were filled with cold water at that time of year. Furthermore, only one decent road ran even part of the way north through the forest, complicating the advance of the artillery, ammunition, and supplies. As expected, the Germans added immeasurably to the area's natural strength, turning it into a veritable fortress of trenches, deep dugouts, barbed wire (in places 100 meters wide), and *chevaux de frise*, all protected by interlocking machine-gun emplacements and preregistered artillery. Although the sector was lightly held in manpower, it was still a nightmare for would-be attackers.[5]

The Argonne must have seemed particularly daunting to the men of the 77th, still exhausted and somewhat demoralized from hard duty along the Vesle and Aisne. Then, between 22 and 25 September, the division received four thousand replacement troops. Any hope that these fresh troops would increase the morale of the division was quickly tempered by an assessment of replacements' skills. Due to an unlucky series of events and a strained training and replacement system, many of the new men had been drafted only weeks before and quickly shipped to France. They had received hardly any training at all, and reports from experienced officers in the division confirmed that a number lacked even the most basic combat skills. Some apparently did not know how to load and shoot a rifle.[6]

Despite the challenges of terrain, the strength of the German defensive positions, the tiredness and relative inexperience of his own men, and the absolute incompetence of the replacements, Alexander wanted to carry out a campaign of maneuver in the Argonne. After failing to locate even a single "outstanding tactical" feature upon which to formulate an elaborate divisional scheme of maneuver, he felt forced into ordering "a straight push forward of the whole line." But, in ordering such an attack, Alexander insisted he was merely depending "upon the initiative of the subordinate commanders, specifically the platoon and company commanders, for the proper maneuvre of their units when the necessity for such maneuvre became apparent."[7]

---

5 Alexander, "Operations of the 77th Division: From the Argonne to Sedan," 144; *History of the 77th Division*, 59–60.

6 Although officers were encouraged to use the least trained men in less important positions, such as ammunition carriers, most were soon expected to perform as experienced riflemen. C.G., 154th Infantry Brigade, to C.G., 77th Division, Subject: "Report of Operations," 15 November 1918, Folder 33.6, Box 17, 77th Division Historical File, RG 120, NA; Capt. Albert T. Rich, Asst. Inspector General, First Army, to Inspector General, First Army, Subject: 77th Division, cutting off of the seven companies and one machine gun company, October 3, 1918, 8 October 1918, in "Personal File of Major H.A. Drum, Papers Relating to Lost Battalion, 77th Division," Box 16, Hugh A. Drum Papers, USAMHI.

7 Alexander, "Operations of the 77th Division: From the Argonne to Sedan," 148.

Alexander accompanied his emphasis on fighting a battle of movement with statements minimizing the importance of firepower in the forest. Although it was true that the thick woods, steep hills, and deep ravines all worked against the effective employment of artillery, mortars, and machine guns, Alexander greatly exaggerated those difficulties when he later claimed that "practically no assistance whatever could be rendered to the infantry by the artillery against the enemy front line" and that in the end, "the infantry of the 77th Division won their way through the Argonne by sheer fighting ability, by the use of the infantry weapons proper, aided in some cases by hand-grenades and the 37 milimetre gun, but, above all, on account of the inflexible determination to conquer which animated the Division as a whole."[8] In fact, there is no record of the division commander ever asking for more artillery support from the corps, nor did he show much interest in maximizing the firepower at his disposal. As in previous engagements, this latter task was left to his subordinates, and they regularly attempted to use the limited means at their disposal to maximum effect. As for Alexander, in his emphasis on maneuver and his minimization of the value of firepower, he demonstrated his commitment to the open-warfare ideal, even in the face of a host of surrounding factors that promised to work against his efforts.

Despite the significant problems of using artillery in the Argonne, the initial attack of 26 September relied heavily on a short but intense bombardment from a massive number of guns to ensure success. For the 77th Division, it also was practically the only attack during the three-week fight in which all guns fired according to a centrally organized plan. The 77th also received significant augmentation in guns, giving it a total of nearly 170 pieces, plus as many as 190 French trench mortars. During the 3-hour preparatory bombardment, all of the divisional guns fired short gas concentrations before shifting to destructive and neutralizing fire on enemy strong points, front-line positions, and assembly areas. The trench mortars and big howitzers cut wire, smashed concrete shelters, and knocked out command posts. Then, 25 minutes before H hour, all the 75mm guns fired a standing barrage until H hour, when the barrage rolled forward in 50-meter jumps at the rate of 100 meters every 5 minutes. Although this was not nearly slow enough, it was slower than the rate used by the other divisions in the corps. The 155s took up a standing barrage at the same time as the light guns but fired it a little farther, and they also shot a rolling barrage at the same rate, keeping just ahead of the 75s to create a double barrage. The barrage was to carry the infantry to the end of

[8] Ibid., 149.

the first phase of the advance – the "Corps Objective" – at which point further orders were to be issued for both the infantry and the gunners. As events showed, this provided adequate protection for the initial attack and it successfully gained the corps line at light cost.[9]

For their part, the infantry was told to advance behind the barrage but only at a distance of some 500 meters, probably due to a fear of fratricide from tree bursts and short rounds from the unregistered guns. Division orders stressed the need to attack through "lanes of least resistance" and to "turn the front of strong positions by outflanking." Ravines were to be avoided unless needed "to filter by strong points."[10] Each of the four lead battalions had a dedicated engineer team, a machine-gun company, and two 75mm guns to assist the advance.

It was a good plan for taking and holding a finite amount of enemy terrain, but the AEF leadership had bigger hopes. The plan also included other features that showed its overaggressive, open-warfare foundation – most notably its distant, essentially unlimited ultimate objectives. Also, although the corps and division plans called for the troops to be "prepared to advance beyond the Corps Objective by H plus 4-1/2 hours," no details whatsoever for that phase of the attack were given to the attack troops at the start of the battle. That part of the attack was to be "covered by later orders."[11] This simple, apparently benign statement was significant because it essentially marked the end of the set-piece portion of the attack and the start of the phase in which AEF leaders probably hoped open-warfare principles would become dominant. Whereas this allowed senior AEF officers maximum flexibility in conducting the attack beyond that line (should they have chosen to exercise it), it also ended the period of organized, well-supported, firepower-based attacks. Although army, corps, and division commanders quickly ordered the troops forward from that line, they rarely provided the detailed information, organizational coordination, and artillery augmentation necessary to make those subsequent advances successful. These deficiencies in staff planning and logistical coordination hindered the offensive.

After the initial attack, the fighting in the Argonne descended into a series of grinding local battles in which senior commanders, from

---

9 HQ 77th Division, Field Orders No. 43, 24 September 1918, 1930 hours, Folder 32.0, Box 4, 77th Division Historical File, RG 120, NA.
10 Ibid.
11 HQ I Army Corps, Field Orders No. 57, 22 September 1918, Folder 32.1, Box 23, I Army Corps Historical File, RG 120, NA; HQ 77th Division, Field Orders No. 43, 24 September 1918, 1930 hours, Folder 32.0, Box 4, 77th Division Historical File, RG 120, NA.

Alexander on up to Pershing, became practically irrelevant except for one significant and dubious role – ordering the attacks to continue. In this, they approached the dreadful stereotype of unknowledgeable Allied commanders of 1914–1917. Just as Pershing's decisions contributed to turning the First Army's offensive into a series of disjointed and ill-supported divisional battles after midday on 26 September, so Alexander's decisions allowed his division's operations in the Argonne to become a grueling struggle of individual brigades and sometimes of regiments, battalions, and companies. And, just as some divisions managed to succeed under Pershing's handling of the battle (e.g., the 1st under Charles Summerall and the 4th under John L. Hines) while others foundered (e.g., the 35th, 37th, and 79th), some units within the 77th Division succeeded at times but failed at others. The key point is that Alexander's style of command pushed the management of the battle down to his brigades and regiments, and it is at those levels that the struggle to adapt, learn, succeed, and especially to survive was waged most intensely.

Despite the dire predictions of the attached French liaison officer, who warned Alexander that "the line in your front will not move.... I fear you will not be able to make the advance you hope for," the men of the 77th Division pressed forward on the morning of 26 September and met almost no enemy resistance as they passed through the enemy's first defensive position.[12] The destruction from the preliminary bombardment and rolling barrage was enormous, and it apparently obliterated most of the few unfortunate defenders ordered to offer resistance from the first line. Alexander even thought the artillery might have "over done it" somewhat.[13] The terrain, turned into "the most amazing tangle imaginable" by the bombardment, slowed the attackers much more than any enemy resistance.[14]

The weak initial resistance primarily resulted from most German troops having previously withdrawn to the second defensive position, about 2 kilometers to the rear of the first. The attackers ran into the first significant resistance in late morning when they hit this strong second position, which lay just in front of the "Corps Objective." Even though they had not yet reached this corps line and were then meeting strong resistance, Alexander told them at 1130 that the standing barrage then being fired 500 yards beyond the corps line would begin rolling forward at

---

[12] Alexander, *Memories*, 176.
[13] Ibid., 181.
[14] Ibid., 180.

1300 hours. They needed to catch up and follow it, but none were able to do so. Subsequent attacks that afternoon, apparently made with ad hoc artillery support, only carried the advance closer to the corps line. Sometime after 1500, Alexander passed along a corps order affirming that the division still needed to gain the "American Army" line, more than 3 kilometers ahead, that night. At 1735 hours, though no further advance had been made, Alexander sent another order reminding his brigadiers to take the same line.[15] There are no records of attacks even being made, much less succeeding, that night.

At 0100 the next morning, the I Corps directed that the advance would continue at 0530. By then, the "American Army Objective," still more than 3 kilometers away, was identified as merely an "intermediate objective," and the goal of the second-day's attack was the "Combined Army First Objective," a line some 15 kilometers to the front. Alexander passed along the order and called for a 30-minute preliminary bombardment as well as a rolling barrage at the same rate as the first day. Beyond the artillery preparation and the rolling barrage, two other details suggest that Alexander may have sensed the difficulty of the task he was assigning his men. First, he ordered that no troops should "advance beyond the intermediate objective" until given further orders; and, second, his instructions stressed that "full use must be made of all the infantry arms placed at their disposal."[16] This might have been, for Alexander, a rare reference to the problem of relying too *much* on the rifle and not using the auxiliary weapons enough. In the morning attack, Wittenmyer's 153rd Brigade gained another half kilometer on the right, while Johnson's brigade made smaller gains on the left. At this point, apparently having concluded that his centralized attack plans were not working, Alexander decided to turn the light-gun regiments over to his brigadiers to let them run practically individual battles. From that point forward, Alexander continued to order his men forward, but he offered little support, planning, or coordination.[17]

Alexander's delegation of the Argonne battle to his subordinates complicated any effort by the division to coordinate attacks and mass firepower. Only he, as the division commander, had the staff and command capability necessary to coordinate the brigade's attacks and develop

[15] ABMC, *77th Division Summary of Operations*, 33–4.

[16] HQ 77th Division, Field Orders No. 46, 27 September 1918, 0100 hours, Folder 32.0, Box 4, 77th Division Historical File, RG 120, NA.

[17] Although Alexander generally retained direct control of the heavy howitzer regiment, even that was delegated directly to the brigade commanders for many of the attacks. ABMC, *77th Division Summary of Operations*, 35.

detailed and mutually supporting fire plans. Most likely, the substantial challenges to using artillery in the dense forest and hilly terrain helped convince Alexander that massed barrages were of limited effect and that more valuable support could be arranged on an ad hoc basis at the brigade level. He later admitted that in the rare instances when he did direct a division-wide rolling barrage, he "expected more moral than material result" from the fire.[18] In any event, the tendency to delegate such responsibility seems to have been part of his style of command.

Despite the challenges of doing so, the brigadiers, regimental commanders, and junior officers labored to support their attacks with firepower. Even after the general failure of the early attack on 27 September, this pattern became apparent. Ordered by Alexander to continue the assault, both brigadiers made additional attacks later that day, utilizing short intense preliminary bombardments and rolling barrages. One such attack by the 154th Brigade pushed the line forward 1 kilometer in the early evening.[19]

Alexander played a minimal role over the next number of days, issuing no significant field orders or attack plans, even though the brigades fought forward 2 kilometers on the 28th, another 1 on the 29th, and another 1 on the 30th. These attacks were always preceded by preliminary bombardments of 30 or 60 minutes and usually were covered by rolling barrages as well. There is no record that troops in any of these attacks ever attempted to move beyond the covering range of the artillery fire. During some attacks, small units made short advances, halted when enemy resistance developed, and only continued the advance after artillery fire was brought back on the enemy strong point. In fact, this latter style of advance seemed to typify the 77th Division's fighting throughout the Argonne and even beyond it.[20]

The brigade and regimental reports on the operations in the Argonne show a repetitive pattern to the fighting. Alexander ordered attacks to be made, often stating simply that "the 152nd F.A. Brigade will furnish such additional artillery support as may be required by Infantry Brigade Commanders."[21] The brigade commanders each identified local objectives to be taken, coordinated an artillery preparation and fire-support plan, and ordered the infantry to attack behind a rolling barrage. At times, some commanders even pulled back their most forward troops to more safely deluge the closest enemy positions with fire. Such tactics were used despite

[18] Alexander, "Operations of the 77th Division: From the Argonne to Sedan," p. 150.
[19] ABMC, *77th Division Summary of Operations*, 36.
[20] Ibid., 37–43.
[21] HQ 77th Division, Field Orders No. 49, 1 October 1918, 2130 hours, Folder 32.0, Box 4, 77th Division Historical File, RG 120, NA.

being officially prohibited by Alexander, who despised the idea of even temporarily giving up ground previously taken. The infantry also made maximum use of their most powerful weapons both before and during attacks, often finding – despite the limitations on the use of all direct-fire weapons in the dense forest – that the 37mm guns, trench mortars, machine guns, and grenades of all types (especially white-phosphorous rifle grenades) produced a greater effect than the Springfield rifle. Nevertheless, many of these attacks led to short gains, at which point they appear to have been quickly stopped, and more fire support was arranged before further attempts were made. Sometimes the advance progressed successfully for 1 or 2 kilometers, usually with the infantry reporting little or "no resistance," until they hit a new enemy line. At that point, attacks again appear to have been quickly stopped, the lines consolidated, and new brigade and regimental plans prepared for an attack the next day.[22]

Operations reports suggest that despite the best efforts of the junior officers to find "paths of least resistance" and outflank enemy strong points, in the end, the troops resorted to slowly blasting their way through the German positions.[23] In addition to getting all possible support from

[22] For the brigade reports, see C.G., 153rd Infantry Brigade, to C.G., 77th Division, Subject: Report of Operations 26 September, 1918, to 8th November, 1918, 19 November 1918, Folder 33.6, Box 15, 77th Division Historical File, RG 120, NA; and HQ 154th Infantry Brigade, "Report of Operations of the 154th Inf. Brigade 77th Division in the Argonne Forest from September 26th to October 17th, 1918," 29 October 1918, Folder 33.6, Box 17, 77th Division Historical File, RG 120, NA. For the regimental reports, see "Operations Report, 305th Infantry, September 26th–November 12/18," Folder 33.6, Box 21, 77th Division Historical File, RG 120, NA; "Operations Report of the 306th Infantry From September 26 to November 8, 1918," Folder 33.6, Box 23, 77th Division Historical File, RG 120, NA; "Report of Operations of the 307th Infantry from September 26th, 1918 to November 8th, 1918," Folder 33.6, Box 26, 77th Division Historical File, RG 120, NA; and HQ 308th Infantry "Report on Operations," Folder 33.6, Box 9, 77th Division Historical File, RG 120, NA. For the reports of the artillery units, see HQ 152nd Field Artillery Brigade, "Report of Operations of the 152nd Field Artillery, September 26th, 1918 to November 11th, 1918," and HQ 152nd Field Artillery Brigade, Memorandum, 10 November 1918, both in Folder 33.0, Box 29, 77th Division Historical File, RG 120, NA; "Summary of Operations, 304th Regiment Field Artillery, 26 Sept. '18–8 Nov. '18," Folder 33.0, Box 29, 77th Division Historical File, RG 120, NA; HQ 305th F.A. Regiment, Memorandum for the C.G., 152nd F.A. Brigade, 4 February, 1919, Folder 11.2, and HQ 305th F.A. Regiment, "Report on Operations," 18 November 1918, Folder 33.6, both in Box 30, 77th Division Historical File, RG 120, NA; "Report of Operations of the 306th Field Artillery from September 26, 1918 to November 8th, 1918, inclusive," Folder 33.6, Box 30, 77th Division Historical File, RG 120; NA.

[23] After repeated failed efforts to work around the flanks of machine-gun nests to his front, one exasperated company commander reported that he could not outflank them because "there is no flank to the dam [sic] things." "Operations Report, 305th Infantry, September 26th–November 12/18," Folder 33.6, Box 21, 77th Division Historical File, RG 120, NA.

the artillery, they made maximum use of other weapons – especially trench mortars and rifle grenades – neither of which was expected by GHQ officers to be of paramount importance in open warfare. In the 77th, as in other divisions throughout the AEF (as well as in the British, French, and German armies), infantry officers were learning that the so-called auxiliary weapons were indispensable in assaults. As for the standard rifle, one officer in the 305th Infantry claimed that it was "used for anything but firing by our infantry."[24] In one typical attack, the commander of the 305th Infantry massed all his Stokes mortars, as well as a number of larger mortars from the 1st Gas Regiment, and concentrated their fire on a 200-meter front during the preattack bombardment to allow for a successful advance through this very narrow zone. The preparation kept all enemy fire down for the first 10 minutes of the attack, during which the troops advanced 150 meters, then dug in when the Germans got their machine guns set up and firing again.[25]

By 2 October, such a system of attacks had brought the two brigades forward 7 kilometers to the German second main defensive position. On this strong line, the defenders determined to make a stand and they successfully resisted numerous attacks during the next five days. The 1-kilometer advance of Major Charles Whittlesey's battalion (made behind an effective rolling barrage), which was quickly cut off and surrounded on the far left of the line, was the only successful attack during this period. During the course of the next four days, a number of attacks by the rest of the 154th Brigade, often made in conjunction with the French on the left flank, failed to crack the enemy positions and relieve Whittlesey's command (see Map 20).

The fascinating story of this so-called Lost Battalion became one of the great tales of the American war effort, but it also highlighted two significant aspects of the Liberty Division's operations in the Argonne. First, the successful resistance of the isolated command against repeated enemy assaults – often hurled at them with much superior firepower – simply confirmed the tremendous tactical advantages held by a determined group of defenders operating in dense woods. The 2nd Division learned this lesson in Belleau Wood, other AEF units learned it elsewhere during the Meuse-Argonne Offensive, and Whittlesey's command simply proved this truth worked for American units as well. Although totally cut off, completely out of food after the second day, without cold-weather clothing, short on

[24] Ibid.
[25] Ibid.

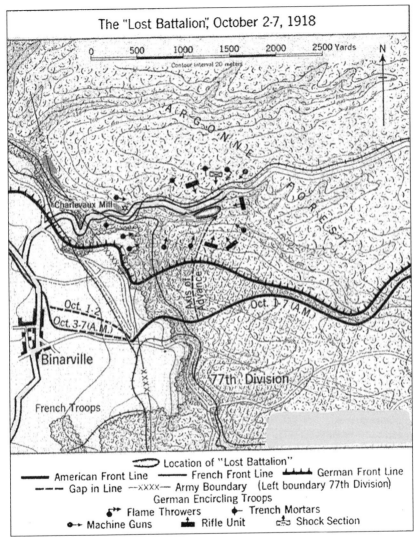

MAP 20: The "Lost Battalion" of the 77th Division in the Argonne.

ammunition, and forced to defend itself with only eight machine guns, a few Chauchats, and five hundred service rifles (and ultimately much less), the command beat back no less than seven enemy attacks supported by artillery, trench mortars, and flamethrowers. Although the command suffered tremendous casualties (i.e., 65 percent of those cut off), it survived the ordeal intact and proved in its own way the enormous challenge that the 77th Division was undertaking by trying to drive a determined enemy out of prepared positions in those same woods.[26]

American operations to reconnect with the "Lost Battalion" demonstrated the other important lesson of those events – the increasing amount of firepower the division employed to break the German lines. After repeatedly failing to get Johnson's brigade to push through to Whittlesey, despite having Johnson personally direct one of the attacks, Alexander finally resorted to the same method that the 2nd Division ultimately used to take Belleau Wood – massive artillery saturation. From midnight until 0600 hours on 7 October, the entire regiment of 155s maintained "special concentrations" on key German positions. The two light-gun regiments also carried out an intense 3-hour bombardment that morning to weaken German resistance. Finally, five days into the effort to relieve the isolated command, the fire from all the divisional guns was coordinated in an effort to break the German lines (see Map 21). Although the Germans surrounding Whittlesey's command withdrew primarily because Liggett was finally able to order a long-overdue flank attack into the woods by the 28th and 82nd Divisions, investigation of the saturation bombardment by corps and division inspectors determined the fire caused "such losses to the enemy in men and material" that it contributed to the enemy withdrawal that day.[27] In fact, this massing of firepower was really just a division-level form of what the brigades and regiments had been trying to do on a smaller scale since the afternoon of the first day.

The fighting of the men in the Argonne was marked by one other characteristic, and it went hand in hand with an increasing reliance on

---

[26] The exact number of men in Whittlesey's command is disputed, but he probably started out with between seven hundred and eight hundred men and lost about a hundred during his advance. An account by Whittlesey claimed 554 men were trapped the first night. He also insisted 194 men were unscathed when relieved on the afternoon of 7 October, while 107 were killed and 159 were wounded. The balance were killed or captured while serving as runners. See L. Wardlaw Miles, *History of the 308th Infantry, 1917–1919* (New York, n.p., 1927), 170. Another excellent source is Capt. Nelson M. Holderman, "Operations of the force known as the 'Lost Battalion', from October 2nd to October 7th, 1918, Northeast of Binarville, in the Forest of Argonne, France," Company Officer's Class 1924–1925, The Infantry School, Fourth Section, Committee "H," Fort Benning Ga. (student monograph) in Folder 18.2, Box 3, 77th Division Historical File, RG 120, NA. Holderman commanded an infantry company in the surrounded force and was awarded the Congressional Medal of Honor for his actions.

[27] HQ 152nd Field Artillery Brigade, "Report of Operations of the 152nd Brigade, Field Artillery, September 26th, 1918 to November 11th, 1918," and HQ 152nd Field Artillery Brigade, Memorandum, 10 November 1918, both in Folder 33.0, Box 29, 77th Division Historical File, RG 120, NA.

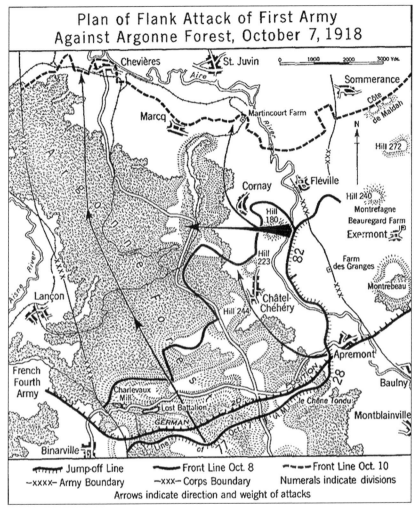

Plan of Flank Attack of First Army
Against Argonne Forest, October 7, 1918

MAP 21: On 7 October, the 77th Division made its first significant advance since the initial attack in September, thanks to a flank attack by the 28th and 82nd Divisions.

firepower – caution. Although many contemporaries – German, French, British, and even American – as well as numerous historians have correctly asserted that inexperienced American troops regularly displayed a level of individual recklessness that matched their bravery, the records of the 77th's experience in the Argonne lead to the inescapable conclusion that the men of that division had learned better than to impetuously run headlong into machine-gun fire. Despite Alexander's callous orders that objectives were "to be gained without regard to losses," the men and junior officers demonstrated a willingness to regulate the intensity and persistence of their attacks. In the most dangerous sense, at least militarily, this resulted in a relatively high rate of "straggling" in the division, and commanders from Alexander on down seemed incapable of stopping it.[28]

However, in a more general sense, many commanders reported that even those officers and troops who courageously fought in the front lines throughout the weeks in the woods typically demonstrated more discretion than aggressiveness in their attacks. In some cases, orders to attack were not followed up by any effort to advance at all but, more often, the attacks were attempted and pressed forward until the troops' tolerance for enemy fire was exceeded.[29] They then stopped and dug in. Alexander knew well that his men did not share his level of aggressiveness in attack, and he bemoaned this fact to Liggett during the battle. Liggett's aide recorded that Alexander claimed to be

about at the end of his rope. He had tried coaxing and kicking and every expedient to make his men move. He had sustained losses, but not heavy, and he had many stragglers and men drawn from the city, who knew nothing about the woods and fighting of this character, but he thought they were all in, and was greatly distressed that he could report no better progress.[30]

He tried firing commanders, from lieutenants to colonels, when he heard that attacks were not pushed to his satisfaction, further repeating the stereotypical pattern of earlier Allied commanders. On 27 September, he ordered that a company commander in the 307th Infantry be relieved and sent "to the rear echelon under arrest with charges against him for

[28] On 4 October, the I Corps chief of staff, Malin Craig, reported to Hugh A. Drum at First Army HQ that the 77th had "a great many stragglers . . . Gen. Alexander says he knows it and has had two straggler lines and in addition to that the Corps has one; but in the woods they get away." Field Messages, Folder 32.16, Box 19, I Army Corps Historical File, RG 120, NA.

[29] The historian, William Langer, who was briefly attached to the 77th Division as a member of the 1st Gas Regiment, described more than one instance of the infantry not attempting to attack after his unit had fired a preparation of thermite, smoke, and high-explosive mortar rounds. He also described attacks that were carried out. In many cases, infantry failed to attack on time simply because they had not yet received the order to do so. William L. Langer, *Gas and Flame in World War I* (New York: Alfred A. Knopf, 1965), 63–4.

[30] Entry for 5 October, Stackpole Diary, p. 250. Apparently only on this late date, well into the second week of the battle, did senior commanders realize it was a serious mistake to send a division of men drafted almost exclusively from New York City to fight in the thickest woods in France, when units filled with men from Michigan and Wisconsin had been available.

disgraceful conduct in the face of the enemy" after the officer supposedly "permitted his entire company to be held up by the fire of a few
snipers."[31] Apparently this did not successfully motivate the other officers and men, because the caution did not disappear or even decrease.
Even senior officers admitted the necessity of prudence in the attack,
though only when more enemy firepower was present. One regimental
colonel openly reported "the impossibility of advancing in the face of a
continuous line of machine-guns which had a good field of fire."[32]

The indirect evidence of the division's casualty and prisoner of war
(POW) statistics confirm that the unit was not overly aggressive in most
of its attacks. Recalling that AEF divisions had an authorized strength of
twenty-eight thousand officers and men, it is instructive to compare the
77th and other divisions. Between 26 September and 19 October, when
it received an eleven-day break from the front lines, the division suffered
4,115 casualties – about 15 percent of its authorized strength.[33] Although
these were by no means insignificant losses, when the difficulty of the
mission and the number of days in line are considered, they prove to
be relatively moderate. During the first week of the attack, the division
suffered an average of 206 casualties a day. It lost 177 a day during the
second week and 144 a day in the final week. In contrast, during this
same period, the 1st Division fought for about twelve days in the Meuse-
Argonne and suffered 7,772 losses (i.e., 28 percent of division strength) –
an average of 648 a day. The 2nd Division fought for about nine days
near Blanc Mont, losing 6,327 men (i.e., 23 percent) – about 703 a day.
The 77th Division itself averaged 202 losses a day during its first week
along the Vesle, when it made no major attacks whatsoever. Regarding
prisoners, the Liberty Division captured just 631 enemy troops during its
three weeks in the Argonne sector. Although not insignificant, that figure
compares unfavorably to the fourteen hundred taken by the 1st Division
during its much shorter fight in the Meuse-Argonne.[34]

[31] Operations Messages, 27 September 1918, Folder 32.11, Box 6, 77th Division Historical
File, RG 120, NA.
[32] "Operations Report, 305th Infantry, September 26th–November 12/18," Folder 33.6,
Box 21, 77th Division Historical File, RG 120, NA.
[33] One source lists the division's actual strength on 26 September as 25,709 officers and
men. If that is correct, the division's losses were 16 percent. *History of the 77th Division*,
137.
[34] These rates pale in comparison to the losses suffered by the 1st and 2nd Divisions at
Soissons, where each lost an average of about fourteen hundred men a day. Also, more
than half of all the prisoners taken by the 77th during the Argonne fighting were taken
on 14 October, when it seized the town of St. Juvin. ABMC, *77th Division Summary of
Operations*, 21; ABMC, *American Armies and Battlefields*, 327, 369.

The operations report from the 306th Infantry, which included the number of casualties suffered in each minor attack in the Argonne, highlights what these general statistics meant on the small-unit level. On 28 September, after a substantial preliminary bombardment and behind a rolling barrage, the regiment drove through a German defensive line and advanced nearly 3 kilometers. Yet, the capture of just one enemy prisoner and the loss of just ten casualties (and none killed) suggest that the Germans probably did more withdrawing than shooting. More telling are the reports of failed attacks. The regimental attack on 2 October broke down after a minor advance, but the unit reported only three killed and ten wounded. Four days later, the regiment failed to take the same objective, and although it reported "entire day spent attacking machine gun nests," it lost only two men killed and five wounded.[35] Although each casualty was individually tragic, losses of this scale during failed attacks by a regiment with more than two thousand soldiers at its disposal suggest that the attackers, far from being overly aggressive, were erring on the side of caution.[36]

Despite the foregoing analysis, it would be wrong to conclude that the officers and men of the 77th Division were shirkers and that no attacks were pressed with vigor. The men of the 77th engaged in much difficult fighting in the Argonne. They worked hard to outflank and envelop enemy strong points. Occasionally, they advanced in the face of withering machine-gun fire, and some assaults ended in fierce hand-to-hand fighting. But, on balance, the system of attack, the rate of advance, and the numbers of casualties suffered and prisoners taken suggest that the men of the 77th attacked with more caution and maybe with less skill than the best AEF divisions. They tended to make successful advances of any depth only after massing enough firepower and pounding the enemy lines long enough to convince the defenders to withdraw. However, it is only fair to note that considering the original plan to have the 77th make slow but steady holding attacks through the woods while other American and French divisions outflanked the defenders, the men and junior officers of the 77th did a better job of sticking with the original scheme of attack than Pershing, Liggett, or Alexander.

Shortly after the 77th Division emerged from the Argonne, the I Corps, by then commanded by Joseph Dickman, ordered it to attack the outpost

[35] "Operations Report of the 306th Infantry from September 26 to November 8, 1918," Folder 33.6, Box 23, 77th Division Historical File, RG 120, NA.
[36] By 8 October, even the thoughtful and self-possessed Liggett exclaimed that he was "out of patience with the apparent supineness and lack of initiative of the 77th." Stackpole Diary, p. 255.

positions of the *Kriemhilde Stellung*, just north of the Aire River. Corps orders directed the 77th to drive forward just slightly, primarily to protect the left flank of the 82nd Division on the right. The division ultimately made two partially successful attacks, one on 14 October that took the town of St. Juvin on the right and then another attack on the 15th that led to the partial occupation of Grandpré on the left (see Map 22). In both attacks, Alexander continued to stress maneuver over firepower, while the brigades again showed a tendency to maximize firepower and make cautious advances.

Alexander's plan to take St. Juvin called for his eastern brigade, the 153rd, to make a demonstration to the immediate front with some troops while swinging another battalion through the rear area of the 82nd Division to the right so it could hit St. Juvin from the eastern flank (see Map 23). The 154th, on the left, was apparently to take Grandpré by direct attack. For fire support, the division orders directed a 2-hour bombardment and a massed machine-gun barrage and specified that the light-gun regiments were "subject to the call" of the infantry brigadiers. McCloskey's artillery plan laid out a detailed schedule of fire support that attempted to incorporate both a slow rolling barrage (i.e., 100 meters every 6 minutes) and a series of shifting fires on successive areas. However, the coordination of this fire plan, complicated by the wide flanking maneuver directed by Alexander, required better liaison than the division could maintain in the attack to keep the artillery shifts coordinated with the infantry advances. Despite these problems and some confusion on the part of the troops carrying out the attack, the flanking troops ultimately took St. Juvin and Hill 182 beyond it, capturing three hundred German soldiers while suffering just seventy-eight casualties. For its part, the 154th failed to cross the Aire in its attack.[37]

That evening, Dickman ordered his corps to continue attacking the next morning and to drive forward about 4 kilometers, which would have taken it through the *Kriemhilde Stellung*. Alexander directed both brigades to attack at 0730 hours and allowed a 1-hour artillery

[37] The details of the St. Juvin battle are sketchy, due as much to a lack of records as to conflicting evidence in those that are available. Although Alexander later wrote that he decided against simultaneous attacks on St. Juvin and Grandpré because his "artillery was not sufficient for both tasks at the same time," his field orders seem to direct both brigades to attack on 14 October; other sources confirm that they did. Nor do reports agree on the specific nature of the artillery support. Alexander, Memories, 244; ABMC, *77th Division Summary of Operations*, 69–70; HQ 306th Infantry Regiment, "Report of the Capture of St. Juvin & Hill 182 by 306th Infantry," 19 October 1918, Folder 33.6, Box 23, 77th Division Historical File, RG 120, NA.

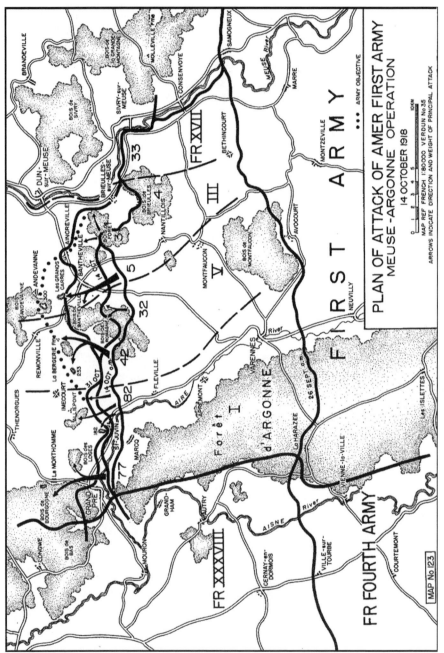

MAP 22: The First Army's 14 October attack.

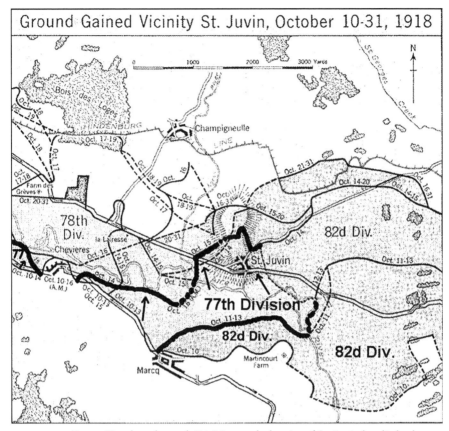

MAP 23: On 14 October, the 77th Division took the city of St. Juvin but little else.

preparation, which focused on Grandpré and Champigneulle, the two large towns in the attack sector. The 155s were to continue pounding those towns until the attacking infantry came within 800 meters of them and then shift to other targets. Alexander's penchant for delegation continued, and he allowed his infantry brigadiers to "employ the regiments of 75s at their disposal in such a manner as they deem expedient from H minus one hour on."[38] In fact, McCloskey gave each infantry brigade the dedicated support of a battalion of 155s as well, retaining direct control

---

[38] HQ 77th Division, Field Orders No. 56, 14 October 1918, 2200 hours, Folder 32.0, Box 4, 77th Division Historical File, RG 120, NA; HQ I Army Corps, Field Orders No. 73, 14 October 1918, Folder 32.1, Box 23, I Army Corps Historical File, RG 120, NA.

of only one battalion of howitzers. With all the guns delegated to the infantry commanders, the artillery fire plan included little more than a list of targets and a rare warning that "due to difficulties of ammunition supply all fire should be observed. Where this is impracticable, there will be a minimum expenditure of ammunition."[39] The infantry commanders added the fire of their 37mm guns, accompanying 75s, and machine guns to the preliminary fire as well as the attack.

Just like the day before, this attack did not go as planned and was only partially successful. The 153rd Brigade spent the entire day repelling a strong enemy counterattack and made no advance. The troops of the 154th advanced well to the Aire before being held up for hours trying to cross that unfordable river (see Map 24). Eventually, after dark, a few companies crossed the Aire and successfully entered Grandpré.[40] Operations reports claimed losses were light thanks to the excellent use of infiltration tactics by the infantry and the fire of the artillery, which was – despite the fear of a lack of shells – described as "splendid throughout."[41] In fact, Johnson wrote a special letter to McCloskey declaring that "had it not been for the effective and efficient support which was given to me by both the heavy and the light arty...the taking of Grand Pre by the troops of my command...would have been an impossibility....the success of the operation was due in large measure to the effective Artillery support."[42]

That very day, 16 October, the division was relieved by the 78th Division, and it marched back into the Argonne forest for a two-week period of rest, refitting, reconstituting, and training before taking part in the final

---

[39] HQ 152nd F.A. Brigade, Field Orders No. 11, 2120 hours, 14 October 1918, Folder 32.1, Box 29, 77th Division Historical File, RG 120, NA.

[40] The question of which division captured Grandpré was a controversy during and after the war. Although many officers in the 77th Division, including Alexander, claimed units of the 77th completely occupied Grandpré, they appear to have only maintained firm control of the southwest portion on the town. The 78th Division, which relieved the 77th on 16 October, engaged in bitter fighting throughout most of the town for many days. See the transcript of the discussion between Liggett and Alexander in Maj. Gen. Alexander, "Operations of the Divisions, 26th of September to the 11th of November" (lecture delivered on 3 February 1919), Folder 50.9, Box 11, 77th Division Historical File, RG 120, NA.

[41] C.O., 307th Infantry, to C.G., 154th Brigade, Subject: Attack on Grand Pre, October 15/16th 1918, 18 October 1918, Folder 33.6, Box 26, 77th Division Historical File, RG 120, NA.

[42] C.G., 154th Infantry Brigade, to C.G., 152nd F.A. Brigade, Subject: Use of Artillery during recent operations, 18 October 1918, Folder 11.4, Box 2, 77th Division Historical File, RG 120, NA.

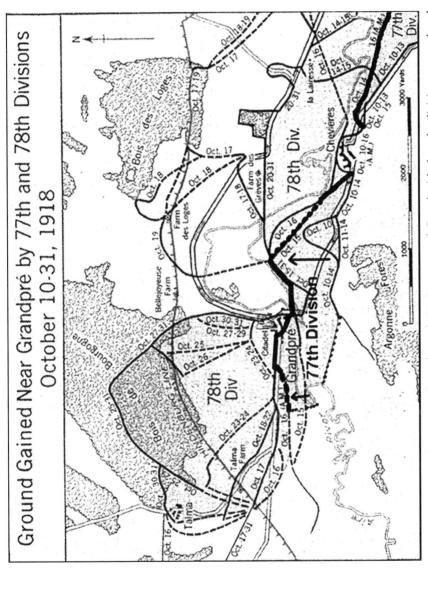

MAP 24: On 15 October, troops from the 77th Division entered Grandpré before the division was replaced by the 78th Division and finally given an opportunity to rest and refit. They had been attacking almost continuously since 26 September.

First Army attack of the war on 1 November. The Liberty Division had been in the front lines continuously since 21 September and was thoroughly exhausted. In grinding its way through the Argonne forest, it had successfully if slowly completed one of the more trying missions of the war by any AEF division. Despite the restrictions and limitations on the offensive use of firepower, from both internal and external factors, the men of the 77th struggled to maximize all the weaponry at their disposal to blast their way forward. Far from demonstrating the reckless aggressiveness that led to heavy losses in the Vesle-Aisne operations, the infantrymen showed a level of caution in their advances that troubled senior commanders but also kept casualty rates below those of units in other major offensives. The division continued to demonstrate those tendencies in the minor operations at St. Juvin and Grandpré and did so even more clearly in its final operation in November.

To the Meuse, 1–11 November 1918

During its brief period out of the front lines, the depleted 77th received its second large contingent of replacement troops. Many were almost as unprepared for combat as those that had arrived in September. For this reason especially, the division officers felt that the days between attacks had to be dedicated to training rather than rest. Alexander ordered that after three days of rest, "intensive training" would begin throughout the division. He stressed the training of "leaders of small groups" in maneuver, as well as "the use of the rifle" and its combined use with "the auxiliary arms." The men were to correct weaknesses identified during the Argonne fighting: lack of skill in outflanking machine guns, too much "useless grouping of men," and too little use of cover. Alexander then admitted that "even of more importance is the necessity for securing fire superiority. Men must be taught the necessity of immediate fire whenever a target presents itself so as to secure at once the overwhelming benefit which immediately results from fire superiority of all kinds."[43]

These words may have been merely an extension of the prewar ideas of gaining fire superiority by having more riflemen fire at the enemy, or they might be a sign that Alexander had developed a greater appreciation for the amount and kinds of firepower necessary to secure superiority on the

[43] HQ 77th Division, G-3 Memorandum, No. 2 (Training), 17 October 1918, Folder 50.9, Box 12, 77th Division Historical File, RG 120, NA.

modern battlefield; the former seems more likely. Elsewhere, Alexander insisted that his experience in the Argonne merely "confirmed" existing opinions.[44] During the training period, he reissued the official "Combat Instructions" memorandum that George Marshall wrote in August, which was based on the fighting in the Aisne-Marne Offensive. He also passed along Pershing's latest version of "Combat Instructions," issued on 12 October, that complained of forward units hesitating "where there has been little opposition" and officers not grasping "the extreme importance of constant aggressiveness."[45]

In the materials he disseminated throughout his division, as well as in his own writings, Alexander proved himself a firm adherent of the official AEF doctrine developed in 1917. He seems to have never lost faith in the almighty power of the rifle, and his postwar references to the more firepower-intensive infantry weapons, including machine guns, automatic rifles, 37mm guns, mortars, and grenades, as "merely adjuncts" suggests he learned little.[46] He criticized his men for "a disinclination to utilize to its full potential power the infantry rifle" and a "dependence ... upon machine guns, grenades and other auxiliaries." The latter weapons, he dismissively wrote, may have been "useful in their way" but the "intelligent use of the infantry rifle wins battles when no other instrumentality will suffice."[47] Alexander may have remained a greater devotee of the standard service rifle than Pershing himself.

But, considering Alexander's style of command, lesson learning by subordinate commanders may have been more important to the remaining operations of his division. The development of the infantry brigadiers, Johnson and Wittenmyer, became a moot point during this period because both moved to other assignments and the division received two new brigade commanders. Colonel William R. Smedberg, an experienced regimental commander, left the 305th Infantry to command the 153rd Brigade and Brigadier General Harrison J. Price arrived from the 82nd Division to lead the 154th Brigade.[48] The regimental commanders were all men who

[44] Alexander, *Memories*, 265.
[45] A First Army document entitled "Combat Instructions," 12 October 1918, was included in HQ 77th Division, G-3 Memorandum, 18 October 1918, Folder 50.9, Box 12, 77th Division Historical File, RG 120, NA. See also HQ 77th Division, G-3 Memorandum, 20 October 1918, Folder 50.9, Box 12, 77th Division Historical File, RG 120, NA.
[46] Alexander, *Memories*, 17.
[47] Alexander, "Operations of the 77th Division: From the Argonne to Sedan," p. 155.
[48] Wittenmyer was promoted and given command of the new 7th Division. For unknown reasons, Johnson asked to be reassigned from the 77th and took command of a brigade in the 79th Division.

had experienced the Argonne as part of the division. They carried out Alexander's orders to improve the skills of the officers and men by completing a regimen of drill, tactical talks, and lots of firing practice into the hills of the Argonne. They found it especially important to ensure that the new troops knew how to use not only their rifles but also rifle and hand grenades, a sign of their appreciation of those weapons in the previous fighting.[49] Finally, some members of Alexander's own staff issued documents to the division that expressed a greater understanding of the role of firepower. The 77th Division's operations chief (G-3) issued a memorandum on 26 October that stressed the importance of artillery liaison officers as well as the use of rifle grenades and Stokes mortars. He also made this surprising admission: "Remember that the men cannot do anything against material. Against wire entanglements artillery preparation is necessary to open the road to the infantry, otherwise the infantry will be needlessly sacrificed."[50]

By the last week of October, planning for the final attack of 1 November was in full swing. The division was reassigned to Dickman's I Corps and was to advance about 5 kilometers to protect the left flank of Summerall's V Corps, which was expected to make the primary effort and the deepest penetration (see Map 25).[51] Although the 77th Division was only attacking in a supporting role, its orders called for a breaching of the main enemy line of defense along the *Kriemhilde Stellung*, certain to be a difficult task.

As with previous attacks, Alexander turned to maneuver to secure his advance. He later wrote that "Under no imaginable circumstances would a direct attack upon so strong a position ... be advisable unless there was no other alternative." Convinced there was "a promising opportunity for maneuver" by going into the territory of the neighboring 80th Division on the right, he ordered that his leading battalions advance from that direction and envelop the main enemy line, which lay 2 kilometers to the front, from the east.[52] Alexander stacked all his regiments so that only the

[49] C.G., 154th Brigade, to C.G., 77th Division, Report on Training, 31 October, 1918, Folder 50.9, Box 12, 77th Division Historical File, RG 120, NA; "Dickman-Smedberg Interview," 9 November 1918, in HQ American First Army, Memorandum for Chief of Staff, Subject: Investigation of Action of 77th Division on November 1, 1918, 12 November 1918, Folder 66.0, Box 14, 77th Division Historical File, RG 120, NA.

[50] HQ 77th Division, G-3 Memorandum Order No. 122, 26 October 1918, Folder 32.13, Box 5, 77th Division Historical File, RG 120, NA.

[51] HQ I Army Corps, Field Orders No. 85, 28 October 1918, Folder 32.1, Box 15, I Army Corps Historical File, RG 120, NA.

[52] Alexander, *Memories*, 268–9. However, there is some doubt regarding some senior leaders' assessments of the strength of the German positions to the front. I Corps orders

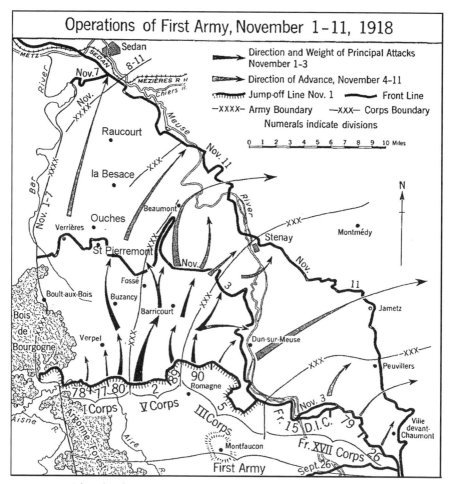

MAP 25: After the slow start on 1 November, the 77th Division fought its way to the Meuse River by November 6. But even this advance was characterized more by caution and a reliance on firepower than by the official AEF doctrine on open warfare.

305th Infantry would make the initial assault. The attack was to occur in three phases: one that led to the capture of the main enemy line and the

for the 1 November attack included "Battle Instructions" that stressed "the difference in the tactical methods to be employed and the preparation required for the assault on a highly organized position, *as compared with a hastily or partially organized position such as at present confronting the Corps*" [emphasis added]. Yet, McCloskey later wrote that the resistance around Champigneulle on 1 November "was more severe than we had expected." HQ 152nd Field Artillery Brigade, "Report of Operations of the 152nd

town of Champigneulle with the flanking attack from the east, the second in which the infantry drove north to an identified line, and the third that covered the final push to the corps objective.[53]

The fire-support plan included 30 minutes of preliminary fire by the divisional guns (though the corps preparation began at H minus 2 hours) and a rolling barrage advancing 100 meters every 6 minutes – a fairly slow rate. During the preparation, the 305th Field Artillery fired a thousand gas rounds into an enemy strong point, while corps guns flooded suspected enemy artillery positions with gas. Throughout the preparation and the attack, the 304th Field Artillery was placed "under orders" of the infantry brigade commander, but it was to take part in the prepared fire plan unless it received specific missions directly from the infantry. McCloskey retained command of the other two regiments as well as the twenty-four additional 75s given to the division for the attack. The firing schedule was completely prearranged for the first phase of the attack, which was expected to last 1 hour. But, after the infantry took Champigneulle, it was to signal the artillery that the fire for the next phase was to start. As for the infantry weapons, Alexander directed his officers to "insure full use" of 37mm guns and Stokes mortars during the attack, and a machine-gun barrage was incorporated into the fire plan.[54]

Although not as comprehensive and powerful as the plan formulated by Summerall for the attack of his divisions in the V Corps, this plan represented some improvement over previous division plans. However, its effort to employ a wide lateral flanking maneuver in the initial phases was complicated, necessitating excellent coordination with its neighboring division on the right and close liaison between the infantry and the artillery between phases. As it happened, mistakes in the former area prevented the division from ever completing the first phase of the attack. Apparently, no senior officer assured that the advance of the division's

Brigade, Field Artillery, September 26th, 1918, to November 11th, 1918," Folder 33.0, Box 29, 77th Division Historical File, RG 120, NA.

53 Although Alexander claimed he secured approval from the commander of the 80th Division, neither he nor his staff ensured that the two advances were suitably coordinated at the small-unit level. Whereas Alexander wrote that he developed this plan of maneuver and that Dickman merely approved it, Dickman later claimed that the plan of attack "was given" to the division commander. It might be the only time in recorded history when two commanders claimed credit for the same failed attack. HQ 77th Division, Field Orders No. 59, 25 October 1918, Folder 32.1, Box 5, 77th Division Historical File, RG 120, NA; HQ American First Army, Memorandum for Chief of Staff, Subject: Investigation of Action of 77th Division on November 1, 1918, 12 November 1918, Folder 66.0, Box 14, 77th Division Historical File, RG 120, NA.

54 HQ 77th Division, Field Orders No. 59, 25 October 1918, Folder 32.1, Box 5, 77th Division Historical File, RG 120, NA.

right flank was coordinated with that of the left of the 80th Division – a terrible failure in an attack in which the right flank was to maneuver through the area of the neighboring division. Just before the attack, the respective platoon and company commanders discovered a time differential of 12 minutes between the advances of the two divisions' adjacent units. Even this small time difference was sufficient to cause the troops on the right flank of the 77th to miss their barrage. When they attacked, they met a wall of machine guns and the attack broke down. Throughout the day, these troops eventually worked their way forward about 500 meters, but they never made their all-important flank attack from the east. The advance of the rest of the division, dependent on this maneuver, never progressed sufficiently either.[55]

As in the Argonne, the caution of the junior officers and men in pressing their attacks also contributed to the lackluster advance of the 77th Division. On the afternoon of 1 November, even Marshall, far away in the First Army HQ, noted that reports from the I Corps front brought word of "no further advance, little firing, and few casualties."[56] Other reports confirmed his insinuation. The 80th Division, stopped by the same German positions that held up the 77th, managed to regroup and reattack later in the day, effectively reducing the enemy strong points holding up the advance. While the officers and men of the Liberty Division actually did a fair job of fighting that day, arranging for special fire from machine guns, 37mm guns, Stokes mortars, and the field artillery, they simply did little advancing. No records show how many enemy were killed or wounded by the fire of the division that day, but the 77th Division suffered fewer than 250 casualties during the entire day's effort.[57]

After Alexander fired Smedberg for supposedly not ensuring that the attack was carried out as ordered, he directed that the offensive be continued the next morning. The artillery support was similar to that of the first attack, with the important addition of a heavy bombardment of the enemy positions throughout the night.[58] Because the 80th Division was actually ahead of the 77th, the attacking infantry had a much easier time

---

[55] HQ, American First Army, Memorandum for Chief of Staff, Subject: Investigation of Action of 77th Division on November 1, 1918, 12 November 1918, Folder 66.0, Box 14, 77th Division Historical File, RG 120, NA.

[56] Marshall, *Memoirs*, 184.

[57] The ABMC summary accounts for just 291 total casualties for the division's operations on both 1 and 2 November. Probably most but not all of these were suffered during the first attack. "Operations Report, 305th Infantry, September 26th–November 12/18," Folder 33.6, Box 21, 77th Division Historical File, RG 120, NA.

[58] HQ 77th Division, Field Orders No. 61, 1 November 1918, 2200 hours, Folder 32.1, Box 5, 77th Division Historical File, RG 120, NA.

using the former's sector as a maneuver ground to take the enemy position from the east. This attack was a walkover, and the infantry claimed that the only thing that kept them out of Champigneulle until 0800 was the fire of the American artillery still pounding the village. By 1015, the division had driven forward 4 kilometers and taken Verpel. By the end of the day, the infantry had established a new line 9 kilometers away from the jump-off.

Alexander claimed this success vindicated his original maneuver-based plan to outflank the German lines from the east:

... the maneuver, identical in principle with that ordered for the 1st, had proven brilliantly successful. The enemy's line was broken and his troops driven in rout before us. It is not unreasonable to believe that the same result would have followed on the 1st and with equal promptness had the orders for that day been carried out with like intelligence and vigor.[59]

Actually, the success of the 77th on 2 November was a result of the excellent flanking position gained by the 80th Division on the 1st, which in turn was a direct result of the brilliant success achieved by Summerall's V Corps. That corps had driven such a salient into the enemy lines on the first day that the Germans in front of the 77th Division withdrew all but a thin rear guard that night.

Alexander was only slightly more correct when he claimed that, from 2 November on, "the pursuit of the fleeing enemy was consequently as rapid as human endurance could compass ... whatever the difficulties, fortified positions or none, the immediate and pressing demand upon us was for vigorous pursuit, unrelenting and remorseless."[60] Although the division did make a relatively rapid advance to the Meuse River over the next few days, the junior officers and men in the vanguard of the advance did not carry out a campaign consistent with GHQ's idealistic view of open warfare – a recklessly aggressive drive of a self-reliant infantry.

According to both the unit histories and the operations reports, the 77th Division's officers below Alexander had learned to meet every instance of any enemy resistance by halting the advance and employing sufficient firepower to blast out the defenders. As with the fighting in the Argonne, the statistics confirm this assessment. The fact that the division suffered fewer than six hundred total casualties over the next ten days

[59] Alexander, *Memories*, 276.
[60] Ibid., 277.

while capturing just eighty-nine prisoners (most of whom were stragglers and wounded) suggests that the 77th Division's pursuit was almost as cautious and reliant on firepower as it could have been.[61]

An attack of the 306th Infantry on the morning of 3 November demonstrated the extent of the adaptation and innovation that characterized this final operation. After an advance of just 4 kilometers, the 306th Infantry stopped in front of a hastily organized enemy line near the village of St. Pierremont. The regiment had netted just sixteen prisoners that day and suffered only three casualties, yet the leading troops made no effort to close with and destroy the enemy rear guard until suitable firepower had caught up. Later that day, a number of light guns moved into position and, while sections of machine-gunners fired their own barrages, the artillerymen sent nearly a thousand rounds into the enemy positions near St. Pierremont, forcing the rear guards to fall back.[62]

The fact that these guns were able to provide such support within a reasonable period was itself a result of important changes made in the artillery brigade. The preceding day, McCloskey had reorganized the entire artillery brigade to ensure that the infantry had at least some fire support during the pursuit phase. Because each of his artillery regiments was so short of horses, McCloskey ordered each regiment to form one fully mobile "provisional battalion" – with all the horses and men necessary to keep a battalion of guns and sufficient ammunition within range of the infantry. By 3 November, this ingenious gamble had paid off, and the infantry received the support they needed to make cautious firepower-based advances even in a more fluid open-warfare environment.[63]

---

[61] The 77th Division suffered fewer than nine hundred casualties from 1 to 11 November, with the majority of them slightly wounded, and it captured just eighty-nine German soldiers and thirty-six guns. For comparison, the 80th Division, on its immediate right, suffered more than twelve hundred casualties, even though it was relieved on 5 November. The two divisions in the V Corps, the 2nd and 89th, suffered 3,282 and 3,864 casualties, respectively, during their drives to the Meuse. The 2nd Division also captured 1,700 Germans troops and 105 guns.

[62] C.G., 153rd Infantry Brigade, to C.G., 77th Division, Subject: Report of Operations 26 September, 1918, to 8th November, 1918, 19 November 1918, Folder 33.6, Box 15, 77th Division Historical File, RG 120, NA; "Report of Operations of the 152nd Brigade, Field Artillery, September 26th, 1918, to November 11th, 1918," and HQ 152nd F.A. Brigade, Memorandum, 10 November 1918, both in Folder 33.0, Box 29, 77th Division Historical File, RG 120, NA.

[63] "Report of Operations of the 152nd Brigade, Field Artillery, September 26th, 1918, to November 11th, 1918," and HQ 152nd Field Artillery Brigade, Memorandum, 10 November 1918, both in Folder 33.0, Box 29, 77th Division Historical File, RG 120, NA.

That night, the 307th Infantry of the 154th Brigade took over the front line. Attacking at daylight, the troops quickly stopped after gains of just 1 or 2 kilometers when they discovered new enemy positions near the village of Ouches. Again, the artillery was massed and more than a thousand rounds were fired during the day. On the evening of 4 November, the division staff actually drew up a detailed plan of attack for early the next morning to ensure that the enemy rear guard to their front would be overwhelmed. At this point, Alexander put a regiment of the 153rd Brigade back in line and even ordered that all the divisional artillery be massed on its front from H minus 30 minutes until 1 hour after the attack. At that time, half the guns reverted to the control of the 154th Brigade, which could call on them as needed. The 155s also were ordered to pound an enemy strong point near a farm for a full hour during the attack. For Alexander, this represented a different approach.[64]

After starting on time, the 153rd Brigade's advance continued without difficulty on the right for 6 kilometers before it ran into enemy fire near the town of La Besace. Quickly the advance was stopped and machine guns were set up to neutralize the enemy fire with a barrage. On the left, the advance drove forward a few kilometers before meeting enemy fire. The commander of the 154th Brigade ordered the infantry to stop while the artillery pounded the enemy strong points for 15 minutes, drove them off, and allowed the infantry to continue. The operations report of the 307th Infantry succinctly described this action, "Our artillery ceased. The Regiment pressed forward."[65] It was a fitting description for the entire drive after 1 November.

On the morning of 6 November, the advance continued without difficulty, and the 153rd Brigade drove almost unhindered to the Meuse River. On the left, the 154th Brigade ran into enemy fire on two occasions that day, first near Malmaison Farm and later near Raucort. In both cases, the advances were stopped, artillery and machine guns were brought up, and the enemy was blasted out. General Price's operations report makes it clear that in both of these cases, the decision to halt and wait for greater fire support was a conscious one, even though it took

[64] HQ 77th Division, Field Orders No. 63, 4 November 1918, Folder 32.1, Box 5, 77th Division Historical File, RG 120, NA.
[65] C.G., 153rd Infantry Brigade, to C.G., 77th Division, Subject: Report of Operations 26 September, 1918, to 8th November, 1918, 19 November 1918, Folder 33.6, Box 15, 77th Division Historical File, RG 120, NA; "Report of Operations of the 307th Infantry from September 26th 1918 to November 8th 1918," Folder 33.6, Box 26, 77th Division Historical File, RG 120, NA.

"considerable time" to arrange the artillery fire. Both the regimental and brigade commanders agreed that the enemy positions, hastily organized as they were, would only be taken "immediately following artillery fire."[66] By the end of the day, units from both brigades had driven the German rear guards across the Meuse, and the division's fighting was practically over. Although Alexander ordered that bridges be put up across the river that "will be crossed and a foot-hold gained on the north bank," no such attack was ever pressed forward.[67] As in the Argonne and in the recent drive toward the river, the junior officers and men apparently assessed the strength of the German positions opposing them and decided to wait for sufficient fire support.[68]

Conclusions

The experiences of the 77th Division present a detailed picture of an important characteristic of the AEF as a whole. The beliefs and attitudes of the senior leaders, especially regarding combat doctrine, were not necessarily as important as the style of warmaking developed by the more junior officers and men. Although the AEF leadership could not have stressed more the importance of training for open warfare, the 77th Division trained almost exclusively for trench fighting. Although official AEF doctrine was based supposedly on the power of the rifle, assisted where absolutely necessary by "the auxiliaries" (e.g., artillery, machine guns, mortars), the officers and men of the 77th based their attacks on the auxiliary weapons and apparently resorted to the rifle only when necessary. Finally, despite the bellicose words of the 77th's senior leaders and their repetitive emphasis on the importance of aggressiveness in the attack, the men of the 77th rather quickly learned to discard this rhetoric and fight with a level of caution that suited their assessments of the resistance ahead of them and of the resources available to them.

During the brutal days along the Vesle and Aisne Rivers, whatever recklessness and aggressiveness this division had appears to have been

---

[66] C.G., 154th Infantry Brigade, to C.G., 77th Division, Subject: "Report of Operations," 15 November 1918, Folder 33.6, Box 17, 77th Division Historical File, RG 120, NA; *History of the 77th Division*, 100.

[67] HQ 77th Division, Field Orders No. 65, 6 November, 2200 hours, Folder 32.1, Box 5, 77th Division Historical File, RG 120, NA.

[68] Apparently, Liggett agreed with the troops and he directed Alexander to countermand any order sending small groups of men, unsupported, across the river. Alexander, *Memories*, 293.

shot out of them. The men may have learned the hard way, but they did learn. Despite Alexander's impractical pronouncements and disruptive command philosophy, from then on, both in the Argonne and beyond it, the officers and men of the 77th Division tried to maximize firepower and make cautious advances. Perhaps it became too cautious in the eyes of some AEF leaders. Yet, it might be more fair to say that this most modern and metropolitan of all American divisions, which nonetheless suffered 25 percent more casualties than any other National Army division, made the kind of adjustments to its style of fighting that many military officers might expect a unit to make during and after the next world war. Although Alexander proudly claimed to have learned very little, the officers and men seem to have learned a great deal. And, in the end, it was the combat doctrine that they demonstrated, more than the one the leaders promulgated, that had the greater impact on the American way of war during the United States' first great crusade abroad.

10

Conclusions

After the armistice of 11 November 1918, all American officers proudly agreed that the AEF had played a crucial role in winning the war. Developing from a small, poorly organized, inadequately equipped, and intellectually unprepared force, the U.S. Army had sent two million men to Europe, organized and equipped itself for modern combat, and bravely delivered powerful attacks against a much more experienced enemy. American officers were convinced that the AEF had provided the margin of victory for the Allied armies. There was less agreement on the role that U.S. Army doctrine had played in bringing about that victory. Although GHQ attempted to develop and disseminate doctrine, including some important tactical reforms, the most significant adaptation occurred within the individual combat divisions.[1]

---

[1] Dennis Vetock shows that the AEF developed the U.S. Army's "first wartime system of gathering, evaluating, and applying ongoing experience." Vetock notes that this process was officially managed by GHQ, where "modern U.S. Army lesson learning emerged in the American Expeditionary Forces." The most significant way GHQ attempted to learn lessons was through its use of inspectors that monitored operations within the divisions. GHQ gathered reports from these inspectors – Vetock calls them "doctrinal commissars" – and on four occasions in the summer and fall of 1918 (after the Aisne-Marne Offensive, the St. Mihiel Offensive, and the first and last phases of the Meuse-Argonne Offensive) issued short publications entitled, "Notes on Recent Operations." Whether GHQ considered the operations reports of battalion, regimental, brigade, or division commanders is unknown. GHQ also issued two "Combat Instructions" pamphlets. The first, in June 1918, was just three paragraphs long and dealt only with defending trench positions. The second, Pershing's *Combat Instructions* of September 1918, had fifty-five thousand copies printed, almost as many as all the "Notes" pamphlets combined. Dennis J. Vetock, *Lessons Learned: A History of US Army Lesson Learning* (Carlisle Barracks, Penn.: U.S. Army Military History Institute, 1988), 37, 48.

The Role of Pershing and GHQ

Despite the increasing doctrinal and operational independence of the AEF combat divisions, Pershing and GHQ were far from irrelevant – a charge sometimes leveled at some senior commanders in the French and British armies. Yet, few studies of the AEF, whether positive or negative accounts, have shown the nature of GHQ's relevance to American combat on the Western Front, or the limits of that significance. First, GHQ initially established an inadequate doctrine and then modified that doctrine more slowly and less completely than officers in the combat divisions. This initial acceptance of prewar American doctrine, and GHQ's continuous stress of the importance of that doctrine, meant that combat officers who accepted the instruction often employed faulty tactics during inadequately supported attacks based on poorly prepared attack plans.[2] Second, in accordance with the fundamental tenets of AEF doctrine, the attack plans for both the St. Mihiel and the Meuse-Argonne Offensives were extraordinarily ambitious. Especially in the latter campaign, this led to serious problems for the inexperienced divisions ordered to make the initial attacks. Third, GHQ did not withhold AEF units from combat until satisfied that they were adequately trained, a significant failure under any circumstances, but particularly egregious considering the admittedly high level of expertise that was essential to success with the most advanced open-warfare tactics. And, despite all the talk of open-warfare methods in the AEF, the official American ideas for open warfare compared unfavorably to those demonstrated at times by the best Allied and German units. The AEF GHQ had its successes during the war, but the failures placed particular burdens on the American divisions. Yet, some divisions overcame these challenges and became excellent combat units, while others seem to have been well on their way.

Doctrinal and Operational Adaptation in AEF Divisions

Each of the four divisions in this study, like all those in the AEF, had a unique training program, varied experiences in the line and in battle, and unit commanders that responded differently to the challenges of the Western Front (see Map 26). However, they shared some important

---

[2] In addition to the poor tactics and insufficient emphasis on firepower shown at Belleau Wood, Soissons, and the Vesle, countless other instances occurred. For some of these, see Infantry School, U.S. Army, *Infantry in Battle* (Washington, D.C.: The Infantry School Press, 1934), 297, 314–19.

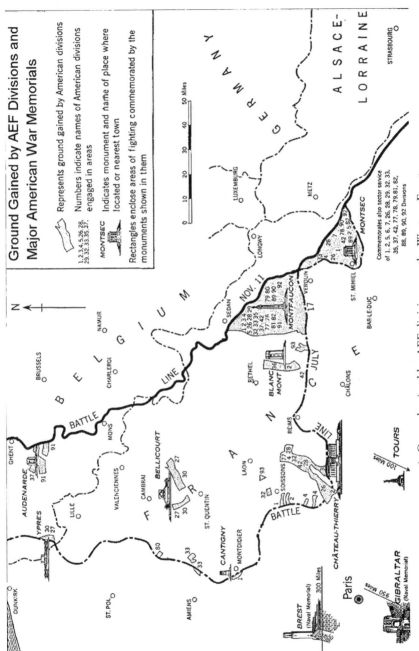

Ground Gained by AEF Divisions and Major American War Memorials

Represents ground gained by American divisions

Numbers indicate names of American divisions engaged in areas

MONTSEC — Indicates monument and name of place where located or nearest town

Rectangles enclose areas of fighting commemorated by the monuments shown in them

MAP 26: Ground gained by AEF divisions on the Western Front.

similarities, especially the recognition of the need for improved infantry tactics, communications during battle, and a reliance on firepower.

In the 1st Division, Pershing's favorite, doctrinal development began under Robert Bullard and was continued by Charles Summerall. As early as the battle of Cantigny on 28 May, the division demonstrated that it had the ability to execute limited set-piece attacks. Near Soissons, it showed just as clearly the limits of its ability to wage open warfare. By the end of that battle, and increasingly during the St. Mihiel and Meuse-Argonne Offensives, the division based its attacks more on firepower than on manpower and on the latest trench-warfare tactics rather than GHQ's open-warfare ideal.

The 2nd Division changed the way it fought in much the same way. Efforts to employ open-warfare tactics and techniques at Belleau Wood led to horrific casualties and small gains. But, by the end of June, the division had learned a number of lessons. Its assault of Vaux was as well planned and executed as the 1st Division attack on Cantigny, and it showed an understanding of trench-warfare tactics that impressed even experienced French observers.[3] Like the 1st Division, the 2nd struggled to employ open-warfare methods during the Aisne-Marne Offensive in July, and it paid the price in casualties. Then, under John Lejeune's leadership, the 2nd Division made distinct efforts to fight its remaining battles according to the formula used so successfully at Vaux – meticulously planned set-piece attacks based on massive firepower to advance relatively short distances and seize limited objectives. Although few divisional officers explicitly admitted as much, these attacks represented a rejection of the official AEF doctrine that stressed a minimum of operational planning, a reliance on "riflepower," and the benefit of unlimited objectives. But, such attacks were similar to the "bite-and-hold" attacks that some British and French commanders used with increasing success in 1917–1918.

The experiences of the 26th Division, after one strips away the layers of controversy surrounding Clarence Edwards and the Regular-Guard hostility, tell a similar story of doctrinal and operational adaptation. Although the Yankee Division struggled in its early operations, its officers and men quickly discarded their initial recklessness while attacking. This led to

[3] According to Robert Bullard, General Degoutte told French Premier Georges Clemenceau that the 2nd Division's preparations for the Vaux attack were better than the French work for the Malmaison attack, which was a successful, highly regarded French attack in October 1917. Robert L. Bullard, *Fighting Generals: Illustrated Biographical Sketches of Seven Major Generals in World War I* (Ann Arbor: J. W. Edwards, 1944), 188.

slower advances but it saved lives. The reports of the unit commanders in the 26th confirm that they rapidly gained an appreciation for the possibilities and challenges of the Great War battlefield. They, and the men they led, instituted most of the same doctrinal developments as the 1st and 2nd Divisions. If the 26th failed to achieve the same level of operational expertise, that was more the result of differences in training, discipline, leadership, and treatment from senior AEF commanders and staff officers at the corps, army, and GHQ levels.

The 77th Division's wartime experience differed significantly from the 1st, 2nd, and 26th Divisions in many ways, but it too made important doctrinal and operational improvements in its relatively short period of combat. Whereas the latter three divisions did almost all of their training in France, the 77th completed most of its training in the United States. But, the nature of that training, heavily focused on fighting in and around trenches, as well as the strong influence of Allied instructors, was very similar to the others. The 77th struggled operationally and suffered heavily in its first battles in the Vesle valley, as other divisions did in their first battles. Like the men of the 26th Division, those in the 77th became more cautious and deliberate in their attacks. Perhaps the most significant difference between the 77th Division and the others in this study was the influence of the commanding officer. Whereas commanders such as Bullard, Summerall, Lejeune, and Edwards adjusted prewar doctrine and tactics to match the Great War battlefield and the abilities of their units, Robert Alexander remained proudly committed to his prewar ideas. Although Alexander's doctrinal traditionalism may have limited and restricted adaptation and development in the 77th Division, it did not stop it. More junior commanders, from brigades to companies, made the changes at their levels, and they made many of the same improvements as the best AEF divisions.

Although the wartime experiences of these four divisions were different, detailed examination of the training, operations, and after-action reports shows that many of the combat officers learned similar lessons and made comparable adjustments to the way they fought. Commanders at various levels opened up infantry attack formations and made them more flexible; they stressed the importance of communication up and down the chain of command, as well as with neighboring units, during battle; they increasingly appreciated the benefits of comprehensive attack plans designed to take and hold relatively small portions of enemy defensive positions (and eliminate the defending troops within those limited areas); and, perhaps most important, they began to see firepower as the *sine qua non* of battlefield success. In all of these ways, combat officers moved far beyond and sometimes directly in opposition to official AEF doctrine, but the results of these developments comprise a much more accurate picture of the way the AEF fought than any study that focuses on Pershing, GHQ, or single battles.

This study cannot positively assert that the lessons learned by these four divisions, each among the most active and experienced in the AEF, were apprehended by officers in all other divisions. Certainly, few other AEF divisions, if any, achieved the level of operational capability demonstrated by the 1st and 2nd Divisions from September to November 1918. But, some evidence suggests that most AEF units were learning many of the doctrinal lessons demonstrated by the 1st, 2nd, 26th, and 77th Divisions. One reason for this was the dispersion of experienced officers from these divisions into positions of authority in others: Beaumont Buck left the 1st to command the 3rd Division, and he was soon replaced at the 3rd by Preston Brown, formerly the 2nd Division's chief of staff; John Hines left the 1st to command the 4th, and then took his ideas with him to command the III Corps in October 1918; George Duncan, also from the 1st, commanded both the 77th and 82nd Divisions; Hanson Ely, who led a regiment in the 1st and a brigade in the 2nd, commanded the 5th Division for the last three weeks of the war.[4]

Other more direct evidence further suggests that many AEF divisions experienced significant doctrinal and operational development. In a post-war lecture, the commander of the 29th Division, Major General Charles G. Morton, stressed that both he and the officers in his combat units discarded old ideas for new ones. He claimed that before any attack, "preparation fire was habitually used on enemy strong points and the barrage preceded the troops." He stressed the importance of automatic weapons in the attack, asserting that "this war has disposed of the old theory that machine guns have their greatest use in defense.... their greatest use is in the offensive.... One principle adopted early in the game was that machine gun fire to have full effect must be of great volume, and ammunition was expended without stint." He then admitted that at least one of his brigade commanders openly deprecated "the value of the ordinary rifle" and that his subordinate commanders made "no mention" of the use of the bayonet in their operations.[5]

[4] ABMC, *American Armies*, 499–500.
[5] Charles G. Morton, "Lecture Delivered by Commanding General, 29th Division," 10 February 1919, Box 30, Edwards Papers, MHS.

The 32nd Division, commanded by Major General William G. Haan, earned a reputation as a powerful combat unit that blasted its way forward from one limited objective to another with massive firepower. In his postwar book, *Fighting Generals*, Robert Bullard told of Haan's heavy use of Allied instructors to train his division to make short trench-to-trench attacks. Bullard notes that in one of the division's first battles, Haan employed an elaborate "triple barrage" to neutralize enemy machine guns, and he summed up Haan's style of fighting by stating that his battles "were carried through plainly upon well-thought-out plans that won confidence and fulfillment by his subordinates."[6] The U.S. Army's official tactical study manual during the postwar period, *Infantry in Battle*, cites the 32nd Division's heavy use of machine guns and artillery in the Meuse-Argonne. Similar development occurred in other AEF divisions.[7]

Two of the four divisions examined in this work, the 1st and the 2nd, achieved undeniably superior combat records. Although neither the 26th nor 77th Divisions had as much operational success, they too adapted their methods and in certain respects exceeded reasonable expectations. Furthermore, by some accounts, the 42nd, 32nd, 3rd, 28th, 82nd, and 89th Divisions earned better operational reputations than the 26th and 77th Divisions, suggesting that they also made substantial adjustments to their doctrine and methods.[8]

Innovation in the AEF: Combat Divisions and GHQ

This study suggests a number of important points that may apply more generally to other military forces, at other times and places. First, it exposes the value and the limitations of preliminary training. Although American training in the United States and France was far from a waste of time and effort, it was nonetheless inadequate in quality and duration. Although many American recruits received about as much individual training as some Allied replacements in 1917–1918, the latter completed their training and underwent their initiation into battle in combat units composed of veterans with many months or even years of operational

---

[6] Bullard, *Fighting Generals*, 241, 243.
[7] Officers credited the 5th, 28th, and 90th Divisions for their extensive use of machine-gun barrages for infantry attacks in Meuse-Argonne. *Infantry in Battle*, 58, 306–10.
[8] See especially Paul Braim's divisional ratings, *Test of Battle*, 147–9; also Trask, *Coalition Warmaking*, 176; and James J. Cooke, *The Rainbow Division in the Great War, 1917–1919* (Westport, Conn.: Praeger, 1994), 239.

experience on the Western Front.[9] In the AEF, until the final few weeks of the war, green American troops joined new units filled with officers and men who were only slightly more experienced in modern warfare. Some evidence indicates a few AEF units emerged from their initial training reasonably capable of executing limited trench-warfare attacks – considered by some officers to be the simplest form of warfare. But, many AEF divisions were not even prepared for those kinds of operations when GHQ released them for unrestricted front-line duty. Those divisions especially, and even the best trained ones to some extent, learned their difficult tasks more by fighting than by training. AEF training was important; the two AEF divisions that seem to have trained the most and hardest – the 1st and the 2nd – became the most proficient. But, organized training in the AEF was generally insufficient, and it certainly did not prepare American divisions to fight according to the official AEF doctrine. Rather, it presented a somewhat confused amalgam of European trench-warfare methods and traditional prewar U.S. Army practices. And, the practical combat training – which focused on attacking and defending – was almost completely based on the former. American divisions ultimately learned how to fight by fighting.

Second, this examination indicates not only that many American divisions experienced significant doctrinal adjustment and operational improvement during the war but also that the most practical and extensive learning in the AEF occurred from the bottom up – at least with respect to divisions, corps, armies, and GHQ. As AEF units fought, they gained an appreciation for the limited, set-piece attacks associated with trench warfare, and they proved increasingly capable of executing such attacks. Few showed any particular aptitude for open warfare and most experienced divisions showed a diminishing taste for it. But, these developments occurred almost exclusively within the combat divisions and only at the corps, army, and GHQ levels as individual officers moved from one level to the other. GHQ recognized that it had the important

---

[9] For example, new recruits to the British Army in 1917–1918, including the various Dominion forces, entered a standardized twelve-week course for basic individual training in individual and platoon drill, firing rifles and Lewis guns, shooting and throwing grenades, bayonet fighting, use of gas masks, and wiring defensive positions. During the fall of 1918, when casualty rates in the BEF far outstripped the number of replacements graduating from the twelve-week courses, the training was reduced first to ten, then to nine weeks. However, in all cases, after this initial training, British and Canadian soldiers were sent into experienced combat units to conduct additional small-unit training. I thank historians Tim Travers and David Campbell for this information on training in the British and Canadian forces.

role of disseminating doctrine, tactical reforms, and lessons-learned, and it attempted to perform that mission. But, in practice, doctrinal adjustment was *not* a top-down process. Although GHQ might have been more successful than the senior headquarters staff in any previous American war at disseminating doctrinal information and tactical advice, its commitment to pass along information and instructions that conformed to its theoretical ideal, and in opposition to the lessons learned *within* the combat divisions, seems to have limited its effectiveness. Apparently, only the intimate understanding of the battlefield as experienced by officers within the battalions, regiments, brigades, and divisions seems to have encouraged acceptance of more practical methods. In many cases, more senior commanders and staff failed to acknowledge the significance of the divisional changes. They sought to be teachers before they themselves had learned the crucial lessons of the battlefields of 1917–1918.

This hints at the third lesson – the importance of individual commanders. Some division commanders, such as Bullard, Summerall, and Lejeune, were quick to understand the challenges of the Western Front and successful in transforming their divisions and their operational methods to meet those demands. But, not all divisional officers learned the same lessons. James Harbord seems to have been a slow learner in this regard, although he led a brigade and a division in combat. Robert Alexander, the 77th Division commander, proved particularly inflexible throughout many weeks of combat, and he may have finished the war more committed to prewar doctrine than some corps commanders, such as Hunter Liggett. Yet, even in the 77th Division, the commanders of the brigades, regiments, battalions, companies, and platoons made important adjustments at their levels and had a dramatic influence on the pace and nature of the fighting in their units.

Fourth, this study shows the limits of established doctrine in the fast-paced changes of modern warfare. Doctrine is important, but it must evolve to remain applicable. The old interpretation of the Great War that viewed the bloody stalemate of the Western Front as a result of almost complete doctrinal and tactical stasis is a great simplification.[10] Even the traditionally minded AEF GHQ made numerous doctrinal and tactical changes, but those adjustments were all minor modifications of the existing doctrine. In his study of the intellectual milieu of the British Army before and during the Great War, Tim Travers has employed Thomas

---

[10] See Alan Clark, *The Donkeys* (London: Hutchinson, 1961); and Norman F. Dixon, *On the Psychology of Military Incompetence* (Aylesbury: Futura, 1979).

Kuhn's theory of the paradigm – a controlling set of ideas – to explain why the BEF leadership struggled for so long to make the kinds of dramatic changes seemingly demanded by the conditions of the Western Front.[11] Kuhn contended that problem solving occurs within a given paradigm until a problem cannot be solved and then, other individuals, often younger or newer to the field, will pragmatically shift to a new set of ideas to solve the problem.[12] As in the BEF, many senior American officers sought answers from within the existing paradigm – as exemplified by the prewar view of battle. Summerall and Lejeune pushed the American doctrinal paradigm to and perhaps beyond the limit; their views on firepower employment and set-piece attacks were heretical by prewar standards. Officers in the emerging armored and airpower weapon systems, such as Billy Mitchell and George S. Patton, were less successful in effecting a substantive change in official American combat doctrine during the war. Unwilling or unable to work outside of the existing paradigm, many senior American officers treated doctrine like dogma and failed to understand that the true test of doctrine was the reality of battle and that doctrine had to be refined – even radically altered if necessary – to be useful. This may be taken as an almost universally applicable principle when an army must enter the uncertainty of battle against an innovative foe with approximately equivalent numbers and technologies.[13]

Epilogue: The AEF Legacy and U.S. Army Doctrine

When the war ended, a serious debate began over the future of U.S. Army doctrine. Many veteran combat commanders were convinced that the best way to take objectives and keep casualties to a minimum was to overwhelm the enemy with firepower. Others, especially those who served on staffs, in positions of high command, or in units that saw very little combat, found little to upset their faith in American prewar doctrine. They retained the traditional views that placed man over machine, infantry over artillery, and maneuver over firepower.

In the immediate aftermath of the war, numerous venues existed for officers to voice their opinions of the war's crucial lessons. Many sat on

---

[11] Travers, *Killing Ground*, xix.

[12] See Thomas Kuhn, *The Structure of Scientific Revolutions*, second ed. (Chicago: University of Chicago Press, 1970).

[13] Historian Edgar F. Raines, Jr., makes this same point in his book, *Eyes of Artillery: The Origins of Modern U.S. Army Aviation in World War II* (Washington, D.C.: Center of Military History, 2000), 326.

special boards that the AEF convened to examine the war and recommend appropriate changes in the areas of material, organization, and doctrine. Dozens of articles flooded the professional journals as officers of all ranks sought to share their experiences and convictions with others. Eventually, a small group of officers was directed to write a completely new edition of the *Field Service Regulations* so that the Army's official doctrine could reflect the lessons learned on the Western Front.

The most significant military committee to meet in Europe after the war was the AEF Superior Board on Organization and Tactics. Officially charged with examining "the lessons to be learned from the present war in so far as they affect tactics and organization," the board had the difficult task of achieving some level of consensus between those who still adhered to the traditional human-centered doctrine and the new firepower clique that viewed the massive employment of modern weaponry as more crucial to success than either infantry training or morale. The board itself, composed of one major general from each of the three main combat branches (i.e., infantry, cavalry, and artillery), two brigadier generals from army and corps level staffs, and one colonel each from the engineer and signal corps, had seen, with one exception, little of the struggles in the front lines.[14] They all would have been well aware of the institutional allegiance, especially of Pershing and his closest officers, to the continued relevance of the prewar regulations and doctrine. Yet, they also had trouble denying the reality of the modern battlefield.

In mid-1920, the Superior Board produced a lengthy report that attempted to maintain the Army's focus on infantry as the most important arm while also admitting the need for massive use of firepower. In some ways, the report was contradictory, claiming both that "infantry must be self-reliant" and that to be successful, a "great mass of [artillery] guns is used to smother [the enemy's] front line troops and neutralize his artillery."[15] The infantry was instructed to maximize "the use of

[14] The board members were Major General Joseph T. Dickman, a cavalryman who commanded a division and corps during the war; Major General John L. Hines, an infantry officer who commanded a regiment, brigade, division, and corps; Major General William Lassiter, an artilleryman who finished the war as Chief of Artillery for the Second Army; Brigadier General Hugh A. Drum, the chief of staff for the First Army; Brigadier General Wilson B. Burtt, the chief of staff for the V Corps (commanded by Charles Summerall for the final four weeks of the war); Colonel George R. Spaulding, an engineer; and Colonel Parker Hitt, who represented the Signal Corps. See U. S. Army, American Expeditionary Forces, Superior Board on Organization and Tactics, *Report of the Superior Board* [1920], U.S. Army Military History Institute, Carlisle Barracks, Penn.

[15] *Report of the Superior Board*, 20, 38.

automatic and auxiliary weapons" but warned against relying too much on "the auxiliary arm and not enough on the means within the infantry itself." The board evidently worked off two different foundational beliefs, one rooted in the traditional, prewar American doctrine and the other in the AEF's wartime experiences. Board members sought to preserve the Army's historical understanding that "the infantry remains the predominant and basic arm," but the board also realized that the battlefield had changed and that new weapons like the machine gun, rapid-fire artillery, gas, airplanes, and tanks demanded modifications to prewar fighting concepts. Somehow, the Army had to make use of the new weapons technologies to overcome the defensive challenges while preserving the infantry as the dominant and most decisive arm.

The Superior Board's answer was to move beyond the myopic focus on the rifle-and-bayonet brandishing infantryman and give the infantry direct control of every new weapon that it could possibly employ. Infantry units were to be given more automatic rifles and machine guns, twice the number of 37mm guns, their own light howitzers, and, of course, tanks. Whereas before the war, the machine gun was "an emergency weapon" with limited utility, the members of the Superior Board could no longer "conceive of a situation" that would not require it. They asserted that the modern infantry battalion could not even be considered "a complete unit" without machine guns.[16] Although the magazine rifle would remain the standard weapon for most infantrymen, the postwar infantry units would integrate firepower to an unprecedented degree. In doing so, the board lodged its disapproval with those specialists who sought to form elite machine-gun and tank corps and with artillerymen who thought artillery pieces were better controlled and employed solely by artillerymen. In the end, the Superior Board had produced a document that preserved the role and position of the infantry while incorporating the use of more firepower on the modern battlefield.

When Pershing forwarded the Superior Board's report to the Secretary of War, he included his own comments on the board's findings, and they were highly critical. Pershing claimed that "the work of this Board was undertaken so soon after the close of hostilities that the members were unduly influenced by the special situation which existed...in the World War. Thus...the recommendations...are based upon the necessities of *stabilized warfare* in Western Europe rather than upon the requirements of warfare of the character and in the theater upon which we are

[16] *Report of the Superior Board*, 21–3, 26–7.

most likely to be engaged" [emphasis added].[17] Specifically, he took issue
with the board's advocacy of the large AEF division. Pershing asserted
that "mobility" was "one of the first requisites of organization" and in
a remarkable conclusion, he stated that the U.S. Army was "most likely to
operate on the American Continent and mobility is especially necessary
under all probable conditions of warfare in this theater." Pershing wanted
a division of about seventeen thousand men, "rigidly" cutting it so as to
include "only those units which are *always* essential to enable it to fight
and live under the most probable conditions."[18] It is not surprising that
Pershing concluded that "the first cut must be made in auxiliaries, and
within the limits of strength allowed the division, the infantry must be kept
at the greatest number practicable." He insisted that the current organization contained an "absurdly unnecessary number of auxiliaries in the
division" for any probable campaign in North America, such as another
expedition in Mexico. Admitting that such cuts would not reduce the division enough to allow for adequate operational maneuver, he advocated a
triangle structure based on three infantry regiments instead of the AEF's
square division.[19] Although he advocated a machine-gun company in each
regiment and small contingents of tanks and airplanes in each division, he
also suggested reducing "the artillery permanently assigned the division
to the lowest possible limits" (he would have eliminated two thirds of the
guns!) and went on to criticize the prevalence of detailed attack plans,
well-defined division attack sectors, and both intermediate and limited
objectives.[20] In many ways, Pershing refuted the style of fighting used
most successfully by the AEF's best divisions.

Both before and after the convening of the Superior Board, the professional journals were publishing articles from American officers that had
widely divergent opinions on the correct lessons of the war. Generally,
these doctrinal articles fell into three categories: those arguing that the
war confirmed the value of the Army's existing, prewar doctrine; those
insisting that the Army needed to understand the inherent value of massive firepower; and a middle group that focused on incorporating as much
firepower into the infantry as possible to keep it as the primary arm, while
admitting that new weapons and technologies had increased the importance of heavy firepower in battle.

[17] John J. Pershing to the Secretary of War, "Wrapper Indorsement, Forwarding Report of
A.E.F. Superior Board on Organization and Tactics," 16 June 1920, p. 1.
[18] The emphasis is in the original. Ibid., 2.
[19] Ibid., 3.
[20] Ibid., 4–5.

The traditional position was best demonstrated by Captain Francis A. Woolfley in his 1922 article, "Queen of Infantry Weapons." Woolfley began by stating,

With the development of the automatic arms (the machine gun and the automatic rifle), the one-pounder accompanying gun (37mm), the light mortar, as well as the rifle and hand grenade, a number of officers and men of the military establishment, to say nothing of the vast majority of the civilian population, consider the rifle and bayonet relegated to a secondary position among the infantry weapons ... this is strengthened by the belief that high Army authorities hold the same opinion. Nothing could be further from the truth. *The rifle and bayonet are still the dominant arms of the Infantry* [emphasis added].

Woolfley went on to cite existing training regulations to remind his readers that "whatever auxiliary methods are employed ... the final method is the physical encounter with *bullet and bayonet*; the human element is the decisive one" [emphasis in original].[21]

Woolfley attempted to prove his point by referring not so much to the lessons of the world war but rather to an Army tradition developed in wars fought decades and centuries before:

The fame of the American rifleman is traditional and historic. The effectiveness of the rifle on the American frontier is well known and the story of the American rifle recalls such types as Daniel Boone, David Crockett, Simon Kenton, and Kit Carson. It is an American tradition that our rifleman does not shoot at random; he picks his man and the direct aim of his rifle speaks certain death.[22]

For Woolfley and those who agreed with him, "Infantry must be mobile ... aggressive ... trained in marksmanship, placing confidence in the fire power of the rifle and in the moral and destructive power of the bayonet. ... The machine gun, the 37mm gun, the light mortar – all auxiliary weapons of the Infantry – are not mobile enough to keep pace with the rifleman." These traditionalists saw no danger from defensive firepower; to them the integration of firepower-based weapons into the infantry was

---

[21] Capt. Francis A. Woolfley, "Queen of Infantry Weapons," *Infantry Journal* 21 (September 1922): 308. I have been unable to determine where and in what capacity Woolfley served during the war.

[22] Woolfley discussed the use of the rifle at "King's Mountain in the War of Revolution," in the War of 1812, and the Mexican War. His only reference to the world war was the claim, of dubious historical accuracy, that "the heroism and deadly aim of our Infantry checked the Germans at Château-Thierry, saved Paris, and turned the battle forever in favor of the Allies." Actually, the machine guns of the 3rd Division, at least as much as its rifles, stopped the Germans at Château-Thierry in early June. And, despite the sporadic fighting between 1 and 5 June, the German soldiers engaged by the 2nd Division at Belleau Wood had ended their offensive by the time the Marines attacked them on 6 June. Ibid., 308–9.

an unnecessary hindrance. They believed that the infantryman "armed with the rifle and bayonet alone" was "a complete fighting machine in himself."[23]

It would be easy to classify these anachronistic words as the nostalgic sentiments of a single, out-of-touch, junior officer, except for the fact that the exact same argument was made by Major General Charles S. Farnsworth, the U.S. Army's Chief of Infantry, just two months later in the same journal.[24] Farnsworth repeated many of the same points, in *exactly* the same words, in a brief article that was meant to quash the growing sentiment that all infantrymen should be given an automatic weapon in place of the rifle and bayonet. Despite the experience of the world war, some officers still wanted to hold on to the old human-focused, prewar doctrine.[25]

On the other side of the spectrum were those officers who wanted the Army to develop a doctrine that accentuated the role and value of fire-power to the absolute maximum, regardless of the impact on the roles of any Army branch or the traditional understanding of American styles of fighting. These officers, many of them artillerymen, believed that the only way to fight on the modern battlefield was to use massive numbers of the most powerful weapons available. They were convinced that the experi-ence of Great War combat proved this approach to be superior to any other.

It is not surprising that Charles Summerall led the way for these unapologetic firepower advocates. Although an artilleryman, Summerall

---

[23] Ibid.

[24] "Notes from the Chief of Infantry," *Infantry Journal* 21 (November 1922): 563. Farnsworth was not a stranger to the Western Front. He commanded the 37th Divi-sion, a Guard division from Ohio, for more than four months in France and led it during its attack in the first phase of the Meuse-Argonne Offensive, as well as in later operations near Ypres as part of the French Sixth Army.

[25] The editorial pages of the *Infantry Journal* often presented this position: "The old thesis of the superiority of the fighting Infantry is thus restated: 'Battle is normally determined by physical encounter with the bayonet and the fear thereof; all other agencies of destruc-tion, such as artillery, machine guns, and aircraft, are auxiliary in their effect, however potent, and serve to make possible the advance of the foot soldier to hand-to-hand encounter.... The War Department is seeking to combat the heresy 'that any material means can ever replace in war the individual soldier who is willing and able to fight.' It ought to have little trouble in disposing of that heresy. The Great War was not won by new inventions – by heavy artillery, mine throwers, improved machine guns, tanks and airplanes, though all of them were of importance – but by the valor of the foot soldiers. It was, as Foch says, a contest of wills, a moral struggle, and victory went to the side which was determined to hold out longer." Editorial Department, *Infantry Journal* 21 (September 1922): 341.

included all types of weapons in the effort to overwhelm the enemy: field
artillery, heavy artillery, and machine guns, as well as the accompanying
artillery, 37mm guns, and light mortars. As he stated most succinctly in a
report on his successful attack of 1 November, "If we are to be econom-
ical with our men, we must be prodigal with guns and ammunition."[26]
For Summerall, this was the supreme lesson of the war. Morale mattered
but it was not enough. The infantrymen, attacking with rifles and bayonets, were important but no longer sufficient. Attacks by unsupported
infantry against even hastily organized enemy positions often resulted in
heavy casualties. Yet, despite the challenges of the modern battlefield,
Summerall was optimistic about the continued power of the offensive in
war. Whereas the conventional view of the First World War, both then and
now, often focuses on the futility of the attack, Summerall insisted, "The
war has ... repeatedly demonstrated that any position, however strong,
can be neutralized and captured, with a sufficiently powerful fire, and that
invariably the lack of sufficient superiority of fire is paid for in losses to
the Infantry and even in failure."[27] Massive use of coordinated firepower,
more than anything else, was the answer to the challenge of successful
offensive on the modern battlefield.

Other officers followed Summerall's lead and they shared his concern
that the Army had not learned the proper tactical and organizational
lessons from the war.[28] Major W. E. Burr insisted that when the Army
changed its tables of organization after the war, it failed to increase the
number of artillery pieces required to adequately support the infantry.
The result was a "dangerous" lack of firepower. He shared the belief that
when it came to weaponry and organizational structure, "extreme fire

---

[26] Charles P. Summerall, "Comments by the Corps Commander upon the Operations of the
Fifth Army Corps," Folder 32.11, Box 17, V Army Corps Historical File, RG 120, NA;
Summerall, "Recent Operations from the standpoint of employment of Artillery with
particular reference to co-operation between Infantry and Artillery" (lecture given to
Army Center of Artillery Studies, 16 December 1918), Box 14, Army Center of Artillery
Studies Files, Entry 371, RG 120, NA.

[27] Summerall to Deputy Chief of Staff, AEF, Subject: Artillery, 4 January 1919, Folder 32.11,
Box 17, V Army Corps Historical File, RG 120, NA.

[28] Another significant contributor to the firepower doctrine was Col. Conrad Lanza, who
served in the First Army artillery. Although his articles were often written later, some as
late as the mid-1930s, he was an adamant firepower advocate who believed that powerful
American artillery support was the only means to prevent severe infantry losses in battle.
See Conrad Lanza, "The Artillery Support of the Infantry in the A.E.F.," *Field Artillery
Journal* 26 (January–March 1936): 62–85; "Counterbattery in the A.E.F.," *Field Artillery
Journal* 26 (July–September 1936): 454–79; and "Note on the Artillery in the Battle of
Buzancy, November 1, 1918," *Field Artillery Journal* 22 (March–April 1932): 157–60.

power" was the "main factor" needed.[29] Colonel H. G. Bishop, an officer on the General Staff in 1922, wrote an odd article that, while repeating the Army's predominant perspective on the primacy of the infantryman in combat, also pressed the point that the dominant lessons of the war were "the preponderant role of machines" and the fact that "in a majority of cases superior technology determined success." In the established combat arms, such as infantry and artillery, as well as new ones, such as tanks and airplanes, the war witnessed the "substitution of a collective machine for the individual arm." After a survey of the technological developments that either had already occurred or were then taking place, such as the semiautomatic rifle replacing the bolt-action rifle and larger artillery with projectiles of "greater range, penetration, and explosive effect," Bishop highlighted that they all tended to increase firepower and, if wisely implemented, provided a substantial increase in "offensive power."[30] These officers all would have agreed with Summerall when he wrote, "To my mind, superiority of fire is the most important element of success in war and the one which demands our greatest study."[31]

Between these two doctrinal positions – the traditionalists like Woolfley and the proponents of mass firepower like Summerall – was a large group of officers who followed the pattern of the Superior Board and attempted to integrate as much technology and firepower into the Army as possible, while maintaining the predominant role and position of infantry. These officers, although believing in the value of tradition, were generally closer to Summerall than to Woolfley, as evidenced by their desire not only to maximize the use of firepower by the infantry but also in their clear belief that in modern war, the infantrymen, even heavily armed, could not do it alone. They believed that the successful attack on the modern battlefield required greater coordination of all the arms and weapons than ever before, and they increasingly referred to the need for a "combined-arms" approach based on firepower more than ever before to succeed.

The case for integrating as much firepower as possible into the infantry itself was presented clearly by Major Owen Meredith in an article advocating the prewar heresy of relegating the traditional rifleman to a supporting role. Meredith believed that future combat should "be built around small

[29] Maj. W. E. Burr, "Some Aspects of Field Artillery," *Field Artillery Journal* 12 (May–June 1922): 180–1.

[30] Col. H. G. Bishop, "What of the Future?" *Field Artillery Journal* 12 (September–October 1922): 366, 369–72.

[31] Quoted in the Editor's Note to "Notes on the Employment of Artillery and Machine Guns in Offensive Operations," *Field Artillery Journal* 9 (April–June 1919): 137.

units of great firepower whose key weapons would be a machine rifle."
He cited the German Army's use of stormtroopers during the war and
the postwar acceptance of such units by the French. Although Meredith
admitted that the rifle and bayonet would still have their role on the battlefield, he claimed that the Army needed to admit that "the entire history
of the development of weapons hinges upon fire power" and that "fire
power properly applied is the essence of success in battle." He understood
that the only thing holding the Army back was an irrational "traditional
conservatism" that blinded it from seeing the "plain lessons" of the last
war.[32] Other officers agreed with him and advocated that the infantry
adopt all the firepower possible and minimize the traditional role of the
marksman and bayonet fighter.[33]

The absolute necessity for a true "combined-arms" team on the modern battlefield was presented by Lieutenant Colonel Paul B. Malone, an
infantryman who had served at AEF GHQ before seeing plenty of combat while commanding an infantry regiment and brigade. Whereas many
officers focused on bringing to the infantry all the firepower available,
such as automatic rifles, machine guns, 37mm guns, grenades, mortars,
and even "infantry howitzers," Malone went one step farther, stressing
that the modern battlefield required almost instantaneous support of even
heavier weapons. Claiming that the war proved the necessity of having
"such cooperation" between the infantry and field artillery that the two
merge together "into a single fighting unit," Malone wanted the attacking
infantry commander to be given command of the supporting artillery during certain phases of an attack. The result, according to Malone, would be
a "true infantry artillery team" and one "which time and service heresies
should not be allowed to destroy."[34]

The 1923 edition of the *FSR*, like the Superior Board before it,
attempted to incorporate some of each position into American doctrine
and did so with a surprising level of success. Although the firepower
advocates had not yet convinced the Army leadership to drop statements
claiming that the principal weapon of the infantry was "the rifle and

---

[32] Maj. Owen R. Meredith, "If Not, Why Not!" *Infantry Journal* 21 (October 1922):
419–21.

[33] See Lt. Col. Jennings C. Wise, "Automatic and Semiautomatic Rifle Fire," *Infantry Journal* 20 (February 1922): 133–5; and Maj. Henry H. Burdick, "Development of the Half-
Platoon as an Elementary Unit" *Infantry Journal* 15 (April 1919): 799–807.

[34] Lt. Col. Paul B. Malone, "Infantry-Artillery," *Field Artillery Journal* 10 (January-
February 1920): 1, 11; and Lt. Col. T. W. Brown, "The Infantry School at Camp Benning,"
Infantry Journal 15 (May 1919): 861–77.

the bayonet," the rest of the 1923 *FSR* contained more concepts of a firepower-based doctrine than anything before in American military history. In three critical ways, the *FSR* showed the integration, if not quite the full acceptance, of the firepower gospel.

First, the *FSR* actually changed the very meaning of the word *infantry* in the U.S. Army. Despite the occasional phrases about the "rifle and bayonet," those weapons no longer were the defining characteristic of American infantry. In 1923, the infantry became "the arm of close combat." It would henceforth employ a wide array of weaponry, especially firepower-based weapons, to accomplish its missions as efficiently as possible. Automatic weapons, light cannon, and even tanks were added to the standard armament, and the regulations stressed the use of firepower in achieving the conditions that allowed the infantry to maneuver on the modern battlefield.[35]

Second, while the firepower gospel changed the very definition of infantry, in the 1923 *FSR* it helped significantly change the conventional understanding of the relative value of artillery in combat. Army doctrine now made it clear that artillery possessed "great power of destruction and neutralization" and was even the "principal means of attack" against certain objectives. Summerall must have applauded the statement that artillery, when properly concentrated and employed, was "capable of being directed with annihilating effects against critical objectives in the zone of combat." Its crucial role in supporting infantry before, during, and after any assault was made very clear.[36]

Third, the regulations repeatedly stressed the importance of combined arms in modern warfare. Although this may seem to be a neutral statement regarding firepower, when placed within the context of traditional Army thinking, it was not. This was the Army's official response to officers like Malone who demanded an "infantry–artillery team" to deal with the modern battlefield. The *FSR* section on the combatant arms began not with the infantry section, as it had in 1914, but rather with a brief section on "The Combined Arms," which asserted that "no one arm wins battles." The chapter on "Combat" stated that the artillery must "open the way for the infantry" and be coordinated with machine guns, infantry cannon, tanks, and airplanes to support an attack "through the depth of the hostile position." Although the 1923 *FSR* retained the Civil

---

[35] U.S. War Department, Office of the Chief of Staff, *Field Service Regulations United States Army 1923* (Washington, D.C.: GPO, 1924), 11–13.

[36] Ibid., 14–15.

War–esque section on "the meeting engagement," it added substantial sections on "attacks of a fortified position" and "attack on a stabilized front," both of which freely discussed the employment of artillery on a Great War scale, to include the use of powerful preliminary bombardments and rolling barrages. The new doctrine stressed the use of combined arms because the First World War had proven the necessity of employing massive amounts of well-coordinated firepower on the battlefield.[37]

Although American combat doctrine would continue to expand the use of firepower in combat, the great shift that put the U.S. Army on that road occurred in 1918. American officers went into combat on the Western Front with a doctrine that stressed the traditional human dimension, exemplified by the preeminent role of rifle-and-bayonet–brandishing infantrymen. According to the prewar vision of battle, these marksmen and masters of "cold steel" played the dominant role in "meeting engagements" in which mobility, maneuver, and morale, along with some well-timed fire support, were the keys to success.

Despite Pershing's hopes of driving the Germans out of their trenches and defeating them in "open warfare" with "self-reliant infantry," the challenge of the modern battlefield forced many American officers to finish the war with very different ideas. These men experienced the reality of industrialized combat; saw the futility of pitting men and morale against machine guns, high explosives, and shrapnel; and developed their own opinions of how American soldiers should fight the enemy. They increasingly saw machines, and especially those technologies that maximized firepower, rather than flesh as the proper means of waging war in the modern era.

Officers returned from the trenches to sit on boards and committees, write articles in professional journals, and eventually contribute to a new doctrine. Although most were not willing to go as far as Summerall, they began to integrate his firepower-based concepts into the heart of official doctrine. The infantry attempted to assimilate and employ any firepower-producing weapon that they could conceivably carry forward and even a few that they could not, such as the infantry cannon and the tank. The artillery was given an unprecedented role in battle. And, the need for all the combat arms to combine their capabilities to achieve victory in the quickest manner and with the lowest cost in American lives was both stated explicitly and woven throughout the 1923 *FSR*.

[37] Ibid., 11, 83–4, 94–9.

The U.S. Army struggled to continue down this road throughout the lean years before the next great war. The path was chosen but the journey was not complete. As William Odom shows in his study of doctrine between the wars, Army doctrine did not progress smoothly and continuously during the 1920s and 1930s. He notes that the results of the Army's Field Manual Project, begun in 1927 by then chief of staff Charles Summerall, led to the creation in 1930 of the *Manual for Commanders of Large Units (MCLU)*, a document that relied heavily on French doctrine and advocated the French Army's firepower-based concept of "methodical battle." The *MCLU* was heavily influenced by Major General Frank Parker, another veteran commander of the Great War and of the 1st Division, and was officially accepted over the protests of a number of senior officers only by Summerall's strong support.[38] Possibly, this bursting forth of the firepower gospel coincided with the rise in rank and prominence of a number of officers who had a more intimate understanding of the industrialized battlefield of the Western Front. However, it is necessary to remember that throughout the 1920s and much of the 1930s, most discussion of war and combat doctrine was essentially theoretical because few expected another major war in the near future, and even fewer expected the U.S. Army to have to wage a second "great crusade" in Europe to win it.

Only after the start of World War II would America commit the massive resources necessary for its military forces to test, try, fail, and ultimately succeed at building and employing a doctrine based thoroughly on the use of overwhelming firepower. In more fully developed tanks, trucks, artillery, and airplanes, American forces would find technologies that combined the modern soldier's insistence on firepower with the traditional allegiance to mobility and maneuver.

Ironically, although the resistance to adhere strictly to the firepower gospel advocated by officers such as Summerall both during and after the war may have had negative consequences on AEF battles, it also may

[38] As Odom notes, the *MCLU* was based on a 1921 French Army document entitled *Provisional Instruction on the Tactical Employment of Large Units*. Parker's influence in this project was pervasive and probably a result of his intimate relationship with the French Army. In 1903, Parker attended the French Cavalry School; in 1912 and again from 1914–1915, he studied at the Ecole de Superieure de Guerre; he was an observer with the French Army and ultimately chief of the American mission there between 1915 and 1917; and in 1920, he finally graduated from the Ecole de Superieure de Guerre and then stayed on as a professor there. Odom, *After the Trenches*, 118–23. For information on Frank Parker, see the summary of the Frank Parker Papers, Southern Historical Collection, University of North Carolina, Chapel Hill.

have saved the U.S. Army from following France, Canada, and Britain down a road that led them to enter the Second World War with doctrines based entirely on firepower and set-piece operations. Patton's dramatic successes in northern France in the summer and fall of 1944 might have been, at least in part, one result of the unwillingness of his AEF superiors to wholeheartedly accept certain lessons of the first Great War. But, then, even Patton once admitted that he did not need to tell an audience of combat veterans "who won" the second Great War. He claimed they knew as well as he that "the Artillery did."[39]

The legacy of the AEF lived on after the Second World War. The firepower doctrine entered the second half of the twentieth century stronger than ever, proving itself again in the Korean War. Whether it exerted too much influence on the conduct of the Vietnam War or the other "small wars" that followed is the subject of other studies. Regardless, as America closed out the twentieth century, there could be little doubt that its reliance on firepower has been one of the Great War's fundamental legacies on American combat doctrine.

---

[39] Patton made these comments at a May 1945 artillery conference in Bad Tolz, Germany. He is quoted in U.S. Army Field Artillery School, *Right of the Line: A History of the American Field Artillery* (Fort Sill, Okla.: U.S. Army Field Artillery School, 1977), 31.

References

Primary Sources

Archival Material

Citadel Archives and Museum, Charleston, S.C.
    Richard J. Eaton Papers
    Charles P. Summerall Papers
    A. G. D. Wiles Papers
Combined Arms Research Library (CARL), Fort Leavenworth, Kans.
    Caffey, B. F., Jr. "A Division G-3 in the World War: The 1st Division, AEF, in the Meuse-Argonne, 26 September–11 Oct, 1918." Student Monograph IR-15-1932.
    Cornish, George R. F. "The Twenty-Sixth Infantry (U.S.) in the Meuse-Argonne Offensive." Student Monograph IR-104-1931.
    Davis, George A. "A Critical Analysis of the Aisne-Marne Offensive." Student Monograph IR-99-1933.
    Johnston, Edward S. "A Study of the Nature of the United States Infantry Tactics for Open Warfare on July 18, 1918, and of Their Points of Difference as Contrasted with the United States Army Tactics as Taught in 1914." Student Monograph IR-124-1931.
    King, Henry L. P. "A Critical Analysis of the Employment of Signal Communications by the 1st American Division at Soissons." Student Monograph IR-61-1933.
    Waltz, Welcome P. "Personal Experience of a Machine-gun Officer at Cantigny, 28th–30th May 1918." Student Monograph, IR-6-1933.
    Whitson, R. K. "Study of the Operation of the First Division in the Soissons Offensive, 16–25 July 1918." Student Monograph IR-98-1931.
Donovan Research Library, U.S. Army Infantry School, Fort Benning, Ga.
    Allen, Oliver. "The 18th Infantry in the St. Mihiel Offensive." 1923.
    Huebner, Clarence R., Jr. "The Operations of the 28th Infantry in the Aisne-Marne Offensive, July 17–23, 1918." 1923.

Keiser, Lawrence B. "The Operations of the 1st Corps (U.S.) in the 1st Phase of the Meuse-Argonne." 1923.

Legg, Barnwell. "The First Division in the Meuse Argonne, September 26th–October 12th, 1918." 1923.

Metcalf, James. "Operations of the First Corps, Second Phase of the Meuse-Argonne." 1923.

Raymond, Senius J. "Operations of the 5th Corps in the 2nd Phase of the Meuse-Argonne." 1923.

Library of Congress, Washington, D.C.

Robert L. Bullard Papers

John L. Hines Papers

John J. Pershing Papers

Charles P. Summerall Papers

MacArthur Memorial Archives, Norfolk, Va.

Douglas MacArthur Papers

William E. Severe Papers

Cleon Stanley Papers

George C. Marshall Library, Virginia Military Institute, Lexington, Va.

Pierpont L. Stackpole Diary, typescript copy loaned to author.

Massachusetts Historical Society, Boston, Mass.

Clarence R. Edwards Papers

The Colonel Robert R. McCormick Research Center, First Division Museum, and the First Division Foundation, Cantigny, Ill.

Butler, Alban B. "Journal of Operations, December 23, 1917 through October 12, 1918."

Summerall, Charles P. "The Way of Duty, Honor, Country." Unpublished memoir.

National Archives, Washington, D.C., and College Park, Md.

Record Group 120, Records of the American Expeditionary Forces, 1917–23

Record Group 165, Records of the War Department General and Special Staffs

Record Group 200, John J. Pershing Papers

Southern Historical Collection, University of North Carolina, Chapel Hill, N.C.

Frank Parker Papers

U.S. Army Military History Institute, U.S. Army War College, Carlisle Barracks, Penn.

William J. Donovan Papers

Hugh A. Drum Papers

John L. Hines Papers

Lanza, Conrad H. *The Army Artillery, First Army.* 2 vols. Undated typescript unit history, prepared for the War Department.

Dennis E. Nolan Papers

R. Kirkham Safford Papers

U.S. Army, American Expeditionary Forces, Superior Board on Organization and Tactics, *Report of the Superior Board.* Chaumont, France, 1919.

World War I Veterans Survey

Published Documents and Manuals

Army Service School. *Instructions for the Training of Divisions for Offensive Action.* Fort Leavenworth, Kans.: Army Service Schools Press, 1917.

GHQ, AEF. *Notes on Recent Operations, No. 1.* France, 7 August, 1918.

GHQ, AEF. *Notes on Recent Operations, No. 3.* France, 12 October, 1918.

GHQ, AEF. *Notes on Recent Operations, No. 4.* France, 22 November, 1918.

Headquarters, Department of the Army, *FM 100-5 Operations.* Washington, D.C.: GPO, 14 June 1993.

Headquarters, Department of the Army, *FM 101-5-1 Operational Terms and Graphics.* Washington, D.C.: GPO, 1997.

Infantry School, U.S. Army. *Infantry in Battle.* Washington, D.C.: The Infantry School Press, 1934.

Pershing, John J. *Combat Instructions.* AEF Document No. 1348. France: GHQ, AEF, 5 September 1918.

U.S. Army, Chief of Field Artillery. *The School of the Battery Commander: 75m/m gun and 155m/m howitzer.* From the pamphlet at the Saumer Artillery School, France. Fort Sill, Okla.: November 1918.

U.S. Army Field Artillery School. *Right of the Line: A History of the American Field Artillery.* Fort Sill, Okla.: U.S. Army Field Artillery School, 1977.

U.S. Army, 1st Division. *World War Records of the First Division A.E.F. (Regular).* 25 vols. Washington, D.C.: Army War College, 1930.

U.S. Army, 2nd Division. *Records of the Second Division (Regular).* 10 vols., (some in several parts). Washington, D.C.: Army War College, 1924.

U.S. Department of the Army, Historical Division. *United States Army in the World War 1917–1919.* 17 vols. Washington, D.C.: GPO, 1948. Reprint, Center for Military History, 1990.

U.S. Infantry Association. *Infantry Drill Regulations, United States Army 1911, with Changes 1–18.* Philadelphia: J. B. Lippincott, 1917.

U.S. War Department. Document No. 394, *Infantry Drill Regulations, United States Army, 1911.* Washington, D.C.: GPO, 1911.

U.S. War Department. *Field Service Regulations: United States Army, 1914, Corrected to July 1, 1914.* Washington, D.C.: GPO, 1914.

U.S. War Department. *Field Service Regulations: United States Army, 1914 (with Changes Nos. 1 to 7).* Washington, D.C.: GPO, 1917.

U.S. War Department. *Field Service Regulations: United States Army, 1914, Corrected to July 31, 1918.* Washington, D.C.: GPO, 1918.

U.S. War Department. *Field Service Regulations: United States Army, 1923.* Washington, D.C.: GPO, 1924.

U.S. War Department. *Order of Battle of the United States Land Forces in the World War.* 3 vols. Washington, D.C.: U.S. GPO, 1937. Reprint, Center for Military History, 1988.

U.S. War Department. *Provisional Field and Service Regulations for Field Artillery (Horse and Light), 1916, Corrected to April 15, 1917.* New York: Military Publishing Company, 1917.

Contemporary Journal Articles

Anderson, John B. "Are We Justified in Discarding 'Pre-War' Methods of Training?" *Field Artillery Journal* 9 (April–June, 1919): 222–30.

"Bayonet Training." *Infantry Journal* 13 (May 1917): 733–50.

Bishop, H. G. "What of the Future?" *Field Artillery Journal* 12 (September–October 1922): 366, 369–72.

Briggs, Allan L. "Bayonet Training." *Infantry Journal* 14 (October 1917): 336–40.

Broad, C. N. F. "The Development of Artillery Tactics – 1914–1918, Part I." *Field Artillery Journal* 12 (September–October 1922): 375–96.

Brown, T. W. "The Infantry School at Camp Benning." *Infantry Journal* 15 (May 1919): 861–77.

Burdick, Henry H. "Development of the Half-Platoon as an Elementary Unit." *Infantry Journal* 15 (April 1919): 799–807.

Burr, W. E. "Some Aspects of Field Artillery." *Field Artillery Journal* 12 (May–June 1922): 180–1.

Cherfils, Gen., French Army. "Infantry Fire in the Present War." *Infantry Journal* 12 (November 1915): 347–49.

"Current Field Artillery Notes." *Field Artillery Journal* 7 (April–June, 1917): 198–204.

Department of Gunnery, School of Fire for Field Artillery. "American Drill Regulations and 'Artillery Firing.'" *Field Artillery Journal* 8 (July–September, 1918): 363–9.

Drennan, L. H. "The Psychology of the Bayonet." *Infantry Journal* 11 (September–October 1914): 169–71.

Editorial Department, "The Battle of the Future," *Infantry Journal* 12 (November–December, 1916): 357–61.

Editorial Department, "The Character of the Present War," *Infantry Journal* 12 (November–December, 1916): 352–7.

Editorial Department. *Field Artillery Journal* 7 (January–March, 1917): 71–4.

Editorial Department. "The Function of Fire." *Infantry Journal* 12 (November 1915): 487–91.

Editorial Department. *Infantry Journal* 12 (December 1915): 513.

Editorial Department. *Infantry Journal* 21 (September 1922): 341.

Editorial Department. "Rifle and Bayonet." *Infantry Journal* 12 (February 1916): 734–6.

Editorial Department. "Some General Deductions." *Infantry Journal* 11 (November–December 1914): 433–6.

"Effect of the New Tactics on the Operations of Infantry." *Infantry Journal* 11 (September–October 1914): 242–6.

Fleming, A. S. "The Mission of the School of Fire for Field Artillery: Address to Incoming Class by Commandant, Col. A. S. Fleming." *Field Artillery Journal* 7 (October–December, 1917): 383–90.

Frink, James L. "Methods of Training Troops." Infantry Journal 12 (September–October, 1916): 139–55.

"General Pershing's Opinion of Infantry." *Infantry Journal* 11 (July–August 1914): 83.

"German Artillery." *Field Artillery Journal* 8 (October–December, 1918): 578–85.

Hobbs, Percy. "Bayonet Fighting and Physical Training." *Infantry Journal* 14 (August 1917): 79–85.

Irwin, George LeR. "Notes on the Training and Handling of Divisional Artillery in France." *Field Artillery Journal* 9 (November–December 1919): 489–507.

Kelly, T. Howard. "Why General Edwards Was Sent Home." *New McClure's* (November 1928): 54–5, 120–6.

Lanza, Conrad H. "The Artillery Support of the Infantry in the A.E.F." *Field Artillery Journal* 26 (January–March 1936): 62–85.

Lanza, Conrad H. "Counterbattery in the A.E.F." *Field Artillery Journal* 26 (July–September 1936): 454–79.

Lanza, Conrad H. "Note on the Artillery in the Battle of Buzancy, November 1, 1918." *Field Artillery Journal* 22 (March–April 1932): 157–60.

Locke, E. M. "Artillery in Europe." *Field Artillery Journal* 7 (July–September 1917): 294–301.

Malone, Paul B. "Infantry-Artillery." *Field Artillery Journal* 10 (January–February 1920): 1, 11.

"Measures Taken by the German Artillery to Carry Out Preparations for Attack Without Betraying the Intentions of the Command." *Field Artillery Journal* 8 (July–September 1918): 504–12.

Meredith, Owen R. "If Not, Why Not!" *Infantry Journal* 21 (October 1922): 419–21.

Moore, J. M. "Bayonet and Bayonet Combat." *Infantry Journal* 12 (March 1916): 908–19.

"New Field Artillery Classification." *Field Artillery Journal* 7 (January–March 1917): 25–30

"Notes from the Chief of Infantry." *Infantry Journal* 21 (November 1922): 563.

"Notes on Artillery." *Field Artillery Journal* 7 (April–June 1917): 164–97.

"Notes on the Employment of Artillery and Machine Guns in Offensive Operations." *Field Artillery Journal* 9 (April–June 1919): 137.

"Organization of a Rolling Barrage in the German Army: Translation of a German Document." *Field Artillery Journal* 8 (July–September 1918): 417–21.

Reilly, Henry J. "Fontainebleau in War Time." *Field Artillery Journal* 7 (April–June, 1917): 109–18.

Sawyer, C. N. "The Stiff Bayonet." *Infantry Journal* 12 (November 1915): 396–405.

Spaulding, O. L. "Infantry under Artillery Fire." *Infantry Journal* 11 (March–April 1915): 641.

"The Scientific Preparation of Fire in the German Army." *Field Artillery Journal* 8 (October–December 1918): 527–34.

Upton, L. S. "Bayonet Melee." *Infantry Journal* 13 (July–August 1916): 32–5.

Wilbur, William H. "Bayonet Instruction." *Infantry Journal* 14 (December 1917): 414–21.

Williams, Roger H. "Bayonet Combat Instruction." *Infantry Journal* 11 (November–December 1914): 390–1.

Wise, Jennings C. "Automatic and Semiautomatic Rifle Fire." *Infantry Journal* 20 (February 1922): 133–5.

Woolfley, Francis A. "Queen of Infantry Weapons." *Infantry Journal* 21 (September 1922): 308.

Memoirs and Other First-Hand Accounts

Adler, J. O., ed. *History of the Seventy-Seventh Division, August 25th 1917–November 11th 1918*. New York: 77th Division Association, 1919.

Albertine, Connell. *The Yankee Doughboy*. Boston: Branden Press, 1968.

Alexander, Robert. *Memories of the World War, 1917–1918*. New York: Macmillan, 1931.

Allen, Hervey. *Toward the Flame: A War Diary*. Pittsburgh: University of Pittsburgh Press, 1934, 1968.

Blake, Robert, ed. *The Private Papers of Douglas Haig*. London: Eyre & Spottiswoode, 1952.

Brannen, Carl Andrew. *Over There: A Marine in the Great War*. College Station: Texas A&M University Press, 1996.

Bullard, Robert L. *American Soldiers Also Fought*. New York: Longmans, Green and Co., 1936.

Bullard, Robert L. *Fighting Generals: Illustrated Biographical Sketches of Seven Major Generals in World War I*. Ann Arbor, Mich.: J. W. Edwards, 1944.

Bullard, Robert L. *Personalities and Reminiscences of the War*. Garden City, N.Y.: Doubleday, Page and Co., 1925.

Chambrun, Jaques and Charles Marenches. *The American Army in the European Conflict*. New York: Macmillan, 1919.

Clark, George B., ed. *His Time in Hell: A Texas Marine in France: The World War I Memoir of Warren R. Jackson*. Novato, Calif.: Presidio Press, 2001.

Currie, A. W. *Canadian Corps Operations During the Year 1918*. Ottawa: Department of Militia and Defence, 1919.

Dickman, Joseph T. *The Great Crusade*. New York: D. Appleton and Co., 1927.

Evans, Martin Marix, ed. *American Voices of World War I: Primary Source Documents, 1917–1920*. London: Fitzroy Dearborn, 2001.

Evarts, Jeremiah M. *Cantigny: A Corner of the War*. n.p., The Scribner Press, 1938.

Foch, Ferdinand. *The Memoirs of Marshal Foch*. Translated by T. Bentley Mott. Garden City, N.Y.: Doubleday, Doran, 1931.

Harbord, James G. *The American Army in France, 1917–1919*. Boston: Little, Brown, 1936.

Harbord, James G. *Leaves From a War Diary*. New York: Dodd, Mead, 1925.

Langer, William L. *Gas and Flame in World War I*. New York: Alfred A. Knopf, 1965.

Lejeune, John A. *The Reminiscences of a Marine*. Philadelphia: Dorrance and Co., 1930.

Liggett, Hunter. *A.E.F.: Ten Years Ago in France*. New York: Dodd, Mead, 1928.

Liggett, Hunter. *Commanding an American Army*. New York: Houghton Mifflin, 1925.

MacArthur, Douglas. *Reminiscences*. New York: McGraw-Hill, 1964.

Mackin, Elton E. *Suddenly We Didn't Want to Die: Memoirs of a World War I Marine*. Novato, Calif.: Presidio Press, 1993.

Mangin, Charles M. E. *How the War Ended*. Paris: Plon-Nourrit, 1920. Reprinted and Translated at Fort Leavenworth, Kans.: General Service Schools, 1924.

March, Peyton C. *The Nation at War*. Garden City, N.Y.: Doubleday, Doran, 1932.

Marshall, George C. *Memoirs of My Services in the World War, 1917–1918*. Boston: Houghton Mifflin, 1976.

Meehan, Thomas F. *History of the Seventy-Seventh Division in the War, 1917–1919*. New York: Dodd, Mead, 1921.

Miles, L. Wardlaw. *History of the 308th Infantry, 1917–1919*. New York, n.p., 1927.

Monash, John. *The Australian Victories in France in 1918*. London: Imperial War Museum, 1993.

Otto, Ernst. *The Battle at Blanc Mont*. Translated by Martin Lichtenburg. Annapolis: U.S. Naval Institute, 1930.

Palmer, Frederick. *Our Greatest Battle*. New York: Dodd, Mead, 1919.

Pershing, John J. *My Experiences in the World War*. 2 vols. New York: Frederick A. Stokes, 1931.

Reilly, Henry J. *Americans All: The Rainbow at War*. Columbus, Ohio: F. J. Heer, 1936.

Smith, Henry W. *A Story of the 305th Machine Gun Battalion*. New York: Modern Publishing, 1941.

Snow, William J. *Signposts of Experience*. Washington, D.C.: U.S. Field Artillery Association, 1941.

Society of the First Division. *History of the First Division in the World War, 1917–1919*. Philadelphia: John C. Winston, 1931.

Taylor, Emerson Gifford. *New England in France: 1917–1919: A History of the Twenty-Sixth Division U.S.A.* Boston: Houghton Mifflin, 1920.

The Ninth U.S. Infantry in the World War. [Neuwied a. R.: L. Heusersche buchdr. 1919].

Wright, William M. *Meuse-Argonne Diary: A Division Commander in World War I*. Edited by Robert H. Ferrell. Columbia: University of Missouri Press, 2004.

Secondary Sources

Books

Abrahamson, James L. *America Arms for a New Century: The Making of a Great Military Power*. New York: Free Press, 1981.

American Battle Monuments Commission. *American Armies and Battlefields in Europe: A History, Guide, and Reference Book*. Washington, D.C.: GPO, 1938. Reprint, Center for Military History, 1995.

American Battle Monuments Commission. *1st Division Summary of Operations in the World War*. Washington, D.C.: GPO, 1944.

American Battle Monuments Commission. *2nd Division Summary of Operations in the World War*. Washington, D.C.: GPO, 1944.

American Battle Monuments Commission. *26th Division Summary of Operations in the World War*. Washington, D.C.: GPO, 1944.

American Battle Monuments Commission. *77th Division Summary of Operations in the World War*. Washington, D.C.: GPO, 1944.

Armstrong, David A. *Bullets and Bureaucrats: The Machine Gun and the United States Army, 1861–1916*. Westport, Conn.: Greenwood Press, 1982.

Asprey, Robert B. *At Belleau Wood*. New York: Putnam's Sons, 1965; reprint, Denton, Tex.: University of North Texas Press, 1996.

Asprey, Robert B. *The German High Command at War: Hindenburg and Ludendorff Conduct World War I*. New York: William Morrow, 1991.

Ayres, Leonard P. *The War with Germany*. Washington, D.C.: GPO, 1919.

Bailey, J. B. A. *Field Artillery and Firepower*. Oxford: The Military Press, 1989.

Bartlett, Merrill L. *Lejeune: A Marine's Life, 1867–1942*. Annapolis: Naval Institute Press, 1996.

Bean, C. E. W. *The Official History of Australia in the War of 1914–1918: Volume VI, The Australian Imperial Force in France During the Allied Offensive, 1918*. Sydney: University of Queensland Press, 1942.

Beaver, Daniel R. *Newton D. Baker and the American War Effort, 1917–1919*. Lincoln: University of Nebraska Press, 1966.

Bidwell, Shelford, and Dominick Graham. *Fire-Power: British Army Weapons and Theories of War, 1904–1945*. London: Allen and Unwin, 1982.

Braim, Paul F. *The Test of Battle: The American Expeditionary Forces in the Meuse-Argonne Campaign*. Newark: University Press of Delaware, 1987.

Brown, Ronald J. *A Few Good Men: The Fighting Fifth Marines: A History of the USMC's Most Decorated Regiment*. Novato, Calif.: Presidio Press, 2001.

Bruce, Robert. *Machine Guns of World War I*. London: Windrow and Greene, 1997.

Bruce, Robert B. *A Fraternity of Arms: America and France in the Great War* (Lawrence: University Press of Kansas), 2003.

Cochrane, Rexmond C. *Gas Warfare at Belleau Wood, June 1918*. Army Chemical Center, Md.: U.S. Army Chemical Corps Historical Office, 1957.

Cochrane, Rexmond C. *The 26th Division in the Aisne-Marne Campaign, July 1918*. Army Chemical Center, Md.: U.S. Army Chemical Corps Historical Office, 1957.

Cochrane, Rexmond C. *The Use of Gas in the Meuse-Argonne Campaign, September–November 1918*. Army Chemical Center, Md.: U.S. Army Chemical Corps Historical Office, 1958.

Cochrane, Rexmond C. *The 26th Division East of the Meuse, October 1918*. Army Chemical Center, Md.: U.S. Army Chemical Corps Historical Office, 1960.

Coffman, Edward M. *The Hilt of the Sword: The Career of Peyton C. March*. Madison: University of Wisconsin Press, 1966.

Coffman, Edward M. *The War to End All Wars: The American Military Experience in World War I*. New York: Oxford University Press, 1968.

Cooke, James J. *The Rainbow Division in the Great War, 1917–1919*. Westport, Conn.: Praeger, 1994.

Cooke, James J. *The U.S. Air Service in the Great War, 1917–1919*. Westport, Conn.: Praeger, 1996.

Cooke, James J. *Pershing and His Generals: Command and Staff in the AEF*. Westport, Conn.: Praeger, 1997.

Cooke, James J. *The All-Americans at War: The 82nd Division in the Great War, 1917–1918*. Westport, Conn.: Praeger, 1999.

Dancocks, Daniel G. *Spearhead to Victory: Canada and the Great War*. Edmonton: Hurtig, 1987.

Dastrup, Boyd S. *King of Battle: A Branch History of the U.S. Army's Field Artillery*. Fort Monroe, Va.: U.S. Army Training and Doctrine Command, 1992.

Dennis, Peter, and Jeffrey Grey. *1918: Defining Victory*. Canberra: Army History Unit, Department of Defence, 1999.

DeWeerd, Harvey A. *President Wilson Fights His War: World War I and the American Intervention*. New York: Macmillan, 1968.

Dooly, William G., Jr. *Great Weapons of World War I*. New York: Walker and Co., 1969.

Doughty, Robert. *The Seeds of Disaster: The Development of French Army Doctrine 1919–1939*. Hamden, Conn.: Archon Books, 1985.

Edmonds, James E. *History of the Great War: Military Operations: France and Belgium, 1918*. Vols. 3–5. London: HMSO, 1947.

Eisenhower, John S. D. *Yanks: The Epic Story of the American Army in World War I*. New York: The Free Press, 2001.

Ellis, John. *Brute Force: Allied Strategy and Tactics in the Second World War*. New York: Viking, 1990.

English, John. *On Infantry*. Westport, Conn.: Praeger, 1984.

Falls, Cyril. *The Great War, 1914–1918*. New York: Capricorn Books, 1961.

Ferrell, Robert H. *Woodrow Wilson and World War I, 1917–1921*. New York: Harper & Row, 1985.

Ferrell, Robert H. *Collapse at Meuse-Argonne: The Failure of the Kansas-Missouri Division*. Columbia: University of Missouri Press, 2004.

Finlayson, Kenneth. *An Uncertain Trumpet: The Evolution of U.S. Army Infantry Doctrine, 1919–1941*. Westport, Conn.: Greenwood Press, 2001.

Finnegan, John Patrick. *Against the Specter of a Dragon: The Campaign for American Military Preparedness, 1914–1917*. Westport, Conn.: Greenwood Press, 1974.

Grotelueschen, Mark E. *Doctrine Under Trial: American Artillery Employment in World War I*. Westport, Conn.: Greenwood Press, 2001.

Gudmundsson, Bruce I. *Stormtroop Tactics: Innovation in the German Army, 1914–1918*. Westport, Conn.: Praeger, 1989.

Gudmundsson, Bruce I. *On Artillery*. Westport, Conn.: Praeger, 1993.

Hallas, James H. *Squandered Victory: The American Army at St. Mihiel*. Westport, Conn.: Praeger, 1995.

Heller, Charles E. *Chemical Warfare in World War I: The American Experience, 1917–1918*. Leavenworth Papers No. 10. Fort Leavenworth, Kans.: U.S. Army Combat Studies Institute, 1984.

Herwig, Holger H. *The First World War: Germany and Austria-Hungary 1914–1918*. London: Arnold, 1997.

Holley, I. B., Jr. *General John M. Palmer, Citizen-Soldiers, and the Army of a Democracy.* Westport, Conn.: Greenwood Press, 1982.

Holley, I. B., Jr. *Ideas and Weapons.* New Haven, Conn.: Yale University Press, 1953. Reprint, Washington, D.C.: GPO, 1997.

Huelfer, Evan Andrew. *The "Casualty Issue" in American Military Practice: The Impact of World War I.* Westport, Conn.: Praeger, 2003.

Johnson, David E. *Fast Tanks and Heavy Bombers: Innovation in the U.S. Army, 1917–1945.* Ithaca, N.Y.: Cornell University Press, 1998.

Johnson, Douglas V., II, and Rolfe L. Hillman, Jr. *Soissons, 1918.* College Station: Texas A&M University Press, 1999.

Liddell Hart, B. H. *The Real War 1914–1918.* Boston: Little, Brown, 1930.

Lupfer, Timothy T. *The Dynamics of Doctrine: The Changes in German Tactical Doctrine During the First World War.* Leavenworth Papers No. 4. Fort Leavenworth, Kans.: Combat Studies Institute, U.S. Army Command and General Staff College, 1981.

McClellan, Edwin N. *The United States Marine Corps in the World War.* Washington, D.C.: GPO, 1920.

Millett, Allan R. *The General: Robert L. Bullard and Officership in the United States Army, 1881–1925.* Westport, Conn.: Greenwood Press, 1975.

Millett, Allan R. *Semper Fidelis: The History of the United States Marine Corps.* New York: Macmillan, 1980.

Millett, Allan R. *In Many a Strife: General Gerald C. Thomas and the U.S. Marine Corps, 1917–1956.* Annapolis: Naval Institute Press, 1993.

Millett, Allan R., and Peter Maslowski. *For the Common Defense: A Military History of the United States of America*, rev. ed. New York: Free Press, 1994.

Nenninger, Timothy K. *The Leavenworth Schools and the Old Army.* Westport, Conn.: Greenwood Press, 1978.

Nicholson, G. W. L. *The Official History of the Canadian Army in the First World War: Canadian Expeditionary Force, 1914–1919.* Ottawa: Queen's Printer, 1962.

Odom, William O. *After the Trenches: The Transformation of U.S. Army Doctrine, 1918–1939.* College Station: Texas A&M University Press, 1999.

Page, Arthur. *Our 110 Days Fighting.* Garden City, N.Y.: Doubleday, Page, 1920.

Paschall, Rod. *The Defeat of Imperial Germany, 1917–1918.* New York: Da Capo Press, 1994.

Pogue, Forrest C. *George C. Marshall: Education of a General, 1880–1939.* New York: Viking Press, 1963.

Powell, Geoffrey. *Plumer: The Soldier's General.* London: Leo Cooper, 1990.

Prior, Robin, and Trevor Wilson. *Command on the Western Front: The Military Career of Sir Henry Rawlinson, 1914–18.* Oxford: Blackwell, 1992.

Prior, Robin, and Trevor Wilson. *Passchendaele: The Untold Story.* New Haven, Conn.: Yale University Press, 1996.

Raines, Edgar F., Jr. *Eyes of Artillery: The Origins of Modern U.S. Army Aviation in World War II.* Washington, D.C.: Center of Military History, 2000.

Samuels, Martin. *Doctrine and Dogma: German and British Infantry Tactics in the First World War.* Westport, Conn.: Greenwood Press, 1992.

Samuels, Martin. *Command or Control?: Command, Training, and Tactics in the British and German Armies, 1888–1918*. London: Frank Cass, 1995.

Schreiber, Shane B. *Shock Army of the British Empire: The Canadian Corps in the Last 100 Days of the Great War*. Westport, Conn.: Praeger, 1997.

Sheffield, Gary. *Forgotten Victory*. London: Headline, 2001.

Sheffield, Gary, and Dan Todman, eds. *Command and Control on the Western Front: The British Army' Experience 1914–1918*. Staplehurst, UK: Spellmount, 2004.

Smith, Leonard V. *Between Mutiny and Obedience: The Case of the French Fifth Division during World War I*. Princeton, N.J.: Princeton University Press, 1994.

Smythe, Donald. *Guerrilla Warrior: The Early Life of John J. Pershing*. New York: Charles Scribner's Sons, 1973.

Smythe, Donald. *Pershing: General of the Armies*. Bloomington: Indiana University Press, 1986.

Spaulding, Oliver, and John W. Wright. *The Second Division, American Expeditionary Force in France, 1917–1919*. New York: Hillman Press, 1937.

Stallings, Lawrence. *The Doughboys: The Story of the AEF, 1917–1918*. New York: Harper & Row, 1963.

Strachan, Hew. *The First World War: To Arms*. New York: Oxford University Press, 2001.

Terraine, John. *To Win a War: 1918, the Year of Victory*. London: Sidgwick and Jackson, 1978.

Thomas, Shipley. *The History of the A.E.F.* New York: Doran, 1920.

Trask, David F. *The AEF and Coalition Warmaking, 1917–1918*. Lawrence: University Press of Kansas, 1993.

Travers, Tim. *The Killing Ground: The British Army, the Western Front and the Emergence of Modern Warfare, 1900–1918*. London: Unwin Hyman, 1987.

Travers, Tim. *How the War Was Won: Command and Technology in the British Army on the Western Front, 1917–1918*. London: Routledge, 1992.

Twitchell, Heath, Jr. *Allen: The Biography of an Army Officer, 1859–1930*. New Brunswick, N.J.: Rutgers University Press, 1974.

Vandiver, Frank E. *Black Jack: The Life and Times of John J. Pershing*. College Station: Texas A&M University Press, 1977.

Vetock, Dennis J. *Lessons Learned: A History of US Army Lesson Learning*. Carlisle Barracks, Penn.: U.S. Army Military History Institute, 1988.

Weigley, Russell F. *The American Way of War*. Bloomington: Indiana University Press, 1977.

Weigley, Russell F. *History of the United States Army*. Bloomington: Indiana University Press, 1967.

Wilson, Dale E. *Treat 'em Rough! The Birth of American Armor, 1917–1920*. Novato, Calif.: Presidio Press, 1989.

Wilson, John B. *Maneuver and Firepower: The Evolution of Divisions and Separate Brigades*. Washington, D.C.: Center of Military History, 1998.

Woodward, David R. *Trial by Friendship: Anglo-American Relations, 1917–1919*. Lexington, Ky.: University Press of Kentucky, 1993.

Zabecki, David T. *Steel Wind: Colonel Georg Bruchmüller and the Birth of Modern Artillery*. Westport, Conn.: Praeger, 1994.

Book Chapters and Journal Articles

Beattie, Taylor V. "Whittlesey's 'Lost' Battalion." *Army History* 54 (Winter 2002): 21–9.

Herwig, Holger H. "The Dynamics of Necessity: German Military Policy during the First World War." In *Military Effectiveness*. Volume I: *The First World War*, eds. Allan R. Millett and Williamson Murray, 80–115. Boston: Allen and Unwin, 1988.

Herwig, Holger H. "The German Victories, 1917–1918." In *The Oxford Illustrated History of the First World War*, ed. Hew Strachan, 253–64. New York: Oxford University Press, 1998.

Howard, Michael. "Men against Fire: The Doctrine of the Offensive in 1914." In *Makers of Modern Strategy from Machiavelli to the Nuclear Age*, ed. Peter Paret, 510–26. Princeton: Princeton University Press, 1986.

Kennedy, Paul. "Britain in the First World War." In *Military Effectiveness*. Volume I: *The First World War*, eds. Allan R. Millett and Williamson Murray, 31–79. Boston: Allen and Unwin, 1988.

Kennett, Lee. "The A.E.F. Through French Eyes." *Military Review* 52 (November 1972): 3–11.

Millett, Allan R. "Cantigny, 28–31 May 1918." In *America's First Battles, 1776–1965*, eds. Charles E. Heller and William A. Stofft, 149–85. Lawrence: University Press of Kansas, 1986.

Millett, Allan R. "Over Where? The AEF and the American Strategy for Victory, 1917–1918." In *Against All Enemies: Interpretations of American Military History from Colonial Times to the Present*, eds. Kenneth J. Hagan and William R. Roberts, 235–56. Westport, Conn.: Greenwood Press, 1986.

Nenninger, Timothy K. "American Military Effectiveness in the First World War." In *Military Effectiveness*. Volume I: *The First World War*, eds. Allan R. Millett and Williamson Murray, 116–56. Boston: Allen and Unwin, 1988.

Nenninger, Timothy K. "Tactical Dysfunction in the AEF, 1917–1918." *Military Affairs* 51 (October 1987): 177–81.

Porch, Douglas. "The French Army in the First World War." In *Military Effectiveness*. Volume I: *The First World War*, eds. Allan R. Millett and Williamson Murray, 190–228. Boston: Allen and Unwin, 1988.

Rainey, James W. "Ambivalent Warfare: The Tactical Doctrine of the AEF in World War I." *Parameters: Journal of the US Army War College* 13 (September 1983): 34–46.

Rainey, James W. "The Questionable Training of the AEF in World War I." *Parameters: Journal of the US Army War College* 22 (Winter 1992–93): 89–103.

Showalter, "Manœuvre Warfare: The Eastern and Western Fronts, 1914–1915." In *The Oxford Illustrated History of the First World War*, ed. Hew Strachan, 30–45. New York: Oxford University Press, 1998.

Spector, Ronald. "The Military Effectiveness of the US Armed Forces, 1919–1939." In *Military Effectiveness*. Volume II: *The Interwar Period*, eds. Allan R. Millett and Williamson Murray, 70–97. Boston: Allen and Unwin, 1988.

Trask, David F. "The Entry of the USA into the War." In *The Oxford Illustrated History of the First World War*, ed. Hew Strachan, 239–52. New York: Oxford University Press, 1998.

Travers, Tim. "The Allied Victories, 1918." In *The Oxford Illustrated History of the First World War*, ed. Hew Strachan, 278–90. New York: Oxford University Press, 1998.

Williams, T. Harry. "The Military Leadership of North and South." In *Why the North Won the Civil War*, ed. David H. Donald, 38–57. Baton Rouge: Louisiana State University Press, 1960. Reprint, New York: Simon & Schuster, 1996.

Unpublished Dissertations and Theses

Johnson, Douglas Valentine, II. "A Few 'Squads Left' and Off to France: Training the American Army in the United States for World War I." Ph.D. diss., Temple University, 1992.

Rainey, James W. "The Training of the American Expeditionary Force in World War I." Master's thesis, Temple University, 1981.

Shugart, David A. "On the Way: The U.S. Field Artillery in the Interwar Period," Ph.D. diss., Texas A&M University, 2002.

Index